Rocking the CLASSICS

Rocking the
CLASSICS

English Progressive Rock
and the Counterculture

Edward Macan

New York   Oxford   Oxford University Press   1997

2006.003175

Oxford University Press

Oxford   New York
Athens   Auckland   Bangkok   Bombay
Calcutta   Cape Town   Dar es Salaam   Delhi
Florence   Hong Kong   Istanbul   Karachi
Kuala Lumpur   Madras   Madrid   Melbourne
Mexico City   Nairobi   Paris   Singapore
Taipei   Tokyo   Toronto

and associated companies in
Berlin   Ibadan

Copyright © 1997 by Oxford University Press, Inc.

Published by Oxford University Press, Inc.,
198 Madison Avenue, New York, New York 10016

Oxford is a registered trademark of Oxford University Press

Page vi is an extension of the copyright page.

Macan, Edward L., 1961–
Rocking the classics: English progressive rock
and the counterculture/Edward Macan.
p. cm.   Discography: p.
Includes bibliographical references and index.
ISBN 0-19-509887-0
ISBN 0-19-509888-9 (pbk.)
1. Progressive rock music—England—History and criticism.
I. Title.
ML3534.M28   1996   781.66—dc20   95-49637

1   3   5   7   9   8   6   4   2

Printed in the United States of America
on acid-free paper

Contents

Lyrics Credits

Prelude

Despite having authored what is to my knowledge the first comprehensive study of progressive rock, I must admit that my involvement in the progressive rock scene has heretofore been as an objective observer, not as a participant. To be sure, I was a fan during the music's commercial heyday of the mid-to late 1970s—although I never was involved to the point of joining any band's fan club—and I have attempted to remain abreast of developments in the progressive rock scene. On the other hand, in recent years my efforts as a musician have been centered in other areas. I have made my living as a music educator, teaching music history, music theory, and piano courses, as well as directing various jazz-based instrumental ensembles. I have devoted significant energy to the classical tradition as a recitalist on piano and the mallet instruments, especially as a performer of my own compositions. I have participated in gospel music and hymnody as an amateur. My training as a musicologist, I might add, geared me exclusively towards engaging the art music tradition. So why write a book about progressive rock?

The answer, I suppose, is that while this book is about progressive rock, it is also about a number of other issues that are of considerable importance to me in my work as a music educator and musicologist. In many ways, the origins of this book can be traced back to 1990–1991, when I read two books that permanently altered my philosophy of music: Henry Pleasants's *Serious Music: And All That Jazz*[1] and Christopher Small's *Music of the Common Tongue: Survival and Celebration in Afro-American Music.*[2] These books challenged virtually every assumption that my academic training had imbued in me: that Western art music was inherently "better" than popular music, that this superiority was the result of Western art music somehow existing beyond the realm of social considerations and therefore being "timeless," and that this superiority is demonstrable through reference to the notated score. Granted, I do not agree with everything in these books; I believe Small in particular sometimes advances arguments that reach the realm of ideological hysteria (for instance, his unfortunate suggestion that classical music is a tool by which imperialistic capitalists oppress the downtrodden masses). Nonetheless, I am grateful for the way in which these books forced me to come to terms with the unstated assumptions that permeate the whole positivistic model of post-secondary music education as it traditionally has been practiced in the United States.

There were three convictions that the Pleasants and Small books brought home to me especially strongly; since they permeate this book as well, it is probably best to enumerate them here. First, no music exists outside of society: Bach and Beethoven were just as much creatures of a specific time and place as were Blind Lemon Jefferson or Charlie Parker. Second, if no music can really be asocial, no music can be "timeless," either. No matter how powerfully a musical style may affect contemporaneous audiences or even listeners several generations down the road, societies change, and a time comes when every musical style loses its grasp on mass culture and enters the realm of historical artifact, to be cultivated by a smaller, more specialized audience of initiates. Finally, the European approach to musical analysis not only neglects the relationship between music and audience (surely the ultimate measure of a music's power) by concentrating exclusively on the sounds themselves, but it also limits itself to those elements (harmony, melody, meter, and structural organization) which the European notational system can accurately convey. Using these criteria, a Beethoven symphony is obviously "superior" to jazz or the blues; however, when one considers the timbral and rhythmic subtleties which notation is unable to capture, this "superiority" becomes harder to maintain unambiguously.

There were other realizations—if not revelations—that occurred to me as a result of reading these books. First, I was forced to acknowledge explicitly what I had long recognized implicitly: popular music has an affective power on contemporary audiences that classical music no longer has, and it would be difficult to state the criteria by which this could be construed as a favorable reflection on the current classical music scene. Over the years I have had occasion to observe the powerful responses that rock, jazz, and gospel musics frequently evoke from their respective audiences. I have not seen anything approaching this kind of rich audience/performer interaction in the largely uncommunicative ambience of the concert hall, where any genuinely spontaneous audience reaction to a performance is castigated as "inappropriate" by the custodians of high culture. I find it difficult to believe that Mozart or Liszt would have rejoiced over the current state of affairs, since it clearly does not resemble audience/performer interaction in their eras. Indeed, it was not always like this, since the taming of the classical music audience that took place in the early twentieth century is by now well documented.[3]

Second, I came to the realization that traditional musicology, and the whole system of music education of which it is an outgrowth, is becoming antiquated on a number of fronts. Some of the limitations of traditional musicology are by now well known: its questionable but pervasive assumptions that "serious" music is categorically "better" than "popular" music, that the music of an artistic elite is inherently "richer" than the music of the uncouth masses, and, most pervasively, that Western art music occupies a different realm qualitatively than any other body of music.

However, other weaknesses of musicology as it traditionally has been practiced are less universally recognized, and therefore, potentially more pernicious. For instance, since one of the elemental assumptions of traditional musicology has been that classical music is timeless and exists beyond society, no methodology was developed for examining the relationship between a musical style and its social context. For years musicologists showed remarkably little curiosity about either the ethnographic identity and the social motivations of the audiences of pre-twentieth-century art music, or about how these factors might have played a role in shaping musical style. William Weber's *Music and the Middle Class*[4] was the first work to expose a particular art music audience (in this case the audiences of Schumann, Chopin, and Liszt) to the type of ethnographic analysis taken for granted in popular music studies; Weber's book appeared only in the mid-1970s, and even then remained unique for some time. Needless to say, as long as the myth of European classical music existing beyond time and place endured, discussions of the roles played by social class, gender, race or ethnicity, and other social variables in the formation of musical style were difficult at best, and frequently did not take place. Paradoxically, though, it was only by ignoring these factors that the myth of an "asocial" music could be maintained.

Another potential pitfall of traditional musicology is that while its existing models of musical analysis are quite successful in demonstrating how specific examples of Western art music work on a purely musical basis, they are usually inadequate for a comprehensive analysis of non-Western music or Western popular music. The reason is that these analytical methods tend to focus on those features of the music that the European system of notation can capture with fidelity: harmony, melody, meter, and large-scale structure. The timbral and rhythmic subtleties that are a major—often *the* major—attribute of non-Western musics or Western popular music tend to be ignored, since these musical parameters cannot adequately be conveyed by the European notational system. This state of affairs has led to the frequently heard comparisons of Western art music's "richness" and "complexity" with the "simplicity," even "banality," of other styles—when, in fact, use of a different analytical system that is not so completely tied to Western art music might lead to a very different set of conclusions.

As a result of its insistence upon the "objective" existence of music in some sort of ideal world outside of time and society, traditional musicology has tended to isolate the music it attempts to illuminate from the realm of everyday experience. As a result, it has increasingly become a hermetic pursuit of no interest to anyone but other musicologists, and has had difficulty in engaging issues that are truly meaningful to contemporary society. Roger Rideout has stated the problem quite eloquently:

> My contention is that the Jeffersonian and Whitmanesque democratic ideals of our country have continued to evolve in this century, while our techniques for analyzing and evaluating music have not, nor have they ever addressed this perspective. The German model [of music education and scholarship] was fully formed, a part of academia a century ago, and not based on those ideals. As our students confront the greater moral, political, and existential ambiguities of modern society, the simplistically clear guidelines of the German model only appear irrelevant and confound their efforts to understand the aesthetic ends of twentieth-century music.[5]

The positivism which permeates the German model of musical thinking had already received a powerful boost early in the century when in his autobiography Stravinsky made the infamous remark that music was incapable of expressing anything.[6] It reached its zenith in the 1950s, however, when figures such as Milton Babbitt and Pierre Boulez insisted on confusing music with physics and other "objective" sciences. (Babbitt's notorious essay "Who Cares if You Listen" marks the high-water mark of this strain of thought.)[7] In pondering the arguments of Pleasants and Small, I came to an explicit realization that music exists as a form of communication between people of a certain time and, most often, a certain place. To be sure, it does not communicate abstract ideas in the same way as language: this is why I believe studies such as Deryck Cooke's *The Language of Music* must be taken with a grain of salt.[8] Nevertheless, its ability to communicate emotion and experience, to forge a sense of community, to bring mind and body into a greater unity, cannot be doubted. Yet while it is these qualities that make music meaningful for the vast majority of people, it is often these attributes that are given short shrift by traditional musicology.

What I sought, then, was a new approach to musicology based on the premise that analyzing the sounds should not be an end in itself. The ultimate goal of musicology, in my view, should be to document the relationship between music and society, because people do not exist for music: music exists for people. I felt that only through reconnecting music to real people in specific times and places could musicology connect with society at large, engage it in a symbiotic dialogue, and thus avoid the death by social irrelevance to which a continued reliance on unexamined positivism will surely condemn it.

I found the model for this kind of musicology in the field of popular music studies. In examining the scholarship of Christopher Small, John Shepherd, Richard Middleton, and others, I sensed that a different type of musicology, which could engage musicologists and nonmusicologists (even nonmusicians) with a force that the traditional musicology could not, was on the cusp of emergence. It was at this point I realized that if I were to continue as a musicologist—or for that matter, as a music educator—I would have to come to terms with this "new musicology."

I will wait until the introduction, where I present my methodology, to give my specific interpretation of this "new musicology." Suffice it to say that while I longed to apply it to the art music repertoire, I came to sense that first I would have to apply it to a musical style with which I had not only musical familiarity, but social grounding as well. As it turned out, there had been a small section at the end of my dissertation on Vaughan Williams and Holst which dealt with the similarity of harmonic style between these composers, later British composers such as Britten and Tippett, and English progressive rock of the late 1960s and 1970s. This section was eventually expanded first into a paper that was read at a meeting of a local chapter of the American Musicological Society, then into a published article. At some point I made the decision to expand the content of this article into a full-blown investigation of progressive rock.

I knew that the new approach to musicology which I hoped to pursue necessitated a familiarity with the social and cultural setting out of which the music emerged; I was able to draw upon my days as a fan and listener to supply this context. As I will argue again and again, progressive rock can only be understood as a product of a hippie/post-hippie culture. As someone who, to a certain degree at least, had been part of this culture, was no longer part of it, and could view it without undue sentimentality, I felt I was ideally positioned to say something relevant about progressive rock not only as a musical style, but also as a social phenomenon. The result of my endeavors is the book you are now reading.

In writing this book, I have tried to avoid an attitude of nostalgia—of "those were the days"—that one could easily slip into in a work of this type. I do feel quite strongly that the late 1960s and early 1970s was a period of unusually potent musical creativity: it is my opinion that the ten-year period of 1966 to 1976 may have witnessed more ferment, more far-reaching musical innovation than any other comparable period in the twentieth century. In this sense, I suppose, one could call it a "golden age" of sorts. Yet, I have mixed feelings about the hippie legacy of which this music played such a major role. On the one hand, I think the hippies' critique of mainstream society was in many ways sound; there is no doubt that the materialistic excesses, the spiritual complacency, and the sense of rootlessness and alienation which the counterculture found so disturbing in the late 1960s remain with us today, and are clearly not the signs of a healthy society. On the other hand, their "solutions," such as recreational drugs (to expand the limits of consciousness) and free love (to renounce the possessiveness of materialistic society), created a whole new set of problems. These are most clearly evident in the rise of a veritable empire of illegal drug trade, which has wrought untold havoc in the social fabric of Western culture, and the blight of illegitimacy and broken families which has visited so much misery on all levels of society. In this sense, I think Jim Curtis is correct to argue that the most enduring legacy of the counter-culture has been "to legitimize hedonism as part of the American way of life."[9] I have said all this because I believe that without understanding both the positive and the negative aspects of the counterculture, one cannot understand progressive rock. As Allan Moore has remarked,

> As with any artistic movement, both cultural and artistic factors can be cited to account for its existence and ultimate demise. "Progressive" rock was initially dependent on the existence of an "underground" culture, spawned by the drug era before its deleterious side-effects were discovered, spurred on by the illusion that individual enlightenment was on the point of being attainable by all, and that global enlightenment could be effected by the youth of all nations if only they could agree on their aims, as exemplified in their reactions to the Viet Nam War. It became public because the boom times of the late 1960s gave record companies the confidence to indulge their more experimental artists (an attitude rare today), aligning rock even more with middle-class attitudes.[10]

The contributions of a number of individuals have been crucial to the success of this book. Several figures who were of considerable importance to the British progressive rock scene of the 1970s have taken an interest in this project at one point or another, and deserve my thanks: Dave Stewart, Keith Goodwin, Eddie Jobson, Mike Pinder, Paul Whitehead, and above all Bill Bruford, who consistently went out of his way to be helpful.

I owe David Overstreet, owner of the Art Sublime label, a great debt of gratitude. He tirelessly assessed the manuscript in its various stages, and offered many helpful suggestions; he also provided me an invaluable service by helping me trace the whereabouts of a number of other individuals who eventually played a key role in the success of this project. Chuck Oken, long-time drummer of Djam Karet and general manager of Rhino Records, Claremont, California, was very helpful in orienting me to the various developments of the 1980s and conceptualizing the overall outline of the final chapter; he also held the keys of introduction to several others that figured in the writing of this book. Greg Walker, owner and general manager of the Syn-Phonic label, unselfishly shared his expertise concerning the neo-progressive movement, and made available to me a number of rare albums from his personal collection.

Nick Barrett of Pendragon offered his impressions of London's Marquee Club and his recollections of the role played by the late Tony Stratton-Smith in the neo-progressive movement, in both cases giving me information that was unavailable elsewhere. Marc Ceccotti of Edhels kindly supplied me with material pertaining to his band that I could not have obtained otherwise. Stephan van de Ven, editor of *Background Progressive Rock Magazine,* and David Robinson, author of *The British*

Progressive Rock Directory, wrote and offered encouragement for this project; David's personal recollections of the subcultural scene that surrounded the English neo-progressive movement during the early 1980s were particularly illuminating. Novelist Barry Harrington was another who offered unsolicited encouragement, read through the manuscript, and provided me with unpublished material of considerable interest.

I must extend thanks to two of my colleagues, Dean Suzuki (San Francisco State University) and John Koegel (Nebraska Wesleyan University) for their input, constructive criticism, and helpful advice. I want to thank Clifford Loeslin, Mike Tiano (creator of "Notes from the Edge," an Internet-only Yes fanzine), and Tim Morse (author of *Yes Stories*) for their help in locating a suitable cover photo. Thanks are due to Mike Stobbie for letting me reproduce the cover art of Pallas's *The Sentinel;* I am also grateful to Phil Carson of Victory Records, artist extraordinaire Paul Whitehead, and Ian Moss of Island Records for allowing me to reproduce the cover art of ELP's *Tarkus,* Genesis's *Foxtrot,* and Jade Warrior's *Floating Worlds,* respectively. I would like to thank Bill Bruford, Eddie Jobson, David Kean, Greg Pawelko, Mike Spindloe, and Mike King for contributing photos to this project; to Ed "Bear" Morgan for supplying the photo which appears on the cover; and Mike Pinder, Brian Emerson of Leadchoice Limited, Terry Whittaker of Carlin Music, and Pink Floyd Music Publishers for their kindness in granting me permission to reprint the lyrics of the Moody Blues, ELP, Van der Graaf Generator, and Pink Floyd, respectively. A special nod of gratitude goes to David Anderson, Paul Schlotthauer, and especially Soo Mee Kwon at Oxford University Press, who worked closely with me at every stage to insure the success of this project.

Finally, I must extend thanks to my wife, Connie, and to my daughters, Nicole and Catherine, for their patience during the sometimes arduous, four year process of completing this book, and to my parents, Thomas and Lena Macan, for their consistent help over the years. I dedicate this book to God, without whom it would never have been possible.

Eureka, Calif.   E. M.
April 1995

Rocking the CLASSICS

Introduction

Few styles of popular music have generated as much controversy as progressive rock. This style, which emerged in the wake of the counterculture, today is best remembered for its gargantuan stage shows, its fascination with epic subject matter drawn from science fiction, mythology, and fantasy literature, and above all for its attempts to combine classical music's sense of space and monumental scope with rock's raw power and energy. Its dazzling virtuosity and spectacular live concerts made it hugely popular with fans during the 1970s, who saw bands such as King Crimson, Emerson, Lake and Palmer (ELP for short), Yes, Genesis, Pink Floyd, and Jethro Tull bringing a new level of depth and sophistication to rock. On the other hand, critics branded the elaborate concerts of these bands as self-indulgent and materialistic. They viewed progressive rock's classical/rock fusion attempts as elitist, a betrayal of rock's populist origins. Not only has progressive rock been largely despised by the rock critics, it has also been largely ignored by popular music scholars. This is probably because it does not prominently chronicle minority or working-class disaffection in the manner of punk or reggae, and therefore does not easily lend itself to the neo-Marxist interpretations which have been the hallmark of popular music scholarship.

It seemed to me, then, that the time has been ripe for quite some time for a comprehensive study that would offer a balanced perspective, while challenging a number of key assumptions which have surrounded the style. But while the lack of attention given to the genre by previous writers has provided me with significant opportunities in writing this book, it also has raised certain problems. In searching for a model upon which to construct my study, I found that I was venturing to a certain degree upon terra incognita; while this book unites elements of musicological analysis, cultural/subcultural theory, and music criticism, strictly speaking it falls comfortably into none of these categories. For this reason, I think it is best to open by explaining my methodology.

First, I have resisted the musicologist's temptation to make this book primarily an analytical study of progressive rock.[1] I believe that rock, like jazz or country-and-western, is as much a cultural practice as a musical style, and that the sonic element—the music itself—is not necessarily the primary "text" one must grapple with when surveying a particular style. One must also address visual elements (which range from album cover art to concert staging to the clothing worn by musicians and fans), verbal elements such as lyrics, and a whole underlying cultural context in which issues of lifestyle and worldview figure prominently.

Unfortunately, musical analysis as it is currently constituted (including both traditional analysis and more recent approaches such as Schenkerian methods and pitch-set theory) does not enable one to examine music's relation to extramusical elements such as visual iconography, much less its social meaning. Rather, its primary function is internal, to explain how a piece of music works on a purely musical basis. My chief goal, on the other hand, has been twofold. First, I have attempted to examine how progressive rock creates its artistic messages through specific combinations of music, visual imagery, and verbal expression. Further-more, I have set out to explore the social meanings of these artistic messages, especially in terms of the relationship between progressive rock as a style and the English hippie subculture of the late 1960s and early 1970s. Thus I do not resort to musical examples, and my musical analysis is of a descriptive rather than a graphic nature. I recognize some might therefore criticize my analysis as cursory. I can only respond that musical analysis for its own sake is not central to the arguments I advance here, and that not resorting to graphic analysis enables me to address a diverse audience—readers with backgrounds in sociology, cultural theory, the sixties, or rock history and criticism—who are united mainly by their lack of grounding in musicology.

Since much of my analysis of the progressive rock style is social, I have, not surprisingly, drawn a great deal from the methodology of subcultural theory in general (a field which was reconstituted during the 1980s as "cultural studies"), and from the so-called Birmingham school in particular. From Paul Willis's sem-inal ethnographic study of English hippies, *Profane Culture*,[2] I have taken the prac-tice of applying structural homology to musical styles. Homological analysis, as defined by Willis, "is concerned with how far, in their structure and content, particular items parallel and reflect the structure, style, typical concerns, attitudes, and feelings of the social group."[3] Dick Hebdige defines structural homology a bit more succinctly, as "the symbolic fit between the values and lifestyles of a group, its subjective experience and the musical forms it uses to express or reinforce its focal concerns. . . . For instance, it was the homology between an alternative value system ('tune in turn on, drop out'), hallucinogenic drugs, and acid rock which made the hippie culture cohere as a 'whole way of life' for individual hippies."[4]

From Hebdige's groundbreaking *Subculture: The Meaning of Style*[5] I borrow the notion of applying semiological analysis to musical style. Hebdige argues that subcultures engage in "semiotic guerilla warfare" by borrowing existing cultural artifacts from mainstream society and then subverting their accepted meanings as a gesture of resistance; he believes deconstructing a subculture's music, visual iconography, clothing, etc., holds the key to unlocking its central concerns and values. To Stuart Hall and the other writers of *Resistance through Rituals*[6] I owe my understanding that subcultural styles do not have a single meaning or even a single description, but constitute a "bricolage," that is, a loose compound of different elements held together by interdependence, affinity, analogy, and aesthetic similarity. Thus progressive rock's amalgamation of rhythm-and-blues, folk styles, classical music, science fiction and fantasy iconography, surreal verse, and Eastern mysticism might at first seem illogical; however, a central goal of this book will be exploring the very specific ways in which the component elements of this bricolage interlock to convey well-defined worldviews and lifestyles.

I am indebted to later studies as well for certain aspects of my methodology. I learned much from the "classic" sociological approach to popular music studies exemplified by Will Straw's "Characterizing Rock Music Culture: The Case of Heavy Metal"[7] and Deena Weinstein's *Heavy Metal: A Cultural Sociology*.[8] Like the work of Willis, Hebdige, and Stuart Hall, these studies have a central weakness: since the authors are neither musicologists nor practicing musicians, their discussions of the music itself are not particularly revealing. On the other hand, Straw and Weinstein are penetrating in their analyses of the relationship between musicians and fans, in their examination of the mediating role played by the music industry (including music critics), and in their considerations of factors such as class, gender, and national or regional differences in the formation of musical style. While I am not a professional sociologist, I too have attempted to address these factors as well as I am able; I have come to believe that only when musicology and sociology are fully integrated will popular music studies and the "new" musicology have fully come of age.

I have mentioned in the Prelude the musical/social criticism of Henry Pleasants and Christopher Small, largely ignored in musiciological circles, and its impact on my work. Two other studies of the 1980s, while seldom mentioned by musicologists or cultural theorists, have also made a mark on my approach. Jim Curtis's *Rock Eras: Interpretations of Music and Society, 1954–1984*[9] is a unique study which I think deserves more attention than it has received. Strongly influenced by Marshall McLuhan's "Laws of the Media" and its postulation of a continuous cycle of enhancement/obsolescence/retrieval, Curtis examines popular music's role in mirroring and influencing American cultural history between 1954 and 1984. While Curtis shows an intuitive grasp of cultural theory (he eschews most of its jargon), he avoids the common assumption of many cultural theorists that artists are merely passive conduits of social tensions. Rather, he examines the confluence of social context and individual temperament in evaluations of a slew of artists ranging from Bing Crosby and Frank Sinatra to Michael Jackson and Bruce Springsteen, all the while examining the music against the backdrop of quintessentially American concepts such as the covenant and the frontier.[10] While he sometimes goes rather far afield in his search for cause and effect between cultural or political events and musical developments (such as his curious attempt to link the rise of disco to the fall of Richard Nixon), he is usually on the mark. The sheer breadth of musical styles addressed is impressive, and in many ways I find Curtis's study a more thoughtful and penetrating history of rock than the accepted standard, *Rock of Ages: the Rolling Stone History of Rock & Roll.*[11]

Another work which has influenced my approach—and which I also feel has been unfairly neglected—is Davin Seay and Mary Neely's *Stairway to Heaven: The Spiritual Roots of Rock 'n' Roll.*[12] The underlying premise of this book—a premise I fully agree with—is that the counterculture was primarily a religious and humanistic, rather than a political or ideological, movement. The viewpoint expressed in the book is clearly Christian, but it lacks the polemic edge of other books on rock music by Christian authors such as Bob Larson. Seay and Neeley are interested not in lambasting rock as the devil's music, but rather in investigating how it mirrored a generation's quest for some sort of metaphysical depth, and examining to what degree (if any) rock can be seen to articulate a coherent theological viewpoint. While there is on occasion a somewhat smug tone to the writing that some might find unappealing, I believe this book is an important corrective to the field of popular music studies; the Marxist background of cultural theory which underlies so many of the major popular music studies has led many authors to insist on materialist/ideological interpretations of musical style at the expense of other equally valid considerations.

Three books appeared in 1993—when my own study was well on its way to completion—which merit mention here. A collection of essays edited by Neil Rosenberg, *Transforming Tradition: Folk Music Revivals Examined,*[13] offers an excellent overview of the various folk movements of the twentieth century, which (as I will argue) had a significant impact on the rise of progressive rock. Robert Walser's *Running with the Devil: Power, Gender, and Madness in Heavy Metal Music*[14] attempts to bridge the gaps between sociology, cultural theory, and musicology in many of the same ways as my own study. Walser's grasp of cultural criticism is potent, and I find his discussion of the music to be equally illuminating. My one concern is that while he energetically challenges the motives of heavy metal's "right wing" critics, he is strangely silent concerning the genre's equally vociferous "left wing" foes. This is especially surprising in light of Deena Weinstein's very thorough consideration in her study of why two such politically and socially different groups would voice such similar criticisms of the music. I must confess that I found myself somewhat disquieted by the kid-gloves treatment that Walser extended to the school of rock criticism exemplified by Dave Marsh and Simon Frith. The reason I was troubled is that these critics are probably more responsible than anyone else for the construct of "authenticity" which has become part and parcel of rock's mythology, as well as for the establishment of the criteria by which a particular style's "value" is determined. Therefore, it seems to me that declining to thoroughly examine the premises behind their viewpoints means leaving unexamined (and therefore unchallenged) some of the key assumptions underlying matters of reception, critical interpretation, and definitions of "authenticity" in rock music. It is for this reason that I have gone out of my way to examine in detail the critical reception of progressive rock in chapter 8.

The third major popular music study to appear in 1993, Allan Moore's *Rock: The Primary Text. Developing a Musicology of Rock,*[15] is an ambitious work which attempts nothing less than to create the first stylistic survey of rock from its inception to the present. For reasons which I have already discussed in the Prelude, I have a fundamental disagreement with Moore's statement that "although the sounds of rock cannot, ultimately, be divorced from their setting, they must be loosely separated in the interim, if the listening act is to receive adequate attention in any discussion of the cultural practices of rock."[16] As I have already said, I believe that a new musicology will fully come of age only when musicology and sociology are adequately integrated. In fact, I suspect there are portions of Moore's study which could have been strengthened if he had proved more willing to consider the social roots of the musical developments that he addresses.[17] Nonetheless, Moore's study will likely serve as an important launching point for any future discussion of rock as a musical style; since he sees progressive rock as playing a pivotal role in the stylistic evolution of rock music, his study is especially important to any meaningful discussion of progressive rock. Furthermore, his warnings concerning the limitations of homological analysis are well taken, although I remain convinced that there are several clear and very real homologies to be drawn between the hippies as a subculture and progressive rock as a musical style.

Finally, I have been somewhat influenced by John Shepherd's methodology, set forth in his *Music as Social Text,*[18] for deconstructing messages of gender identity and relations in popular music. Shepherd took as his starting point Angela McRobbie's pioneering articles of the late 1970s and early 1980s, "Rock and Sexuality,"[19] cowritten with Simon Frith, and "Settling Accounts with Subcultures: A Feminist Critique."[20] These studies emphasize that any analysis of a style that does not address gender relations is incomplete. Drawing on Roland Barthes's concept of "readerly" and "writerly" texts,[21] Shepherd classifies timbres in terms of their "openness" and "closedness" to facilitate an understanding of gender types encoded in music. While Shepherd's methodology has both practical limitations (it was created to deal exclusively with vocal music) and theoretical limitations (it rests on metaphor rather than empirically measurable categories, since "openness" and "closedness" are relative concepts), it inspired me to construct a related but different typology based on acoustic (i.e., "open") and electronic (i.e., "closed") timbres. I believe exploring the relationships created between electronic and acoustic timbres in progressive rock's structural approaches will illuminate the manner in which the hippies of the late 1960s and early 1970s postulated an ideal society in which the best elements of "matriarchal" and "patriarchal" societies are harmoniously integrated.

Despite my obvious debt to cultural theory, however, I must emphasize that this book is not intended to be a "pure" subcultural/cultural study. A genuine subcultural study should be able to tell one many things about a subculture that its music cannot possibly encode: what its members do for a living, how they live if they don't work (as was the case for many hippies), at what age they enter and leave the subculture, how marriage and childbirth affect one's place in the subculture, and so on. While I am very much interested in how progressive rock mirrors the concerns and worldviews of the subculture that created it, my ultimate concern here is not with the subculture, but with the style itself. I think that this is where, as a musicologist, I can make a contribution that a social scientist cannot. Sociologists and cultural theorists who write about musical styles all too often tend to see style as a cypher which passively reflects society and has no internal dynamic of its own. Traditional musicology, of course, has tended to go to the opposite extreme, viewing a piece of music as a law unto itself, arguing that a piece's structure is its content, that it has no dependence whatsoever on society for its "meaning."

My view is halfway between these two extremes. On the one hand, it cannot be denied that musical style is created by social pressures, reflects important aspects of the society (or the segments of society) that created it, and is ultimately dependent on society for its meaning. While I am certain that Leonard Meyer was correct to stress the importance of interrelationships between aesthetic and psychological factors in shaping music's meaning in his *Emotion and Meaning in Music*, I would argue that the psychological factors which shape the aesthetic of a given style are at least in part socially conditioned, and thus vary from culture to culture. Meyer seems to assume basic musical patterns should always be goal-oriented (since he postulates that the success of "great" music results from how it heightens expectations and postpones resolution), when in fact this is true largely of Western music from the common-practice era, or music written according to common-practice conventions. Meyer's theory does not account for why non-Western listeners, or even contemporary Western listeners, would find music that raises no harmonic expectations in the first place (be it organum, minimalism, or any number of world musics) emotionally meaningful. While more work needs to be done in this area, it seems clear to me the idea that "meaning" in music is totally asocial—which Meyer and his followers seem to have assumed—can no longer be sustained.

On the other hand, a musical style does have an internal dynamic. Sociologists who write about popular music have been slow to realize that musical symbols are not arbitrary in the manner that many other semiotic symbols of a culture (including language) are, that musical events such as shifts in tempo, rhythm, or dynamics produce remarkably similar affective reactions from culture to culture, since these events affect the body directly. Furthermore, I believe that structural interrelationships between various elements of a piece of music (for instance, between the ear-splitting *fortissimo*, strident, distorted timbres, and heavy beat of a heavy metal song) often allow for a more objective "reading" of the music's meaning, even without an understanding of its social context, than writers of the music-as-social-cypher persuasion would allow for. It is for this reason that I have philosophical difficulties with the writings of certain sociologists-turned-music commentators, especially Simon Frith. I see Frith's strident insistence that the text itself has no meaning other than the subjective meaning an individual or social group may read into it—since, in his view, the only meaning a text really has is imparted through mediation—as a tacit admission of his own inability to evaluate the musical text as an objective entity. It seems to me, then, that "meaning" is a combination of internal factors present in the text itself and external factors brought into play by the context in which the text is mediated.

Besides drawing rather extensively on elements of subcultural/cultural theory, I also devote a good deal of the text to music criticism, especially in the final two chapters. To be sure, this book is not a record review, nor is it, strictly speaking, a critical survey of the major English progressive rock bands. I do not compare bands; I will leave it up to the individual reader to decide whether Van der Graaf Generator or Renaissance, King Crimson or Genesis, Soft Machine or Yes is the better band. However, I do make aesthetic judgments in terms of suggesting why some progressive rock pieces are better than others; why some directions explored by the genre have been more valid than others; and why some offshoots of the "classic" progressive rock style are likely to be more successful than others. I realize that objectivity is usually prized in studies of this type. It is my firm belief, though, that musicology has abrogated a certain sense of social responsibility by attempting to be totally objective. I therefore draw both on the philosophical/social tradition of criticism exemplified by Pleasants and Small and more conventional approaches to popular music criticism. I assume most readers will have little problem differentiating empirical fact from critical opinion, and I take full responsibility for the latter.

Finally, while this book serves as a history of English progressive rock, I do not attempt to give exhaustive biographical coverage of individual musicians or bands. Rather, I am concerned primarily with the music itself, with allied ideas in the realm of verse and visual art, and with the cultural and social factors that shaped the music. I realize that this approach sacrifices the "live-at-the-scene" feeling that would have resulted from interviewing major participants: musicians, managers, technicians, record company executives, roadies, and groupies. Here I can only confess that in this sense another book is needed to round out the picture, a book that tells the story of the progressive rock scene as opposed to surveying the music itself. In the meantime, though, there are good biographies of several major progressive rock bands which can at least partially fill this void; there are also a number of good reference sources for demographic data, and the appendix of this book offers discographies and personnel listings of a number of progressive rock bands.[22]

Paradoxically, however, in order to examine the sociological and cultural factors surrounding progressive rock I have had to focus on bands whose music has given rise to a body of critical and biographical documentation. This has meant in effect that I have focused mainly on commercially successful bands, or at least on bands that achieved a considerable cult following: a number of musically accomplished bands are given less extensive coverage simply because there is so little written documentation surrounding them. While I have tried to draw attention to a number of relatively unknown bands that made some excellent music, I must reiterate again this book is not a record guide, but in large part a study of progressive rock as a cultural force: one can argue endlessly whether ELP or Egg were a "better" band, but there will be no argument that ELP exerted the greater cultural (and therefore musical) influence. I suspect there will be relatively little debate concerning the bands from the 1960s and 1970s that I have chosen to discuss, since for the most part a consensus has emerged concerning which bands from this period made the most important contributions to progressive rock as an idiom. However, no comparable consensus has emerged concerning the major neo- or post-progressive rock bands of the 1980s and 1990s. This situation is compounded by the fact that commercial success can no longer be used as a measure of importance now that progressive rock is a cult style, so it is likely that I may neglect to mention contemporary bands whose contributions to the genre and its offshoots may eventually prove important.

As the title indicates, this book serves as a study of English progressive rock. There may be some readers who feel that it is a mistake not to give equal coverage to Continental European and American progressive rock bands, and who will point out that the work of the finest of these bands is probably on par with that of contemporaneous English bands. Nonetheless, I believe my decision to limit my field of inquiry to English groups is justified on several grounds. The genre originated in England and achieved its "classic" form at the hands of English bands during the early 1970s; even the neo-progressive revival of the early 1980s began in England. Furthermore, limiting myself to England allows me to explore the relationship between progressive rock, its subcultural context, and its cultural role in more specific terms than would be possible if I were to attempt to survey the progressive rock scene of a number of different countries. Finally, much of what I say concerning the sonic, visual, and verbal conventions of English progressive rock in chapters 2 through 4 can be applied to European and American bands as well. The contributions of Continental European and American musicians to progressive rock as an idiom are summarized in chapter 9.

Unlike a standard historical study, the book's arrangement is roughly, rather than strictly, chronological, which better enables it to approach progressive rock from the interdisciplinary perspective outlined above. The first chapter opens by describing the cultural conditions which gave birth to the progressive rock style; I examine the emergence of the genre from the psychedelic and folk styles of the mid- to late 1960s, and trace its development through its golden age of the early to mid-1970s. During this period the progressive rock style is seen to pass through two distinct stages. Psychedelic bands such as the Moody Blues, Procol Harum, the Nice, and Pink Floyd laid the foundation of the progressive rock style between 1966 and 1970. The release of King Crimson's album *In the Court of the Crimson King* in October 1969 signaled the emergence of the mature progressive rock style, which reached its artistic and commercial zenith between 1970 and 1975 in the music of bands such as Jethro Tull, Yes, Genesis, ELP, Gentle Giant, Van der Graaf Generator, and Curved Air.

Chapters 2–5 provide a detailed survey of the stylistic conventions of progressive rock as they emerged during its "golden age." This survey explores the conventions that govern the music itself (chapter 2), the conventions pertaining to the genre's visual dimension in the realm of album cover art and the visual aspects of the progressive rock concert (chapter 3), and the conventions pertaining to the genre's verbal dimension of lyrics and conceptual themes (chapter 4). The nineteenth-century composer Richard Wagner coined the term *Gesamtkunstwerk* (unified art work) to describe the equal importance of music, words, scenery, lighting, and costume design to his music dramas. In chapter 5 I examine four well-known progressive rock pieces in order to explore the manner in which the progressive rock bricolage constitutes a kind of *Gesamtkunstwerk* in which music, visual motifs, and verbal expression are inextricably intertwined to convey a coherent artistic vision. This vision encapsulates countercultural ideology; it simultaneously protests the soulless bureaucracy which the hippies believed is crushing every trace of spiritual life out of Western culture, and suggests an ideal society in which technology and nature, past and future, matriarchal and patriarchal social values can be harmoniously interwoven.

At the time of progressive rock's appearance, the various subgenres of rock music were much more fluid, much more subject to change, and much more difficult to define with precision than is now the case. Chapter 6 gives me the opportunity to justify my definition and categorization of progressive rock as a specific genre by comparing and contrasting it with several overlapping styles which both influenced it and were influenced by it to a degree: jazz-rock, folk-rock, heavy metal, electronic music, and minimalism. I also point out how progressive rock's eclecticism worked to draw together a diverse taste public. Chapter 7 addresses progressive rock from a sociological perspective, exploring the backgrounds of the musicians and fans on an ethnographic basis. I consider why progressive rock could have hardly developed outside of a bohemian, southeastern English youth sub-culture; point up the manner in which the musicians simultaneously celebrate and subvert the values imposed by their middle-class upbringings; and explore the reasons behind progressive rock's huge popularity among its large North American fan base between the early and mid-1970s.

Chapter 8 considers the largely antagonistic relationship that has existed between progressive rock and the rock music press. Besides examining the merits of the "accepted" critical view that progressive rock is elitist and traditionalist, I examine the motives behind these criticisms by exploring the critics' notions of authenticity (especially in terms of evaluating a style based on how closely it reflects an R&B heritage), social relevance, and commercial contamination. I argue that the ac-cepted critical stance ultimately tells us more about the critics than it does about progressive rock, and has tended to obscure a realistic (as opposed to idealistic) survey of the cultural history of the 1970s as conveyed through popular music.

The final chapter considers the history of progressive rock since the 1970s, which is seen to pass through two distinct phases. The first phase, evident between the mid-1970s and the early 1980s, witnessed the decline, fragmentation, and disso-lution of the "classic" progressive rock style, which in turn mirrored the simultaneous unraveling of the hippie subculture that created it. The second phase, which began in the early 1980s, has been marked by three distinct trends. First, there is the continued (or in some cases revived) activity of the major bands of the 1970s. Second, there is the rise of the neo-progressive movement, spearheaded by Marillion and other younger bands who have sought to introduce a more con-temporary sensibility to the classic progressive rock style. Finally, there is an eclec-tic, or "post-progressive," approach inaugurated by King Crimson with their *Discipline* LP of 1981 and pursued by later bands who have sought to fertilize the "classic" progressive rock style with entirely new influences such as minimalism and ethnic music. Besides examining the impulses which have shaped each of these developments, I attempt to summarize what progressive rock's current state might tell us about its future, and what it might tell us about the present state of affairs in the progress of popular music.

Two themes recur again and again throughout this book in the manner of a Wag-nerian leitmotif. The first involves the intimate relationship between progressive rock and classical music. The defining features of progressive rock, those elements that serve to separate it from other contemporary styles of popular music, are all drawn from the European classical tradition. These hallmarks include the continuous use of tone colors drawn from symphonic or church music, the employment of lengthy sectional forms such as the song cycle or the multimovement suite, and the preoccupation with dazzling metrical and instrumental virtuosity. The continuous references progressive rock musicians make to classical music are, in turn, emblematic of the musicians' middle- and upper-middle-class backgrounds. Progressive rock as an idiom can be understood as a forum in which the musicians attempt to forge a dialectical relationship between the high culture of their parents and the popular culture that they grew up in, dominated by African-American musical forms. In turn, the constant appeal made in progressive rock to the music of high culture is one of the major reasons that many rock critics, professed "populists," disliked the idiom so intensely.

The second recurring theme involves the intimate relationship between progressive rock as a musical style and the counterculture of the late 1960s and early 1970s. The proto-progressive bands of the late 1960s played a direct role in the countercultural scene, while the major progressive rock bands of the 1970s drew their mass audience from a post-hippie extension of the counterculture. The subject matter of the lyrics is above all an expression (sometimes direct, most often veiled) of countercultural ideology. Likewise, the surrealism of the lyrics and the album cover art, even the elaborate light shows at concerts, can be understood to stem directly from the psychedelic zeitgeist of the period, particularly from the impact of hallucinogenic drugs.

The main elements of the music itself reflect important aspects of the counterculture as well. The heavy reliance on tone colors derived from the Western art music tradition reflects the sense of importance and even ritual that the hippies attached to the music, while the consistent use of lengthy forms such as the programmatic song cycle of the concept album and the multimovement suite underscores the hippies' new, drug-induced conception of time. The intricate metrical and wayward harmonic schemes of the music, as well as the frequent appeals to instrumental virtuosity, reflect the elements of surprise, contradiction, and uncertainty that the counterculture prized so highly, as well as serving as a gate that separated the "real" hippies from the uncomprehending "straights" (i.e., non-hippies). Furthermore, the juxtaposition within a piece or an album of predominantly acoustic with predominantly electric sections, one of the hallmarks of the progressive rock style, seems to encapsulate many of the conflicts that were of great significance to the counterculture. For instance, it is possible to see in the style's acoustic/electric dichotomy the contrast of the pastoral and organic with the technological and artificial, the conflict between matriarchal and patriarchal values, between ancient and modern ways of life, and between the folk and psychedelic musical styles that progressive rock drew from.

Finally, the rise and fall of progressive rock as an idiom with mass popularity reflects the rise and fall of the counterculture itself. Both appeared as oppositional forces to mainstream society during the mid-1960s, were gradually absorbed into the mainstream between the early and mid-1970s, and dissolved beyond recognition between the mid- and late 1970s. A contemporaneous idiom like heavy metal that has remained the nexus of a thriving subculture has been able to retain its aesthetic and commercial viability into the 1990s. While progressive rock offshoots have continued to undergo stylistic evolution into the 1980s and 1990s, the difficulty the genre has experienced as a commercially viable idiom since the late 1970s is a reflection of the fragmentary nature of the fan base that has surrounded it since the dissolution of the counterculture. For this reason, while the "classic" progressive rock bands of the 1960s and 1970s may continue to sell millions of records for some time to come, the new strains of progressive rock that have developed since the mid-1970s are likely to remain cult styles with no mainstream commercial viability (like classical and most jazz styles, for instance) for the foreseeable future.

The Birth of
Progressive Rock

I remember vividly *Sergeant Pepper* coming out—there was this incredible buzz of sheer disbelief. Wherever you went people would be playing it. Suddenly, with this astonishing music anything seemed possible.[1]

This remark by Van der Graaf Generator's David Jackson nicely sums up the wave of euphoria that greeted the 1967 release of the Beatles' album *Sergeant Pepper's Lonely Hearts Club Band:* the conviction that an as yet unnamed music was being born out of a fusion of rock, classical, jazz, folk, and Indian styles, and a belief that this new music could at once be creative and popular. Jackson's quote also illustrates the shock that many felt at the appearance of a style of rock—which eventually became known as "progressive rock"—that drew heavily on, of all things, the classical tradition of Bach, Mozart, Wagner, and Stravinsky. After all, well into the 1960s conventional middle-class wisdom held that rock-and-roll was a primitive music, largely the domain of the lower classes, of no particular aesthetic merit. Many even considered it to be a likely cause of juvenile delinquency. In the space of scarcely a decade, how could the admittedly raw, artless music of Elvis Presley, Jerry Lee Lewis, and Chuck Berry have been transformed into the complex, monumental, multidimensional progressive rock style? This question can only be answered by considering the sudden emergence during the mid-1960s of the counterculture, a youth-based subculture that first appeared in isolated urban areas such as the Haight Ashbury district of San Francisco and London, and from there spread across much of the Western world.

As it has now been over a quarter century since the counterculture spilled out of Haight Ashbury and into international consciousness during the "Summer of Love" during 1967, a brief description of it for the uninitiated is probably warranted. The counterculture consisted largely of young, middle-class white people who had consciously rejected the lifestyle of their parents in favor of more exper-

imental paths. So much as the "hippies," as members of the counterculture were
called, had an organized agenda—and hippies were notorious for their dislike of
organization—they sought the political and spiritual transformation of mainstream society. Hippies placed much emphasis on uncovering new realms of perception and consciousness, especially through the use of hallucinogenic drugs and
the adoption of Eastern or "mystical" religious practices such as transcendental
meditation. Politically, the counterculture opposed the institutionalized materialism of capitalist society. Hippies often refused to work, lived nomadic lifestyles,
experimented with various forms of communal living, and generally despised the
nine-to-five routine of "straight" society. A notable aspect of the American counterculture in particular was its vehement opposition to the military and law en-
forcement arms of government, which it regarded as tools of oppression and
totalitarian manipulation. This opposition surfaced most forcefully in the sometimes violent demonstrations against the Vietnam War.

Mainstream society—the Establishment, as the counterculture called it—considered the hippies to be dangerous to the status quo on a number of counts. Their
widespread advocacy of drug use, expressed most infamously by drug guru Timothy Leary's dictum "Turn on, tune in, drop out," raised hackles, and led to a
series of never-ending skirmishes between the hippies and police drug squads.
Their practice of free love and their flouting of conventional sexual mores was
another cause of widespread concern. So was their seeming opposition to any form
of organized authority, evident not only in the political turbulence that swept
American college campuses in the late 1960s, but also in youth-led agitations
against the governments of France, Greece, and Mexico. By 1968—almost certainly
the high-water mark of the counterculture's political and cultural clout—mainstream society had come to perceive it in terms of that notorious triumverate of
sex, drugs, and rock-and-roll. Whether or not one considers this characterization
to be fair, there is no doubt that the Establishment's fear was not misplaced; the
counterculture of the late 1960s ushered in the most powerful cultural revolution
the Western world had seen since the end of World War I, nearly fifty years earlier.

Although music was ultimately the most important source of the counterculture's self-identity, there were other important elements of the hippie persona as
well. Especially obvious was clothing. Shoulder-length hair (for both men and
women), tiny dark glasses, eccentric hats, paisley shirts, flowers, beads, and faded
bell-bottomed blue jeans served to identify one as a hippie immediately. The men's
long hair and the women's miniskirts, in particular, were prized as a slap in the
face of the Establishment. The influence of hallucinogens upon the counterculture's taste in visual art cannot be underestimated: the bright-colored clothing, the
intricate linear designs and surrealism of the album covers and poster art, and the
growing popularity of light shows in conjunction with concerts during the late
1960s can be traced above all to the impact of lysergic acid diethylamide, LSD for

short. "Acid," as it was called, affected verbal expression as well—the lyrics of American folk/rock musician Bob Dylan and the Beatles from the mid-1960s on show a tendency toward surrealism and elliptical statement that was quite new to popular music, but that was thoroughly representative of the hippies' general approach to verbal communication. Furthermore, the seriousness of the subject matter dealt with in these lyrics—the social protest of Bob Dylan giving way to the cosmic speculations of the Beatles during the late 1960s—also became characteristic of much of the counterculture's creative expression.

Nonetheless, despite the importance of dress, visual, and verbal expression, it was above all in the realm of musical style that the counterculture forged its self-identity. The psychedelic style, as it came to be known, represented a decisive challenge to the styles that dominated the pop airwaves between the early and mid-1960s. Psychedelic music was loud; it drew its propensity for amplification and its heavy beat from rhythm-and-blues. The British blues revival of the early 1960s, spearheaded by Alexis Korner's Blues Inc. and John Mayall's Bluesbreakers, exerted a particularly powerful effect on English psychedelic music for at least two reasons. First, it gave many young British musicians their first live exposure to the electric blues style of black American artists such as Muddy Waters (a.k.a. McKinley Morganfield), Howlin' Wolf (a.k.a. Chester Burnett), and B. B. King. Second, the British blues movement attracted a number of slightly older musicians who had begun their careers in the British jazz scene of the late 1950s: Graham Bond, Brian Auger, and Ginger Baker, to name but a few. The improvisational abilities these musicians had developed during their jazz days were to prove of considerable importance when psychedelic music began to come into its own during the mid-1960s.

While psychedelic music's emphasis on soloing and lengthy instrumental sections was obviously indebted to R&B and jazz, though, its eclecticism, its mixing of different styles, was something quite new. Writing about psychedelic music in 1968, Harvey Pekar commented that "what we may be witnessing is the creation of a new, as yet unlabeled form of music, as America around the turn of the century saw the development of jazz. . . . Among the elements being melted down are blues, country-and-western, near Eastern, Indian, and baroque forms. Increasingly important is the technique of producing novel, exciting effects by using the potential of tape."[2] (Indeed, one must add that psychedelic music could not have emerged without the technological advances in music equipment that took place during the 1960s.) At least partly because of the use of hallucinogenic drugs that was integral to the counterculture from its inception, psychedelic music was "head music"— music to be listened to—rather than dance music, which furthered its tendency toward musical experimentation.

Around 1966 and 1967 a series of clubs opened in London, San Francisco, and other major countercultural centers specializing in the presentation of psychedelic music. The relationship between performers and audiences at these clubs was extremely close; for instance, when the Sunday afternoon "Spontaneous Underground" series was introduced at London's Marquee club in February 1966, there was no division between stage and audience. It was this type of symbiotic relationship between the audience and the band members, who were themselves products of the counterculture, that proved crucial to the formation of the musical, visual, and verbal conventions that later became part of the mature progressive rock style.

The fact that the psychedelic style literally exploded out of the clubs had a profound impact on the musicians' relationship with the record industry as well. Initially, the record companies could not tailor the music to the masses, as they did with so many other styles of popular music; they could only react to demands for the new music by signing a wide range of acts and carefully monitoring what sold and what didn't. Of course, the record industry subsequently established ever greater control over rock as a product; as writers such as Simon Frith (in *The Sociology of Rock*) or Reebee Garofalo and Steve Chapple (in their *Rock 'n' Roll Is Here to Pay*) argue, the history of rock can only be adequately understood against the backdrop of capitalist economics. Nevertheless, there is no doubt that record company "turbulence" during the late 1960s and early 1970s gave artists recording at this time a creative control over their music that was virtually unprecedented in the history of popular music. There is also no doubt that without this leeway for experimentation, the economic conditions would have never existed for progressive rock's appearance.

The underground press and underground radio stations that emerged around psychedelic music during 1966 and 1967 were the final two elements necessary for the birth of progressive rock. Not only did they lead to a further dissemination and crystallization of psychedelic music as a distinct style, they also fostered a sense of critical appreciation, connoisseurship, and artiness that had previously been reserved for more "developed" forms of music such as classical music and jazz. Without this specific alignment of cultural and economic forces—the appearance of the counterculture, the formation of the psychedelic style, the rise of a network of clubs, radio stations, and publications around the music, and an entirely new relationship between the musicians and the record companies—the progressive rock style never could have emerged.

Psychedelic music of the 1966-1970 period was considered at the time to be a single style, and certainly there are common elements which unite the music of the psychedelic era. Long pieces (ten minutes or more was not uncommon) with prominent instrumental sections and lengthy solos became a hallmark of psychedelic music. So did a fascination with electronic experimentation: the exploitation of feedback, the use of echo machines and other effects devices that appeared during the late 1960s, and the utilization of then novel tape effects such as multitracking and splicing. References to North Indian classical music—the use of instruments such as sitars and tablas, the employment of exotic modes drawn from Indian ragas, the utilization of ornamental, melismatic lines in instrumental solos—also became common among some psychedelic bands of this period and exemplified the powerful influence exerted by Eastern spirituality upon the counterculture.[3]

Nonetheless, despite these similarities, one can already detect in psychedelic music of this period the roots of a number of new genres that erupted around 1970 with the fragmentation of psychedelia. The appearance of this slew of new styles (including, for instance, progressive rock, heavy metal, jazz-rock, glam-rock, and southern rock) is in turn indicative of the fragmentation of the essentially unified youth culture that existed between 1966 and 1970 into a number of distinct subcultures along national, regional, and class lines. As I will show later, these factors all had a great impact on the development of progressive rock as a style. Progressive rock could have never emerged from the working-class milieu that was responsible for the formation of genres such as heavy metal and later, punk rock; throughout the 1970s, progressive rock's audience consisted largely of a middle-class, post-hippie extension of the counterculture. Likewise, it is difficult to imagine the progressive rock style having developed in the United States rather than England (although it eventually did achieve great popularity there), just as, for instance, the southern rock of bands such as the Allman Brothers could have never developed outside of the southeastern United States.

There seem to have been at least three distinct wings of psychedelic music in England. One wing of English psychedelic music, dominated by Cream, the Yardbirds, and Jimi Hendrix (a black American guitarist who rose to prominence in London working with English musicians), was based on a heavy, electric reinterpretation of the blues that the Rolling Stones had already begun to explore by the mid-1960s. Like the Stones, these bands featured simple, blues-based harmonic progressions, repetitive rhythm guitar riffs (usually two or four bars in length), and a driving back beat. To this they added certain devices such as power chords (open fifths played at a crushing volume) and guitar feedback pioneered by Peter Townshend, guitarist of the other seminal English hard rock band of the mid-1960s, the Who. The long instrumental sections and the fiery guitar solos that dominated the live shows of Hendrix and Cream, on the other hand, came less from the Stones or the Who than from the urban blues masters themselves: Cream's Eric Clapton, for instance, has frequently acknowledged his debt to B. B. King. The instrumentation of these bands consisted of one or two electric guitars, bass guitar, and drums; there was usually only one singer, and the massive backdrop of sustained keyboard chords or vocal harmonies which were to figure so prominently in progressive rock was largely absent. (In this sense the Stones were a more obvious precedent to Cream or Hendrix than the Who, whose rich vocal arrangements on songs like "I Can See for Miles" offer a more obvious sonic link to progressive rock.) By 1970 this wing of psychedelic music had developed into the heavy metal style, exemplified most prominently by Led Zeppelin, Black Sabbath, and (beginning with their *Machine Head* album of 1971) Deep Purple.

A second wing of English psychedelic music, which also grew out of the British blues revival, drew especially strongly on jazz sources. This wing was represented early on by Traffic, Colosseum, IF, and a group of bands, spearheaded by Soft Machine and Caravan, that sprang out of Canterbury's underground scene of the late 1960s. These bands added wind instruments (especially saxophones and flutes) to the instrumental core of keyboards, guitar, bass guitar, and drums. Their music deemphasized the legacy of the pop song in favor of experimentation with instrumental forms to a degree that was unusual even for psychedelic music. Lengthy, virtuosic solos were de rigueuer, while chord changes and rhythmic patterns were considerably more complex in this music than in the Cream/Hendrix/Yardbirds approach. By the early 1970s this wing of psychedelic music had developed into several interrelated strains of jazz-rock fusion, exemplified especially by the hard fusion of Mahavishnu Orchestra and their followers and the more experimental "Canterbury rock" of the Soft Machine/Caravan school.

The third wing of English psychedelic music was represented by the Moody Blues, Procol Harum, Pink Floyd, and the Nice. Unlike the other two wings of English psychedelic music, these groups were influenced by the later music of the Beatles. The Beatles, of course, predated psychedelic music by several years; however, they steadily moved away from their roots in the straight-ahead pop style of the early 1960s, and by 1966 became a de facto psychedelic band.[4] It was in the Beatles' music of 1966 and 1967—particularly in their album *Sergeant Pepper's Lonely Hearts Club Band*—that many of the elements that later characterized English progressive rock first appear. One sees in this album a self-conscious eclecticism, a mixing of many different musical styles in which devices derived from several styles of classical music figure prominently. If there are references to Baroque chamber idioms ("She's Leaving Home"), there are also references to the avant-garde electronic experimentation of Karlheinz Stockhausen, whose face appears among the crowd that has come to witness the Beatles' "funeral" on the back of the album cover.

One also sees a new concern for large-scale structure. The different songs of *Sergeant Pepper* are part of an overall song cycle unified by the recurrence of the opening song in varied form near the end of the album, by the imaginative use of taped effects to tie the different songs together, and above all by the adherence to a specific concept that is developed from song to song. In short, *Sergeant Pepper* was generally recognized as the first concept album.[5] The practice of tying a series of songs together by using both a recurring melodic theme and a program—that is, a unifying idea or concept which is developed in the lyrics of the individual songs—can be traced back to the song cycles of early-nineteenth-century composers such as Franz Schubert and Robert Schumann. Not surprisingly, critics were quick to comment on *Sergeant Pepper's* "classical" conception of structure.

Several of the English psychedelic bands that followed in the wake of *Sergeant Pepper* drew upon specific characteristics of the band's music most closely associated with classical music, and developed these elements far more single-mindedly than either the Beatles or contemporaneous West Coast psychedelic bands that exhibited certain stylistic affinities (especially the Doors and Jefferson Airplane) were wont to.[6] The Moody Blues, recording their influential *Days of Future Passed* album with the London Festival Orchestra in late 1967, almost singlehandedly established the concept of "symphonic rock." In their later recordings they used the Mellotron, a keyboard instrument capable of reproducing prerecorded string, brass, and choral voicings, to provide a symphonic backdrop; they also developed the Beatles' three-part vocal harmonizations into an even more richly arranged four-part style. Procol Harum, who rose to prominence in 1967 with their ravishing hit single "A Whiter Shade of Pale," pioneered the use of the Hammond organ as a substitute pipe organ—hence the stately pace and cathedral-like ambience of much of their most characteristic music. They also continued to expand the Beatles' utilization of acoustic instruments not previously associated with rock on albums such as *A Salty Dog* (1969). Both bands further developed the idea of the concept album as a type of programmatic song cycle; for instance, according to Hugh Mendl's liner notes the various songs on the Moody Blues' *Days of Future Passed* LP "attempt to paint their picture of everyman's day, which takes nothing from the nostalgia of the past—and adds nothing to the probabilities of the future." Compared to *Sergeant Pepper,* instrumental interludes are longer and more frequent, and musical material is recapitulated more subtly at various points across the album; thus the opening cut of *Days of Future Passed,* "The Day Begins," is entirely instrumental, and forecasts the thematic material of the album's major songs.

The Nice and Pink Floyd were also influenced to some degree by the Beatles, especially on their debut albums. On the other hand, they moved somewhat farther afield from the heritage of *Sergeant Pepper* as a result of their more thorough exploration of purely instrumental music—a tendency which led Pink Floyd, in particular, to be associated with contemporaneous Canterbury bands such as Soft Machine. Indeed, it was an interest in creating lengthy instrumental soundscapes that led these two groups to bring yet another large-scale programmatic form drawn from classical music, the multimovement suite, into the framework of psychedelia. The multimovement suite, as employed by late-nineteenth- and early-twentieth-century composers, is (usually) an instrumental piece in several distinct movements that attempts to convey an extramusical source of inspiration (the "program") by using music to "paint" a picture, "narrate" a story, or "describe" a philosophical concept. Pink Floyd's *A Saucerful of Secrets* (1968) and the Nice's contemporaneous *Ars Longa Vita Brevis* (which does contain one brief vocal) are both four-movement works that are based on "programs" in this sense. *A Saucerful of Secrets* seems to describe a mystical experience, or perhaps space travel—the album's cover art suggests either as a possibility. *Ars Longa Vita Brevis*, which borrows some of its material from the opening movement of J. S. Bach's "Brandenburg" Concerto No. 3, is based on a nebulous philosophical underpinning that is articulated more clearly in the album's brief liner notes than in the music itself.

The interest these two bands showed in instrumental pieces had other important ramifications as well. The Nice's two best-known numbers, "Rondo" and "America," are entirely instrumental and prominently feature Keith Emerson's muscular, flamboyant organ solos. Emerson almost single-handedly provided the model for the classically trained virtuoso that became a central facet of progressive rock; his fondness for creating revved-up, earsplitting arrangements of the classics also had a decisive impact on the genre. Pink Floyd, meanwhile, concentrated on otherworldly sound effects to a degree that was unusual even for a psychedelic band; there is little doubt that their studio wizardry represented an important legacy to progressive rock. To be sure, after 1970 they de-emphasized electronic experimentation and increasingly adopted the structural approaches and instrumentation that eventually became the hallmark of progressive rock. Nonetheless, their characteristic blend of celestial organ backdrops, alternately ethereal and clangorous guitar lines, hypnotically repetitive bass/drum patterns, and avant-garde electronics influenced the development of both the German electronic rock of the 1970s and the electronic New Age styles of the 1980s.

Besides the influence of *Sergeant Pepper*–era Beatles, a crucial link between all of the bands discussed here is their debt to the folk revival of the 1960s. The evolution of the folk movement, with its emphasis on traditional folk songs, rich vocal arrangements (which can be traced back at least to the seminal folk group of the 1950s, the Weavers), and acoustic instruments (especially acoustic guitar), had paralleled the development of rock until the mid-1960s. From the mid-1960s, however, the two formerly separate styles began to intermingle in the music of Bob Dylan, American bands such as the Byrds, and the Beatles themselves. It is from the intermingling of psychedelic and folk heritages in the music of the post–*Sergeant Pepper* bands that one of the most characteristic qualities of progressive rock as a genre emerges: the systematic juxtaposition of acoustic and electric passages, sections, or movements. Indeed, a number of other characteristics which were to define English progressive rock as a style emerged between 1967 and 1970 in the music of these bands as well. These include a persistent use of classically derived tone colors produced on the Mellotron, Hammond organ, and assorted acoustic instruments; rich vocal arrangements; lengthy pieces consisting of clearly articulated sections or movements; long instrumental passages; and a tendency to experiment with electronic effects and new recording techniques.

For these reasons, it is not inappropriate to say that the Moody Blues, Procol Harum, Pink Floyd, and the Nice, while considered proponents of psychedelic music by their contemporaries, actually represent a proto-progressive style, a "first wave," as it were, of English progressive rock. Nonetheless, it is a sign that the genre had yet to fully crystallize that the music of each individual band did not fully incorporate all of these elements. Furthermore, elements common to other types of psychedelic music that were to play no role in the mature progressive rock style, such as a fascination with guitar and organ feedback and the use of quasi-Indian flourishes, are still evident in the music of these bands.

It is only with the emergence of a "second wave" of bands in the closing years of the 1960s that English progressive rock as a genre fully comes of age. Virtually every major English progressive rock band released their first album during this period, including Jethro Tull (1968), King Crimson, Yes, Genesis, and Van der Graaf Generator (1969), and Emerson, Lake and Palmer, Gentle Giant and Curved Air (1970). King Crimson's first album, *In the Court of the Crimson King* (released October 1969), had an especially powerful impact on the nascent progressive rock movement, and just may be the most influential progressive rock album ever released. Unlike the first releases of Yes, Genesis, Van der Graaf, and Jethro Tull, which do not represent a fully matured musical vision, this album displays every major element of the mature progressive rock genre. To be sure, there are obvious references to the music of the proto-progressive bands (the Moody Blues, Procol Harum, Pink Floyd); the achievement of *Crimson King* is to crystallize these elements into a distinctive, immediately recognizable style. Both its melancholy, minor-key passages permeated by acoustic guitar and the Mellotron's symphonic colorings ("Epitaph") and its muscular, polyrhythmic jazz-tinged stylizations dominated by alto sax and fuzzed guitar ("21st-century Schizoid Man") were to reverberate in progressive rock throughout the 1970s. The album exerted a powerful extramusical influence on later progressive rock bands as well: both the apocalyptic subject matter of "Epitaph" and "Schizoid Man" and the medieval imagery and mystical undertones of the title cut greatly influenced later progressive rock bands, as did the album's surrealistic, gothic cover art.

King Crimson's next three studio albums never quite recaptured the magic of *In the Court of the Crimson King,* and it was not until Robert Fripp reorganized the band in 1972 to achieve a sparer and more improvisatory sound that King Crimson again became an influential force in progressive rock. In the meantime, however, the multi faceted influence of Crimson's first album enabled a number of other major progressive rock bands to find their own unique voices in a series of albums released in the early 1970s. Yes and Genesis drew on the stylistic implications of "Epitaph" to create a rich, symphonic strain of progressive rock in which folk-like acoustic guitar lines, massive backdrops of sustained keyboard chords, and (in the case of Yes) complex, almost choral vocal arrangements are blended with more angular electric guitar leads and the power of a rock rhythm section to create quasi-symphonic rock song suites. Albums such as Yes's *The Yes Album, Fragile* (both 1971), and *Close to the Edge* (1972) and Genesis's *Trespass* (1970), *Nursery Cryme* (1971), and *Foxtrot* (1972) developed this style to a high degree of perfection; *Close to the Edge* and *Foxtrot* are particularly outstanding. These albums exerted a massive influence on later bands in a number of realms: the music itself, the fractured narrative verse, and the mythic surrealism of the cover art (Roger Dean's artwork for Yes, in particular, came to serve as a visual symbol of progressive rock in much the same way that occult imagery came to symbolize heavy metal).

At the same time Yes and Genesis were developing their highly influential strain of progressive rock, other bands such as Gentle Giant, Curved Air, and Van der Graaf Generator were drawing not only on the symphonic/folk rock of "Epitaph," but also on the proto-fusion of "Schizoid Man" and the avant-garde improvisatory approach of "Moonchild" to create less influential but more individual variants of the same style. For instance, Gentle Giant added elements of cool jazz and renaissance music to the symphonic/folk framework, creating a dauntingly complex approach characterized by spasmodic rhythms, dense textures, and an extraordinarily varied instrumentation. Their almost manneristic progressive rock can be heard to best effect on *Octopus* (1973) and the excellent *Free Hand* (1975). Van der Graaf Generator, meanwhile, developed the dark undertones of *Crimson King*, framing vocalist Peter Hammill's relentlessly bleak verse with "gothic" organ backdrops, alternately angular and dulcet reeds, and virtuosic drumming. Their dark, brooding progressive rock variant received its most powerful expression on the remarkable *Pawn Hearts* LP of 1971. Curved Air's numerous personnel changes prevented them from developing the highly individual sound of the other bands mentioned here, and many feel they never quite lived up to the promise of their debut album of 1970, *Air Conditioning* (although their *Phantasmagoria* of 1972 comes close). On the other hand, they did introduce the electric violin into the mainstream of rock music, and were also the first major progressive rock band to be fronted by a female lead vocalist.

Emerson, Lake and Palmer and Jethro Tull, two other bands which rose to prominence in the early 1970s, also proved to be important to the formation of the mature progressive rock style, even if they stood a greater distance from the King Crimson legacy. Although Greg Lake was recruited from the original lineup of King Crimson, Emerson, Lake and Palmer's self-titled debut album of 1970, with its keyboard heroics, angrily distorted Hammond organ, and cyborgian arrangements of the classics, draws mainly on Emerson's work with the Nice. Indeed, the keyboards/bass guitar/drums configuration of these two bands popularized the keyboard trio format: later trios featuring multikeyboardists such as Dave Stewart (Egg), Patrick Moraz (Refugee), and Eddie Jobson (U.K.) all show a clear stylistic debt to the Nice/ELP legacy. (Moraz's rhythm section in Refugee, bassist Lee Jackson and drummer Brian Davison, were in fact veterans of the Nice.) On the other hand, ELP were not just a continuation of the Nice under a new name. Greg Lake's sonorous voice and abilities as an acoustic guitarist opened up a range of possibilities never available to the Nice. Furthermore, the trumpet-like blasts of the modular Moog synthesizer, a novelty item before Emerson pioneered its use in live performances, introduced an entirely new sonic element into the mainstream of popular music. The heavier, more exclusively electronic and keyboard-dominated alternative to the Yes/Genesis strain of symphonic progressive rock suggested on *Emerson, Lake and Palmer* was further developed in the band's influential *Tarkus* (1971), and brought to perfection in their masterpiece, *Brain Salad Surgery* (1973).

Meanwhile, Jethro Tull's highly eclectic sound crystallized on their second and third LPs, *Stand up* (1969) and *Benefit* (1970). It was here that Ian Anderson's jazz-inspired flute work and Faginesque persona emerged as the predominant elements of the band's identity. Stylistically, these albums revealed the peculiar amalgamation of English folk music, rhythm-and-blues, renaissance and baroque instrumental music (as opposed to the symphonic and church music sources favored by the other major progressive rock bands) that has marked all of their subsequent releases. The band pursued the most epic (and overtly "progressive") ramifications of this approach on their *Thick as a Brick* and *Passion Play* LPs of 1972 and 1973, respectively.

By 1972, the formation of progressive rock as a distinct style was essentially complete. Nonetheless, even at this time talk of a self-conscious progressive rock "movement" is probably misleading. As Bill Bruford has remarked, "[There was] no sense of alliance or cooperation in a musical movement between the chief players. In 1972–74, for example, no self-respecting member of King Crimson would have been seen dead in a musical movement that contained Genesis."[7] This is not necessarily surprising. Artistic styles are usually recognized as such retroactively; in the early stages of a style, before conventions have hardened, practitioners are often more keenly aware of differences between themselves than in similarities.

Certainly there were a number of differences in the character of the music put forth by these bands. First, there are contrasts in instrumentation. The quasi-symphonic keyboard/guitar-dominated sound of Yes, ELP, and Genesis can be contrasted with the jazzier, woodwind-tinged sheen of King Crimson, Van der Graaf Generator, and Gentle Giant, while the predominantly electronic approach of ELP or *Red*-era King Crimson is quite different from the much more acoustic ambience of early Genesis or Renaissance. Second, there are different levels of virtuosity: the almost overpowering (and occasionally overbearing) virtuosity of ELP, Yes, or the mid-1970s incarnation of King Crimson can be contrasted with the relative lack of virtuosity in the music of Pink Floyd, while bands such as Genesis and Van der Graaf Generator attempted to hew to a middle path. Third, there are different levels of emphasis on singing and playing. Even in the late psychedelic era, one notes a difference between bands such as the Moody Blues and Procol Harum who drew on the tradition of the pop song and were essentially vocal groups, and bands such as Pink Floyd and the Nice who placed greater emphasis on instrumental music and were much more given to experimentation with instrumental forms. This dichotomy is present in the music of the progressive rock bands of the 1970s as well. Finally, there is a difference between what might be termed a "heavier" and a "lighter" ambience, which results both from specific approaches to rhythm, mode, and instrumentation, and from the content of the lyrics (for a discussion of the dichotomy between "Aquarian" and "Existentialist" lyrics, see chapter 4). Suffice it to say that no one is likely to confuse the savage energy of King Crimson and Van der Graaf Generator in their mid-1970s incarnations with the disinterested density of Gentle Giant or the more pastoral, at times delicate, stylizations of Genesis or Renaissance (or even Yes in their quieter moments).

Nonetheless, my chief argument in the next chapter will be that the similarities between these bands outweighed the differences. Further proof of the fact that a distinct progressive rock style was in existence by 1972 is that bands which appeared after this date merely modified the sound of one or more of the already established bands. Thus Renaissance, beginning with their 1972 LP *Prologue*, developed a more pastoral, acoustic version of the guitar/keyboard symphonic stylizations of Yes and Genesis, with the added twist of a female lead vocalist. Camel, who released their first album in 1973, fused the influential Yes/Genesis sound with the jazzier approach of the Canterbury school, especially Caravan. U.K., a group that was formed relatively late in the progressive rock era (1977), created a more fusion-tinged variant of ELP's Hammond- and Moog-dominated sound tapestries.

A word should be said at this point about the term "progressive rock" itself. In the mid- to late 1960s, this term was appropriated by the underground radio stations and applied to psychedelic music in general; the label was used to distinguish music of this type from the pop music of the pre-psychedelic era. Around 1970, however, the term "progressive rock" came to have a more specific meaning, signifying a style that sought to expand the boundaries of rock on both a stylistic basis (via the use of longer and more involved structural formats) and on a conceptual basis (via the treatment of epic subject matter), mainly through the appropriation of elements associated with classical music. It is this new, more specific application of the term which is clearly intended in the liner notes of Caravan's debut LP of 1969: "Caravan belong to a new breed of progressive rock groups—freeing themselves from the restricting conventions of pop music by using unusual time signatures and sophisticated harmonies. Their arrangements involve variations of tempo and dynamics of almost symphonic complexity." In the late 1950s, Gunther Schuller coined the term "third stream" to describe music that fused elements of two formerly distinct traditions to form a new style.[8] Although Schuller was mostly concerned with classical/jazz fusions, progressive rock, which is mainly a classical/rock fusion with some folk and jazz elements included, can also be considered a "third stream" genre (I discuss progressive rock's debt to classical music and folk styles in chapter 2, and its debt to jazz in chapter 6).

Two synonymous terms, "classical rock" and "art rock," have sometimes been used to describe the genre as well. However, the term "classical rock" tends to negate the style's nonclassical sources (i.e., jazz and folk), while the term "art rock" often leads to confusion between the style under discussion here and the highly theatrical, ironically detached glam-rock of David Bowie and Roxy Music, which is also sometimes called "art rock." The editors of *The Rolling Stone Encyclopedia of Rock and Roll* argue that the term "progressive rock" most clearly describes the genre, and I have accepted their definition.[9]

The "first wave" and "second wave" bands can be distinguished from each other on both a chronological and a purely stylistic basis. The Moody Blues, Procol Harum, and the Nice did their most representative work between 1967 and 1971; the Nice disbanded in 1970, the Moody Blues released no new studio albums between 1972 and 1978, and although Procol Harum were intermittently active until 1977, they had no more top forty albums after 1973. On the other hand, the "second wave" bands did their most representative work between 1971 and 1976, the period that must be considered the "golden age" of English progressive rock. Virtually all of these bands released their most critically acclaimed albums during this period: thus Van der Graaf Generator's *Pawn Hearts* and Jethro Tull's *Aqualung* were released in 1971, Yes's *Close to the Edge* and Curved Air's *Phantasmagoria* in 1972, ELP's *Brain Salad Surgery* and Pink Floyd's *Dark Side of the Moon* in 1973, Genesis's *The Lamb Lies Down on Broadway* in 1974, and Gentle Giant's *Free Hand* in 1975. Pink Floyd were the one "first wave" band that continued to transform their style well into the 1970s; they adopted many of the stylistic practices of the "second wave" groups, and remained at the cutting edge of the progressive rock movement.

On a purely stylistic basis, the music of the "second wave" bands is different from that of their predecessors by being more monumental and more complex on virtually every level. Pieces are longer, formal plans are more involved, and correspondingly less emphasis is placed on traditional song forms. Instrumental virtuosity is much more pronounced, and harmonic syntax and textures are more complex. In addition, the relatively square-cut rhythms of the "first wave" bands, which feature a rather predictable emphasis on the downbeat, can be contrasted with the more complex metric schemes and more syncopated rhythmic patterns of the "second wave" bands (which, in turn, may reflect the greater influence exerted by jazz upon these later bands). The one area in which the music of the "second wave" bands is somewhat regressive is electronics. Despite the mass appearance of synthesizers in progressive rock during the 1970s and the great improvement in the quality of recording and sound production during this period, the most adventurous electronic experimentation in English rock actually took place during the late 1960s and very early 1970s, especially in the music of Pink Floyd and some of the early Canterbury bands such as Soft Machine and Egg. The next chapter, which undertakes a detailed stylistic survey of the genre, will explore some of these differences between earlier and later progressive rock on a more specific basis than is possible here.

Another major difference between "first wave" and "second wave" bands involves the forum in which they presented their music. The "first wave" bands began their careers by playing clubs and small venues, mainly in southern England, that were countercultural haunts; the interaction that existed between performers and audiences in such settings was obviously very intense. Many of the "second wave" bands (Yes, Genesis) also started out by playing clubs, but after 1970 the clubs rapidly declined in importance as a feasible revenue-generating source. Large-scale tours were used to promote a group's latest album, and became necessary to generate the huge volume of sales that record company executives increasingly expected; Hugh Hopper once described such tours as "loss-making promotions for platinum discs."[10] The record companies expected their bands to tour North America, which offered a much larger market and much greater potential revenues than Britain; Simon Frith estimates that by the late 1970s the United States accounted for roughly 50 percent of the world's record-buying public, Britain no more than 8 percent.[11] More successful bands headlined concerts at arenas and stadiums, while lesser-known groups opened for a better-known group on their first or second tour (by the third tour a band usually had either broken up or had achieved sufficient record sales to headline its own concert tours).

By the mid-1970s, the most commercially successful progressive rock bands—ELP, Yes, Pink Floyd, Jethro Tull—easily sold out large stadiums and arenas on their American tours; between 1971 and 1976 these four bands had sixteen top ten and four number one albums in the United States between them, arguably making progressive rock the most commercially lucrative style of this period. Even bands with more of a cult following—King Crimson, Gentle Giant, Genesis (which did not become a spectacular commercial success until the late 1970s)—were quite capable of selling out venues that seated several thousand.[12] Groups such as Van der Graaf Generator and Henry Cow that were either unwilling or unable to tour the United States could not emerge as a significant force on the progressive rock scene. Even though these bands commanded a dedicated British and Continental European following,[13] the possibilities for the profitable dissemination of their music in the States were simply too limited, and thus the influence of their music (even though it was highly innovative) was circumscribed.

The short-term effect of this new pattern was to make the bands, and many people associated with them, very rich. However, this trend also contained the seeds of the music's eventual decline and dissolution. The successful bands spent much more time touring America than Britain; furthermore, the nature of the huge venues at which they played decisively limited the interaction between performers and members of the audience, who at really large venues were often hard-pressed to even see the performers. The net result of this trend was to progressively remove the bands from the subcultural scene in which they had originated, and to create the vast gulf between the major acts and their fans which characterized the rock scene of the 1970s. At the beginning of progressive rock's "golden age," the audience for the major progressive rock bands could be described as a genuine subculture, united not only by aesthetic tastes but also by lifestyle and worldview. By 1976, however—the year usually given as marking the implosion of what was left of the counterculture—the audience for these bands increasingly came to re-semble a taste public, united mainly by aesthetic taste rather than by an adherence to a common lifestyle or worldview (indeed, unlike subcultures, taste publics tend to share at least some aspects of their lifestyles and worldviews in common with mainstream society). As a result, the music of the major progressive rock bands was increasingly dictated not by the symbiotic relationship between a specific sub-culture and its musicians, but rather by pressures exerted by the recording industry and other outside commercial agents. The eventual outcome of this situation will be discussed more fully in the final chapter of the book.

The Progressive Rock Style
The Music

We were playing totally new music, something that didn't fit any style. That was the most exciting thing about playing with the Nice. Nobody else did our blend of classical, rock, and jazz.[1]

Although I do not wish to disparage the Nice's originality in any way, the fact is that *many* English bands were experimenting with fusing elements of rhythm-and-blues, jazz, and classical (as well as folk and North Indian) styles during the late 1960s. As I said in the last chapter, the emerging progressive rock idiom was ultimately most indebted to R&B, folk, and the classics. Indian music ended up having relatively little impact on the mature progressive rock style, while jazz made a greater impact on the various fusion styles of the 1970s than on progressive rock. From R&B, and particularly from the heavily amplified British blues of the 1960s, progressive rock drew its propensity for long pieces, the heavy beat and amplification of its electric sections, and its emphasis on instrumental passages and virtuoso solos. From the music of the 1960s folk revival the genre drew its modality, its fondness for acoustic instruments, and the meditative, pastoral ambience of its acoustic sections. To some degree, progressive rock could be described as a marriage between the "masculine" R&B and "feminine" folk styles.

However, such a description would ignore the huge impact that European art music made on the genre. Progressive rock has proved to be highly eclectic, drawing on a number of different musics from within the overall umbrella of the classical tradition:[2] symphonic music, renaissance and baroque sacred music, classical piano and guitar music, even medieval music. These different bodies of music have, in turn, influenced progressive rock in a number of ways: in its instrumentation, its approach to structure, its harmonic and metric practices, and its attitude toward virtuosity. In short, it is the thorough permeation of progressive rock by the European art music tradition that separates it not only from the earlier styles that it developed out of, but also from contemporaneous styles of popular music.

In this chapter I will examine the progressive rock style as it emerged during its "golden age" of roughly 1970 to 1976. The progressive rock style will be shown to be indebted to the classical tradition in the realms of instrumentation, structure, and virtuosity, while a clear link will be demonstrated between the genre's modal harmony and the legacy of folk music. I also highlight a number of clear homologies that can be drawn between progressive rock as a musical style and the counterculture of the late 1960s and early 1970s. For instance, progressive rock's juxtaposition of "masculine" and "feminine" sections can be seen to symbolize many of the conflicts that were of great importance to the hippies. Furthermore, a clear connection can be drawn between the style's wayward modal harmony and the counterculture's acid-induced sense of time (or timelessness). Finally, progressive rock's fondness for virtuosity and compositional artifice fosters the sense of surprise, contradiction, and uncertainty that was so prized by the hippies.

Instrumentation and Tone Color

Perhaps the most readily identifiable characteristic of the progressive rock sound is its persistent use of tone colors drawn from a variety of European art music sources. Again and again, one hears echoes of symphonic music, renaissance and baroque sacred music, classical piano and guitar literature, and medieval and renaissance vocal music in the most representative examples of the style. Merely pointing out the self-evident debt of progressive rock's instrumentation to the classical tradition, however, risks ignoring the deeper significance of the idiom's juxtaposition of "classical" and rock instrumentation. If, as I believe, timbre conveys gender messages more thoroughly than any other element (although I believe rhythm and harmony are also important in this realm), then the genre's electric/acoustic dichotomy is of importance for at least two reasons. First, its systematic contrasts of harsh, closed, "masculine" timbres (produced on electric guitar, distorted Hammond, and synthesizer) with more open, relaxed, "feminine" timbres that lack strong attacks and piercing upper frequencies (produced on the Mellotron and various acoustic instruments) is almost unique. Other contemporaneous styles of popular music have tended to be either "hard" (hard rock, heavy metal) or "soft" (folk, top forty–oriented pop) in their tone colors. As I will point out later, progressive rock's contrasts of "masculine" and "feminine" sections contribute directly to the structure of many lengthy progressive rock pieces, and mirror the conflicts between patriarchal and matriarchal modes of social organization that were of great significance to the counterculture. (Incidentally, I use the terms "masculine" and "feminine" simply as metaphors and archetypes, commonly used by musicologists; I do not attempt to judge whether the characteristics associated with these terms are biologically grounded or socially constructed.)

Furthermore, if past commentators have been correct to assert that contemporary popular musics have played an important role in gender construction, and if I am correct to postulate that progressive rock's audience during the 1970s was largely male (a point I will address in greater detail in chapters 6 and 7), then the style undoubtedly played a role in defining a new type of masculinity for its post-hippie audiences. The hippie subculture was ultimately patriarchal, and hippies did not, as was often supposed at the time, value androgyny or unisexuality. Nonetheless, masculinity as the hippies redefined it contained elements that the Establishment had long considered effeminate: this was most evident in the men's long hair, beads, and flamboyant clothing. However, it is also evident in the music. The hippies retained many elements of previous rock-and-roll styles, such as the distorted guitars and the heavy beat. On the other hand, the heavy borrowing from classical and folk musics that earlier rock-and-rollers would have considered effete showed a new willingness to redefine "masculinity" in contemporary rock. Not coincidentally, contemporaneous genres such as heavy metal that were more exclusively concerned with celebrating masculine power largely rejected acoustic instruments and the classical legacy (a reaction grounded in class as well as gender which will be explored in more detail in later chapters).

Finally, it is important to point out how often progressive rock has drawn on instrumental or vocal stylizations that traditionally have had religious or ritualistic connotations. The idiom's use of the Hammond as a substitute pipe organ, its fanfare-like synthesizer choruses, and it almost choral vocal arrangements are borrowed from the heritage of earlier religious music, especially the musical legacy of the Anglican church. The reasons behind this "ritualistic" instrumentation will become more apparent at the end of the next chapter, when I describe how rock of the late 1960s and early 1970s often played a quasi-liturgical role for its listeners.

The most obvious adoption of classical instrumentation by progressive rock musicians came in the late 1960s and early 1970s, when a number of bands actually recorded with a symphony orchestra. This trend was initiated by the Moody Blues with their influential *Days of Future Passed* LP, recorded late in 1967, and was followed soon after by Procol Harum, the Nice, Deep Purple, Pink Floyd, Yes, and, in the mid-1970s, by Renaissance, Caravan, and ELP.[3] Although the practice of working with symphony orchestras drew much critical attention to progressive rock, not all the recordings that resulted were terribly successful,[4] and at any rate very few groups did more than one album with an orchestra; recordings of this type represent only a small percentage of the overall output of progressive rock bands. Rather, these groups drew on electric and electronic keyboards[5]—many of them creations of the 1960s—to simulate the classical tone colors that were so important to the genre.

Prior to the mid-1960s, the instrumentation of most rock bands consisted of one or two electric guitars, a bass guitar, and drums; a piano was sometimes present, but inevitably was regarded as part of the rhythm section, not as a lead instrument. Only during the late 1960s did the introduction of three specific keyboard instruments—the Hammond organ, the Mellotron, and the Moog synthesizer—make the progressive rock sound possible, and bring the keyboard player to a level of parity with, or even predominance over, the guitarist. Indeed, in the view of former Soft Machine bassist Hugh Hopper, the rise of the keyboardist was the defining event of progressive rock, and may have represented the genre's most important contribution to popular music as a whole:

> One particularly welcome fresh development [of the late 1960s] was the sudden upsurge of keyboard players. From the Fifties the electric guitar—at first a wonderful new sound but, after exposure in thousands of groups, in danger of becoming just another part of the musical wallpaper—had been the standard rock and pop instrument. It is quite easy to achieve a passable level of accomplishment on the six-string guitar. Unfortunately many guitarists of the period never progressed beyond the passable; outstanding players like Hendrix and Clapton simply confirmed how ordinary the majority were.
>
> Perseverance and practice, however, is needed to master any form of keyboard. Survivors of childhood piano lessons have inevitably absorbed plenty of music theory and possess genuine technical ability. Not all the organists and pianists of the great psychedelic era were over-endowed with talent and inspiration; however, the good ones, such as Traffic's Steve Winwood, Curved Air's Francis Monkman, Soft Machine's Mike Ratledge, Van der Graaf Generator's Hugh Banton, and the Nice's Keith Emerson came up with music and new sounds that were a much needed change.[6]

Hopper goes on to note that the introduction of classical influences into psychedelic music happened primarily through the keyboardists: "It should also be said that classically-trained keyboard players often found themselves at loggerheads with more instinctive, less disciplined drummers, singers, and bassists."[7]

As Hopper suggests, the Hammond organ, although not new to the 1960s (the instrument dates back to the mid-1930s), became extremely important to the emerging progressive rock sound—and to British rock in general—during the late 1960s. When used in conjunction with the rotating Leslie Organ Speaker, which gives the instrument a livelier and deeper tone, the Hammond is capable of evoking a cathedral-like ambience. Matthew Fisher's organ part in Procol Harum's "A Whiter Shade of Pale" (1967), which is based on a theme by J. S. Bach, offers an early example of the Hammond as a substitute pipe organ. Other early champions of the instrument such as Keith Emerson used a Marshall amp to exaggerate the key click of the Hammond and create "that warm, dirty, overdriven, mechanically-generated sound"[8] for which the instrument became famous. The Hammond was frequently featured both as a surrogate pipe organ and for its more percussive properties by bands such as ELP, Yes, Genesis, Van der Graaf Generator, Egg, Gentle Giant, and U.K.

The major strength of the Hammond was its versatility. It proved to be an effective textural instrument, capable both of supplying sustained background chords and of stating thematic material. It also proved to be an excellent lead instrument, allowing a Keith Emerson or a Mike Ratledge to create the kind of frenzied, lightning-fast lead lines that had previously been the exclusive property of electric guitarists. Above all, perhaps, it is the instrument that best captures progressive rock's ideal of uniting masculine and feminine musical characteristics. A distorted or fuzzed Hammond organ produces a massive, complex timbre whose power and sustaining capabilities are rivaled only by the electric guitar; Keith Emerson has described it as a "tacky, aggressive, almost distorted, angry sound."[9] On the other hand, played quietly, with no distortion and plenty of chorus, the Hammond can be a more delicate, "feminine" instrument. For its many champions, one of the chief challenges of mastering the instrument was learning to exploit the many timbral shadings between these two extremes.

The Mellotron, invented in the early 1960s, is an organ-like instrument (lacking pedals, however) capable of reproducing prerecorded string, woodwind, and choral voicings. Because the instrument is capable of playing chords (unlike early synthesizers, which could only play one note at a time), the Mellotron was frequently used to create a massive symphonic background of sustained chords; it was also frequently used to present a slow, lyrical melody. Since notes on the Mellotron are produced by running a strip of tape across a replay head, the instrument does not "speak" rapidly enough to make the kind of rapid, flamboyant passagework that worked so well on the Hammond organ a possibility, and as a result the instrument was not used for soloing.

Although the Beatles used the instrument as a background effect as early as 1966 (in "Strawberry Fields Forever"), it was the Moody Blues that first made the Mellotron an integral part of their sound (beginning with *Days of Future Passed*), and thereafter the instrument was often used by King Crimson, Genesis, Yes, Gentle Giant, and a host of other bands. It was most often used in quiet sections, usually to interject a bittersweet or romantic quality (in the same way that Hollywood film composers have long used the string section); if the Hammond was usually progressive rock's "masculine" keyboard, the Mellotron was its "feminine" foil. It faded from use only during the late 1970s, when a number of sturdier, more mechanically reliable polyphonic synthesizers appeared on the market.

The Moog synthesizer played a particularly important role in the progressive rock sound. Indeed, in the early 1970s this instrument was largely the private property of progressive rock groups, before it gradually began to be appropriated into other genres of contemporary popular music. Robert Moog's earliest instruments were both monophonic (that is, incapable of producing more than one pitch at a time) and enormous. However, in 1969 Keith Emerson, while still with the Nice, pioneered the live use of the instrument, thus encouraging Moog to create a smaller, more portable model. After Moog marketed just such an instrument, the Minimoog, in 1971, the synthesizer quickly became integral to the progressive rock sound. By the mid-1970s, when Moog had manufactured the first mass-produced synthesizer capable of playing several notes at once, the Polymoog, a number of competitors had entered the market: ARP, Roland, Oberheim, Yamaha, Korg, and Sequential Circuits.[10] Synthesizers were well on the way to attaining their present role of preeminence in many types of contemporary popular music.

Moog's synthesizers (and those of his contemporaries) were capable of producing a virtually infinite variety of timbres, and most progressive rock bands used the instruments at some time or another to produce otherworldly sounds. However, the most remarkable electronic experimentation in English rock occurred before the mass availability of synthesizers. The mysterious wooshing, buzzing, and pulsating noises that psychedelic groups such as Pink Floyd achieved through feedback, distortion, use of primitive echo devices, and electronic manipulation of natural sounds became less and less evident after 1970, when progressive rock emerged as a genre distinct from psychedelic music.[11] Surprisingly often, progressive rock keyboardists treated the synthesizer as a souped-up Mellotron and pressed the instrument into service to suggest orchestral sonorities. In the hands of Keith Emerson, for instance, the Moog is often used to evoke a supersonic trumpet section, as in the simulated trumpet fanfares scattered across ELP's *Brain Salad Surgery* LP.

Interestingly, progressive rock keyboardists also discovered that the Minimoog could present an astonishingly authentic electric guitar simulation. This may explain why a number of prominent progressive rock bands—notably ELP, Refugee, Genesis, (after 1977), and U.K. (after 1978)—found it possible to dispense with a guitarist. (In ELP and Genesis, the bass guitarist was called on to occasionally double on guitar.) As one might expect, the early monophonic synthesizers were called upon to state thematic material, to supply instrumental commentary between vocal stanzas, and to serve as an alternate lead instrument to the electric guitar. With the advent of polyphonic synthesizers in the mid-1970s, the instrument was increasingly also used to provide a rich harmonic cushion, and thus began to displace both the Mellotron and the Hammond organ.

Even though the progressive rock stylistic code does permit the absence of a full-time guitarist, most progressive rock bands did employ one, although the use of both a lead and a rhythm guitarist—common in many other styles of rock—is very rare in English progressive rock of the 1970s. The progressive rock electric guitar style emphasizes melodic lines, not the kind of chordal riffing associated with other rock subgenres. Hugh Hopper attributes this fact to the presence of the Hammond organ: "Organists introduced the sound of long, sustained notes and thereby relieved many songs of the time-honored accompaniment of staccato guitar-strumming. More sinuous arrangements thus became possible, causing songwriters and vocalists to rethink their styles."[12] Even when in the sonic background, progressive rock guitarists tend to play arpeggios (broken chords) or a melodic ostinato (a short melodic pattern that is repeated over and over), often in unison with the bass guitarist, rather than strumming chords; chords are frequently strummed only on the acoustic guitar. Most progressive rock guitarists modified the sound of their electric guitars with a host of electronic devices such as fuzz boxes, flangers, phasers, and chorus units to create a massive, complex timbre that perfectly complements the quasi-symphonic tone colors of the electronic keyboards.

Despite the prominence afforded to electronic keyboards and (to a lesser extent) electric guitars, acoustic instruments also play a very important role in progressive rock. Indeed, it was part of the genre's stylistic code that keyboardists and guitarists were expected to demonstrate at least near-equal fluency on the acoustic instrument. King Crimson's Robert Fripp was probably the first rock guitarist to place equal emphasis on mastering the electric and acoustic instrument, and also established a precedent by drawing not only on rock but also on classical and jazz guitar techniques. Guitarist Steve Hackett of Genesis, in acknowledging Fripp's influence in this realm, states,

> I could put several guitarists in the same category [as Fripp] perhaps—Steve Howe, Pete Banks [members of two different incarnations of Yes], Jan Akkerman [of the Dutch progressive rock band Focus]. Guitarists in that mold are able to sketch in as many different styles as possible, without necessarily being a virtuoso in any of them. To really be, say, a virtuoso [classical] guitarist, I think you've got to devote yourself one hundred percent to that.[13]

Likewise, progressive rock's piano technique fundamentally modified the pounding, boogie-woogie-derived piano stylizations of early rock. Progressive rock pianists drew on a host of rhetorical devices drawn from the classical piano repertoire of the mid–nineteenth to early twentieth centuries, that is, from roughly Chopin and Liszt to Debussy, Ravel, and Bartók. The progressive rock piano style is marked by virtuoso scalar runs and rolling arpeggios in the right hand, arpeggiated or melodically active accompaniments in the left hand, grandiose block chords, and sustained, impressionistic chordal backdrops that make ample use of the damper pedal to blur and blend notes. There is also a definite influence of J. S. Bach's toccata style in progressive rock: the scalar runs, the sequential spinning out of a particular rhythmic motive, the virtuoso arpeggiation of straightforward chord progressions. However, this influence is most apparent in sections featuring the Hammond organ; Keith Emerson's famous organ solo in "Rondo" contains a lengthy excerpt from Bach's Toccata and Fugue in D Minor, while the Fantasia for unaccompanied Hammond which opens Argent's *Pure Love* suite is also very Bach-influenced.

Two other acoustic instruments that previously had played virtually no role in rock music, the flute and the violin, have also played a major role in the progressive rock sound. Unlike the keyboards and guitars, which function both to provide a harmonic backdrop and to supply lead lines, these instruments are used either in an obbligato role (most often to supply instrumental commentary between vocal stanzas) or as an alternate lead instrument to the keyboards and guitar. The electric violin, in particular, has been transformed by players such as Eddie Jobson, Darryl Way, and David Cross into a very different instrument than its acoustic counterpart. In many of King Crimson's pieces of the mid-1970s, for instance, Cross's fuzzed and heavily distorted violin is often difficult to distinguish from Robert Fripp's equally aggressive guitar; much the same remark could be made about the interplay of Jerry Goodman's violin and John McLaughlin's guitar in the music of Mahavishnu Orchestra. The flute, on the other hand, is often used to create the same pastoral ambience that it has traditionally been used for in classical music; this is how the Moody Blues' Roy Thomas and King Crimson's Ian McDonald used the instrument. At times, though, players such as Jethro Tull's Ian Anderson and Focus's Thijs van Leer use a breathier, dirtier timbre that would be considered "incorrect" by conservatory standards. (Incidentally, a number of flute players, such as McDonald, Mel Collins, and Van der Graaf Generator's David Jackson, doubled on saxophones and occasionally other reed instruments.)

Certain premodern instruments were drawn on consistently enough that they should also be considered a minor part of the progressive rock soundscape. By far the most important instrument in this respect is the harpsichord, a keyboard instrument whose somewhat metallic, brittle sounds can be heard on the Nice's first album, *The Thoughts of Emerlist Davjack,* on Procol Harum's multimovement suite *In Held Twas in I,* on the Moody Blues' LP *In Search of the Lost Chord* (all dating from 1968), and on assorted cuts by later progressive rock bands such as Yes, ELP, Jethro Tull, and Gentle Giant. Other archaic instruments that are occasionally used by these groups include the flute-like recorder (featured quite prominently at the beginning of Led Zeppelin's "Stairway to Heaven" and throughout Yes's "Your Move"); the lute, a more complex ancestor of the modern acoustic guitar that was championed by Focus's Jan Akkerman; the krummhorn, a buzzing, kazoo-like wind instrument featured prominently on Gryphon's *Red Queen to Gryphon Three* LP; and the regal, a nasal, honking keyboard instrument whose strident sounds can be heard to good effect on Gentle Giant's "It's a Dog's Life." Like the Mellotron, these instruments are often used in conjunction with acoustic guitars to introduce a bittersweet or pastoral ambience in more overtly "feminine" sections.

The rhythm section of bass guitar and drums plays the same crucial role in progressive rock that it does in other rock styles; the drummer ceaselessly reiterates the beat, frequently at an unyielding tempo, while the bass guitarist provides a distinctive bottom sound. Nonetheless, progressive rock modified the role of the traditional rhythm section to its own individual ends. Unlike the heavy metal bass guitarist, whose bass lines are important mainly as a harmonic and rhythmic foundation, the progressive rock bassist frequently enters into the melodic discourse, and the bass guitar of choice is often a Rickenbacker or some other instrument with a thick, trebly sound. Chris Squire of Yes was especially influential in this regard: "The bass," Squire once remarked, "is just as much a solo and melodic instrument as the guitar or even organ."[14]

Likewise, the progressive rock drummer often sees himself as a classical percussionist as much as a drummer per se. Bill Bruford (Yes, King Crimson, U.K.) once commented that "even though I am ostensibly a drumset player, my thinking is more in keeping with that of a European symphony percussionist."[15] Compared to other rock styles, the role of the bass drum is somewhat de-emphasized, and the upper part of the drumset (the snare, toms, cymbals, and high hat) is used to create an intricate set of rhythmic patterns that often contradict the downbeat (usually laid out on the bass drum). Besides the drumset itself, most progressive rock drummers have a vast array of percussive devices at their disposal, both tuned (timpanis, chimes) and untuned (gongs, cowbells, woodblocks). More than in any other genre of rock, these percussion instruments are used not so much to emphasize the beat as to create an interesting, ever-shifting array of tone colors. A special feature of progressive rock, foreign to most other styles (save jazz-rock), is a tendency of the drummer to rhythmically double melodic lines.

Because of progressive rock's strong interest in experimenting with instrumental forms, it is not unusual for individual album cuts to be entirely instrumental, and occasionally an entire side of an album may be devoted to instrumental music. However, the presence of one or more vocalists is an integral part of the progressive rock style—if for no other reason than even in the early 1970s, it was very difficult to get airplay for a cut that contained no vocals. An entirely instrumental album is far more characteristic of progressive rock's "cousin," jazz-rock, with which it otherwise shares a number of common features.

The importance afforded to the vocalist(s) varies from band to band. In some groups, such as Yes, instrumental and vocal passages are given roughly equal weight; in other groups, such as King Crimson, singing is given somewhat less emphasis than playing. Very few progressive rock bands dispensed with vocalists entirely, however, and the exceptions merely proved the rule.

A number of writers have pointed out both the degree to which vocal quality serves to define particular genres of popular music, and the fact that we tend to tune into (or be turned off by) the characteristic qualities of a vocalist's delivery even before we understand the lyrics he or she is singing.[16] It is important, then, to consider the tonal properties most frequently cultivated by the style's vocalists.

The lead singer of a progressive rock band is usually a tenor, often a high tenor capable of hitting notes in the higher end of his range without resorting to falsetto (Yes's Jon Anderson). However, low tenors or baritones (Jethro Tull's Ian Anderson, Caravan's Richard Sinclair) are not uncommon; the rare female lead vocalist may be either an alto (Curved Air's Sonja Kristina) or a soprano (Renaissance's Annie Haslam). Despite the style's ties with classical music, the progressive rock lead singer seldom resorts to the rich chest tones and heavy vibrato of singers of Italian opera. Likewise, the progressive rock vocal style is separated from that of hard rock and heavy metal by its avoidance of rasping vocals that emphasize growling, wailing, or other "masculine," blues-derived vocal stylizations.

Rather, a straight, pure head tone with relatively little vibrato is preferred. The progressive rock vocal style shows a strong preference for tempered singing, with relatively little slipping and sliding to and from pitches. It lacks the microtonal richness of the blues singing styles and the supple vocal melismas of black gospel music (there are a few exceptions, such as the Ray Charles–inspired vocals of Procol Harum's Gary Brooker), although its rhythmic diction is often extraordinarily subtle. While this vocal style was foreshadowed by a number of singers active in the folk movement of the early to mid-1960s, I suspect its roots ultimately lie in the Anglican and Catholic choral traditions rather than folk music. Bob Dylan's nasal, reedy voice and highly constricted range has a closer link to genuine folk singing than the soaring soprano of Joan Baez or the angelic tenor of Art Garfunkle; however, it was the style of these latter singers that progressive rock vocalists usually chose to emulate. The resulting vocal quality is curiously platonic and asexual, and fits well within the framework of masculine/feminine instrumental juxtapositions which progressive rock favors.

The progressive rock vocal style is also affected, of course, by the nature of the melodic material. In much progressive rock, there is a tendency to alternate between lyrical tunes and relatively unmelodic lines that are mainly concerned with setting the text's rhythms as naturally as possible. While this latter kind of melodic line is relatively rare in popular music, it is quite common both to certain types of folk music and to opera, where it is used in the recitative sections. By drawing on techniques associated with these musics, many progressive rock vocalists mastered a kind of virtuoso declamation that involved moving back and forth between an infinite variety of shades of speech and song. Peter Gabriel and Van der Graaf Generator's Peter Hammill became especially adept at this technique (Hammill was also very good at moving quickly between the "choirboy" vocal style and a more rasping, hard-rock type of delivery), and it is also apparent in the singing of a number of the genre's other lead vocalists.

While some progressive rock bands (ELP) had only one singer, most had two, three, or even four, and passages sung by the lead singer alternate with choruses sung in three- or four-part harmony by all the group's vocalists. If a band had only one singer, he would often layer his voice on studio albums to create three- or four-part choruses of this type (Greg Lake's overdubs on ELP's "Lucky Man," John Wetton's overdubs on King Crimson's "Easy Money"). The Moody Blues, with four vocalists, were perhaps the first group to try to obtain an almost choral effect with their vocal arrangements; listening to their *In Search of the Lost Chord* LP, one is struck by the hymnlike quality of the climax of "Legend of a Mind" and the wordless vocal interlude of "Ride My See-Saw." Yes, Caravan, and Gentle Giant further developed this approach to vocal arranging, cultivating both homophonic arrangements in which the voices move in note-against-note motion with each other, and contrapuntal arrangements where two and even three separate vocal melodies are presented at the same time. Two pieces in particular by Gentle Giant, "Knots" and "On Reflection," employ four-part vocal counterpoint of staggering complexity; the vocal arrangement at the conclusion of Yes's "Parallels" is also quite dense.

The genre's fondness for rich vocal arrangements can probably best be explained in the context of English music history. From the thirteenth century on, English singers showed a great delight in creating smooth, sonorous vocal arrangements; throughout the medieval and early renaissance periods, the English style of vocal arranging was widely admired and imitated throughout Europe. In this sense, English rock can be seen as tapping into a long and venerable musical tradition—a point I will make in greater detail in chapter 7 when I consider the connection between progressive rock and Anglican church music.

Classical Forms

Anyone who has even a passing familiarity with progressive rock is usually aware that it represents an attempt to harness classical forms into a rock framework, to combine the classical tradition's sense of space and monumental scope with rock's raw power and energy. Understanding the role classical forms have played in progressive rock, then, is essential to understanding the genre as a musical style. I noted in chapter 1 that the Beatles' pioneering concept album *Sergeant Pepper* was in fact a modern-day recasting of the nineteenth-century song cycle: a group of songs are tied together conceptually, by a common concept or program that threads its way through the lyrics of each song, and musically, by the recurrence of one or more melodic ideas during the course of the song cycle/concept album. Since the concept album approach has remained very important to progressive rock throughout its existence—one immediately thinks of the Moody Blues, Pink

Floyd, and a host of later bands that have organized the songs on their albums along these lines—it cannot be denied that the nineteenth-century song cycle was an important legacy to progressive rock. Nonetheless, when commentators discuss "classical forms" in progressive rock, they are usually referring to instrumental forms. But why, one might ask, would rock musicians draw on classical forms in the first place?

This question can best be answered by considering the legacy of psychedelia. Driven equally by their exploration of hallucinogens and of instrumental styles such as jazz and Indian ragas that emphasized a great deal of improvisation, the psychedelic bands filled their songs with ever-longer instrumental sections. There is certainly a connection at some level between these lengthy improvised passages and acid trips—a sense that the flow of time is being suspended, that the tyranny of goal-directed movement is being replaced by a new emphasis on momentary sensation. As the musicians had become aware by the late 1960s, however, this approach was not without its shortcomings. When listening to the long instrumental jams of even the most gifted psychedelic bands—the Hendrix Experience, Cream, the Nice—one is initially wowed by the musicians' daunting virtuosity, but after two or three minutes a certain numbness sets in: one wishes for a greater variety of instrumentation and dynamics, a better balance between virtuoso solos and a more melodic approach, and ultimately a sense that the music was "going somewhere." Needless to say, in the hands of lesser musicians this type of jamming could prove insufferable: Iron Butterfly's "Inna Gadda Da Vida," with its interminable drum solo, is a perfect example. For musicians of the late 1960s who wished to continue with instrumental music—and these were increasingly drawn to the emerging progressive rock, jazz-rock, and heavy metal styles—the question became how to bring a sense of organization, variety, and climax to the music without completely destroying the spontaneity and sense of timelessness which characterized the best psychedelic jams.

The musicians who pioneered progressive rock found their answer in limiting the role of improvisation to one or two sections of a piece, and carefully organizing the rest of the material along the lines of nineteenth-century symphonic forms. This is not as surprising as it may at first appear. Nineteenth-century music and psychedelic music are both Romantic in the fullest sense of the word, sharing the same cosmic outlook, the same preoccupation with the infinite and otherwordly, the same fondness for monumental statement (often conveyed through very long pieces), and the same concern with expressing epic conflicts.[17]

The two nineteenth-century genres that seem to have particularly interested these musicians are the programmatic multimovement suite and the symphonic poem. Both genres are, of course, lengthy orchestral works that consist of either a number of discrete movements (the multimovement suite) or several distinct but interlocking sections (the symphonic poem), and exemplify that quintessentially nineteenth-century phenomenon, program music—that is, instrumental music that attempts to convey an idea or story, or perhaps aims to depict a landscape or a visual image. The movements or sections of these pieces are given musical coherence by the appearance of one or more melodic ideas which are transformed throughout the course of the piece; the manner in which a piece's principal theme or themes are transformed from section to section is often crucial to conveying its extramusical program. Variety is achieved by taking different approaches to musical elements such as tempo, rhythm, orchestration, texture, and harmonic character in each movement or section.

Although there are progressive rock multimovement suites such as Pink Floyd's *Atom Heart Mother* and Camel's *The Snow Goose* that are almost completely instrumental (both contain some wordless vocalises), most of progressive rock's lengthier pieces combine instrumental and vocal sections, and actually represent something of a hybrid between the song cycle and the instrumental programmatic approaches. Likewise, the distinction between multimovement suites and pieces that adhere to the single-movement sectionalized approach of the symphonic poem is not always clear-cut; length is the chief distinguishing factor. Progressive rock pieces between six and twelve minutes in length usually adopt the contours of the single-movement sectionalized forms—examples such as Yes's "Roundabout," ELP's "Trilogy," and Genesis's "Firth of Fifth" create the impression of a song that has been expanded to enormous proportions by the inclusion of lengthy instrumental preludes, interludes, and postludes, as well as one or more contrasting bridge sections.

On the other hand, most of progressive rock's multimovement suites occupy at least one side of an album and are twenty minutes long at the minimum, far too long to be perceived of as "mere" songs. In pieces of this sort, instrumental sections are stretched into full-length movements, while vocal sections take on the character of quasi-independent songs; it is here that the genre reaches truly symphonic dimensions. Progressive rock's first three multimovement suites appeared in 1968: Pink Floyd's *A Saucerful of Secrets*, the Nice's *Ars Longa Vita Brevis*, and Procol Harum's *In Held Twas in I*. Multimovement suites became especially popular with these bands around 1969 and 1970, when a number of them recorded with symphony orchestras: witness the Nice's *Five Bridges Suite* (1969) and Pink Floyd's *Atom Heart Mother* (1970). Even after 1970, when enthusiasm for recording with symphony orchestras waned sharply, this approach remained very important to progressive rock, and a partial listing of progressive rock multimovement suites would include some of the genre's best-known pieces: *Tarkus* and *Karn Evil 9* by ELP, *Close to the Edge* and *Tales from Topographic Oceans* by Yes, *Supper's Ready* by Genesis, *A Plague of Lighthouse Keepers* by Van der Graaf Generator, *In the Dead of Night* by U.K., *Lizard* by King Crimson, *The Snow Goose* by Camel, and *Scheherazade* by Renaissance. It is important to point out, though, that even as progressive rock became increasingly identified with pieces of symphonic scope, it never entirely abandoned the legacy of the pop song. Most progressive rock albums contain at least a few songs of three to four minutes in length which follow the conventions of standard pop-song forms fairly closely, although more emphasis might be placed on contrasting instrumental middle sections than was usual in other genres.

By drawing on the legacy of nineteenth-century program music, progressive rock was able to address two of the major challenges posed by the long instrumental sections of psychedelic rock: how to bring a sense of variety and a sense of direction to the music. Progressive rock's answer to this first challenge involves systematic juxtapositions of what can best be termed masculine and feminine sections; while this approach is not unusual in symphonic music, it is rare in most other rock styles, and thus became one of progressive rock's defining characteristics. Tony Banks of Genesis, a band especially well known for this kind of juxtaposition, has noted that "you make a soft bit prettier by putting it next to a loud bit. Our playing on 'Musical Box' is just an exercise in dynamics. 'Supper's Ready' is another example of that."[18]

The type of dynamics shifts referred to by Banks also involve tone-color contrasts, since quieter sections primarily involve acoustic instruments, while the louder sections are dominated by electric/electronic instruments. Significantly, electronic and acoustic passages each have their own characteristic and mutually exclusive approach to musical elements such as harmony, rhythm, melody, and texture. For instance, in passages using acoustic instruments, the rhythm section of drums and bass guitar is often de-emphasized or entirely absent; as a result, the heavy, rock-steady beat of electric sections is replaced by a gentler, more flexible, classically oriented conception of rhythm. Furthermore, acoustic sections tend to be slower and to feature longer, more lyrical melodies, simpler harmonic progressions, and more open textures, while electric sections tend to be faster and to emphasize less tuneful melodic material, denser textures, and more complex harmonies.

Clearly, in progressive rock the alternation of electronic and acoustic sections creates a set of dialectical opposites. Acoustic passages suggest the meditative, pastoral, traditional, and "feminine," electronic passages the dynamic, technological, futuristic, and "masculine." The masculine/feminine analogy goes deeper than one might think, since masculine and feminine sections complete each other, contributing to the expansion and contraction, the movement toward and away from climaxes, that was such a central facet of progressive rock structure. Furthermore, this masculine/feminine dialectic allows for a symbolic playing out of many of the conflicts that were of great significance to the hippies. It symbolizes how a whole set of cultural opposites—high and low culture, European and African-American creative approaches, a futuristic technocracy and an idyllic agrarian past, or matriarchal (creative, intuitive) and patriarchal (rational, carefully organized) modes of society—might be integrated into a larger whole. As will be seen, the concern with reconciling these seemingly irreconcilable cultural opposites is a major concern of the genre, and strongly informs its lyrics and cover art as well.

Progressive rock is also able to achieve an impressive variety by drawing on a number of different types of melodic expression. While vocal sections often consist of tunes in the commonly understood sense of the word, instrumental sections tend to de-emphasize full-blown tunes in favor of other types of melodic material. Large-scale structure in instrumental progressive rock results from the repetition of brief melodic ideas or chord progressions, and the combination of such fragments to produce larger, more complex units. One often encounters short, four- or eight-bar fanfare-like instrumental themes that recur periodically throughout a movement or section; repeated ground-bass patterns or chordal ostinatos that are overlaid with virtuoso passagework, short thematic fragments, or a combination of the two; and folksong-like or chant-like melodic edifices that are created by splicing together short phrases of unequal length. This last approach, which may be transferred to vocal sections as well, results in melodic structures which contain virtually none of the four-square repetitions of phrase rhythms or phrase lengths normally associated with rock.

Progressive rock was able to solve yet another challenge posed by the psychedelic jam—how to create a sense of direction—by drawing on nineteenth-century symphonic music's fondness for building up tension until a shattering climax is reached, abruptly tapering off, and then starting the whole process anew. In progressive rock, this process is most frequently achieved by beginning with a quiet (often acoustic) passage, usually without the rhythm section, and then gradually layering in electric/electronic instruments, and ultimately the bass and drums, until a powerful climax is achieved. Yes's music offers a number of highly successful examples of this approach (especially the second part of "Awaken"), and the technique can also be observed in the more progressively-oriented passages of non-progressive rock bands such as Led Zeppelin (whose "Stairway to Heaven" is virtually a textbook example of the approach). An effective extension of this technique involves marking off a climax by using electronic instruments to give a heavy rock treatment to a theme that had initially been stated quietly in an acoustic setting (notice once again the feminine/masculine dynamic at work here). ELP's "Trilogy," U.K.'s "Thirty Years," Gentle Giant's "His Last Voyage," and Genesis's "Firth of Fifth" all use this device to great dramatic effect.

Besides serving a dramatic purpose, this kind of transformation of melodic material from movement to movement or section to section gives lengthy progressive rock pieces a coherence that was usually not apparent in the lengthy psychedelic jams. At times, key themes or musical ideas that were stated in the first movement are recalled almost verbatim in the last: ELP's *Tarkus* and Camel's *The Snow Goose* offer good examples of this approach. At other times, material is transformed when it is recalled: the melodic material of the final movement of Genesis's *Supper's Ready*, for instance, is created through imaginative transformations of melodic ideas drawn from the opening two movements. Sometimes cross-references of this sort involve inner movements instead; the pastoral, lyrical tune which opens King Crimson's *Lizard* is transformed into a jazzy bolero in the second movement, but is not heard again in the last two movements.

Some commentators charged that progressive rock's adoption of nineteenth-century programmatic forms caused it to lose much of the spontaneity of psychedelic jams, and this is probably true. On the other hand, nineteenth-century formal approaches are quite loose compared to the earlier classical forms (such as sonata form) of Haydn, Mozart, and Beethoven, so even when progressive rock musicians perform their lengthy pieces note-for-note, a somewhat improvisatory quality is present. Furthermore, the musicians often try to leave at least one section open for improvised solos; in these sections forward motion tends to be temporarily suspended by the presence of a ceaselessly reiterated ostinato pattern and/or chord progression underneath the solo, so for a moment at least the timeless, acid-imbued ambience of the psychedelic jam is evoked.

It is above all a firm grasp of large-scale structure that separates the best progressive rock bands from their lesser imitators. Comparing Yes's long suites with those of Rick Wakeman is a case in point. Wakeman, who was in fact Yes's long-time keyboardist, released a number of solo albums during the 1970s in the same general style as his band's; these albums show Wakeman to be a virtuoso performer with a formidable working knowledge of the analog equipment at his disposal. Unfortunately, there is not as much substance beneath the surface brilliance of the music as one would hope for. Wakeman tends to move rapidly from one idea to another, often creating a pastiche-like effect in the process; since individual ideas are seldom developed, and tend to run into one another rather haphazardly, there is seldom a chance to build up much intensity.

The situation in Yes's best multimovement suites is quite different. The band uses material quite economically; for instance, in *Close to the Edge* the same melodic material is constantly being reworked, varied, and expanded in the first, second, and fourth movements. At the same time, musical ideas do not follow one another haphazardly, but are carefully arranged so there is a sense of one idea expanding into the next; since instrumentation and dynamics are carefully managed as well, there is a powerful sense of forward motion, an inexorable movement to and from climaxes. It is this clearly defined movement—which is, again, a legacy of nineteenth-century symphonic music—that gives the music of Yes a sense of drama and expansiveness that Wakeman's records usually lack (although there are a few exceptions, such as "Judas Iscariot" from his *Criminal Record* LP). Many progressive rock bands worked in large-scale forms during the 1970s; however, only the best of them had the compositional sophistication to pull off fully successful pieces on this type of epic scale.

Virtuosity

Progressive rock also drew on classical music's legacy of virtuosity. This tradition stems initially from the romantic flamboyance of such nineteenth-century figures as the violinist Nicolò Paganini (whose amazing exploits on his instrument led some to suspect that he was possessed by the devil) and the pianist Franz Liszt. After 1920, jazz absorbed the whole tradition of the Romantic virtuoso; from here the tradition passed on into rhythm-and-blues, and finally to psychedelic music, which witnessed the rise not only of virtuoso guitarists (Jimi Hendrix, Eric Clapton, Jimmy Page, Jeff Beck), but also virtuoso bass guitarists (Jack Bruce) and drummers (Ginger Baker). In all of these musics, virtuosity has served the same general function: the soloist takes on the role of Romantic hero, the fearless individualist whose virtuoso exploits model an escape from social constraints (represented by the orchestra in nineteenth-century music, and by the rhythm section in jazz and the blues).

Interestingly, the psychedelic bands that most emphasized virtuosity—the Hendrix Experience, Cream, the Yardbirds—influenced the development of heavy metal much more than progressive rock. In fact, members of proto-progressive bands such as the Moody Blues, Procol Harum, and Pink Floyd (or the Beatles, for that matter) were not known as brilliant soloists; the one major exception was Keith Emerson, the Nice's organist/pianist. Emerson received extensive classical training as a child and also dabbled in jazz during his teens; his experience working with a leading British blues band, the T-Bones, during the British blues revival of the mid-1960s exposed him to yet another genre that put extensive emphasis on instrumental virtuosity. Already on the Nice's first album, *The Thoughts of Emerlist Davjack* (recorded in late 1967 and early 1968), there is a notable tension between Emerson's long, carefully conceived solos, dominated by lightning-fast passagework and an unusually sophisticated sense of long-range planning, and the psychedelic noodlings of the band's guitarist, David O'List.[19] O'List left during the recording sessions for the band's second album, *Ars Longa Vita Brevis,* thus giving full rein to Emerson's quasi-classical leanings. Emerson almost single-handedly propelled keyboards to the forefront of the progressive rock sound, and created the model of the virtuosic, classically trained musician that virtually ever major progressive rock multikeyboardist that came after him attempted to follow.

Indeed, Emerson served as a role model for nonkeyboardists as well. Guitar virtuosos of the psychedelic era such as Hendrix and Clapton were influenced mainly by the guitar masters of the urban blues: Muddy Waters, Howlin' Wolf, B. B. King. On the other hand, progressive rock's guitar virtuosos—Robert Fripp (King Crimson), Steve Howe (Yes), Jan Akkerman (Focus)—were influenced just as strongly by classical guitar music and the jazz guitar style of players such as Barney Kessel, and became equally adept on the acoustic instrument. Fripp's rapid-fire cross-picking technique, clearly drawn from classical models (although Fripp used a plectrum), proved widely influential. Progressive rock even witnessed the rise of virtuoso bass guitarists (of which Chris Squire of Yes was the most influential) and virtuoso drummers (ELP's Carl Palmer, Bill Bruford, and Guy Evans of Van der Graaf Generator, arguably the genre's finest drummers, were all influenced very strongly by classical percussion techniques and jazz drumming).[20] In other words, Emerson's model of the classically trained virtuoso instrumentalist, often with some jazz experience as well, exerted a profound influence on the entire progressive rock movement.

Most progressive rock bands devoted a fairly sizable portion of album space to featuring the band's various soloists, with keyboards, guitars, and other lead instruments (flutes, saxophones, violins) given pride of place. Passages prominently featuring the bass guitarist or drummer in a solo role are more unusual, but by no means unheard of.[21] When skillfully woven into the piece's overall structural fabric and when not overextended, such solos can be ecstatic in the truest sense of the word, generating a great deal of excitement. However, there is no doubt that progressive rock solos were often overextended, were not always skillfully tied into the piece of which they were a part, and were sometimes rote and formulaic. Not surprisingly, when critics attacked progressive rock's "self-indulgence," they were often referring to its propensity for lengthy solos.[22]

Another aspect of progressive rock that is separate from, yet not unrelated to, its emphasis on instrumental virtuosity is its fondness for unusual meters. The vast majority of popular music—indeed, the vast majority of European art music of 1600 to 1900—is in duple or triple meter, with beat groupings falling into regularly recurring patterns of two, three, or four. Both asymmetrical meters (that is, meters that fall into beat groupings of five, seven, eleven, thirteen, or occasionally a higher prime number) and shifting meters (which involve constant shifts between bars of two, three, four, and six) were introduced into European art music during the late nineteenth and early twentieth centuries by composers such as Musorgsky, Rimsky-Korsakov, Stravinsky, and Bartók. These composers were in turn heavily influenced by Eastern European folk song, where such meters are used to capture the natural rhythms of the text as closely as possible. Asymmetrical and shifting meters were first systematically introduced into American popular music around 1960 by jazz pianist/composer Dave Brubeck, who had studied with the French composer Darius Milhaud (who in turn was strongly influenced by Stravinsky).[23] By the mid-1960s the Beatles began using shifting meters in some of their songs (notably "Strawberry Fields Forever," recorded in late 1966), and their "Within You, without You" (from the *Sergeant Pepper* LP of 1967) provides an early example of the use of quintuple meter in a rock framework.

Two factors contributed to the emergence of meters of this type in psychedelic music. The first was the use of a type of blank verse and free verse by the lyricists that virtually demanded the use of irregular meters in order to accurately capture the flow of the text. The second factor contributing to the use of unusual meters in this music was the relative de-emphasis of dance in live presentations of the music. As early as 1966 Pink Floyd's Rick Wright observed that during the band's performances "Most people just stand and listen at first. What we really want is that they should dance *to* the music and *with* the music and so become a part of us."[24] However, between 1966 and 1970 dance was if anything de-emphasized even further as a result of the audience's pervasive fondness for ingesting hallucinogens, the corresponding emphasis placed on light shows, and the growing complexity of the music itself. Although some psychedelic music was danced to (invariably with freaky freeform movements), by the time progressive rock emerged as a distinct style it was fairly well understood that the genre was not about music for dancing, and the following disclaimer from the liner notes of Egg's first album of 1970 was largely unnecessary: "The music on this LP is not dancing music, but basically music for listening to. It is harmonically and rhythmically complex, designed to be as original as possible within the confines of the instrumental lineup; so it's pretty demanding on the listener's attention."

Without question, progressive rock has explored unusual meters more systematically than any other style of popular music. Keith Emerson, who was strongly influenced by Brubeck (the Nice's first album contains an epic arrangement of Brubeck's *Blue Rondo à la Turk*), penned his first piece in $\frac{5}{4}$, "Azrael, the Angel of Death," in 1968. Jethro Tull's "Living in the Past" of 1969, their first hit single, is another early example of quintuple meter in a progressive rock context. After 1970, meters in five and seven became commonplace among progressive rock bands; over the next decade virtually dozens of progressive rock pieces utilized one of these meters, and some of the genre's best-known pieces grew out of experimentation with unusual time signatures. Keith Emerson remarks that "In the case of *Tarkus* [drummer] Carl [Palmer] was very struck by different time signatures. He told me that he'd like to do something in $\frac{5}{4}$, so I said I'd keep that in mind and started writing *Tarkus* from there."[25] Complex mazes of shifting meters also became common in progressive rock after 1970; the first movement of *Tarkus*, "Eruption," alternates between sections of $\frac{5}{4}$ and passages in which there are meter shifts every several bars.

By the early 1970s, even more complex asymmetrical meters began appearing in progressive rock. As early as 1969, Caravan experimented with $\frac{11}{8}$ in "Where but for Caravan Would I Be," and the same meter also crops up in parts of Van der

Graaf Generator's "Man-Erg" and Gentle Giant's "Pantagruel's Nativity" (both 1971). Parts of Egg's "I Will Be Absorbed" (1970) are in $\frac{13}{8}$, as is the closing section of the first side of Jethro Tull's "Thick as a Brick" (1972) and much of the central section of King Crimson's "Starless" (1974). A passage from ELP's *Karn Evil 9*, 1st Impression, part 1 (1973) is in $\frac{15}{8}$; again, however, Caravan had experimented with this meter by 1970 ("Warlock" from the *Can't Be Long Now* suite). By the end of the decade even more exotic meters were being utilized; U.K.'s *In the Dead of Night* suite contains an instrumental refrain in $\frac{21}{16}$, while National Health's "Tenemos Roads" contains some extremely intricate passages in $\frac{25}{16}$.

The complexity of progressive rock's rhythmic schemes goes beyond the use of asymmetric and shifting meters. After 1970, syncopation—the use of rhythmic patterns in which notes consistently fall between rather than on the beat—became an important element of the progressive rock style. The tension generated by the frequent refusal of syncopated melodic lines or chord progressions to "resolve" into the rhythm section's downbeat gives much progressive rock (especially its faster passages) an urgent forward momentum. The use of polyrhythms (that is, two distinct meters juxtaposed simultaneously in two different parts), yet another technique frequently resorted to by these bands, often creates a nervous, off-balance effect.[26] The prototypical progressive rock rhythm can in fact be regarded as a fusion of the steady beat and syncopated rhythms of African-American popular music (especially jazz) and the asymmetrical and shifting meters of European folk music, mediated through the music of twentieth-century nationalist composers such as Stravinsky, Bartók, Holst, and Vaughan Williams. The ability to negotiate complex rhythmic and metric patterns took on the same importance for the progressive rock musicians of the 1970s that the ability to improvise a fugue had for an organist in Bach's day, or the ability to improvise a solo over complex chord changes had for the bebop musicians of the 1940s. As Geddy Lee of Rush (a Canadian band that was strongly influenced by English progressive rock) once remarked,

> We've played in seven almost as much as we've played in $\frac{4}{4}$, you know. So for us to be into seven is the most natural thing in the world. It's probably as natural to us as it is for Bill Bruford to play in five. He can make it seem so smooth. . . . But it depends on how familiar you are with that particular feel and how much you [have] thought out the music . . . so it doesn't feel herky-jerky.[27]

Besides the emphasis on instrumental and metrical virtuosity, progressive rock musicians often placed an emphasis on what might be called compositional virtuosity. One example of this is the preference shown by these bands for lengthy multimovement formal plans. Effectively tying together twenty or thirty minutes of music on both a musical and conceptual basis is a genuine compositional achievement, and a well-constructed multimovement suite is able to impart a sense

of monumentality and grandeur, to convey the sweep of experience (very important to the counterculture) in a manner that a three- or four-minute song simply
cannot.

A number of these bands also liked to flex their compositional muscles by drawing on archaic forms such as canon or fugue in which several independent melodic
lines are unfolded at the same time. To be sure, progressive rock has for the most
part utilized the four-part homophonic texture common to other rock styles, in
which one principal melody is supported by a bass line, chordal filling, and percussive backing. Nonetheless, a number of examples of full-fledged fugues can be
found in progressive rock, including the fourth movement of the Nice's *Five Bridges
Suite;* the second movement of ELP's *The Endless Enigma* suite; the seventh movement of Renaissance's *Scheherazade;* the opening of Van der Graaf Generator's
"Meurglys III (The Songwriter's Guild)"; and the opening and closing sections of
Gentle Giant's "On Reflection" (canonic progressive rock pieces include Jethro
Tull's "Round" and Caravan's "Asforteri 25"). Furthermore, bands such as Gentle
Giant also experimented with more modern types of polyphonic textures drawn
from composers such as Stravinsky and Holst, in which several short, repetitive
melodic fragments are superimposed against each other to create intricately inter-
locking ostinato networks.

The final type of virtuosity inherent to progressive rock is electronic and technological in nature. As I noted earlier, progressive rock bands were largely responsible for introducing synthesizers into the mainstream of contemporary
popular music, and throughout the 1970s the genre remained at the cutting edge
of keyboard technology. The production quality of the albums of the best-known
progressive rock bands was state of the art; for years ELP's eponymous debut album
and Pink Floyd's *Dark Side of the Moon* were used to test stereo systems. Many of
the innovative studio techniques utilized in the Beatles' later albums by engineer
George Martin—panning a particular part from speaker to speaker, dividing parts
stereophonically, overdubbing, electronically manipulating natural sounds to create radically new effects, slipping various taped effects into the sonic background—
were taken to a high degree of perfection by progressive rock engineers. Like
Martin, the contributions of some of these engineers, notably Alan Parsons (Pink
Floyd) and Eddy Offord (ELP, Yes), made them virtually an additional band member. Stereophonic sound systems and headphones first became common among
the listening public during the late 1960s, and more than any other style of popular
music progressive rock records were conceived to cater to either an individual
listener with a set of headphones, or to a small groups of listeners in an intimate
setting where listening to music was the primary activity. Jim Curtis's remark about
the implied listening audience toward which the more complex psychedelic albums
of the late 1960s were geared is equally pertinent to the progressive rock of the
1970s:

The archetypal implied listeners on a classic late sixties album like the Doors' *Strange Days* would be a group of friends sitting on the floor in a candlelit room passing around a joint. This experience of music in an intimate environment retrieved the setting, if not exactly the ambience, in which people listened to the radio in the 1920s.[28]

It also has obvious parallels to the nineteenth-century salons at which Schubert, Chopin, Liszt and others performed—yet another parallel between the hippie and the Romantic movements. This tendency reflects the degree to which listening to music became a form of personal meditation and spiritual exploration for many members of the counterculture.

In its tendency toward virtuosity (be it instrumental, metrical, or technological), its interest in compositional problems for their own sake, and its eclecticism—its delight in mixing unlikely stylistic sources—progressive rock showed a predilection toward art for art's sake that is absent in most other types of contemporary popular music. This served as a constant source of irritation for many rock critics, who were quick to point out that the style's preoccupation with virtuosity seemed directed neither toward art nor toward communication, but toward cleverness and ingenuity for their own sake. Sometimes this was almost certainly true; more often, though, it was not.

Indeed, although many critics were slow to realize it, there is no doubt that virtuosity played an important cultural role in psychedelic music and in a number of styles such as progressive rock and jazz-rock that stemmed from it. The hippies despised the Establishment-approved top forty music for its predictability, conformity, and (in their view) banality. Progressive rock's attachment to dense arrangements, complex mazes of shifting meters, and spasmodic solos created the sense of unpredictability, tension, and nonconformity which the hippies found so spectacularly lacking in the Establishment-approved pop styles. Furthermore, its complexity served as a symbol of resistance against the Establishment, as a gate that separated the uncomprehending "straights" from the mysteries of the hippie subculture.

Modal Harmony

Progressive rock's modality—that is, its use of the church modes and occasionally more exotic modes to create the melodic and harmonic substance of a piece—stems largely from the folk revival of the 1960s, and to a lesser degree, perhaps, from the classical music of North India which was popular in certain countercultural circles during the late 1960s. It may therefore be useful to ask, what was the point of the folk movement in the first place? I would suggest that for both middle-class English and white American audiences, by the 1960s the folk movement had come to signify a vague protest against the depersonalizing tendencies of modern society. It represented a nostalgic look back at a stable preindustrial European and North American agrarian society where men and women lived "closer to the earth," shared a genuine sense of community, and were privy to a spiritual insight that has since been lost. I do not wish to speculate here as to what degree this notion is actually true and to what degree it is wishful thinking. I will only point out that without an understanding of the impulses that shaped the folk movement (and there is no doubt that a similar desire to recover lost spirituality powered the hippies' interest in things Eastern), one cannot understand the significance of folk music's most important legacy to progressive rock, modal harmony.

In European classical music, the ancient church modes fell out of use near the beginning of the seventeenth century, when they were replaced by the modern major and minor scales. Marxist-influenced commentators such as John Shepherd see the rise of functional harmony (that is, harmony based on the major-minor system) as symbolic of the near-simultaneous rise of modern industrial society.[29] According to Shepherd, functional harmony's hierarchy of chords, stemming from a central chord (the tonic) and expanding outward to take in other levels of successively weaker chords, captures capitalist society's insistence upon maintaining a strict hierarchy in the workplace, and measuring social relationships according to this hierarchy. Shepherd sees functional harmony's inexorable drive away from and back to the tonic chord as mirroring industrial society's concept of progress through spatialized time toward some sort of clearly defined goal, and its regular harmonic rhythm (that is, regularly recurring chord changes) as encapsulating our society's preoccupation with the passing of an objectively measured chronological time.

Modality, on the other hand, has its roots in the distant past—in folk music and in European church music of the medieval and renaissance periods, while Indian classical music, of course, brings with it a geographical distance as well— and in some ways mirrors certain values of an earlier period which the hippies of the 1960s wished to resurrect. Above all, modality proved capable of capturing the hippies' acid-induced sense of freedom from time in a way that functional harmony could not. While modality and the I–IV–V blues progression coexisted uneasily in British rock during the early days of psychedelia, by the late 1960s progressive rock musicians had largely abandoned the rigid framework of the blues progression in favor of modality's greater flexibility. (Significantly, post-psychedelic hard rock/heavy metal styles, which had a weaker connection to the hippie ethos, continued to strongly emphasize the blues progression.) Functional harmony (from which the blues progression is derived) is built from the bass line up, and melodies must conform to the framework of the chord progressions; on the other hand, modal harmony tends to build from the melody down (often through the technique of melodic doubling), and the only "framework" is provided by the melody itself. Furthermore, unlike functional harmony, modal harmony does not have a regular harmonic rhythm. Rather, it is characterized by stark alternations between static harmonic rhythm, where a drone or ostinato pattern may be prolonged underneath a keyboard or guitar solo for several minutes at a time, and rapid harmonic rhythm, where chords change quite frequently (often every second or two) and chord progressions slip almost imperceptibly from one key center to another.

Finally, even when its harmonic rhythm is relatively regular, modal harmony is more wayward and unpredictable than functional harmony, since the relationship between chords in the modes is more ambiguous and less hierarchically determined than in the major/minor system. Progressive rock musicians often choose to accent this sense of unpredictability even further by drawing on techniques such as modal borrowing, or mixing chords drawn from different modes (for instance, drawing on B♭-major and D-major chords while in A aeolian), and using cross relations, chromatic variants of a note (such as C and C♯) which occur at or near the same time in different parts. (Cross relations are forbidden in functional harmony because they introduce an ambiguity deemed unacceptable.)

The actual modes used by progressive rock musicians vary. Modes tend to be chosen for their expressive qualities; bands such as Yes or Genesis that favor a more sunny, open sound tend to emphasize major modes, while bands that gravitate towards a darker ambience—Pink Floyd, Van der Graaf Generator, King Crimson—resort more frequently to minor modes. The most frequently used minor modes in progressive rock are the aeolian and dorian modes; the even darker phrygian mode, with its distinctive lowered second degree, is used somewhat more infrequently, but is by no means rare. The three most common major modes are the mixolydian mode, the ionian mode, and a hybrid mode that contains a lowered seventh and alternately raised and lowered third and sixth degrees. Two of the church modes, the lydian and locrian modes, have seldom been used in progressive rock.

Certain more experimentally inclined progressive rock musicians have used not only the church modes, but also more unusual, exotic modes that appear to be of Eastern European or Mideastern origin. Thus ex–Soft Machine drummer and songwriter Robert Wyatt has commented that the modes he uses are

> Discarded versions of Greek modes, perhaps from someplace like Macedonia. You hear it in Bulgarian folk music to this day, which is probably closer to ancient Greek music than we realize. I've always liked scales that had an ambiguity about whether they were major or minor. What I like about flamenco is they use gypsy scales, where the second note is only a half-step up [from the tonic note] . . . that half step's a North African thing, because a lot of Egyptian scales are like that.[30]

As already observed, it is likely that at least some of the more unusual modes favored by progressive rock musicians are of Indian origin, and can be traced back to the psychedelic period's interest in Indian music.

A large percentage of the chords used in any given progressive rock piece are simple triads. Progressive rock has remarkably little use for dominant ninth, eleventh, and thirteenth chords, or for other rich chords with dominant implications such as augmented sixth and diminished seventh chords, since these chords create the strong goal-oriented harmonic movement that the genre usually eschews. The two types of seventh chords that are frequently used in progressive rock, the minor seventh chord (e.g., D-F-A-C) and the major seventh chord (e.g., C-E-G-B), have no strong tonal implications and thus fit comfortably into the essentially wayward ambience of progressive rock harmony; so do the suspended second and suspended fourth chords that these musicians favor. For the most part, the standard progressive rock harmonic syntax is not a great deal more complex than the harmony of other rock genres; it is certainly simpler than that of jazz-rock.

On the other hand, a number of the more adventurous progressive rock musicians also drew on more advanced harmonic techniques that are clearly a legacy of twentieth-century English and Eastern European nationalist composers. Roughly half a century before the emergence of the urban folk movement of the late 1950s and early 1960s, composers such as Béla Bartók, Ralph Vaughan Williams, Igor Stravinsky, and Gustav Holst drew on European folk culture to resurrect an authenticity and spirituality which they felt was being lost to industrialization; Bartók and Vaughan Williams, in particular, used folk song as the basis for creating a more sophisticated harmonic language. Many of these composers exerted a powerful influence on progressive rock musicians. Jon Anderson cites the influence of Stravinsky and Jean Sibelius on Yes's music,[31] King Crimson's Robert Fripp has expressed admiration for the music of Bartók and Stravinsky,[32] while Kerry Minnear of Gentle Giant has evinced a fondness for the music of Vaughan Williams.[33] Dave Stewart has drawn attention to the impact of Holst's and Stravinsky's music on Egg;[34] Keith Emerson arranged works by Bartók, Sibelius, and Leoš Janáček for the Nice and ELP.[35] King Crimson performed an arrangement of "Mars," the first movement of Holst's The Planets, during their American tour of 1969,[36] and Emerson arranged "Mars" for the Emerson, Lake and Powell LP of 1986. Manfred Mann's Earth Band, an unclassifiable group that mixed blues-based hard rock, fusion, and a highly electronic progressive rock in a series of albums during the early and mid-1970s, had a British hit in 1973 with "Joybringer," based on a tune from another movement of The Planets, "Jupiter."

It was undoubtedly from the music of Bartók, Stravinsky, Holst, and others that progressive rock musicians drew the more dissonant harmonic techniques with which they spiced up their basically simple modal harmony: polytriads, quartal harmony, whole-tone harmony, and bitonality. For example, Keith Emerson has remarked that he found the "unsettled" nature of the fourth appealing,[37] and quartal harmony (that is, progressions of chords built on stacked fourths rather than thirds) plays an important role in ELP's *Tarkus* (especially the first, fifth, and seventh movements) and *Pirates*. Polytriads—that is, two distinct triads or parts of two distinct triads that are fused together—are sometimes used by these musicians at the end of a phrase to swing the music into a new key center. They may also be used to create a dramatic cadence such as can be found at the conclusion of *Tarkus*, when a pungent F-major/F$^\sharp$-minor polytriad unexpectedly converges into F major to end the piece.

Indeed, the practice of enlivening simple triadic progressions in the right hand with nonharmonic tones in the left hand became a central element of the progressive rock keyboard style. Gary Brooker of Procol Harum comments that "I've always been quite a lover of playing the wrong note in the bass to alter the sound of a chord."[38] Tony Banks of Genesis states that "the idea is that you come up with interesting changes when you change chords simply by changing the bass notes . . . like in the introductory bit to "The Eleventh Earl of Mar." One of the chords in that is basically a G-minor chord with an A$^\flat$ in the bass. That sounds unlikely, but it sounds great in context."[39] Likewise, Keith Emerson admits that he often favors using "the open major chords played off against the root next door. For example, you've got an A root against a G-major chord, a D root against an E major, a C root against a D major, and an F against G."[40]

Progressive rock musicians also occasionally resort to whole-tone harmony and bitonality. The emphasis that whole-tone harmony places on the tritone, a harmonic interval that has traditionally been considered dissonant and unstable (medieval theorists called it *diabolus in musica*, "the devil in music") lends it a wry, somewhat knotty ambience. King Crimson's "Red" and "Fracture" feature this type of harmony extensively; in these pieces whole-tone harmony is combined with guitar and bass guitar distortion and a bulldozer-like backbeat to create the aura of lurking and menace that characterized so much of the band's output between 1972 and 1974. Bitonality, which involves the simultaneous juxtaposition of parts in two different keys, is occasionally encountered in progressive rock as well: in pieces such as the third movement of ELP's *Tarkus* suite, "Iconoclast," bitonal harmony and motoristic rhythms are combined to create a metallic, machine-like effect. Bitonality also plays a major role in the central section of ELP's "Infinite Space" and at the close of their *Endless Enigma* suite, as well as in the opening sections of Egg's *Symphony No. 2* and *Long Piece No. 3*.

Postscript: The Taming of the Acid Trip

Modal harmony's importance to progressive rock can only be fully understood when considered in conjunction with the genre's reliance on large-scale structures drawn from symphonic music. On a cultural level, psychedelic music's reliance on modal harmony and its more dissonant extensions can be seen to mirror the counterculture's drug-triggered rebellion against industrial society's conception of chronological time and goal orientation. At the same time, though, progressive rock's adoption of programmatic forms is a tacit acknowledgement that some sort of order, however loose, would be necessary after all in order to avoid total incoherence; there was simply no other way to impose order on the meandering instrumentals of the psychedelic era. In this sense, then, progressive rock poignantly mirrors the hippies' ultimate accommodation to the conventions of industrial society. Despite Timothy Leary's talk of "the politics of ecstasy," the mass youth culture of the late 1960s and early 1970s was ultimately forced to admit that the sense of "freedom" and "timelessness" induced by hallucinogens was illusory—just as illusory, in fact, as the construct of chronological time which the hippies had hoped to overthrow.

The Progressive Rock Style
The Visuals

Robert Fripp What's the implication of building a formal structure on the golden mean and Fibonacci progressions, rather than on traditional formal symmetry of the Western classical tradition? Again, what would the implication be of working in five rather than four beats?

Tom Mulhern You wouldn't get much pop radio airplay.

Robert Fripp Well, that's probably true.[1]

Although progressive rock did receive a certain amount of airplay during its heyday, radio was never a particularly important medium for disseminating the genre to potential audiences.[2] Even in the early 1970s, before format conventions hardened, radio programmers showed little enthusiasm for playing fifteen- or twenty-minute tracks; the progressive rock songs that did get airplay tended to be shorter and often (as in the case of ELP's "Lucky Man") more pop-oriented than the standard progressive rock fare. It was mainly through the acquisition of albums and through the concert experience that progressive rock audiences were able to experience the music of their favorite groups.

Both the albums and the concert experience have a strong visual dimension; in progressive rock certain conventions are repeated often enough both in album cover art and in concerts that it is not inappropriate to speak of a visual style that governs the genre. I have divided the following discussion into two categories, album cover art and the concert experience, to reflect the two principal manners in which audiences encountered progressive rock. In both realms I will point out how the hippies' fondness for hallucinogens fostered the development of a surrealistic visual style; I will also address the way in which progressive rock's music and visuals are coordinated to convey a unified artistic vision and, in live performances, to create a ritualistic, almost liturgical experience.

Cover Art

Prior to the late 1960s, the main purpose of an album cover in popular music was to show the performers. However, the album cover underwent a significant change of function during the late 1960s. As in so many other realms, the primary innovators in this area were the Beatles. Beginning with their *Sergeant Pepper* LP of 1967, the cover art was used to help convey the album's concept; the fact that the mysterious cover of this album is open to different interpretations is not necessarily incongruous, since the same is true of the album's lyrics. Significantly, *Sergeant Pepper* was the first rock music album sleeve that contained the lyrics to all of the album's songs. Clearly, the Beatles intended this first concept album to be a *Gesamtkunstwerk* (a "unified" or "complete art work") in which music, words, and visual art are all combined to convey a specific concept or program (it is again useful to point out that rock musicians of the late 1960s and 1970s used the term "concept" in exactly the same sense that nineteenth-century composers used the term "program").

Since the concept album played a more central role to progressive rock than virtually any other genre of popular music, it is hardly surprising that extreme care was often lavished on the cover art of progressive rock albums. The cover art usually reflected the album's concept; if the album was not a concept album, the cover art usually tied in with the LP's longest or otherwise most significant track. Progressive rock album covers, whether involving photography, drawing and painting, or a combination of the two, are often decisively surreal, reflecting the influence of psychedelia and, by extension, hallucinogenic drugs—marijuana, mescaline, hashish, psilocybic mushrooms, and above all LSD. The visual effect of an LSD, or acid, trip—which became almost a rite of passage into the counterculture for many during the late 1960s—was overpowering:

> On the surface, there were all those distorted images, the fireworks, the color displays. That was not from "seeing"; it bypassed the optic system, blind people had the same displays. And then there were the images, winged beasts, mythic animals, everything eating everything; the perspectives and the colors and the images went into the art and the music. College bookstores sold posters by Magritte and Dali and Man Ray—and M. C. Escher; the perspectives suddenly looked familiar.[23]

In the early years of psychedelia—especially 1967 and 1968—album covers tended to feature brilliant splotches of colors and lines that writhe and overlap in an infinite variety of patterns, reflecting the LSD experience at its most elemental level: the cover art of the Moody Blues' *Days of Future Passed*, Cream's *Disraeli Gears*, and *Iron Butterfly Live* are representative examples of this approach. By 1969 and 1970, however, even as progressive rock emerged as a distinct style, a more subtle approach, reminiscent of Salvador Dali's style of surrealism, became apparent in both the photography and the artwork of many album covers—a realist's meticulous attention to detail is used to depict impossible landscapes and to juxtapose unrelated objects in unexpected situations. Most progressive rock album covers from 1970 on are surrealistic in exactly this sense.

Within this overall umbrella of surrealism, two types of subject matter are used over and over again: science fiction and fantasy/mythological scenes. Science fiction imagery, in turn, usually involves outer space scenarios, bizarre, futuristic machinery, or a combination of the two; the cover paintings of two ELP albums, *Tarkus* and *Brain Salad Surgery*, offer especially memorable (and well-known) depictions of technology gone awry. William Neal's cover art for *Tarkus* depicts a half-armadillo, half-tank creature rolling across a vast psychedelic landscape that is empty except for the bleached bones of its victims; the album's inner gatefold contains several additional scenes in which "Tarkus" is depicted destroying a number of other cybernetic creatures, before finally being disabled by a Manticore. The cover art ties in directly with the album's *Tarkus* suite, which occupies all of side one; the lyrics of the piece suggest that "Tarkus" symbolizes a technology that has escaped the control of moral and spiritual strictures. (I will take this up in greater detail in chapter 5.) Likewise, the cover art of ELP's *Brain Salad Surgery* LP, designed by the noted Swiss surrealist H. R. Giger, forcefully depicts the conflict between technology's depersonalizing tendencies and human self-awareness that dominates the entire album. The outer cover features a skull imbedded in a bizarre mechanical device; clearly this scene is intended to depict the triumph of technology over spirituality. However, when one opens the two halves of the cover, another painting emerges which renders the apparent triumph of machine over man more ambiguous: a sleeping woman with the infinity sign on her forehead.

Two of Roger Dean's covers for Yes involve outer space scenes. The cover of *Fragile* shows the Earth breaking up into fragments. In a series of tableaux on the *Yessongs* album (released in 1973, two years after *Fragile*) these fragments are guided by a spaceship through outer space, and are shown being peopled by new life on a time frame "which we cannot wholly grasp; this is the material of myth."[4]

These two albums represent one of several examples where the artist makes reference on one album to the artwork of an earlier album. Thus Paul Whitehead's artwork for Genesis' *Foxtrot* makes reference to his cover art for the group's earlier *Nursery Cryme* LP, while William Neal, in the inner sleeve of ELP's *Pictures at an Exhibition* makes a veiled reference to the psychedelic landscape he depicted on the band's *Tarkus* LP of the previous year. The practice of using artwork to tie two or more albums of a group together also points up the way in which specific artists often became associated with particular groups. Roger Dean became particularly closely associated with Yes (for many, Dean's mythic landscapes became a visual symbol of progressive rock), while William Neal and Paul Whitehead were associated with ELP and Genesis, respectively, in the earlier part of their careers. Indeed, one particular design firm that worked out of London, Hipgnosis, designed album covers for a number of well-known progressive rock bands: Yes (after their association with Dean temporarily ended), Genesis, ELP, Caravan, Renaissance, and above all Pink Floyd. The founding members of Pink Floyd and of Hipgnosis (Storm Thorgerson, Aubrey Powell) were associated with each other from the early days of the countercultural scene in London; Hipgnosis designed virtually every Pink Floyd album cover through *Animals* (1977).

In addition to science fiction motifs, fantasy/mythological motifs were also extremely prominent in progressive rock cover art. Fantasy imagery usually centers on a landscape; the surrealistic element may stem from the landscape itself, or may result from the inclusion of strange people and/or objects. In Roger Dean's widely acclaimed painting for Yes's *Close to the Edge* album (which appears on the inner gatefold, not on the cover), the landscape itself is the protagonist. We view this landscape—which appears to be a world separate from our own—from a mountaintop (on our world?); a long, narrow, treacherous-looking bridge stretches over a foggy abyss into this "other" world. The surrealistic element of this landscape results from the fact that although it is apparently an island, it is surrounded by fog, not water, and is bordered on its outer edges not by land, but by sea. Other than its strangeness, the most notable aspect of this landscape is that even from the great distance of our vantage point, it is clearly pristine and unspoiled. The suite *Close to the Edge,* which occupies the first side of the album, is based on Hermann Hesse's *Siddhartha,* and centers on the individual's quest for spiritual truth. Thus Dean's painting seems to mirror the piece's concept: truth and spiritual enlightenment (symbolized by the pristine landscape) are fabulously difficult to reach (hence the narrow, treacherous bridge), but once attained, are the source of peace and contentment.

An extremely different landscape, setting a very different mood, is created by Storm Thorgerson's cover photography for Pink Floyd's *Animals* LP. Under a gray sky in one of metropolitan London's grimiest areas, the Battersea Power Plant belches soot from its four enormous smokestacks. Over the top of the power plant floats a large pig. The oppressive, even menacing, mood set by this unlikely juxtaposition of objects—the factory, the rundown surrounding environs, the polluted sky, the airborne pig—effectively conveys the album's bleak depiction of an Orwellian society that consists only of "sheep" (mindless followers), "pigs" (self-righteous and tyrannical moralists), and "dogs" (power-hungry and violence-prone manipulators).

The surrealistic element of fantasy landscapes in progressive rock's cover art may well have reached its zenith with Paul Whitehead's paintings for the covers of Genesis's *Nursery Cryme* and *Foxtrot* albums of 1971 and 1972, respectively, which offer especially striking examples of bizarre landscapes peopled by strange inhabitants. On the *Nursery Cryme* cover, two young ladies in Victorian garb play what at first appears to be an ordinary game of croquet; a close inspection of the playing field, however, reveals that severed human heads, rather than croquet balls, are being used. In the distance, a large Victorian manor (based on Coxhill in the Woking area of Surrey, where lead singer Peter Gabriel grew up) is visible. This surrealistic, rather grotesque scenario is based on the song "The Musical Box," which occupies half of the album's first side. On the *Foxtrot* cover, several bizarre characters dressed in fox-hunting garb (one resembles a monkey, another a space alien) sit solemnly on a hill overlooking the sea. One member of this strange group weeps because the quarry, a strange creature with a fox's head and a woman's body (dressed in a long red evening dress, no less), has eluded them and is floating out to sea on an iceberg. Behind the hill on which the "fox hunters" sit, the grotesque game of croquet that had been depicted on the cover of the *Nursery Cryme* album is plainly visible; only now there is a large hole where "Coxhill" once stood. The cover art of these two albums set a standard in surrealism and plain weirdness that later artists often strived to match, but were hard-pressed to equal.[5]

Besides the science fiction and fantasy subject matter discussed above, medieval and Eastern motifs were sometimes drawn on as well. The cover art of King Crimson's *Lizard* LP, Gentle Giant's *The Power and the Glory*, Gryphon's *Red Queen to Gryphon Three*, and the *Trespass* album by Genesis all employ medieval imagery; the *Lizard* album is even done in the style of a medieval manuscript illumination. King Crimson's *Lark's Tongue in Aspic*, *Scheherazade* by Renaissance, and virtually every album by Jade Warrior draws on Indian or (in the case of Jade Warrior) Chinese symbology.

In the last chapter I noted how the whole progressive rock musical style, with its masculine/feminine contrasts, can be understood in terms of juxtaposing (or at times merging) cultural opposites such as technology and nature; progressive rock's visual imagery can often be seen to play a similar role. For instance, Roger Dean's mythic landscapes can be understood as symbols of an idealistic, holistic society toward which the hippies aspired; mythological, medieval, and Eastern subject matter often carries the same kind of idealistic overtones as well. On the other hand, much of the science-fiction imagery that depicts technology gone awry (for instance, the cover art of ELP's *Tarkus* and *Brain Salad Surgery* LPs) symbolizes the nightmarish, manipulative totalitarian society which the counterculture feared was overtaking us. In the next chapter, I will point out how these cultural opposites were played with and explored in the lyrics as well.

The Concert Experience

The progressive rock concert experience was impacted by psychedelia just as strongly as was the cover art of progressive rock albums. Synesthesia, the ability to "see" sounds as colors, was a fairly common experience for those who had ingested LSD, and therefore it is not surprising that early in the psychedelic era bands began experimenting with light shows which to some degree at least were meant to suggest the LSD experience. Pink Floyd, the first English band to experiment with making their concerts a multimedia event, were especially important in this regard. At first, the group's "light shows" were rather rudimentary, and consisted of slides projected onto group members. By late 1966, however, when the band had hired a student named Joe Gannon from London's Hornsey College of Art, their light show had become much more sophisticated: "Flashing lights, slide projection, thunderous atmospheric sounds and incense were the essence of the psychedelic Pink Floyd concerts . . . on either side [of the band], sets of filtered spots sprayed various colors over the stage whilst modern art slides were projected behind."[6]

Although the technology used by Pink Floyd during this period was not as sophisticated as that used by contemporary Haight-Ashbury bands (the Grateful Dead, Jefferson Airplane), these bands hired independent outfits to run their light shows, while Pink Floyd designed their own, so that from the beginning, "the Floyd's lights were far more closely integrated with [their] music."[7] By the time Pink Floyd had emerged as part of the nascent progressive rock movement around 1970, light shows—and by extension the perception of the concert as a multimedia experience—had become an essential part of the genre. The lengths to which extramusical props were taken by the genre can be grasped by briefly considering the concerts of three of the most commercially successful English progressive rock bands of the 1971–1976 period: ELP, Pink Floyd, and Yes.

ELP's world tour of 1973 and 1974 proved to be one of the most visually ambitious projects of the entire progressive rock era. Keith Emerson's huge modular Moog synthesizer appeared to "blow up" during the middle of the concert; the effect was reinforced by the smoke which drifted up from the apparently disabled instrument. Emerson's grand piano was catapulted across the top of the stage, while Carl Palmer's drum rostrum revolved in a 360-degree circle during his drum solo, spraying laser lights throughout the auditorium (laser lights, along with fog machines and flashpods, became a regular feature of Yes's and Genesis's concerts during the mid-1970s as well). In a concert the band gave at New York's Madison Square Garden on Christmas Eve 1973, "snow" fell from the rafters during their rendition of "Silent Night."[8]

After Pink Floyd reached megastar status with their *Dark Side of the Moon* album (1973), they augmented (and to a certain degree replaced) their already sophisticated light show with a series of increasingly audacious technical props. Their concerts at Earl's Court Exhibition Hall in London on May 18 and 19, 1973, are described as follows:

> The concert opened with the familiar "Set the Controls for the Heart of the Sun" and "Careful with that Axe, Eugene." Dry ice smoke falling like a waterfall on

"Echoes" led to the interval. *Dark Side of the Moon* was played in its entirety. The stage was littered with landing beacons and spotlights searched the sky for airplanes. Finally a plane appeared followed by a spot[light] as it slowly flew over the audience and crashed into the stage, exploding in a ball of fire. The audience went wild. . . . [9]

Another concert the band gave at London's Rainbow Theatre on November 4 of the same year is described in similar terms:

The four-foot model airplane flew down from the balcony and burst into flames and a huge balloon suspended above the audience had pictures of the moon projected upon it. The concert ended with a huge ball of mirrors hanging over the stage reflecting thousands of needles of light into the audience and emitting colored fog at suitable times.[10]

During Yes's *Tales from Topographic Oceans* Tour of 1974, the stage itself—designed by Roger Dean and his brother Martyn—was the most important visual element of the concert: "The stage for the *Topographic Oceans* tour was composed of ambiguous shapes that were meant to be transformed by the lighting [like ELP and Pink Floyd, Yes utilized an ambitious laser light show], so that sometimes they appeared like flowers, sometimes like animals, or machines, or an inanimate landscape."[11]

The musical concert as a multimedia experience is a concept that has been pursued throughout much of the twentieth century—as early as 1911 the Russian composer Alexander Skryabin called for colored lights to flood the concert hall during the performance of his symphonic poem *Prometheus*—and is certainly a worthy goal. We have already seen that progressive rock was the first style of popular music to exploit synthesizers in a systematic way; the genre also must be given credit for developing psychedelic music's conception of the concert as a multimedia experience more thoroughly than any other contemporary genre of popular music. Yet there seems to be little doubt that the visual elements of these concerts became something of a two-edged sword for these bands. It is hard to disagree with this pronouncement by Roger Dean: "To consider that people come to concerts for music alone would imply a very limited idea of what music [one suspects that what Dean really means here is the concert experience] is capable of. Songs can tell a story, music can create moods or atmospheres and obviously, emotional responses; it can also enhance and be enhanced by images."[12]

However, Dean's statement assumes that the music and the images have some sort of organic relationship to each other. The problem with ELP's catapulting pianos and Pink Floyd's crashing airplanes is that the relationship between music and image became increasingly tenuous. As often as not, image was employed as a spectacle in and of itself, as an attempt to make up for the loss of a meaningful symbiotic relationship between musicians and audiences that occurred when progressive rock bands made the move from clubs and small venues to arenas and stadiums. Some progressive rock musicians were quick to realize that by the mid-1970s the formerly close relationship between music and stage show was being lost. Eric Tamm notes that Robert Fripp was particularly quick to see potential problems: "[Fripp] had grown suspicious of the visual "trickery" associated with [King Crimson's] British tour of 1971, "however fine it might have been. I'm thinking of the lights, and the general blood and thunder." In other words, Fripp wanted the band to be judged on its purely musical merits."[13] By the late 1970s—when many other aspects of the progressive rock style had undergone profound changes as well—the visual aspect of many progressive rock concert tours was scaled back somewhat, Pink Floyd's extremely elaborate setup for their *The Wall* tour of 1980 notwithstanding.

Progressive rock never really developed a definitive dress code in the manner of certain other styles of popular music (i.e., the leather-studded biker gear of heavy metal or the androgynous, gender-bending outfits of glitter rock). The typical accouterments of the counterculture—shoulder-length hair, hats from thrift shops, tiny dark glasses, paisley shirts, beads and bells—remained popular into the early 1970s. A simple jeans and T shirt approach was common as well, and various "mystical" apparel derived from psychedelia (flowing robes, capes, kaftans, etc.) was also worn. Brightly colored clothing—another obvious legacy of psychedelia—was not uncommon. Another legacy of the counterculture, long hair, was de ri-geuer among progressive rock performers (who were overwhelmingly male—the infrequent female performer had long hair as well) through the mid-1970s. However, unlike certain other genres of popular music (heavy metal, for instance), long hair did not prove to be really essential to the progressive rock image, and by the late 1970s some progressive rock performers were appearing with closely cropped hair.

Compared to performers of other rock genres, progressive rock performers have tended to be relatively static and motionless on stage. There are several reasons for this. The music itself is often very complex, and the type of hyperkinetic motion engaged in by heavy metal guitarists, for instance, is simply not feasible. Indeed, two of progressive rock's most significant guitarists, Robert Fripp and Steve Hackett, performed seated; most progressive rock guitarists and bass guitarists have performed standing, however. Keyboardists, in particular, often had to move rapidly between several keyboards, and excess motion was a liability to successfully realizing their parts.

Furthermore, at the zenith of the progressive rock era—the mid-1970s—the visual aspect of the concert experience had become so elaborate that audiences often spent far more time concentrating on the laser lights, the dry ice fog, and the other elaborate visual effects than on the performers themselves. When Mike Tait, Yes's lighting director throughout the 1970s, designed the band's stage show, he did so with the specific assumption that the musicians would be relatively motionless, and the lights and effects would provide the focus of visual attention:

> The performers in Yes are not great movers (they can't be or they might move out of the carefully pre-set lighting cue positions), and no one minds if the fans watch something else.... Yes is a symphonic band, Tait believes, and there is no more reason why Yes musicians should leap about ... than there is for the members of the London Philharmonic to attempt a mid-air splits during a performance of a Shostakovich piano concerto. The important thing is that the effects should provide the visual dynamic.[14]

Nonetheless, the performance approaches of two progressive rock performers—Keith Emerson and Peter Gabriel—deserve further comment.

While still with the Nice, Emerson became famous for his flamboyant stage show which he derived from both Jimi Hendrix and a virtually unknown organ player named Don Shinn—beating his organ with a whip, stabbing it with knives, turning it on its side, leapfrogging over the top of it.[15] Some of these antics actually did serve a musical purpose—the knives were carefully inserted in the keyboard to hold down specific notes which served as pedal points during solos, while turning the organ on its side caused the instrument to feed back (some of the most fascinating electronic effects of the psychedelic era were produced by guitar or organ feedback). After Emerson formed ELP, he adopted a somewhat more static mode of performance in response to the band's ever-more spectacular stage props; ironically, Emerson's violent stage show with the Nice (as well as some of his flamboyant outfits) exerted a much more profound influence on heavy metal performers than on progressive rock musicians, who seldom resorted to histrionics of this type.[16]

A completely different approach was taken by Peter Gabriel, lead singer of Genesis until 1975. While lead singers (especially those who do not play an instrument) have more freedom of mobility that other band members, no other progressive rock lead singer took advantage of this mobility to the extent of Gabriel. By 1972 he had begun the practice of donning an outrageous new outfit for each piece, which he acted out as he sang. He took this approach to its logical conclusion during the band's tour for *The Lamb Lies Down on Broadway* (1974–1975), a concept album of nearly an hour and a half in length. Gabriel's performance of the piece turned *The Lamb* into virtually a one-man opera, as he acted out the various metamorphoses undergone by Rael (the song cycle's hero) during his journey through a surreal Manhattan. Again, Gabriel had much less impact on progressive rock—which seldom set out to be "theatrical" in this sense—than on English glitter rock. The irony and sense of self-detachment fostered by this genre made it a more hospitable format for the development of this almost Brechtian conception of theatre, and Gabriel's approach was developed to its logical conclusion by glitter rock's most important exponent, David Bowie.

Postscript: Progressive Rock as Liturgy

David Shumway, in his interesting article "Rock and Roll as Cultural Practice," draws attention to two extremes in rock performance which he describes as "theatrical" and "liturgical."[17] David Bowie would certainly be a primary example of a "theatrical" performer; Shumway also cites Madonna's "Blond Ambition" tour, with its lip-synching and extremely stylized choreography. As an example of the rock concert as a "liturgical" experience, he cites the Grateful Dead: "Dead concerts seem less like shows than rituals, including a standard repertory of music, a community of devoted followers, and even a pacing that strikes one as liturgical."[18]

There is an undeniably liturgical and ritualistic facet of the counterculture as a whole. Paul Willis, for instance, has noted the sense of ritual that surrounded drug use; taking LSD, in particular, became a quasi-liturgical act for many hippies.[19] It would seem that many rock performances of the late 1960s and early 1970s, in conjunction with hallucinogens, often served as a ritual means of transporting listeners into other realms of consciousness. Stephen Davis, in his biography of Led Zeppelin, notes William Burroughs's surmisal as to the ultimate goal of that band's concerts: "Burroughs compared Led Zeppelin's loud music to the trance music of the Master Musicians of Jajouka in Morocco, who also played loud blaring themes with horns and thundering drums. Just as Moroccan music is used as a psychic hygiene, Burroughs suggested, so Led Zeppelin's music was used by its audience for astral travel and spiritual regeneration."[20]

I would suggest that the performances of many of the major progressive rock bands of the 1970s have the same liturgical overtones as do Grateful Dead or Led Zeppelin concerts. Others have also drawn attention to the liturgical nature of much progressive rock. Dan Hedges has characterized Yes's *Close to the Edge* as a "thundering, sonic impression of Chartres Cathedral on Easter Sunday morning,"[21] while more to the point, Robert Fripp remarked during the early 1970s, "I'm not really interested in music; music is just a means of creating a magical state."[22]

In the last chapter, I pointed out how progressive rock has shown a great fondness for drawing on instrumental or vocal stylizations—be it majestic pipe organ-like passages produced on the Hammond, fanfare-like trumpet choruses realized on the Moog, or massive, almost choral vocal arrangements—that have strong ties with earlier religious styles, especially the music of the Anglican and Catholic churches. Certainly the visual aspect of many progressive rock concerts can be seen to have liturgical overtones as well. The laser lights, flashpods, and fog machines that played such an important role in these concerts function in much the same way that candles and incense have in other religious rites throughout the centuries. As Aldous Huxley noted, light has traditionally been used for "transporting the spectators to that other World which lies at the back of the mind.... [P]reternatural light evokes, in everything it touches, preternatural color and preternatural significance."[23] Even Keith Emerson's knifing of his Hammond organ at the conclusion of each Nice concert always struck me as a ritualistic act; Emerson seems to play the role of a tribal shaman or priest performing a ritual sacrifice or some other magical rite.

Yet another "liturgical" aspect of progressive rock is its relative de-emphasis of the individual performer. Jim Curtis has noted that the status of the individual performers in progressive rock tends to mirror the status of the individual performers of other types of religious music: "Religious music glorifies something greater than an individual, so that the individual performers mostly serve as a medium for the transmission of the music. Rick Wakeman once admitted that he was a star, and added, 'But when somebody says, "Yes," you think of the music and not so much of the people in the band.' "[24]

Of course, one might argue that progressive rock's emphasis on instrumental virtuosity—and thus on individualism—is not really in keeping with religious music's de-emphasis on the individual performer. I would suggest that this tension is resolved by progressive rock's ideal of collective virtuosity. One can see this ideal at work even in the music of ELP, the progressive rock band that most frequently threatened to blur the distinction between "overpowering" and "overbearing." One critic noted,

> Together, Emerson, Lake and Palmer have always made chartered, flowing sense; a strong concept of team play and tonal unity has aborted any pomposity. Their masterworks—Take a Pebble, Karn Evil 9 and most of the Tarkus suites—have proven to be a capably representative easel for Emerson's bombastic figurines, Palmer's tympanic conceptions and Lake's latent folkie yet exquisite chords and smooth voice.[25]

This emphasis on collective virtuosity separates the progressive rock band from both the top-forty–oriented pop styles where a famous singer is accompanied by faceless instrumentalists, and from the hard rock/heavy metal styles in which the lead singer and lead guitarist are clearly predominant. (I think it is significant, for instance, that well into the 1980s heavy metal produced no virtuoso bassists.) I would add that the tendency of many progressive rock bands to alternate statements sung by the lead vocalists with "choral" affirmations sung by many or all of the group's vocalists shows the same concern with negotiating individual and communal interests that can be seen in a wide array of religious styles—from African-American gospel music to Baroque oratorios and cantatas.

Finally, if the rock concert of the late 1960s and early 1970s played an almost liturgical role for its participants, it is because the counterculture had fully accepted the Romantic notion of the Artist as Prophet or Seer. Perhaps Richard Wagner or the Russian composer Alexander Skryabin would not have cared for the music heard at one of these concerts; they would almost certainly have recognized and approved, however, of the priestly role which the audiences had assigned to the musicians. Significantly, the Romantic movement emerged at just that point in the early nineteenth century when the upper-middle-class intelligentsia had begun to question inherited religious dogma. Likewise, it does not seem coincidental that it was at that juncture when traditional religious practice—and especially denominational Christianity—was coming under unprecedented attack in mass culture at large (one thinks, for instance, of *Time* Magazine's dramatic "Is God Dead?" headline of April 1966) that the rock concert began to function as a full-blown liturgy for many young people. The band members played the role of both high priests and temple musicians; the music took on the function of prophetic revelation; hallucinogens provided a rite of entrance into the mysteries of the temple; and the lights and other stage trappings created a suitably imposing background.

The Progressive Rock Style
The Lyrics

The Onyx, the *I Ching*, tarot cards, and God's eyes. (Hesse's) *Steppenwolf* (and) *Siddhartha*, (Tolkien's) Middle Earth, and Merlin. The peace sign, yin/yang, astrology, and yoga . . . from the welter of American Indian lore, Arthurian daydreams, Oriental smoke rings, science fiction ciphers, and their own growing compendium of psychedelic syllogisms, the hippies seemed on the verge of achieving a grand synthesis, striking the final harmonizing metachord.[1]

In this passage from his book **Stairway to Heaven: The Spiritual Roots of Rock'n'Roll,** Davin Seay criticizes what he perceives as the hippies' emphasis on symbolism over substance. He goes on to argue that the hippies' "theology," so far as it existed, was so syncretistic, so given to trying to reconcile imcompatible beliefs and practices, that it was ultimately nothing more than an empty set of symbols that could never contribute to the formation of a genuine religion.

Seay may be right, although it seems to me that the hippies' pantheistic Eastern-inspired sense of the oneness of things, of an overarching superawareness in which all consciousness is joined—ultimately, a belief that each man and woman is God—has contributed to the formation of the modern New Age movement. Nonetheless, in this chapter I will not primarily be concerned with exploring to what degree—if any—the hippies' belief system can be said to constitute a "religion." Rather, I will explore how the symbols mentioned by Seay—drawn from mythology, fantasy and science fiction literature, and a host of sacred texts from the past—are used in progressive rock lyrics as symbols of resistance and protest: used to symbolize both an idealized society toward which we might strive and a nightmarish technocracy which the hippies believed is on the verge of overwhelming us. I will also consider the impact of surrealism on progressive rock lyrics, and explore how progressive rock and heavy metal each came to develop certain mutually exclusive elements of the psychedelic legacy.

Surrealism in Progressive Rock Lyrics

More often than not, the lead singer of a progressive rock band was also its lyricist: thus Jon Anderson of Yes, Ian Anderson of Jethro Tull, Greg Lake of ELP, Mont Campbell of Egg, Peter Gabriel of Genesis, and Peter Hammill of Van der Graaf Generator all wrote their own lyrics. However, this was not always the case. Roger Waters of Pink Floyd, who usually sang backing rather than lead vocals, wrote virtually all of his band's lyrics. Procol Harum initiated an important precedent by making Keith Reid, a lyricist who neither sang nor played an instrument, a full member of the band. Later groups that followed this approach included King Crimson, whose music featured lyrics by Peter Sinfield and later Richard Palmer-James, and Renaissance, whose lyrics were provided by Betty Thatcher.

Reference has already been made to the impact of surrealism on the visual realm of progressive rock; it is therefore hardly surprising that progressive rock lyrics often show a strong tendency toward surrealism as well. The role played by hallucinogens in the formation of a surrealistic poetic style cannot be underestimated. Furthermore, just as album cover designs often made reference to the styles of surrealist masters such as Dali, progressive rock lyricists often sought out the works of literary surrealists. Jon Anderson of Yes was an avid reader of Hesse, whose influence can be detected most directly on *Close to the Edge*;[2] Peter Gabriel of Genesis was deeply impressed by T. S. Eliot's *The Wasteland*, which strongly influenced the group's *Selling England by the Pound* LP.[3]

Like Hesse and Eliot, progressive rock lyricists often try to strike a delicate balance between stating certain key ideas clearly, so they cannot be misinterpreted, and presenting other ideas in such a manner that meaning is conveyed through ambiguous imagery and is thus open to several possible interpretations. Some bands, notably Yes, resort to surrealistic imagery so frequently in their lyrics that the meaning of a particular piece often rests with the listener and is the result of free association, rather than being inherent in the lyric itself. Jon Anderson, Yes's lead singer and principal lyricist, has commented,

> Sometimes I'd just use a series of tantalizingly-sounding words, but sometimes I'd get deeper into meaning and statement. Like in "Starship Trooper," there's a line that says, "Loneliness is a power that we possess to give or take away forever." That's kind of a one-liner, a statement that I like to do now and again. I don't think it's far from the truth if you think about it. On the other hand, "Cause it's time, it's time In time with your time" from "Your Move" is a very danceable lyric. It doesn't actually *mean* that much . . . but it varies, you know? I've had incredible conversations and get letters from people telling me what they think my words are all about. Who knows? Maybe they're right.[4]

On the other end of the spectrum, groups such as Pink Floyd tend to use surrealistic imagery rather sparingly, so that the objective message of a lyric will not be impaired (especially in their later albums). The lyrics of most progressive rock bands fall between these two extremes. It is ironic that the more "meaningless" a lyric becomes (in terms of the ambiguity of its imagery), the more it is open to interpretation on several different levels of meaning.

Simple rhyme schemes, which have always predominated in popular music, do appear fairly frequently in progressive rock lyrics. However, as a result of the legacy of psychedelia and surrealism, there was a surprisingly frequent tendency to resort to blank verse utilizing unequal syllabic schemes. Two excerpts from Van der Graaf Generator's "Lemmings" will illustrate this tendency well (numbers indicate syllables per line):

> The clouds are piled in mountain shapes   (8)
> And there is no escape except to go forward.   (12)
> Don't ask us for an answer now—   (8)
> It's far too late to bow to that convention.   (12)
> What course is there left but to die?   (8)

One notes the emphasis on interior rhymes (shapes/escape, now/bow) at the expense of more conventional rhyme schemes, and the uneven distribution of syllables from line to line. Another excerpt from the same song is similar:

> I know our ends may be soon   (7)
> But why do you make them sooner?   (8)
> Time may finally prove   (6)
> Only the living move her and—   (8)
> No life lies in the quicksand . . .   (7)

I noted previously that shifting and asymmetrical meters were often used as a vehicle for virtuosity by progressive rock bands, especially in instrumental sections. Shifting meters were, however, often called upon to play a purely functional role in setting lyrics such as these, since only by constant shifts between groups of two, three, four, and six beats can the natural rhythms of texts of this sort be captured with complete fidelity. Thus Robert Wyatt stated, "I got fed up with songs where the main accents would make you emphasize the words in a way you wouldn't if you were just saying them, and I got interested in the technique of writing songs where the melody line fits the way you'd say the words if you were just talking."[5] When Rick Wakeman was asked "Why has this band [Yes] always gone for what some might consider show-offy metrical pyrotechnics?" he answered,

> The major problem is Jon [Anderson] and myself. . . . [I]t might be the nature of the way I play that encourages Jon to come in at one or another point. That tends to dictate the meter of the piece, because I'll have to change something to adapt to where Jon comes in. When you look at it, it means I'm playing $\frac{4}{4}$, $\frac{5}{4}$, $\frac{7}{8}$, $\frac{4}{4}$, $\frac{5}{4}$—something like that. Phrasing is very important.[6]

Likewise, when David Gilmour of Pink Floyd was asked how bandmate Roger Waters had come to compose "Money" in $\frac{7}{4}$, he answered that

> [Waters] was always a big fan of John Lennon, and was very keen on changing rhythms in the middle of songs. And Syd [Barrett, Pink Floyd's first leader and songwriter]. Syd used to sing a lyric till he finished it and then change. There are old songs of Syd's in which you can't tell how many beats are in the bar—drummers would have hell trying to get through these things.[7]

Often the lyricist/lead singer had no idea what time signatures his material used, and was only concerned with capturing the flow of the text as naturally as possible. This is evident in Peter Hammill's description of how Van der Graaf Generator worked through "Gog," one of the songs from his solo album *In Camera:*

> As far as I was concerned, having played it, it just sort of had the rhythm and I never bothered to actually work out time signatures—I'm hopeless at it. . . . I just know [the rhythm of] "Gog" although I couldn't tell what time it's in—it just goes [sings]. And that seems natural to me, solo all the way. . . . When we came to rehearse it with the band the first ten times [drummer] Guy [Evans] and [organist] Hugh [Banton] had to count all the way down through the song because it turned out to be so complicated.[8]

Two distinct approaches to vocal melody developed in English progressive rock, each appropriate to a particular type of lyric. Texts with simple rhyme schemes tended to be set to a carefully balanced, lyrical tune. Blank verse of the type discussed above tended to be set in a very declamatory, recitative-like style; the natural rhythms of such texts were captured through the use of irregular phrase lengths and/or shifting and asymmetric meters. The emphasis in this type of melodic writing is not on melodic beauty or tunefulness for its own sake, but on presenting the text as naturally as possible.

Countercultural Ideology in Progressive Rock Lyrics

When one thinks of progressive rock lyrics, one usually thinks of mythological narratives, science-fiction apocalypses, or pseudo-ritualistic texts that read like the Tibetan Book of the Dead or William Blake. Most often, one does not think of social protest. And to be sure, progressive rock was never a style that wore its politics on its sleeve—for reasons which will soon become apparent. Nevertheless, there is often a strong protest element hidden beneath the arty, self-consciously literate lyrics; the punk rockers of the late 1970s were mistaken to think that the mythological and sci-fi epics were merely escapist. To tease the social commentary out, though, one has to understand both the hippies' literary tastes and the relationship between music, words, and imagery in progressive rock.

As I have already pointed out, the whole progressive rock musical style is founded on systematic juxtaposition of masculine and feminine elements. This masculine/feminine dynamic, in turn, encapsulates many of the cultural opposites that the counterculture wished to see reconciled: nature and technology, matriarchal (right-brained, creative, intuitive) and patriarchal (left-brained, rational, carefully organized) approaches to society, ancient and modern ways of life, and so on. Progressive rock's visual imagery also plays with this set of opposites. Fantasy landscapes and medieval or Eastern imagery come to represent the idealized society—close to the earth, based on mutual dependence and a strong sense of community, linked with the past—to which the hippies aspired. On the other hand, bizarre sci-fi imagery is often used to represent the oppressive, soulless bureaucracy which the counterculture believed is crushing the life out of contemporary Western culture.

This same general dichotomy is evident in the lyrics as well. On the one hand, many of progressive rock's most representative lyrics draw on mythology, fantasy literature, science fiction, and sacred texts of the past to suggest a model for an ideal society toward which we might strive, most characteristically a society in which technological virtuosity and ancient wisdom are harmoniously reconciled. On the other hand, lyrics which draw on works such as T. S. Eliot's *The Wasteland* and George Orwell's *1984* to protest the cold, inhuman technocracy which Western society seems to be in the process of becoming are also very much a part of the style. I will divide my discussion of progressive rock lyrics into two broad categories to reflect this dichotomy.

Resistance and Protest in Progressive Rock Lyrics

The spiritual impulse that lay at the root of all progressive rock's most representative lyrics is the belief that Western society's spiritual sterility is increasing in direct proportion to its technological prowess. On the one hand, this belief stimulated the hippies' interest in Eastern spirituality, mysticism, mythology, fantasy literature, and other models of a more organic, "natural" mode of society; it also drew them to texts that attacked the spiritual poverty of modern industrial society. As early as 1922, T. S. Eliot had bewailed Western culture's spiritual bankruptcy in his epic poem *The Wasteland;* not surprisingly, *The Wasteland* held considerable resonance for the counterculture. Significantly, Eliot had entertained the idea of converting to Buddhism some forty years before the hippies, although he eventually settled on the Anglican Church instead. The hippies showed a great fondness for books such as Hermann Hesse's *Steppenwolf* or Carlos Castaneda's pseudo-autobiographical Don Juan cycle which depict the spiritually impoverished Westerner seeking spiritual enlightenment from non-Western sources. Even more important to the hippies than *The Wasteland* were novels such as Aldous Huxley's *Brave New World* and George Orwell's *1984*, which depict the rulers of a totalitarian society of the not-too-distant future marshalling all the technological resources at their disposal to brutally repress the slightest signs of nonconformity.

Orwell's novel had a particularly powerful impact on the musical output of the counterculture and its post-hippie extension of the 1970s: a number of major concept albums cast his vision of totalitarian annihilation in terms of a secular apocalypse. For instance, Pink Floyd's *Animals* LP (1977), based loosely on Orwell's *Animal Farm,* sets forth a bleak, Orwellian interpretation of society as consisting solely of "sheep" (mindless followers), "pigs" (tyrannical thought-police), and "dogs" (violent, power-hungry manipulators). At the explosive climax of the album, the "sheep" finally resort to violence to overcome the "dogs." However, in lyricist Roger Waters' pessimistic assessment, the cycle of events is doomed to be repeated, since the "sheep" will end up returning to their same old pattern of mindless obedience:

> Have you heard the news? The dogs are dead!
> You'd better stay home and do as you're told,
> Get out of the road if you want to grow old ...

ELP's most fully realized concept album, *Brain Salad Surgery* (1973), opens with Hubert Parry's "Jerusalem," in which William Blake's dire prophecies of Satanic mills set forth the opposition between man and machine that dominates the entire album.[9] In *Karn Evil 9,* 1st Impression, lyricist Greg Lake depicts a manipulative totalitarian society in which natural phenomena, spirituality, and human emotion alike have been crushed. In *Karn Evil 9,* 3rd Impression, it becomes evident that the tyrannical overlord is in fact a computer (the imagery is taken from Stanley Kubrick's movie *2001,* but there is also an equation of modern bureaucracy with a soulless but ruthlessly efficient machine), and "what's left of humanity" declares a kind of jihad against its oppressor. Even at the apocalyptic climax of the album, when the computer is defeated militarily, victory has not been won; the computer tells its "victor," "I am perfect—are you?" As with Pink Floyd's *Animals* LP, there is a sense that even a complete overthrow of the existing order will not bring about a brave new world, that the cycle is doomed to repeat itself; having trusted in materialism and technology rather than in human spirituality, mankind has created a monster from which there is no escape.

Eliot's vision of an entire society unraveling at its seams also gave rise to a number of progressive rock songs with distinctly apocalyptic overtones that protest industrial society's materialism. Van der Graaf Generator's riveting "Lemmings" (from the *Pawn Hearts* LP of 1971) uses the image of lemmings rushing into the sea as a metaphor for an entire generation—its hope for any real spiritual fulfillment shattered—hurtling blindly on toward its ruin. While Peter Hammill's earlier lyrics were sometimes marred by their affected, bathos-ridden character, here all unnecessary melodrama is eliminated, and his harrowing, existentialist vision emerges with a new urgency. The "lemmings" repeatedly ask, "What course is there left but to die?" and proclaim

Minds surging strong, we hurtle on into the dark portal—
No one can halt our final vault into the unknown maw.

In response to the lemmings' query of "What course is there left but to die," Hammill poses his own rhetorical question:

What choice is there left but to live
In the hope of saving our childrens' childrens' childrens'
Little ones?

As in so many other progressive rock songs that draw on apocalyptic imagery, "Lemmings" portrays technological "progress," with its dehumanizing tendencies, as the source of the crisis:

Yes I know, it's out of control, out of control:
Greasy machinery slides on the rails,
Young minds and bodies on steel spokes impaled . . .

Many progressive rock lyrics protest industrial society's dehumanizing tendencies without resorting to apocalyptic imagery. A central tenet of these lyrics (or, for that matter, of texts such as *The Wasteland* or *1984* which greatly influenced the counterculture) is that protest and resistance are couched in humanistic/religious, rather than overtly political terms. The counterculture, like any other large-scale social movement, had its different wings and certainly contained a radical political element that sought direct political change;[10] however, I would argue that for the bulk of its participants the counterculture was ultimately more about spiritual transformation than political revolution. Materialism was seen as the root of all evil, the source of greed, violence, and social inequality; even war, as heartily despised as it was by the hippies, was ultimately seen to be rooted in materialism. Most members of the counterculture saw little point in replacing one model of society predicated on materialism, capitalism, with communism, a different model of society that was equally materialistic. Indeed, the hippies were convinced that the material world was essentially unreal (an attitude that was strongly fostered by their drug use), and believed that attempts to change this exterior world were ultimately useless.

Rather, the hippies believed that genuine political change could be wrought only through a general raising of consciousness and a widespread spiritual transformation. This belief that inner transformation or spiritual evolution, rather than political activity, was the key to solving society's problems is echoed by many progressive rock lyricists, who often view political revolution with indifference at best and at times with downright hostility. As Mike Pinder of the Moody Blues says in his "Lost in a Lost World,"

> Grow, the seeds of evolution
> Revolution never won
> It's just another form of gun
> To do again what they have done
> With all our brothers' youngest sons.

Likewise, in Van der Graaf Generator's "Lemmings" Peter Hammill expresses his belief that

> There's other ways than screaming in the mob
> That makes us merely cogs of hatred.
> Look at the why and where we are;
> Look to yourselves and the stars, and the end.

Many of these musicians believed that their music itself was potentially a far more revolutionary force than any political system that could be implemented. Thus, Robert Fripp has stated his belief that "music is a high-order language system; i.e., it is a meta-language. The function of a meta-language is to express solutions to problems posed on a lower-order language system. . . . If one were interested in political change one would not enter political life, one would go into music."[11]

It was the counterculture's prevailing belief that spiritual transformation, rather than direct political revolution, held the key to society's salvation that gave rise to the theme of the spiritual quest that dominated so many concept albums of the late 1960s and early 1970s. One already sees this theme being treated in some of the later music of the Beatles, especially in *Sergeant Pepper*. In her frequently cited content analysis of the album, Joan Peyser interprets side one as being about illusion, with the Beatles pointing up specific ways that people go about hiding the truth from themselves. She interprets the lyrics of George Harrison's song "Within You, Without You," which opens side two of the album, as an explicit description of what side one was all about, as Harrison begins the song by remarking "We were talking about . . . the people who hide themselves behind a wall of illusion . . ." Peyser sees the subsequent songs on side two as illustrations of the futility of life lived without illusion, and concludes that the album's final song, "A Day in the Life," suggests that "while man cannot live without illusion . . . man cannot live with it either."[12] In short, she views *Sergeant Pepper* as a search for meaning amid the sterility and quiet desperation of contemporary everyday life.

Early progressive rock bands picked up where *Sergeant Pepper* left off, devoting entire concept albums to the spiritual quest. The Moody Blues' *In Search of the Lost Chord* (1968) opens by depicting the materialism of modern industrial society, exemplified by the nine-to-five lifestyle ("Ride My See-Saw") as the root of spiritual impoverishment. As the album progresses, music ("House of Four Doors"), hallucinogens ("Legend of a Mind," a veritable paean to Timothy Leary), and transcendental meditation ("The Actor") are shown as steps on the road to the attainment of cosmic consciousness, which is depicted in the album's final song, "Om." Today it is hard not to smirk at some of the album's lyrics, which certainly represent flower power at its most naive: the spoken interludes, with their hippie voice-of-God intonation, are especially insufferable. Nonetheless, there is no doubt that the band's quasi-symphonic instrumentation (especially their characteristic juxtaposition of Mellotron and acoustic guitar), their rich vocal arrangements, and the carefully managed buildups to big climaxes evident in a song like "Legend of a Mind," were highly influential.

Procol Harum's nearly contemporaneous *A Salty Dog* (1969) is a much more pensive album which draws on the sea journey as a metaphor for the spiritual quest: "A ghostly guided tour through the feverish hold of a sailing ship, *A Salty Dog* was peopled with a cast of haunted, deluded, and deranged characters, each with a cautionary tale to tell."[13] The ambience of this album is darker than the Moody Blues' *Lost Chord*, the outcome of the quest more ambiguous; in the album's moving final song, "Pilgrim's Progress," the seeker laments that he has forsaken all to take up the quest but "still no hidden truths could I unfold." These two albums display the competing philosophical approaches that are evident in the spiritual quest epics of later progressive rock bands. The optimistic, Aquarian worldview evident throughout the Moody Blues' *Lost Chord*, with its strong debt to Eastern spirituality, was taken up by later bands such as Yes to suggest that the goal of the spiritual quest—an ill-defined cosmic consciousness—can in fact be attained. On the other hand, Procol Harum's searching, troubled vision, with its references to existentialism (very evident in the music of later bands such as Van der Graaf Generator), suggests that while the quest is a noble (and perhaps even a necessary) duty, it is also by its very nature unfulfillable. Rock critics have always gravitated to the "existentialist" school, preferring the dark, brooding visions of Van der Graaf Generator, Pink Floyd, and King Crimson to the "Aquarian" school of thought, which they considered sophomoric and overly naive. There is no doubt that the vision of the "existentialists" meshes far better with the cynical outlook of the 1990s than that of the "Aquarians." However, it is possible that the old school of rock idealism will be at least partially rehabilitated, and the cosmic optimism of bands such as Yes may eventually be seen in a more favorable light.

While the emphasis on a spiritual quest was perhaps the counterculture's most epic means of protest against the values of industrial society, many progressive rock lyrics are concerned with protest on a somewhat less cosmic (and arguably a more immediately effective) scale. As has been seen in examining the progressive rock lyrics that utilize apocalyptic motifs, there was a widespread fear among the counterculture that technology was not benefiting society, but rather depersonalizing it, dehumanizing it, spiritually impoverishing it—thus ELP's parable of computers enslaving mankind in *Karn Evil 9*. Two of the most-studied aspects of the counterculture, its experiments with communal living and its championing of socially disadvantaged groups, stem from the desire to arrive at a more organically relevant, "natural" community. In *Profane Culture*, his seminal ethnographic study of English hippies, Paul Willis makes this highly perceptive observation:

> The move from the scruffy terrace/local street, and all the human density that implied, to the new tower block/impersonal highway, and the human desolation that implied, was paralleled for the hippies in the gigantic move of the whole of Europe from an older hierarchic, ornate order to a standardized, affluent democratic drabness. In the dust and poverty of India the hippie hoped to find those spiritual values and authentic experiences that were so spectacularly lacking in the West.[14]

In Pink Floyd's *Dark Side of the Moon* (1973), lyricist Roger Waters explores just those abstractions of modern industrial society that depersonalize, dehumanize, and ultimately drive people to madness: time (more accurately, industrial society's conception of it), money, war and violence ("Us and Them"), the futility of the nine-to-five career ("On the Run"). In the last song of this great song cycle, "Eclipse," Waters suggests that there is indeed a cosmic blueprint that informs the apparently random events of everyday life; we have simply grown too dull to perceive it. The dehumanizing tendencies of industrial society received frequent treatment by rock groups throughout the 1970s, but seldom with the power and insight displayed here. By the mid-1970s, as the dreams of the counterculture faded, Waters's own lyrics took on an increasingly bitter, pessimistic tone, culminating in the angry pseudo-political stridency of *The Wall* (1979).

Since Britain did not undergo the Vietnam experience, antiwar themes in the music of the British counterculture usually lack the urgency and stridency found in the music of their American counterparts. Nonetheless, lyrics which extol the futility of war and the industrial/military complex can be found throughout the output of English progressive rock bands of the 1970s: "Us and Them" by Pink Floyd (from the *Dark Side of the Moon* album), "Battlefield" by ELP (the sixth movement of their *Tarkus* suite), "Yours Is No Disgrace" by Yes, "21st-century Schizoid Man" by King Crimson, "The Emperor and His War-room" by Van der Graaf Generator, and "One for the Vine" by Genesis. English bands tend to view war from a more philosophical, abstract viewpoint than their American counterparts, seeing it as the inevitable result of society's materialism and its attendant greed and lust for power.

Protests against organized religion—and much more specifically, the Anglican Church, with which many of the middle-class and upper-middle-class English musicians were intimately familiar—were also common. Jethro Tull's concept album *Aqualung* (1971) set the tone for the treatment of this subject. Denominational Christianity is criticized for its glorification of ritual over meaningful experience, its dedication to a rigid hierarchical order at the expense of equality and egalitarianism before God, and its perceived intolerance in terms of doctrinal matters. (Since countercultural spirituality was strongly influenced by Eastern concepts, reality itself was seen as relative and open to individual interpretation, not as absolute and revealed through divinely inspired canon.) Similar ground was covered in ELP's "The Only Way" (1971) and King Crimson's "The Great Deceiver" (1974), which specifically protests the commercialization of the Vatican.

Other social institutions are criticized as well. The copious liner notes of Jethro Tull's *Thick as a Brick* LP (1972), cast in the form of a mock newspaper, purport to tell the story of a boy named Gerald Bostock who had written a rambling, visionary poem called "Thick as a Brick" for a contest sponsored by the Society for Literary Advancement and Gestation (SLAG). After Gerald read his poem live over the BBC, the contest's judges quickly disqualified him and declared him to be a troubled young man in need of immediate psychiatric counseling. The "newspaper" reports that the noted progressive rock band Jethro Tull have agreed to set Gerald's poem to music, hence the album *Thick as a Brick*. Besides providing an amusing explanation for the genesis of his lengthy piece, Ian Anderson uses this clever story line to attack the insistence on conformity and the discouragement, even suppression, of individuality that characterized the English public school (actually a network of exclusive private schools that traditionally have been open only to members of the upper and upper middle classes). Anderson himself has said of *Thick as a Brick* that "I'm just creating a background lyrical summation of a lot of things I feel about being a contemporary child in this age and the problems that one has—the problems of being precocious beyond one's age or having interests beyond one's age, and to some extent being ruled in a kind of heavy-handed, unexplained fashion."[15] A number of English progressive rock musicians were intimately familiar with the institution of the English public school; Genesis actually formed at the highly exclusive Charterhouse. Pink Floyd's "Another Brick in the Wall, Part Two" represents a particularly heated attack on the institution.

Attacks on specific political parties or individual politicians held relatively little interest for progressive rock musicians, since they were regarded as merely symptoms of society's malaise rather than its underlying cause. Nonetheless, occasional exceptions are evident. Gentle Giant's *The Power and the Glory*, released in September 1974, just a month after Richard Nixon was forced to resign the presidency as a result of the Watergate scandal, is a concept album that illustrates the corruption inherent in contemporary political systems. Occasionally individual political figures were attacked: "Pigs" from Pink Floyd's *Animals* LP takes an explicit swipe at Mary Whitehouse, England's self-appointed guardian of public morals during the late 1970s.

Progressive Rock's Utopian Vision: Mythology, Mysticism, and Science Fiction

Many progressive rock lyrics draw on mythology, fantasy literature, science fiction, or sacred texts of the past as metaphors for an ideal society toward which we might strive. Both ancient mythology and fantasy works such as J. R. R. Tolkien's Middle Earth cycle (of which *The Hobbit, The Lord of the Rings,* and *The Silmarillion* are best known) depict societies far different than our own, and to the hippies' way of thinking, far more desirable: pastoral and linked to the earth in a way that we are not, sharing a sense of community and possessing a spiritual insight that we have lost. It was this search after lost spirituality that sparked the counterculture's love affair with Eastern religions, led to popular culture's "discovery" of the Tibetan and Egyptian Books of the Dead during the 1960s, spurred an explosion of cults and sects from Hare Krishnas to Jesus freaks to Gurdjieff adepts, and created a general interest in vanished cultures.[16] In his program notes for the third movement of *Tales from Topographic Oceans,* "The Ancient," Jon Anderson writes, "Steve [Howe]'s guitar is pivotal in sharpening reflections on the beauties and treasures of lost civilizations. Indian, Chinese, Central American, Atlantean [note how the existence of this legendary civilization is here accepted as fact]; these and other peoples left an immense treasure of knowledge."

Yes, more than any other major progressive rock band, stressed the belief that drawing on the distilled wisdom of the ages (I use the term figuratively) is the key to breaking out of our cycle of social strife and entering a new period of cosmic awareness. One sees this theme threading its way through their *Close to the Edge* suite, which is loosely based on Hesse's *Siddhartha;* their enormous *Tales from*

Topographic Oceans, structured around the description of the four-part Shastric scriptures found in Sri Paramhansa Yoganda's *Autobiography of a Yogi*; and their *The Gates of Delirium*, which was supposedly inspired by Tolstoy's *War and Peace*. In all of these pieces, the masculine/feminine musical contrasts for which the band was famous are effectively used to convey the progress from gross materialism to spiritual awareness; while feminine sections introduce an all-important element of reflection and realization, masculine sections introduce the equally important quality of struggle and attainment.

A similar philosophy can be found in the lyrics of a number of other progressive rock bands as well. Genesis's epic *Supper's Ready*, a psychedelic recounting of the New Testament Book of Revelation, presents the New Jerusalem as the model of a perfect, fulfilled society—won, of course, after an epic struggle between the forces of good and evil. Even more characteristically, their "Cinema Show" contrasts the emptiness of a pair of modern-day lovers with the spiritual fullness of the Greek mythological figure Tiresias, who is both male and female; Tiresias seems intended to symbolize that synthesis of patriarchal and matriarchal values which will characterize the hippies' ideal society. (An earlier song by Genesis, "The Fountain of Salmacis," deals with yet another mythological male/female character, Hermaphrodite, although here it is not so clear that the story line has larger social implications.) There is an element of pantheistic or nature mysticism in a number of progressive rock songs that serves a similar purpose to mythological or fantasy imagery. For instance, Yes's "Roundabout," Genesis's "Firth of Fifth," Refugee's "Grand Canyon," and some of the songs from Jethro Tull's folkier albums of the late 1970s (*Songs from the Wood, Heavy Horses*) idealize nature, and see it as a source of quasi-mystical revelation and as a metaphor for spiritual authenticity. In his content analysis of the most famous "pantheist song" of all, Led Zeppelin's "Stairway to Heaven," Robert Walser emphasizes above all this search for authenticity: "Images of nature abound: a brook, a songbird, rings of smoke, trees, forests, a hedgerow, wind . . . Like the music, [the lyrics] engage with the fantasies and anxieties of our time; they offer contact with social and metaphysical depth in a world of commodities and mass communication."[17]

The prevalence of science fiction narratives in progressive rock during the late 1960s and early 1970s may at first seem harder to explain, since there is an obvious tension between the counterculture's generally dim view of technology and their fascination with science fiction in general and space travel in particular. There seems to be two explanations. First, this type of subject matter was very much in the air during the late 1960s: at the time there was a great deal of interest among the public at large in space exploration (Apollo 11 landed on the moon in 1969), and science fiction literature had reached the peak of its cultural resonance. Stanley Kubrick's movie version of Arthur C. Clarke's *2001: A Space Odyssey* was a huge hit in 1968; the books of Isaac Asimov, Ray Bradbury, Robert Heinlein, Frank

Herbert, and other major science fiction writers were extremely popular among the counterculture and the mainstream public alike.

Even more importantly, for the counterculture space travel seemed to be the one realm in which technology could serve a beneficial purpose rather than a dehumanizing one. In concept albums such as the Moody Blues' *To Our Children's Children's Children* (1969), for instance, there is a clear implication that man's conquest of space could bring with it a raising of cosmic awareness and an opportunity for spiritual transformation. In short, hippies saw the science fiction epic as an excellent forum for reconciling Western society's technological virtuosity with the proverbial wisdom of the ages.

Pink Floyd pioneered the space rock epic during the late 1960s with a trio of pieces: "Astronomy Domine," "Interstellar Overdrive," and "Set the Controls for the Heart of the Sun" (the title of the last song was borrowed from one of William S. Burroughs's novels). While Pink Floyd abandoned science fiction subject matter after 1970, a number of other leading progressive rock bands produced at least one major piece involving outer space travel. Especially characteristic were Van der Graaf Generator's "Pioneers over c" (1970), ELP's "Infinite Space" (1971), Yes's "Starship Trooper" (1971), Genesis's "Watchers of the Sky" (1972), and Argent's *Nexus* LP (1974), a hard rock/progressive rock fusion that mixes outer space imagery with Biblical apocalypse. By the mid-1970s, interest in science fiction subject matter, especially space travel, waned considerably among English progressive rock musicians, although some North American stadium rock bands (notably Rush) began treating similar subject matter at about the same time.

It must be admitted that progressive rock's epic subject matter did not necessarily serve as a parable for countercultural values, nor was the hippies' ideology always presented through larger-than-life narratives. On the one hand, progressive rock's supernatural narratives (Procol Harum's "Dead Man's Dream," Gentle Giant's "Alucard," Renaissance's "A Trip to the Fair," Caravan's "C'thlu thlu") or adventure/thriller narratives (Van der Graaf Generator's "Scorched Earth," Genesis's "Dance on a Volcano," Yes's "South Side of the Sky," ELP's "Pirates") make no particular social statement, but seem to be recounted more for the joy of telling a story than for the purpose of proving a point. On the other hand, down-to-earth storylines were sometimes used as parables through which values of the counterculture were expressed. For instance, Gentle Giant's *Three Friends* (1972) is a concept album which traces the progress of three young men from their school years into their maturity. One becomes a manual laborer; one, an artist; one, a highly successful businessman. The third has succeeded, in the eyes of respectable society, far more than the first two, who are both outcasts in their own ways. Nonetheless, in the businessman's monologue, "Mr. Class and Quality," it becomes apparent that of the three men he is by far the most spiritually impoverished. Thus the band uses this concept album to drive home that oft-expressed concern of the counterculture, the corrosive effect of materialism on a person's spiritual well-being.

Postscript: Dionysian Themes in Progressive Rock

There was always an implicit tension in the counterculture between the alleged goals of drug use and free love (opening new portals of consciousness and renouncing the possessiveness of materialistic society, respectively) and the pursuit of these activities as ends in themselves. With the dissolution of psychedelia around 1970, one sees the emergence of what might be called Apollonian and Dionysian responses to this paradox in the two primary subgenres to emerge from the ashes of psychedelia, progressive rock and heavy metal. Progressive rock represents the Apollonian side of the counterculture: the emphasis on the spiritual quest, the critiques of contemporary society, the fascination with sophisticated narratives. Heavy metal, on the other hand, represents the Dionysian side of the counterculture, drawing upon its undeniable hedonistic streak and portraying sex, partying, and the general pursuit of carnal pleasure as a worthy goal in and of itself. In their seminal article of 1978, "Rock and Sexuality," Simon Frith and Angela McRobbie dubbed heavy metal and related hard rock styles as "cock rock" because of their supposedly aggressive celebration of masculine sexuality.[18] While I believe that considering these styles from a single viewpoint (gender) can lead to serious omissions (for instance, one cannot explain how a heavy metal concert differs socially from a football match without examining the "liturgical" overtones of a Led Zeppelin or Black Sabbath performance), Frith's and McRobbie's description does underline the sexually charged nature of much of this music.

Dionysian themes represented a territory that progressive rock musicians largely steered clear of. Several progressive rock musicians—notably Robert Fripp and Ian Anderson—took a strong antidrug stance long before such a view was fashionable among hip society, and the band Yes gained a certain reputation for sobriety after becoming vegetarians and health-food addicts. While there had been occasional veiled references to the consciousness-expanding potentials of hallucinogens in the songs of the psychedelic bands (the Beatles' "Lucy in the Sky with Diamonds," the Moody Blues' "Legend of a Mind," some of the songs on Caravan's debut LP), after 1970 it is next to impossible to find a progressive rock song that glorifies drug and alcohol use in the manner of innumerable heavy metal anthems. Of course, this is not to say that no progressive rock musicians took drugs; obviously, even those who didn't were influenced by psychedelia and the general tendency toward surrealism spawned by hallucinogens.

The topic of sex—which, again, figured prominently in innumerable heavy metal songs—was not frequently referred to in progressive rock. A few bands devoted a token song to the subject—ELP's "Living Sin," King Crimson's "Ladies of the Night," Curved Air's "Not Quite the Same," Genesis's "Counting out Time," Procol Harum's "Souvenir from London." Typically, Van der Graaf Generator's "La Rossa," while nominally about the protagonist's lust for his lady, is ultimately more concerned with his harrowing self-analysis. Jethro Tull made somewhat more frequent references to sex, but Ian Anderson's bawdiness often comes off as a self-conscious stab at adolescent humor when compared to the forceful directness and open obscenity with which many heavy metal bands approached the topic.

If there is one element that unites the lyrics of progressive rock and heavy metal bands, it is the complete seriousness with which the lyrics are presented, without any sense of satire or ironic detachment. (Granted, there is a certain irony and sense of humor in some of the lyrics of Peter Gabriel and Ian Anderson, but it is largely mitigated by the cosmic imagery.) As Will Straw points out in his perceptive sociological analysis, "The Case of Heavy Metal,"[19] a rereading of *Rolling Stone* from the early to mid-1970s reveals that a self-conscious treatment of rock imagery and an ironic detachment from the lyrics are precisely the qualities that the rock critics of this period most admire. As I point out later, this meant that both progressive rock and heavy metal were in for some rough handling by the critics. Indeed, critics writing for *Rolling Stone, Creem,* and similar journals looked upon progressive rock's emphasis on virtuosity, its self-conscious eclecticism, its purely musical interest in compositional problems, and the essentially serious subject matter of its lyrics as proof that the style had committed (in their estimation) the most unpardonable sin of all: it took itself seriously. The animosity evinced by many critics toward progressive rock can be understood at least partially in this light.

ABOVE: The Minimoog (upper keyboard) and the Mellotron Model 400 (lower keyboard) were important components of the progressive rock keyboard arsenal. The Model 400 was used by Yes, Genesis, Gentle Giant, and *Red*-era King Crimson. The Minimoog was used at one time or another by a majority of the major progressive rock bands of the 1970s.

BELOW: The Mellotron Mark II, a larger and more mechanically complicated predecessor of the Model 400. It was used by the Beatles, the Moody Blues, and the early King Crimson lineups. *(Courtesy of David Kean, Mellotron Archives)*

William Neal's painting on the inner gatefold of Emerson, Lake and Palmer's *Tarkus* LP. *(Reproduced by permission of Victory Music, Inc)*

Paul Whitehead's cover art for Genesis's *Foxtrot* LP. *(© Copyright P. Whitehead.*

Roger Dean's cover art for Yes's albums of 1971-1975 gave rise to a genre of mythic land-scape paintings that became closely associated with progressive rock. Dean had many imitators, but Patrick Woodroffe, whose painting for Pallas's *The Sentinel* (1984) is shown here, is one of Dean's few serious rivals in the field. Note the strange geological formations,

the medievalism of the distant city, the Bosch-like flying machines, and the surreal touches (flying boats, birds with human hands). While Dean pioneered a number of these motifs, seldom did they receive the maturity of expression seen here. *(Reproduced by permission of Pallas/Mike Stobbie)*

Emerson, Lake and Palmer in concert in St. Louis, Missouri, March 28, 1974. *(Photos courtesy of Greg Pawelko/Turbulence)*

ABOVE: Keith Emerson playing the Moog.   **BELOW:** Emerson and Carl Palmer. Note Palmer's enormous arsenal of miscellaneous percussion surrounding the drum kit.

Greg Lake

ABOVE: King Crimson in a London studio circa 1973. Left to right: John Wetton, David Cross, Robert Fripp, Bill Bruford. Some critics consider this the finest progressive rock lineup ever assembled. *(Courtesy of Bill Bruford. Photo by Barry Wentzell)*

BELOW: Van der Graaf Generator in concert in London's Marquee Club, July 30, 1976. Left to right: Hugh Banton, Peter Hammill. *(Courtesy of Mike Spindloe/Pawn Hearts. Photographer unknown)*

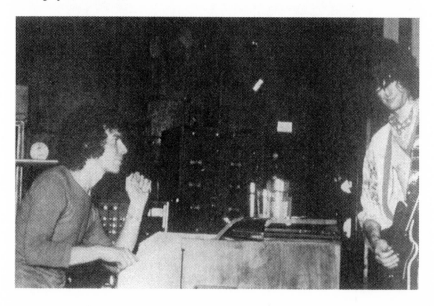

Van der Graaf Generator's David Jackson in concert in London's Marquee Club, July 30, 1976. *(Courtesy of Mike Spindloe/Pawn Hearts. Photographer unknown)*

Jethro Tull's Ian Anderson in concert in Toronto, 1976. *(Courtesy of the Mike King Collection)*

Gentle Giant's Gary Green (left) and Ray Shulman (right) in concert in Toronto, 1976. *(Courtesy of the Mike King Collection)*

ABOVE: Steve Hackett of Genesis in concert at Toronto's Maple Leaf Gardens, 1977. *(Courtesy of the Mike King Collection)*

BELOW: Michael Rutherford of Genesis in concert at Toronto's Maple Leaf Gardens, 1977. Note Rutherford's unique custom-made twelve-string guitar/electric bass. *(Courtesy of the Mike King Collection)*

Eddie Jobson in concert during U.K.'s *Night after Night* tour, 1978-1979. *(Courtesy of Eddie Jobson/Zinc Inc. Photo by Max Takahashi)*

Jade Warrior's *Floating World* LP. This Eckford/Stimpson design is a good example of the Eastern motifs that sometimes appeared in progressive rock cover art. *(Courtesy of Island Records Limited)*

Four Different Progressive Rock Pieces

In the last three chapters, I have separated the sonic, visual, and verbal elements of progressive rock in order to define the general tendencies of each as precisely as possible. Of course, such a separation is artificial; as I stated in the introduction, contemporary popular music styles can only be fully understood when one considers these elements in tandem. Therefore, in this chapter I will put words, visuals, and music back together by considering four particularly representative pieces of the progressive rock era: ELP's *Tarkus* (1971), *Close to the Edge* (1972), Genesis's "Firth of Fifth" (1973), and Pink Floyd's "Wish You Were Here" (1975).

In selecting these pieces, I have attempted to keep several goals in mind. First, I have tried to cover a variety of structural approaches which were of importance to progressive rock. *Tarkus* exemplifies a type of relatively loose multimovement suite that was to appear again and again in progressive rock; *Close to the Edge*, on the other hand, is a tightly knit multimovement suite that bears more than a passing resemblance to that most venerable form of the classical tradition, sonata form. "Firth of Fifth" is cast in a single-movement sectionalized form, and is suggestive of a simple song that has been expanded to enormous lengths by the inclusion of instrumental preludes, interludes, and postludes; on the other hand, its structural pattern suggests parallels with both arch form and sonata form. *Wish You Were Here* is a conflation of the multimovement suite with the song-cycle approach of the concept album.

Second, I have chosen pieces that trace a chronological line from early (1971) to late (1975) in progressive rock's "classic" period. This allows one to witness the manner in which progressive rock gradually developed away from the assumptions which had dominated the psychedelic era. In its early days, progressive rock drew on the hermetic streak of psychedelia, the supposition that music should contain hidden meanings which insiders would be aware of, but which outsiders would be oblivious to. One sees this hermetic element most strongly in *Tarkus*, with its dense maze of visual symbols, verbal imagery, and sometimes unusual music; it is somewhat less evident in *Close to the Edge* and "Firth of Fifth," and is in the process of disappearing by the time of *Wish You Were Here*, where the occasional "trippiness" of the cover art or of isolated snippets of lyrics does not mask the clear, unambiguous message of the lyrics.

I have also attempted to choose pieces which have not received comprehensive discussion elsewhere. For instance, Eric Tamm analyzes a number of King Crimson pieces in his study of Robert Fripp; his analysis of "Starless," arguably the band's finest song, is especially thorough. Allan Moore's most penetrating analyses of progressive rock in his *Rock: The Primary Text* are devoted to the music of Jethro Tull; Nors Josephson's article "Bach Meets Liszt: Traditional Formal Structures and Performance Practices in Progressive Rock" also contains a concise discussion of the structure of Tull's *Thick as a Brick*. (Josephson also discusses Genesis's *Supper's Ready*, Yes's *The Gates of Delirium*, Kansas's "The Wall," and Supertramp's "The Logical Song.") Blair Pethel's study of Keith Emerson contains thorough analyses of ELP's "Abaddon's Bolero" and "Pirates," but says relatively little concerning *Tarkus* (and, unfortunately, virtually nothing about *Karn Evil 9*). In addition to avoiding works that have been discussed elsewhere, I have also decided to discuss pieces which, because of their popularity, made an enduring mark on popular culture at large. This has meant neglecting more obscure works which are probably equally worthy of attention, such as Van der Graaf Generator's "Lemmings" or Egg's "Enneagram."

However, I have attempted to choose pieces that, despite their important surface differences, contain deeper similarities which seem to characterize progressive rock both as a musical style and as a philosophical statement of the counterculture and its post-hippie extension. The structural outlines of all four pieces reveal a tension between a persistent avoidance of goal-oriented harmonies and a persistent embrace of goal-oriented forms. This tension is quite characteristic of progressive rock, and seems to me to nicely encapsulate the hippies' (ultimately futile) struggles to move beyond the conventions of middle-class society, even while retaining important cultural constructs of the society they were ostensibly rebelling against. Each of these four pieces reflect, albeit in different ways, the primary focus of the counterculture in its best moments: the search for some sort of authentic spirituality amid the depersonalizing tendencies and rampant materialism of contemporary Western culture. However, I think there is an irony inherent in all four pieces that speaks volumes about the counterculture's ambiguous relationship with the despised Establishment: the protest against dehumanization was made with the aid of the most expensive, technologically sophisticated arsenal of musical equipment that was available to musicians of that time.

Emerson, Lake and Palmer: *Tarkus* (1971)

The earliest of the pieces to be discussed is Emerson, Lake and Palmer's *Tarkus*, recorded and released in 1971. Side two of the *Tarkus* LP is filled by several relatively short songs that are of somewhat uneven quality; in contrast, *Tarkus* occupies the entirety of side one, and is one of progressive rock's earliest and most influential multimovement suites. The piece was also one of progressive rock's most radical, and caused a great deal of turbulence within the band. In 1970 and 1971, Emerson had been exploring the music of Bartók and Alberto Ginastera (especially the latter's First Piano Concerto), and saw *Tarkus* as a forum in which "to explore some things I had never really done before: percussive keyboard sounds, strong rhythms, atonality."[1] However, according to Emerson, his bandmates—particularly Greg Lake—initially found the piece entirely too radical:

> I had written the opening of *Tarkus* on the piano, and when I took it in to the other guys, Greg said "I can't play that kind of music. If that's what you want to play, then I think you should look for someone else to play with." This kind of shocked me, because I was excited about the new piece, but I told him that if that was what he wanted, I'd find some other musicians.[2]

Eventually one of the band's managers convinced Lake to try the new piece, and as Emerson has remarked, "Greg gradually became turned on to the work, and he added a track of his own, 'The Battlefield.'"[3]

In many ways *Tarkus*, which clocks in at just under twenty-one minutes in the studio performance,[4] is the archetypal progressive rock multimovement suite. The seven individual "movements" move seamlessly, without pause, from one to the next; the longest movement is just under four minutes, the shortest just over a minute. Movements one, three, five, and seven are instrumental, while movements two, four, and six are vocal. The even-numbered "song" movements are the longest, while movements one and seven are fairly substantial as well; it is possible to hear the piece as three semi-independent songs with an instrumental prelude, two short instrumental interludes, and a lengthier instrumental postlude.

The concept of *Tarkus* is conveyed through a combination of cover art, lyrics, and music; the titles of the individual movements are also important in fleshing out the piece's concept. Both the symbolism of the cover art and the imagery of the lyrics are open to more than one "reading"; when these elements are considered in conjunction with the music, yet more possible meanings emerge, and as a result one cannot really insist on a dogmatic interpretation of *Tarkus*. Indeed, such an interpretation would not be in keeping with the whole hermetic *ethos* of the psychedelic era—that is, with the supposition that music contains hidden meanings which need searching out—and it seems likely that the band intended for individual free association to play at least some role in interpreting the piece. (Incidentally, to my knowledge none of the band members have ever discussed the piece's conceptual "meaning" in a published interview.) On the other hand, while some elements of both cover art and lyrics are certainly open to differing interpretations, other elements can be "read" fairly objectively, so I think certain broad conclusions can be drawn about what the band intended the work's "meaning" to be.

William Neal's drawing for the outer cover of *Tarkus*, with its fearsome armadillo/tank mutant, has become one of the better-known visual symbols of progressive rock. Nonetheless, it is Neal's eleven discrete panels on the album's inner gatefold that are crucial to creating a framework through which the piece's concept can be conveyed. The first panel, which corresponds to the opening movement, "Eruption," depicts Tarkus emerging from an egg on the side of a volcano, while lava spews ominously from a nearby crater. The next two panels tie in with the piece's second movement, "Stones of Years"; the first of these panels reveals an indescribably strange cybernetic creature (something like a walking space station), which in the second of the two panels has been blown to bits by Tarkus's fearsome gun turrets. Panels four and five, corresponding to the piece's third movement, "Iconoclast," chronicle the appearance and subsequent destruction of a cybernetic pterosaur/warplane mutant. Similar ground is covered in the panels which correspond to the fourth movement, "Mass"; yet another cybernetic creature (a combination lizard/locust/guided missile launcher) faces down Tarkus, only to be destroyed. The next panel, which is especially large, depicts a Manticore, a mythological beast with the head of a man, body of a lion, and tail of a scorpion; this panel ties in with the piece's fifth movement, "Manticore." The Manticore is the first of Tarkus's foes that is not cybernetic; I will suggest the possible significance of this below.

In the next two panels, corresponding to the sixth movement, "Battlefield," Manticore and Tarkus square off: Manticore stings Tarkus's eye, forcing the latter to retreat. In the final panel, Tarkus is seen floating down a river on its side; blood appears to be flowing from its head, but its gun turrets still appear operable, so it is hard to say to what if any degree it has been incapacitated. The music of the first half of the seventh movement, "Aquatarkus," is reminiscent of a funeral march, therefore suggesting the the beast's demise. However, the final section of the movement recapitulates part of the first movement, "Eruption," suggesting that the resurrection or return of Tarkus remains an ever-present danger: this is an ambiguity that the sudden emergence of F major at the end of a piece otherwise dominated by minor modality does little to clarify.

As useful as these eleven panels are for providing linear continuity to the concept, they obviously cannot be interpreted literally; otherwise, *Tarkus* is merely a musical depiction of a number of weird and fantastic creatures killing and maiming each other. Clearly, the various beasts depicted in Neal's psychedelic album art are symbols; the lyrics and the titles of the individual movements become the vehicles through which the symbols can be "read" with at least a degree of objective certainty. For instance, in "Stones of Years" lyricist Greg Lake draws on imagery that conjures a set of dying cultural traditions. He speaks of time that has been "overgrown, never known," days that have "made you so unwise." He asks

> How can you know where you've been?
> In time
> You'll see the sign
> And realize your sin.

Through the lyrics, then, the meaning of the cover art pertaining to the second movement becomes more apparent: Tarkus has obliterated cultural tradition.

As one continues to correlate lyrics, movement titles, and cover art in this manner, it becomes evident that Tarkus has obliterated most of society's other moorings as well. For instance, while the third movement has no lyrics, its title, "Iconoclast," gives us enough information to interpret the cover art: Tarkus has destroyed the capacity for individuality, for independent thought. Likewise, the cutting lyrics of the fourth movement, "Mass" (the title almost certainly refers to the Roman Catholic liturgical celebration), suggest that even religion cannot survive the assault of Tarkus. "Mass" calls forth some of Lake's angriest, and yet most imaginative, lyrics. It is peopled by a whole cast of unsavory characters: a pilgrim "committing every sin that he could," a "cardinal of grief," a "minister of hate," a "messenger of fear," and a silent choir bringing forth "jaded sound." Lake describes them all with the same recurring refrain: "The weaver in the web that he made." The album art, in conjunction with the lyrics, tells the story: religion, like independent thought and cultural tradition, is unable to withstand the onslaught of Tarkus. But what, exactly, does "Tarkus" symbolize?

This question becomes especially acute when one considers the last three movements and their relationship to the last four panels. Manticore is the first of Tarkus's foes that is not cybernetic, but completely organic. Significantly, while the Manticore is unable to destroy Tarkus, it is at least able to withstand its assaults, to injure it, and to drive it into hiding.

It seems to me that the organic nature of the Manticore holds the key to interpreting the conceptual foundation underlying the *Tarkus* suite. While the symbolism behind "Tarkus" can be "read" more than one way, different readings will tend to be interrelated. Like the creatures it destroys, Tarkus is cybernetic; it is as much machine as it is animal, and hence is "unnatural." Therefore, Tarkus can be seen to symbolize a totalitarian society (one thinks of how Big Brother crushed spirituality, individuality, and tradition in Orwell's *1984*); or, equally, Tarkus can be seen to symbolize technology run amok, out of the control of its creators, visiting misery upon all it touches. Perhaps Tarkus can even be seen to represent materialism, which poisons everything around it. None of these readings are mutually exclusive; perhaps they are all correct, since the hippies certainly saw technology, totalitarianism, and materialism walking hand in hand. The lyrics of the sixth movement, "Battlefield," suggest that Tarkus may well be a conflation of all these evils. The protagonist first crows about "the profits of my victory" (signifying the triumph of materialism), but then grows more pensive upon considering the horrors of war:

> Were you there to watch the earth be scorched?
> Did you stand beside the spectral torch?
> Know the leaves of sorrow turned their face,
> Scattered on the ashes of disgrace.

In the movement's final couplet, Lake offers an especially pregnant bit of imagery:

> Where the blades of grass on arrows rain
> Then there'd be no sorrow, be no pain.[5]

By superseding the technology of war (arrows) with natural phenomena (blades of grass), Lake seems to suggest there is one way to stop the suffering: humans need to short-circuit technological "progress" to reenter a "natural," prematerialistic state.

The Manticore, then, seems to symbolize the "natural" or "spiritually authentic" man or woman—unencumbered by materialism, unbeholden to technology, unafraid of Big Brother.[6] While Manticore may not be able to destroy Tarkus and all it represents (since both the final panel of the album art and the recapitulation of part of the opening movement at the end of the piece suggest that Tarkus will always be capable of returning), it can at least hold Tarkus at bay.

It is the nature of the concept album, however, that one can interpret a given album's concept in a more specific sense if one wishes. For instance, I have heard it argued that Tarkus represents the United States, since the armadillo is an American animal; that Manticore, with its origins in Persian and perhaps ultimately Indian mythology, symbolizes Southern Asia;[7] that the sixth movement, "Battlefield," is actually about the Vietnam War; and that the entire piece is therefore an antiwar protest. On one level, I rather doubt it. While Keith Emerson was once involved in a flag-burning incident during his days with the Nice, by the early 1970s he admitted to having lost interest in protest politics.[8] Furthermore, since Vietnam protest songs were not uncommon around 1970, resorting to a veiled or hidden protest would have been quite unnecessary.

On the other hand, though, even this interpretation is not unrelated to the "readings" I discussed earlier. After all, many of the hippies viewed the Vietnam War as nothing more than the totalitarian oppression of a weak country by a strong one; the Vietnamese were seen as in some ways morally "superior," since they lived in a more "natural" state and were not tainted by materialism to the degree of their American counterparts. If *Tarkus* proves one thing, it is that the imagery and symbolism of concept pieces allowed for a multitude of interpretations, some of which were interrelated and many of which were "correct" on some level or another.

On more than one occasion, Keith Emerson has admitted that his collaborations with Greg Lake were sometimes strained, and often were not completely integrated.[9] For instance, for *Tarkus* Lake penned the lyrics, but wrote the music only for the sixth movement; Emerson wrote the music for the rest of the piece. One result, as Emerson himself pointed out, is that there was never an ELP style so much as there was an Emerson style, a Lake style, or a Palmer style.[10] A second result of this state of affairs is that while the music of *Tarkus* does complement and illuminate the piece's concept, it is more self-contained than concept pieces by other bands where several members contributed musical and lyrical ideas. In short, even shorn of its lyrics and cover art, *Tarkus* makes sense as an abstract instrumental piece.[11] It is worthwhile, then, to examine how the piece is organized on a purely musical basis.

The first organizing principle, discussed above, is the juxtaposition of the odd-numbered instrumental movements with the even-numbered "song" movements. A second organizing principle, clearly drawn from the practice of the "classical" tradition, involves contrasts in tempo. The first three instrumental movements are quite fast; the first and third "song" movements are slow, befitting the essentially mournful character of the lyrics, while the more cutting lyrics of the second "song" movement are set to a faster tempo. The first section of the seventh (final) movement is moderately slow, a reflection of its funeral march-like character; the final section of this movement, however, recapitulates part of the opening, with its fast tempo.

The harmonic practice of *Tarkus* deserves a chapter to itself; here I will simply try to summarize important points. While Emerson had stated that one of his goals in composing *Tarkus* was to explore atonality, the piece is not atonal in the strict sense of the word. However, tonality is established by traditional harmonic relationships between chords only in the vocal movements; in the instrumental movements tonality is established by repeating a drone or ostinato pattern (usually in the bass) in the manner of Stravinsky or Bartók. Therefore, while the instrumental movements are not "atonal," they are often quite dissonant, since the jagged, chromatic melodic motives of the upper register often clash with the ostinato patterns in the bass. Much of "Iconoclast" is bitonal, with two ostinato patterns a tritone apart being juxtaposed against each other; this harmonic approach, in conjunction with the fast tempo, motoristic rhythms, and percussive Hammond organ timbres, creates a "metallic" effect that is also apparent in varying degrees in the first and fifth movement. Emerson often doubles melodic ideas in parallel fourths ("Manticore") or with three-voice quartal harmonies (parts of "Eruption," the march theme of "Aquatarkus"); the instability of the fourth, combined with the fast tempos and jagged, edgy rhythms, lends the instrumental sections of *Tarkus* their characteristic driving quality. Traditional triadic progressions are predominant only in the "song" movements. Even here, though, there is a clear distinction drawn between the relatively simple modal harmony of "Battlefield" and the wry chromatic harmony of "Stones of Years," which unites jazz-based chord voicings otherwise unusual in progressive rock with a pseudo-baroque ground bass.

The harmonic scheme of *Tarkus* plays a major role in imposing a structure that is improvisatory and unpredictable, yet logical and ultimately satisfying. The opening movement, "Eruption," is the most tonally volatile section; unity is provided by the return of a motoristic bass ostinato figure, first in F modal minor,[12] then in C modal minor, finally E modal minor. Linking these three recurrences are episodes which display some of the most careening, unpredictable, and inventive keyboard figurations of Emerson's career. This figuration is created by linking a number of short motives together and is characterized by wide melodic skips and irregular rhythms; musicologists who continue to believe that rock is all four-square rhythms and phrase structures are urged to examine these passages. Toward the end of "Eruption," the music appears to be moving toward B modal major; a transitional passage into the second movement, however, swings the music into a broadly interpreted C minor, where it remains throughout the affective, stately "Stones of Years."

"Iconoclast" opens with a bitonal juxtaposition of the "Eruption" ostinato pattern in F and B modal minor, which accompanies new motivic material; it is the piece's most dissonant section. Toward the end of this movement, another episode of unpredictable keyboard figuration swings the tonality into A modal major. Much of the aggressive fourth movement, "Mass," is in A modal minor; the harmonic syntax of "Mass" differs from the other two vocal movements in that it is dominated by open fifths rather than triads, which complements the more cutting lyrics and more fragmentary vocal line of this movement. The final verse of "Mass" is transposed up a major second, to B minor; this transposition paves the way for a return to the suite's dominant key, C minor, which is signaled by the rolling ostinato figure which opens the frenetic "Manticore." (It may or may not be coincidental, incidentally, that the first movement, representing Tarkus, and the fifth movement, representing the Manticore, stand in a tonic-dominant relationship.) Much of "Manticore" remains in C, although the relentless ostinato figure and its jagged motivic overlay momentarily shift to A phrygian in the middle of the movement. The expansive "Battlefield" opens with a slow, tortured progression of dissonant polytriads; much of the remainder of the movement is in a fairly conventional E aeolian/dorian, although a recurring four-bar "fanfare" refrain hints at the F modal minor of the next movement.

At the beginning of the final movement, "Aquatarkus," this four-bar refrain is taken up and transformed into the solemn march theme which dominates the movement's first section and is repeated a number of times underneath a cascade of improvised Moog fanfares. Carl Palmer's gong strike summons a recapitulation of the second half of "Eruption"; the music careens through C minor, halts momentarily on a grinding F-major/F♯-minor polytriad, and finally resolves into F major upon a final repetition of the "Aquatarkus" march theme to end the piece. If one were to schematize the tonal movement of the piece in a Schenkerian framework (that is, graphing "middle-ground" and then "background" movement), the following schema would result (brackets indicate more transitional tonalities, and smaller-case letters denote minor keys):

	Mvt. 1	Mvt. 2	Mvt. 3	Mvt. 4	Mvt. 5	Mvt. 6	Mvt. 7
"Middleground"	f-c-e-[B]	c	b/f-[A]	a-b	c-[a]-c	e	f-[c]-F
"Background"	f			→c			→F

The tonal scheme is therefore a major factor in the music's coherence. Movements one and two involve a progression from the tonic F to the dominant C; movements three through five retrace this movement, while movements five through seven reverse the tonic-dominant movement.

Tonal movement, tempo shifts, and juxtapositions between instrumental and vocal movements are all factors, then, in creating variety. Another factor is constantly shifting instrumentation. On the one hand, *Tarkus* is rather atypical of lengthy progressive rock pieces in that there are no significant electronic/acoustic shifts; the piece is unusually electronic for the early 1970s. On the other hand, certain instrumental juxtapositions in *Tarkus* play a roughly analogous role to the acoustic/electric dichotomy. In the first, third, and fifth movements, rapid tempos, motoristic rhythms, fragmentary, jagged melodic motives, and dissonance are coordinated with a specific instrumentation: percussive Hammond, a strident, trumpet-like Moog setting, piano (which sometimes doubles the bass guitar and lends a peculiarly "clangorous" effect), bass, and drums. The second and sixth movements feature a different, less percussive approach: Lake's mournful vocals are supported by a pipe organ-like Hammond accompaniment with no percussive piano and relatively little Moog (the sixth movement adds yet another sustained, almost "vocal" line via Lake's lyrical electric guitar solo). The fourth and seventh movements each represents a different instrumentation. In "Mass," the Moog is used to produce a "funky," clavinet-like accompaniment which effectively captures the angry, somewhat biting tenor of the lyrics. "Mass" also contains an extremely percussive Hammond solo in which the instrument almost seems to "spit" the notes out; even Lake's vocals are electronically treated to conform to the generally strident effect. In "Aquatarkus," meanwhile, the Moog is given a mellower brasslike setting which, in conjunction with the quartally doubled march theme and the stepwise bass line, creates a solemn, almost funereal mood.

The most impressive musical achievement of *Tarkus* is the effective tension maintained between impetuous, improvisatory sections and coherent long-range planning. Besides effectively juxtaposing different approaches to tempo, instrumentation, and harmony, *Tarkus* also makes effective use of contrasts in melodic character; the rhythmically smooth, stepwise vocal lines of the second and sixth movements can be contrasted with the jagged, rhythmically irregular motives of movements one, three, and five or the short, incantatory themes of movements four and seven. Contrasts in meter play a role as well, since the instrumental movements tend toward unusual meters (the first and third movements are in five), while the "song" movements are all in common time (i.e., four).

Coherence is provided, on the other hand, by the firmly drawn tonal plan and by the recurrence of themes and motives from movement to movement. The jagged bass ostinato which recurs on three separate occasions in the first movement dominates much of the third movement as well, where it accompanies new motivic material. The four-bar instrumental fanfare refrain of the sixth movement is transformed into the march theme which dominates "Aquatarkus"; even the rolling ostinato figure which permeates "Manticore" appears, to a degree at least, to be an arpeggiation of part of the sixth movement's four-bar instrumental refrain. The final movement, of course, also recapitulates a lengthy section of the opening movement. Only "Stones of Years" and "Mass" do not share melodic material with other movements. Yet another means of creating coherence is the pervasive use of quartal harmony: the first, fifth, and seventh movements are all strongly informed by the melodic and harmonic use of the fourth.

Nonetheless, in certain realms *Tarkus* does not represent the apogee of ELP's output. Engineer Eddy Offord, who played such an important role in creating Yes's characteristic sound during their "classic" recordings of the early 1970s, was never able to achieve the same sense of clarity in his work with ELP. The too-frequent combination of bass guitar with piano, Hammond, and Moog in their lower registers creates a "muddiness" in the lower end of the mix that gives the general production of *Tarkus* a somewhat dated character. (Certain other production effects, such as running Lake's voice or the drums through an echo chamber in specific passages, have also not dated well.) This situation was only resolved on the *Brain Salad Surgery* LP, when the crystalline production of engineers Geoff Young and Chris Kimsey created the definitive ELP sound.

Brain Salad Surgery's *Karn Evil 9* improves on *Tarkus* in at least two other categories. Musical ideas are expanded and developed at a greater length; equally significant, the concept is more straightforward and not hidden so deeply among a dense maze of visual symbols and verbal imagery. Nonetheless, *Tarkus* played a major role in both ELP's development and in the development of progressive rock at large; it remains a significant and memorable example of the style.

Yes: *Close to the Edge* (1972)

Yes's *Close to the Edge* LP, recorded and released in 1972, is the third in a series of albums (the previous two, *The Yes Album* and *Fragile*, having appeared in 1971) that collectively are often viewed as constituting the band's "classic" period. In particular, *Fragile* and *Close to the Edge* were recorded by the lineup that many feel represents the finest Yes incarnation of all: Jon Anderson (lead vocals), Steve Howe (guitars, backing vocals), Bill Bruford (drums, percussion), Chris Squire (bass guitar, backing vocals), and Rick Wakeman (keyboards).[13]

The *Close to the Edge* LP differs from the band's two previous albums in that it contains only three cuts: the title piece on side one, *Close to the Edge*, clocks in at roughly nineteen minutes, while the two cuts on side two, "And You and I" and "Siberian Khatru," are each about ten minutes long. In 1972, cuts of this length were still the exception rather than the rule, even in progressive rock, and devoting an album to three pieces of this duration was considered a major gamble. Nonetheless, the *Close to the Edge* LP is hailed by a large contingent of critics and fans as the most consistently excellent album of the band's recorded output, and the title cut in particular must be considered one of the finest and most influential examples of the progressive rock style.

As with *Tarkus*, the underlying "concept" of *Close to the Edge* is conveyed through a combination of cover art, lyrics, and music. In some ways, *Close to the Edge* is even harder to "read" conceptually than *Tarkus*. There is only one cover painting, rather than a sequence of panels clearly intended to narrate a storyline. Furthermore, the lyrics, by Jon Anderson and Steve Howe, are considerably more given to surrealistic imagery and stream-of-consciousness drift (including disconcerting shifts in viewpoint from second person to first person and from singular to plural) than Lake's. Like *Tarkus*, though, the division into distinct movements (four instead of seven) and the use of movement titles suggest that a veiled narrative is indeed at work.

In the only exhaustive content analysis of *Close to the Edge* that I am aware of, Thomas Mosbø argues that the piece can be interpreted as "a ritual about ritual."[14] He states that "in its four movements, we (1) enter the ritual world on the borders of our own, (2) encounter the new realities found there, (3) assimilate those realities and make them a part of ourselves, and (4) return to the "normal" world with new perceptions and identities, or perhaps pass through the ritual to a new world (as in death)."[15]

As I noted in my discussion of *Tarkus,* rock concept albums or pieces of the late 1960s and early 1970s are very much open to alternate interpretations. Therefore, to attempt to prove Mosbø's content analysis as "mistaken" would be fruitless. On the other hand, though, I believe that while a number of "readings" of a given concept piece may have at least some merit, some interpretations are bound to be more "correct" than others. In the case of Mosbø's reading, I can see two problems. First, the lyrics give a stream-of-consciousness description of experiences as they are actually experienced; this is normally not the stuff of ritual, which tends to formalize and "objectify" experience. Second, Mosbø fails to take advantage of secondary sources which could have cast further light on the matter. For instance, he quotes Jon Anderson as saying, "The lyrical content [of *Close to the Edge*] became a kind of dream sequence in a way. The end verse is a dream that I had a long time ago about passing on from this world to another world."[16] Curiously, Mosbø extrapolates from this quote his conviction that *Close to the Edge* is ritual about ritual. To me, Anderson's remark seems to be just another manifestation of that ultimate hippie concern: the desire to seek the portals to other realms of consciousness, other planes of spiritual reality. In short, it does not seem unreasonable to suppose that the concept of *Close to the Edge* is that most quintessential of countercultural themes, the spiritual quest.

Furthermore, in his *Yes: The Authorized Biography,* Dan Hedges notes that Jon Anderson had taken a keen interest in Hesse's *Siddhartha* about the time of the writing of *Close to the Edge.*[17] *Siddhartha,* of course, was one of the cornerstones of countercultural spiritual thought: it traces an individual's progress from gross materialism to cosmic awareness, very much in an Eastern (and specifically Buddhist) context. While I do not find any direct quotation of *Siddhartha* in *Close to the Edge,* the general framework in which Anderson and Howe present spiritual "progress" in the lyrics is certainly similar. In short, I see *Close to the Edge* as one of the major "spiritual quest" epics to come out of the countercultural scene during the late 1960s and early 1970s—perhaps the most richly developed of all.

Nonetheless, my intent here is not to discredit Mosbø's reading of *Close to the Edge,* but rather to clarify it. It is true that religious ritual is a reenactment of a passage from ordinary to nonordinary reality. In this sense, then, the very act of musically representing the stages of the spiritual quest can perhaps be viewed as a ritual of sorts, a ritual to be reenacted in the concert hall.

The four movements of *Close to the Edge* appear to express distinct stages of the spiritual quest. The first movement, "The Solid Time of Change," depicts what might be termed the calling of the seeker. The protagonist's spiritual bankruptcy is complete; it would take a "seasoned witch" to summon the seeker from his or her disgraceful condition. In contrast to the opening verses, which graphically describe the seeker's spiritual poverty, the refrain "close to the edge" (which is to recur in the second and fourth movements as well) offers hope, pointing up that we are closer to other realms of consciousness, other spiritual worlds, than we frequently imagine. Nevertheless, the first occurrence of the "close to the edge" refrain is followed by the statement "not right away," suggesting that one's initial impulse when confronted by a greater spiritual reality is to flee rather than to follow. It is only the final verse group of the movement, when the seeker has "crossed a line," that a resolve to embark on the spiritual quest clearly has been made.

If the first movement depicts the call, initial hesitation, and eventual resolve to take up the Quest, then the second movement, "Total Mass Retain," deals with both the exhilaration of experiencing new spiritual dimensions and the resistance which can encumber one's progress. There are the wonders one experiences as one enters new spiritual realms, described as "manna from above." There are also new achievements, as the seeker's hate has been "crucified" and his or her hands now hold "the word." Incidentally, this movement offers an especially clear example of Jon Anderson's tendency to appropriate words or images with strong Christian connotations ("manna," "crucified," "word") into an essentially Eastern framework. It is perhaps this aspect of Yes's lyrics—along with the general stream-of-consciousness drift—that has often reminded me of the poetry of William Blake.[18]

With genuine progress in one's path on the Quest comes resistance, which is conveyed through the use of military imagery: "sad courage" has claimed its victims, and "armored movers" have been summoned to block the seeker's progress. Close on the heels of these descriptions of impediments to the Quest comes a particularly urgent repetition of the "close to the edge" refrain, characterized by a more compressed rhythmic setting than previous occurrences. Thereafter, it becomes clear that the resistance has been overcome, since the new verse group offers that the journey now "takes you all the way." Nonetheless, temptation and the possibility of making a wrong turn remain, since the seeker still passes by paths that "climb halfway into the void."[19] At the end of the movement "we hear the total mass retain"; apparently the seeker has absorbed all that he or she is capable of at this point in the Quest.

The third movement, "I Get Up, I Get Down," borrows its title (and the melodic contour of its refrain) from the brief phrase "I get up, I get down" which was appended to the final statement of the "close to the edge" refrain at the end of the first and second movements. Now the music grows slower, less active, more contemplative: the lyrics engage the intense self-questioning, self-doubt, and assimilation which mark yet another stage in the Quest. The seeker poses nagging questions and ponders the difference between saying and doing, between merely seeing the way and coming of age spiritually. The recurring "I get up, I get down" refrain suggests that the seeker has yet to rise above self-doubt, or the tendency to become dismayed by the disparity between the peace of the other worlds, or realms of consciousness, he or she has experienced and the despair that is part and parcel of everday existence on a more material plane.

The final movement, "Seasons of Man," is prepared by a huge instrumental crescendo, achieved mainly on pipe organ and Moog. When the lyrics return, along with the much faster tempo of the first two movements, it is evident that the higher spiritual dimension that had so diligently been sought after has finally been attained. The seeker now stands on a mountain, figuratively speaking, beholding the silence of the valley below, witnessing "cycles only of the past"; the things that formerly stood in the way are now overcome, to be surveyed as part of a past that need not be repeated again. As the piece reaches its grandiose climax, the "close to the edge" refrain occurs one more time in greatly expanded form: the phrase "seasons will pass you by" occurs twice, suggesting perhaps that the person who has attained true enlightenment now stands in a different relationship to chronological time than he or she did before. At any rate, the fourth movement is clearly intended to depict the final stage of the Quest, attainment. I would graph the four stages as follows:

Movement 1, "The Sold Time of Change": The Call

Movement 2, "Total Mass Retain": Adversity and Triumph

Movement 3, "I Get up, I Get down": Self-Examination and Assimilation

Movement 4, "Seasons of Man": Attainment

It is possible, of course, to see this general pattern played out in other concept albums of this period: one thinks, for instance, of any of a number of Moody Blues albums. However, I am convinced that the Spiritual Quest motif had never before been this richly developed in popular music—and perhaps has never been so richly developed again. In this sense, I suppose, *Close to the Edge* might be said to represent contemporary popular music's answer to Wagner's *Parsifal.*

The album art for *Close to the Edge* ties in directly with the title track. Interestingly, Roger Dean's drawing appears in the inner gatefold; the front of the album cover is fairly austere, save for Dean's famous Yes logo (which makes its first appearance at this time), while the back of the cover features album credits and photos of the musicians.

I have already explored the connection between Dean's *Close to the Edge* drawing and the concept of the title piece in chapter 3, so I will not repeat the discussion here. In many ways, I think Dean's description tells the whole story: he describes the drawing for *Close to the Edge* as being "another paradox miniature world."[20] Clearly there is an obvious connection between Dean's surreal landscape—at once impossible and strangely familiar[21]—and the alternate dimensions of spiritual reality described by Jon Anderson in the lyrics of the title track. Interestingly, Dean has said that he rarely has heard the music before doing an album cover:

> I cannot say that the music is ever a direct inspiration for my work. However, the music, the title, and the art work are all related, and must all affect each other to some degree. It's like the relation between a picture and its title. For example, if a picture was entitled "Peace" and the image was of a poppy field the significance would be different than if it was of a wrecked tank or a waterfall. The picture changes the title and the title changes the picture.[22]

Since Jon Anderson and Steve Howe collaborated on both the words and the music for *Close to the Edge,* the correspondence between words and music here is in certain ways more intimate than in ELP's *Tarkus.* On the other hand, the music's organization would not suffer unduly if the words were removed: by any standards, *Close to the Edge* is one of the structural marvels of progressive rock. One of the most frequently made statements about this piece is that it exemplifies the most venerable classic form of all, sonata form.[23] There is in fact a great deal of validity to this comparison: I think it is possible to see *Close to the Edge* as a conflation of the multimovement suite and the one-movement sonata form. I will therefore discuss the music of *Close to the Edge* in the context of its relation to sonata form, exploring both the significance of its debt to sonata form structure and its occasional divergences from that form.

To give a brief explanation for those unfamiliar with it: sonata form is essentially a three-part form consisting of an exposition, a development, and a recapitulation. The exposition, in turn, consists of at least three sections: an opening theme, a transition, and a contrasting second theme (there may be a distinct closing theme as well). The exposition begins in the tonic (or home) key, but moves to a closely related key (the dominant key if the tonic is major, the relative major if the tonic is minor) during the transition from the opening to the second theme. The remainder of the exposition is in this new key. In the classic period style of Haydn and Mozart, the exposition was inevitably repeated. Following the repetition of the exposition comes the development, a section in which the main themes of the exposition are broken up, developed sequentially, stated in imitation, and otherwise varied. A hallmark of the development section is its tonal instability: it modulates constantly, often to keys that are quite distant from the tonic. The recapitulation involves a restatement of the exposition, with the exception that both the opening theme and the contrasting second theme are now heard in the tonic key. Besides these three "mandatory" sections, a sonata form movement might have a slow introduction (since sonata form movements were usually fast in the classic period style, a slow introduction offered a bit of contrast) and a coda, a section after the recapitulation in which the piece "winds down."

Sonata form brings to a head several elements of the European classical tradition as practiced between 1600 and 1900. It is goal-oriented: the music leaves the tonic key, travels on first to a closely related key (in the second half of the exposition) then to more distant keys (in the development) before returning "home" (in the recapitulation). It is also dramatic: the sense of conflict/resolution and tension/repose inherent in the tonal movement of sonata form offers an obvious parallel to the resolution of the plot in opera. Finally, it is narrative: it unfolds in a sequential, logical fashion, offering an opportunity to recall past events, intimate future developments, and either fulfill or thwart expectations.

The four-movement construction of *Close to the Edge* offers a number of clear parallels with sonata form. The first movement can be viewed as the "exposition"; the second, as a varied repetition of the "exposition"; the third, as the "development section"; and the final movement as the "recapitulation." There is also a lengthy introduction that falls into two distinct sections, and a brief coda that refers back to the opening of the piece.

The introduction, nearly three minutes long, is particularly important to the piece's underlying symbolism. The first section of the introduction commences with "bird chirps" (frequency-modulated tones on Wakeman's Moog), "running water," and other "sounds of nature"; a synthesizer drone on the open fifth D-A and gently jangling Moog arpeggios gradually emerge into the sonic foreground. Here is an Edenic vision, the "natural" state of humankind. The second section of the introduction, on the other hand, suggests the confusion and strife brought about by our separation from our "natural" spirituality. It is very fast and dominated by dense linear counterpoint. Howe's jagged motives on electric guitar, with consistent tritone skips that are reminiscent of some of Emerson's keyboard figurations in *Tarkus,* clash often with Squire's ascending harmonic minor scale fragments; Wakeman's busy Moog argpeggios and Bruford's sudden bursts of unpredictable drum patterns provide suitably "chaotic" punctuation. Despite grinding dissonances (produced especially by the contrapuntal clashes between Howe's guitar leads and Squire's running bass figures), a clear D-minor tonality emerges, largely as a result of the bass line and the occasional vocal triads. Thus the introduction is entirely in D; I will suggest the possible significance of this momentarily.

The first movement, or "exposition," is prefaced by an instrumental ritornello that establishes the moderately fast tempo and the general rhythmic and melodic character of the movement although it retains the introduction's D tonality (which shifts, however, to major). The movement proper consists of four sections: a group of two verses, the "close to the edge" refrain, a group of two contrasting verses, and an expansion of the opening refrain. One notes a parallel with the layout of the exposition section in sonata-allegro form: first theme–transition–second theme–closing theme. The tonal scheme of "The Solid Time of Change" suggests sonata form as well. The movement's first set of verses are in A dorian; the first appearance of the refrain acts as a transition to the new key; the set of contrasting verses and the second appearance of refrain are in the relative major, C major.

The contrasts drawn between the first set of verses, the refrain, and the second set of verses are also reminiscent of the sharply etched differences in thematic character which often characterize sonata form. The melodic line which sets the first set of verses is recitational, almost incantational; a two-bar fragment that moves obsessively in a narrow melodic range is repeated throughout. The second verse group, on the other hand, covers a wider melodic range, involves less repetition, and is generally more tuneful. Here one can see the type of contrast often evident in Mozart's expositions between a driving, masculine first theme and a more lyrical, feminine second theme. Both sets of verses tend toward metric regularity (the first in $\frac{12}{8}$, the second in $\frac{3}{2}$). The refrain, on the other hand, utilizes constantly shifting meters, which allows for the continuous expansion, contraction, and rearrangement of the poetic stanzas that Anderson and Howe favor.

Instrumentation serves as yet another means of contrast; Yes "orchestrate" each theme with just as much care as a classical composer would. The first verse group is set in two-part vocal harmony and is accompanied mainly by percussive or plucked sounds: strummed mandolin, a strange wisp of filtered Mellotron that darts in and out of the mix, and staccato keyboard chords. The second verse group, sung by Anderson only, entails a different instrumentation characterized especially by edgy electric guitar riffing and a "piping" ostinato in the upper register of the Hammond. The refrains are set to a richer, more sustained instrumentation: three-part vocal harmonies, sustained Hammond, and electric guitar chords.

The second movement, "Total Mass Retain," corresponds to the repetition of the exposition in a sonata form movement. Much of the first movement's music is repeated to new lyrics; however, some interesting changes are made. The instrumental ritornello which opened the first movement is not repeated. There are several shifts in accompaniment patterns, exemplified especially by Squire's bass line. In the first verse group of the first movement, Squire's bass part is fluid, and rhythmically complements the other parts. In the first verse group of the second movement, however, he begins playing a bizarre rhythmic pattern which is quite different from the rhythm of the vocal lines; he repeats this pattern a number of times. Since Squire's bass pattern is a different length (two and a half bars) than the repetitive two-bar phrases of the vocal part, the two constantly intersect each other at different points, creating a nervous, off-balance effect.[24] The refrain also undergoes significant variation upon its first presentation in the second movement. The melodic contour of the refrain is retained, but the rhythm is compressed and the tune is harmonized in open fourths rather than triads, giving it a more urgent, driving character. Both of the variations mentioned here seem intended to capture the conceptual sweep of the lyrics. The excitement of new spiritual discovery and the subsequent turmoil which result are suggested by Squire's edgy, off-balance bass part. Meanwhile, the "close to the edge, round by a corner" refrain—which signifies our proximity to new portals of consciousness—takes on a more urgent meaning in the second movement on account of the new spiritual discoveries described in the verses, and therefore invites a different type of musical setting.

Comparing the tonal movement of the first and second movements also yields some interesting observations. Both begin in A dorian; but while the second half of the first movement modulates to the relative major, C, the second half of the second movement modulates to the subdominant major, D, referring back to the D tonality of the introduction. The second movement ends with a brief instrumental interlude; over a stepwise ground bass supplied by bass and guitar, Wakeman's organ part recalls and varies the theme of the instrumental ritornello which had preceded the first movement proper.

The third movement, "I Get Up, I Get Down," offers a number of important contrasts with the other movements. The instrumentation is dominated by Wakeman's Moog, Hammond, and (toward the end of the movement) pipe organ, and by some intricate three-part vocal arrangements; the piercing upper frequencies and percussive attacks which characterize much of the rest of the piece are not present here. The movement's tempo is much slower than the rest of the piece; the rhythm section is absent, and there is no hint of the driving rhythms which dominate the other movements. On the other hand, this movement contains the one really memorable tune to emerge from *Close to the Edge*. In short, "I Get Up, I Get Down," is the "feminine" section of *Close to the Edge*. It effectively captures the self-questioning mood of the lyrics with its bittersweet use of modal mixing and its hazy keyboard backdrops, allowing for a moment of contemplation after the hectic activity of the previous movements.

The movement opens with an impressionistic, almost motionless collage of sustained tones and lazily drifting melodic fragments. Thereafter, the outlines of a simple (if flexible) song form emerges, with irregular repetitions of verses and refrains accompanied by slowly pulsing Hammond chords. While the musical material of the verses is new, the music and lyrics ("I Get Up, I Get Down") of the refrain are drawn from a segment of the refrain heard at the end of the first two movements, thus providing a musical and conceptual link to the rest of the piece.

At the very beginning of the movement the tonality settles into E major (the dominant of the A tonality which at this point seems to be emerging as the piece's tonic); unlike the previous sections of *Close to the Edge*, there are no tonal shifts to speak of. Toward the end of the movement Wakeman launches into a pseudo-baroque pipe organ episode. It is interrupted briefly by a final vocal repetition of the "I Get Up, I Get Down" refrain; it is then resumed, developing into a frenetic pipe organ/Moog cadenza that builds up to an impressive climax and momentarily swings the music into B major.

Wakeman's keyboard cadenza segues into "The Seasons of Man," which begins with a repetition of the entire instrumental ritornello which had preceded the first movement. The tonality changes, though; while this section originally appeared in D major, it reappears here in F$^\sharp$ major. The instrumentation changes, too; while the electric guitar had presented the melody in the ritornello's first appearance, accompanied by Hammond chords, now the theme is heard in a "metallic" Moog setting of open fourths (which the guitar quietly doubles), while the rhythm section accompany with a more driving rhythmic figure. The return of the ritornello is followed by a Hammond organ solo by Wakeman over the chord changes of the first verse group, now back in A dorian. Thereafter, the music of the first (and second) movement returns with new lyrics, but with a couple of major differences. First, the refrain that separates the two sets of contrasting verses is dropped. The refrain appears only at the end of the movement, where it appears in greatly expanded form with a more grandiose instrumentation, featuring the only conventional use of the Mellotron in the entire piece.

The second major change involves the tonal scheme. The conventions of the Classic period style demanded that the tonic key reappear at the beginning of the recapitulation, and be retained for the duration of the movement. After the instrumental ritornello in F$^\sharp$ major, the fourth movement proper does indeed open in the "tonic" A dorian; however, it modulates to F major when it reaches the second set of verses, and remains in this key for the remainder of the piece. Since this tends to subvert the illusion of sonata form which the band otherwise worked so hard to maintain, the question is raised, What is the significance of this tonal shift?

I would answer this question in two ways. First, if *Close to the Edge* is about a spiritual quest, about an attempt to reach a higher level of consciousness and spirituality, returning to the tonic would make little symbolic sense. It would suggest that the seeker ends his or her quest by returning to the place he or she started at, rather than having moved on to a higher plane. Thus, while sonata form's potential for depicting conflict and resolution is ideally suited to convey the conceptual substance of *Close to the Edge*, its tonal scheme is not.

Second, while A dorian is the tonic of the first, second, and fourth movements, and while the E tonality of the third movement seems to establish the A tonality even more firmly, it is a mistake to ignore the D-minor tonality of the opening section. The movement from the chaotic D-minor introduction to the majestic F-major conclusion involves a movement from the minor to its relative major— symbolically, from darkness to light. Conceptually, it is attractive to suggest that D minor and F major are the "real" tonics, and A dorian merely an "illusory" tonic that actually functions as the dominant of D. The closing of the piece, which reintroduces the "bird chirps" and other "natural sounds" of the opening, would seem to lend further weight to this suggestion. Nonetheless, I will not insist on this reading. Rather, I will simply point out that *Close to the Edge* is an example of progressive tonality—that is, a piece of music that begins and ends in different keys, and thus has more than one tonic[25]—and leave the rest open to individual interpretation.

There have been so many parallels drawn between ELP and Yes over the years that in closing it will perhaps be useful to compare *Tarkus* and *Close to the Edge* on the basis of the four parameters discussed in chapter 2: instrumentation, structure, virtuosity, and harmonic practice. In terms of harmonic syntax, *Tarkus* is the more "advanced" piece. Yes occasionally resort to parallel open fourths, but not to the quartal harmonies, the pungent polytriads, or the bitonal layerings that permeate *Tarkus*. Only the chaotic introduction of *Close to the Edge* approaches the level of dissonance of "Eruption," "Iconoclast," or "Manticore," which are characterized by the dissonant clashes of a bass ostinato with totally independent keyboard figuration. To the contrary, certain sections of *Close to the Edge* feature a type of "rich" chord with dominant implications, such as augmented sixths and diminished sevenths, that ELP avoid. Such chords appear in the instrumental ritornello that precedes the first movement and in the pipe organ episodes between the third and fourth movements, where they function as expected. Like ELP, in their modal sections Yes tend to establish tonality by means other than functional chord progressions; a favorite method is to circle the tonic triad with triads a step above and below until the tonic is established by repetition. One can hear this approach in the first verse group of the first, second, and fourth movements.

In terms of instrumentation, one can compare and contrast the two pieces. Of course, there are two immediate differences between the bands that informed the instrumentation decisions of *Tarkus* and *Close to the Edge*. First, Yes had four instrumentalists, ELP three; second, Yes had three vocalists, ELP one. This meant, among other things, that ELP often uses sustained keyboard chords to fill registral space that Yes would have filled with vocal harmonies; that Yes had to be more self-disciplined in their arrangements, so that the two lead instrumentalists, Howe and Wakeman, didn't get in each other's way; and that in order to "fatten" their sound ELP often used the drums as a melodic instrument (in terms of rhythmically doubling the keyboards' melodic lines) as much as a timekeeper. ELP also tended to push the drums higher up in the mix than Yes were able to.

Both bands arrived at combinations of instrumental sounds that were genuinely new and innovative in 1971–1972. Emerson and Wakeman arrived at somewhat different, but equally valid uses of the Moog; Wakeman was somewhat more concerned with using it to create totally "new" sounds, while Emerson was more intent on creating interesting variants of recognizable timbres (i.e., synthetic trumpet). *Tarkus* is stronger in its exploration of Hammond timbres (indeed, I cannot think of another album which draws so many subtle shadings out of the instrument); Emerson refused to use a Mellotron on any of ELP's recordings, while Wakeman used the instrument with real imagination on *Close to the Edge*. Because of the presence of a full-time guitarist and three vocalists, Yes on the whole are able to offer a more varied timbral palette than ELP (which makes Emerson's refusal to use the Mellotron all the more puzzling). Interestingly, both albums were engineered by Eddy Offord. I think that the production of *Close to the Edge* is superior to that of *Tarkus,* with its somewhat muddy lower frequencies; on the other hand, ELP's *Brain Salad Surgery* of 1973 was even more crystalline in its production polish than *Close to the Edge.*

ELP and Yes are both virtuosic bands, demonstrating a high level of technical proficiency on their instruments. Of the two bands, though, Yes are probably the more discreet in the way they employ their considerable instrumental prowess. The thematic ensemble interplay in the instrumental sections of *Tarkus* gives the members of ELP ample room to showcase their virtuosity. In addition to these ensemble passages, though, there are three lengthy keyboard solos over short ostinato patterns (in the second, fourth, and seventh movements), as well as a lengthy electric guitar solo in the sixth movement. By the late 1970s, the technique of soloing over a short, repetitive chord progression or bass ostinato had been dangerously overused, and had become one of the banes of progressive rock; even in *Tarkus,* it is hard to avoid the impression that there are too many solos of this type. On the other hand, *Close to the Edge* contains just one lengthy solo over a repeated chord progression, Rick Wakeman's Hammond solo in the fourth movement. Otherwise, there is the "sound collage" which opens the piece, and the rest of the instrumental passages involve thematic ensemble interplay; even the second half of the introduction, with its "speedfreak" guitar lines, has thematic elements, and at any rate avoids literal repetition (the same could be said of Wakeman's Moog cadenza at the end of the third movement).

Finally, there is the matter of structure in *Tarkus* and *Close to the Edge.* My analysis of *Close to the Edge* in the context of sonata form should not blind one to the obvious similarities of its multimovement layout to that of *Tarkus. Close to the Edge* presents a song and then repeats it twice with variations, with a contrasting song (the third movement) and several instrumental preludes, interludes, and postludes included for variety. The episodic nature suggested by this description points up the many very real similarities between the two pieces. The main difference between them is that *Close to the Edge* shows a greater economy of means, a more single-minded development of the primary musical material. It is for this reason that *Close to the Edge* probably represents a more mature example of the progressive rock idiom.

Indeed, there is a sizable contingent of critics and fans that see *Close to the Edge* as the pinnacle of the band's musical evolution. Bill Bruford left the band soon after the album's release; he felt that it reflected a crystallization of the band's style, and that subsequent releases would likely begin a process of self-quotation and self-imitation.[26]

Genesis: "Firth of Fifth" (1973)

"Firth of Fifth" appears on the *Selling England by the Pound* LP of 1973. It represents the third album by the lineup which many of the band's earlier fans feel is the "classic" Genesis incarnation: Peter Gabriel (lead vocals, woodwinds), Tony Banks (keyboards, backing vocals), Steve Hackett (guitars), Michael Rutherford (bass guitar, backing acoustic guitar), and Phil Collins (drums, backing vocals). This lineup was to endure for two more years, until 1975, at which point Gabriel departed to pursue a solo career and Collins assumed the role of lead singer.

As an album *Selling England by the Pound* is probably not as consistently good as *Foxtrot* (1972), which contains the band's epic multimovement suite *Supper's Ready*. On the other hand, *Selling England* contains two somewhat smaller-scale pieces that are among the band's strongest: "Firth of Fifth" and "Cinema Show." "Firth of Fifth" is, in my opinion, the finest nine and a half minutes of music that Genesis ever put down: it exemplifies virtually every major aspect of their Gabriel-era style, is extremely well put together from a standpoint of structure, and represents one of the band's finest achievements in every realm save perhaps the lyrics. An analysis of "Firth of Fifth" will also allow for a consideration of how the single-movement sectionalized form—which was actually much more common in progressive rock than the multimovement suite—could be used to expand a simple song form to vast proportions by the inclusion of instrumental preludes, interludes, and postludes.

There are three elements of the Genesis style of the 1970s that are particularly well represented by "Firth of Fifth." The first involves harmony, and seems especially to be the contribution of Tony Banks.[27] Genesis do not resort to the "advanced" sonorities which pervade *Tarkus*: polytriads, bitonal layerings, quartal harmonies. Nor do they utilize the dissonant linear counterpoint exemplified by the introduction of *Close to the Edge*. To the contrary, their harmony is more unremittingly "functional" than either ELP's or Yes's; tonality is usually the result of relationships between chords rather than of melodic encirclement or of the repetition of a bass drone. Yet it is just this "conservative" element of Genesis's harmony which—in its rock context—lends the band's music its distinctive sound. Unlike *Tarkus* or *Close to the Edge* (or much other progressive rock, in fact), where changes of key are usually sudden and unprepared, "Firth of Fifth" tends to use pivot chords, often quite imaginatively, to shift passages from one key to another. Occasionally an entire two- or four-bar progression is used to unobtrusively pivot the music into a new key; in listening to "Firth of Fifth," one must constantly reevaluate such passages in light of the new harmonic context of which they now appear to be a part.

Despite its frequent instability, though, the harmony of "Firth of Fifth" doesn't resemble the late-nineteenth-century style of Liszt or Wagner. To be sure, diminished seventh chords are used much more frequently by Genesis than by other progressive rock bands, and are usually used as modulatory pivots. Otherwise, though, the band's harmony is largely triadic, with a healthy dose of the major sevenths, minor sevenths, and major triads with added sixths that are part and parcel of the progressive rock harmonic syntax. Rather than resorting to chromatic harmony in the late-nineteenth-century sense, the band uses the relative instability of modal harmony to effect their modulations.[28] For instance, in the bridge of the song proper of "Firth of Fifth" the music there is a passage that begins in E$^\flat$ major; the E$^\flat$-major chord is suddenly reinterpreted as a major triad on the lowered sixth degree of G, which is established through a $^\flat$VI–$^\flat$VII–I progression (E$^\flat$ major–F major–G major). It is above all the band's combination of modal harmony and kaleidoscopic shifts in tonality which lent their 1970s style its distinction.

Another major characteristic of the Gabriel-era Genesis style is the frequent presence of asymmetric and shifting meters. The solo piano overture of "Firth of Fifth" offers perhaps the most daunting example of the band's penchant for shifting meters: at various points in the overture the theme consists of alternating bars of $\frac{6}{8}$ and $\frac{7}{8}$, of $\frac{6}{8}$, $\frac{5}{8}$, and $\frac{4}{8}$, and of $\frac{4}{4}$, $\frac{6}{8}$, $\frac{3}{8}$, and $\frac{2}{4}$. The band avoids overusing this approach, however: the contrasting sections of "Firth of Fifth" are in common time.

A final quintessentially "Genesis" aspect of "Firth of Fifth" is an emphasis on clarity, which makes itself felt in the realms of arrangement and timbre. In terms of timbre, Genesis prefer "clean" sounds. Tony Banks seldom ever resorts to the distorted timbre which characterizes the Hammond sound of the early ELP albums; furthermore, he does not share Emerson's preference for highly percussive Hammond settings. He also uses the Mellotron conventionally to create very full "choral" or "string orchestra" backdrops, and does not resort to the kind of experimentation with the instrument evident in Wakeman's Mellotron parts on *Close to the Edge*. Likewise, Steve Hackett prefers a "warm" electric guitar timbre that is characterized by a controlled fuzz-tone; this sound is evident throughout "Firth of Fifth."

In terms of arrangement, Genesis preferred somewhat more "open" textures than most other progressive rock bands; they had little fondness for the denser style exemplified by Gentle Giant (and on occasion, King Crimson, Yes, or ELP). As a result, their arrangements are, if anything, even more disciplined than Yes's; the guitar is virtually absent on the lengthy keyboard episode in the middle of "Firth of Fifth," while during the guitar lead the keyboard is confined to providing a luxuriant harmonic cushion.

A final aspect of Genesis's characteristic "clarity" is their relative de-emphasis of virtuosity. While Tony Banks and Steve Hackett are capable instrumentalists, as soloists they are not in the same league as a Keith Emerson or a Steve Howe.

Genesis use this to their advantage, however, by avoiding drawn-out solos over a repeated bass line or chord change in favor of thematic ensemble interplay that is often of considerable complexity. An excellent example of this type of episode is the synthesizer section which occupies the center of "Firth of Fifth." The keyboard figuration is intricate, requiring a good deal of technique in performance, and in this sense might be said to be "showy." However, unlike the busy passagework of many other progressive rock solos, it is of thematic importance to the song at large, and contains a great deal of melodic, harmonic, and metric interest. In short, it is the preference for "open" textures, "clean" timbres, and intricate ensemble interplay over virtuosic solos that gives the music of Gabriel-era Genesis its characteristic "clarity." If ELP were the ultra-Romantics of the progressive rock movement, Genesis were the movement's Mozarts. (I can even find certain elements of eighteenth-century keyboard style in the work of Banks which I do not find in the work of other progressive rock keyboardists, a matter I will discuss momentarily.)

Unlike *Tarkus* or *Close to the Edge*, "Firth of Fifth" is not given visual expression through the cover art. Instead, the cover art of the *Selling England by the Pound* LP was intended to tie in with "I Know What I Like," Genesis's first single, which appears immediately before "Firth of Fifth" on the album. Painted by Betty Swanick in a style vaguely reminiscent of Henri Rousseau, the cover art depicts the song's protagonist, a lawnmower, lying on a park bench with his tools of trade carelessly scattered about; in the background, rows of people in stylized gestures exchange meaningless platitudes.

Likewise, the lyrics of "Firth of Fifth" cannot be said to tell a story. As I will show, the narrative power of this song rests in the music itself. What the lyrics can do, however, is to provide suggestive imagery. Like several other songs by Genesis ("The Fountain of Salmacis," "Cinema Show"), "Firth of Fifth" draws some of its imagery from Greek and Roman mythology. In particular, there is much use of water imagery; the song's title, "Firth of Fifth," is in fact a play on the Firth of Forth, a bay on the east coast of Scotland adjacent to Edinburgh. Like Yes's "Roundabout," there is a tendency toward verbal landscape painting and a definite streak of nature mysticism.

For instance, the lyrics juxtapose a number of images of natural beauty associated with the domains of Neptune (the Roman god of water)—trees, sky, lillies, waterfalls, inland seas—with centers of human habitation, which by comparison are described as scenes of death, even as "cancer growths." While some people appreciate the beauty of Neptune's domains and "gaze with joy," others "care not." Indeed, on the whole people are depicted as being indifferent to anything that lies beyond the corridors of their everyday existence; like sheep, they remain in a metaphorical pen, even when they've seen the way out. Here there is perhaps at least a faint suggestion of that driving concern of

Close to the Edge: the other realms of consciousness and spirituality which lay just beyond the boundaries of our everyday experience. Of course, if one interprets the song this way, one must read the nature imagery and the imagery referring to towns, the "homes of men," etc., as symbols of spiritual fulfillment and spiritual sterility, respectively.

The question of how to interpret the water imagery becomes especially acute in the final verse. Here the water imagery takes on the nature of a force that exists on a scale beyond human comprehension; a river dissolves into the sea (representative of eternity, perhaps), and has the capacity to erode the "sands of time." Faced with this power, gods, men, and sheep alike can simply remain "inside their pen" until a higher power—"the shepherd"—leads them on.

If I seem somewhat hesitant to render final judgment on the "meaning" of these lyrics, it is because I don't want to read too much into them. Ultimately, I think the "meaning" of the lyrics of "Firth of Fifth" rests with the individual listener. Unlike "Cinema Show," the mythological imagery is not used as an allegory through which to address the problems of here and now; unlike "The Fountain of Salmacis," mythology is not used as a springboard for presenting a coherent narrative. In this sense, I do not see the lyrics of "Firth of Fifth" as among the band's best. On the other hand, the music itself is so strong that it is able to impose at least the illusion of narrative coherence on the lyrics.

The overall shape of "Firth of Fifth" resembles an arch form, which from its middle proceeds in a mirror direction of its opening; in this case, A B C A C B A. However, the dramatic ideals of struggle, transformation, and attainment seem so central to the piece that it seems sensible to evaluate it in the context of sonata form (even though the tonal scheme is different from what one would expect in a sonata form movement). Viewing "Firth of Fifth" in this context, there is a lengthy instrumental overture (A); an "exposition," which consists of the song proper (B); an instrumental "development," which begins with a new theme (C) and then takes up and develops the A and C themes; a "recapitulation," in which the "song" (B) returns; and a brief instrumental coda (A) which stems from the opening overture. I will structure my discussion of "Firth of Fifth" on the basis of this model.

The instrumental overture which opens "Firth of Fifth" is a lengthy passage for solo piano which very possibly may represent Tony Banks's finest moment on record. In this passage Banks shows a real talent for an eighteenth-century technique called *fortspinnung,* or "spinning out" a musical idea based on figuration presented in the first few measures. Here the model would seem to be the late baroque toccata: a fanfare-like theme is presented in continuous arpeggiation in the right hand, accompanied alternately by a booming bass line and soft chords in a higher register in the left. What is quite contemporary about Banks's theme, on the other hand, is its shifting meters; its use of modal mixtures also would have been quite out of place in eighteenth-century music. The first sixteen measures are built on a metric pattern which involves shifts between a bar of $\frac{4}{4}$, two bars of $\frac{6}{8}$, and a bar of $\frac{2}{4}$. The overture begins in $B^\flat$ major, but as it continues it moves through other keys—$E^\flat$ major, a transitional passage which culminates in $F^\sharp$ major—before finally recalling the opening section in $B^\flat$. Each modulation, in turn, corresponds to a new metric shape: the section in $E^\flat$ is set to a $\frac{6}{8} + \frac{7}{8}$ pattern, while the passage in $F^\sharp$ is set to a pattern of $\frac{4}{4} + \frac{6}{8} + \frac{3}{8} + \frac{2}{4}$. By maintaining the figuration and the general shape of the opening melodic idea, though, Banks imposes an impressive unity on the entire section.

A short transition section swings the music from $B^\flat$ into the key of the song proper, B major, at which point the entire band enters. The song, which corresponds to the "exposition," is much slower than the preceding instrumental overture. It consists of two verses, a lengthy bridge, and a final repetition of the verse. Since Gabriel-era Genesis resorted to vocal harmonizations somewhat infrequently (and not at all here), the keyboards played an especially important role in providing a rich harmonic cushion. In the verses, Gabriel is accompanied by a pipe-organ-like Hammond setting, guitar and bass (which double the bass line), and somewhat "martial" drums; the tonality never budges from B major, although there is some of Genesis's characteristic modal mixing. In the bridge, on the other hand, the rhythm section drops out, and a more pastoral and intimate instrumentation is adopted to accompany the rich imagery of the lyrics: Mellotron, strummed acoustic guitar, and an almost "spectral" electric guitar obligato. The flow of the music here is furthered by a series of extraordinary chord progressions which pass through several keys. The key of B major is reached at the end of the bridge, leading into a final repetition of the verse with the original instrumentation.

The "song" ends, and the music almost comes to a complete halt, save for a few slow arpeggios in the piano; this marks the beginning of the "development." Gradually, as the slow piano arpeggios fall into a more regular pattern and are at length doubled by the bass guitar, Gabriel enters on flute with a new theme (the C section in the arch form scheme above), a slow, wistful tune in E which has elements of both aeolian and diatonic minor tonality. At length, Banks's acoustic piano takes the theme over; the tempo picks up, the rhythm section enters quietly, and in another fine example of *fortspinnung*, he begins to spin out a transitional theme based on a motive drawn from the tail end of Gabriel's flute melody.

This passage leads to the return of the opening overture, the halfway point of both the arch form and the "development" section. The section retains its driving tempo, its shifting meters, its tonalities, and its melodic contour from the opening; it is rescored here, though, for the full band. The thematic material is presented by Banks in a trumpet-like setting on an ARP Pro-Soloist (a Minimoog-like monophonic synthesizer); a block-chord accompaniment is supplied on the Hammond, while the bass guitar and drums provide a rhythmically energetic backing which gives the theme a more driving character than it had before. There is something about the interaction between Bank's synthesizer figuration and Phil Collins's drum kit—which tends to rhythmically double the melodic line or supply an intricate set of complementary counterrhythms on the upper part of the set—that is reminiscent of the interplay between drums and keyboards in ELP.

This section is followed by a development of the flute theme (the C section in the arch form), which proves to be the piece's climax. The piece returns to common time; the drums kick into a harder-rocking rhythm, and the bass introduces a driving, syncopated, two-bar rhythmic ostinato which creates a new sense of energy. Over backing Hammond chords, Hackett commences a lyrical guitar lead dominated by a motive consisting of expressive descending sevenths. He obsessively develops this motive, ascending higher registrally, until he suddenly takes up the flute theme from the earlier C section. Neither the melodic contour nor the E-minor tonality of the tune change. Nevertheless, it does undergo development: the rhythm section's driving accompaniment lends it an energy that is totally new, while Tony Banks's rich Mellotron backdrop realizes harmonic implications of the tune that the earlier presentation had only hinted at. In short, the character of the tune is utterly transformed: what had previously belonged in the realm of the wistful and slightly melancholy now takes on an air of tragedy. Hackett momentarily abandons the tune in favor of more jagged, agitated passagework, but ultimately takes it up one more time, bringing the section to its climax. Thereafter a short modulatory bridge, now in E major, slows the rhythmic motion, and prepares a return of the song proper.

The "recapitulation" of the B section involves the return of the verses, which are recalled with new lyrics. While this section's triumphalism had seemed somewhat out of place upon its initial presentation, it now seems totally justified; there is thus no need for the more "sensitive" bridge section, which is excised. Under the sustained Hammond chords which accompany Gabriel's final words, the acoustic piano which opened the piece returns to the sonic foreground. It is now phased (probably to create an "out-of-focus" effect, as if one were hearing it through the mists); after presenting a fragment of the opening overture in the key of E major, it fades out into the distance.

Like *Close to the Edge*, "Firth of Fifth" is an example of progressive tonality; the harmonic relationships of this piece, however, are even more complex and ambiguous. The overture is in B♭ major; the song proper ("exposition") is in B major. The "development" opens in E minor, moves to B♭ major upon the return of the opening theme, then back to E minor for the guitar restatement of the flute theme. The recapitulation of the song proper is again in B major; the coda closes in E major. These relationships can be graphed as follows:

Overture	"Exposition"	"Development"	"Recapitulation"	Coda
B♭	B	e–B♭–e	B	E

The movement by tritone between B♭ and E is particularly important to the piece, and it is tempting to interpret the move from the E minor of the development to the E major of the coda as a symbolic transition from darkness to light. However, it might be a bit of a leap to declare E as the tonic, especially since the song proper is firmly centered in B upon both of its occurrences. It is probably best to leave the ramifications of this tonal scheme open to individual interpretation.

However one interprets the piece's tonality, though, "Firth of Fifth" is in many ways an almost archetypal progressive rock piece, offering masculine/feminine contrasts on a number of levels:

Feminine	Masculine
Acoustic sections	Electronic sections
Passages without rhythm section	Passages with rhythm section
Slow rhythmic motion	Fast rhythmic motion
Lyrical melodies	Thematic or motivic melodies
Open textures	Denser textures

It is the manner in which these elements intermingle in the repetitions of the various thematic sections which gives this piece its tension, its characteristic quality of developing from one thing into something else quite new. The band recognized it as a particularly successful effort; Steve Hackett in particular has commented that it is one of his favorite Genesis pieces.[29]

Pink Floyd: *Wish You Were Here* (1975)

More than any of the other albums discussed in this chapter, Pink Floyd's *Wish You Were Here* is the product of a fully mature band; by 1975, David Gilmour (guitars, lead vocals), Roger Waters (bass, backing vocals), Rick Wright (keyboards, backing vocals), and Nick Mason (drums, percussion) had been playing together for seven years. The group had, in fact, only gone through one lineup change: Gilmour had been brought on board in 1968 to replace Syd Barrett, the band's original guitarist, lead vocalist, and songwriter, after Barrett had become pop music's most notorious casualty of LSD.[30] Since *Wish You Were Here* concerns itself, at least on one level, with meditations on Barrett's downfall, in some ways it represents the band coming full circle in historical terms.

The album was a milestone in other ways as well. While Waters had become the band's lyricist soon after Barrett's departure, Waters, Gilmour, and Wright (sometimes Mason as well) had tended to collaborate on writing the band's music, and *Wish You Were Here* marked the last (and perhaps the finest) example of this arrangement. Beginning with the transitional *Animals* LP of 1977, Waters increasingly insisted on having total creative control of the band's output; parts of *The Wall* (1979) and all of *The Final Cut* (1983) are essentially Roger Waters solo projects, with the other Floyd members being used interchangeably with a battalion of studio musicians.

Floyd biographer Nicholas Schaffner sees *Wish You Were Here* as the highpoint of the band's creative output because "it struck such an inadvertent balance between Roger's growing conceptual obsessions and Dave and Rick's refinement of the classic Floyd atmospherics that had attracted most listeners to the group in the first place; the album thus ended up capturing the best of both worlds."[31] Certainly it was the last Floyd album to capture the band's "classic" sound: the celestial backdrops of electronic keyboards, the ethereal vocal harmonies, the prevailing adagio tempos, and the characteristic mixture of soft acoustic balladry with state-of-the-art electronic effects.

Since the events of the recording sessions for the album were to have a direct impact on the structural shape of the final product, a brief recapitulation of these events is warranted here. The band initially had planned to record three cuts. The first, a multimovement suite in nine sections entitled *Shine On You Crazy Diamond*, was to occupy the entirety of side one. This piece consists of a multisectional instrumental prelude (parts one through four), a quasi-independent song (part five), a lengthy instrumental interlude (part six), a recapitulation of the earlier song section with new lyrics (part seven), and an instrumental postlude in two distinct sections (parts eight and nine). Side two of the album was to be devoted to two cuts of approximately ten minutes each, "You Gotta Be Crazy" and "Raving and Drooling." (Altered versions of these songs were eventually to appear on the *Animals* LP as "Dogs" and "Sheep," respectively.)

Shine On You Crazy Diamond, the album's magnum opus, was to be a biography of sorts of Syd Barrett (the "crazy diamond" of the title), detailing how the pressures of pop music stardom had shattered this overly sensitive musician's tenuous grip on sanity. The opening lyrics of part five of *Shine On You* deal directly with Barrett's predicament:

Remember when you were young, you shone like the sun.
Shine on you crazy diamond.
Now there's that look in your eyes, like black holes in the sky.
Shine on you crazy diamond.

As Waters remarked, the lyrics were meant to "get as close as possible to what I felt . . . that sort of indefinable, inevitable melancholy about the disappearance of

Syd. Because he's left, withdrawn so far away that, as far as we're concerned, he's no longer there."[32]

However, as the recording sessions wore on, Waters began to feel that "at times the group was there only physically. Our bodies were there, but our minds and feelings somewhere else."[33] In other words, he saw the band's situation mirroring Barrett's: there was a sense of unfulfilled presence. A decision was then made to divide *Shine On You Crazy Diamond* into two discrete halves (parts one through five and parts six through nine), and to sandwich three newly composed songs in between: "Welcome to the Machine" and "Have a Cigar," both scorching attacks on the recording industry, and the more ballad-like "Wish You Were Here."[34] Roger Waters, in particular, believed that the new arrangement of music gave the album a conceptual coherence it would have lacked if the original plan to include the two unrelated songs on side two had been pursued. The three new songs serve as "commentaries" on the lyrics of *Shine On You Crazy Diamond*, since they all address aspects of Barrett's situation. They also function as an autobiography of a band that had become so commercially successful they were struggling for a reason to continue, and had to some degree "lost their fire." Furthermore, the songs take on a more universal meaning by virtue of the fact that the whole Syd Barrett saga can be viewed as symbolic of the sense of alienation and withdrawal that pervades contemporary Western society. In its final shape, then, *Wish You Were Here* functions as a concept album on three distinct levels: as a biography detailing Syd Barrett's withdrawal into madness, as an autobiography of the band's fragmented state after the stunning success of their *Dark Side of the Moon* LP of 1973, and as a commentary on twentieth-century alienation.

Wish You Were Here also marked the most ambitious collaboration between the band and the graphics design firm Hipgnosis. Storm Thorgerson, who was largely responsible for the album's cover art, has stated that what most impressed him about the album's music was "this sense of wide-open spaces of the inner mind, or of some unknown terrain." Thorgerson accompanied the band on their April 1975 U.S. tour in order to thoroughly familiarize himself with the new music's content; he described his job as being "to invent an image related to the music." (One might wish to compare and contrast this view with the collaboration between Roger Dean and Yes discussed earlier in the chapter.) He finally decided that the theme of the album boiled down to "unfulfilled presence in general rather than Syd's particular version of it." He said that in his brainstorming sessions with the band, they were "searching for a powerful metaphor or symbol of absence. We were especially interested in the aspect of absence which involved pretense."[35]

The broadsides against the music industry which fuel "Welcome to the Machine" and "Have a Cigar" were ultimately responsible for suggesting much of the album's cover art. The front of the album depicts two businessmen shaking hands: one is on fire, symbolizing that he has been "burned" (i.e., swindled) by the other.

The handshake, then, while ostensibly a gesture of friendship, here becomes worse than a meaningless ritual: it becomes a means of masking one's more malignant motives. The back of the album cover depicts a salesman hawking Pink Floyd albums in the middle of an empty desert: he has no ankles, no wrists, and no face. He is, so to speak, an empty suit. The inner sleeve is adorned with two further symbols of absence that are more "pastoral" in tone. One depicts a veil blowing across an empty Norfolk grove lined by unremittingly regular rows of trees; the other depicts a splashless diver in California's Mono Lake. Alienation, apparently, recognizes no rural/urban divide. As a final gesture of "absence," the band decided to issue the album in opaque shrink wrap. The band's name and the album title were embossed on a sticker which adorned the shrink wrap; the sticker also included an ominous logo designed by Hipgnosis's George Hardie depicting a handshake between two mechanical hands.

Before discussing the music of *Wish You Were Here*, it seems worthwhile to point up some very real differences that exist between the music, particularly the instrumental music, of Pink Floyd and the other bands discussed in this chapter. ELP, Yes, and Genesis, despite their differences in other areas, tend to create large-scale structure through rather similar means. This is especially true in their instrumental sections, where large-scale structures result from linking together melodic ideas of various types: motives, short themes, and on occasion longer tunes. This material tends to recur periodically—sometimes literally, sometimes transformed—during the course of a piece. Some of this material is relatively slow and lyrical; just as often, however, it is fanfare- or toccata-like, is melodically ornate, and requires considerable technical ability to carry off in performance. Each new "segment" of music (whether a group of motives, a short theme that is repeated several times, or a genuine tune) tends to be in its own key, so key changes in the instrumental progressive rock style of ELP, Yes, and Genesis are frequent.

The Pink Floyd instrumental style evident in *Shine On You Crazy Diamond* is quite different. The members of Pink Floyd were not virtuoso instrumentalists, and were capable neither of the flamboyant solos over a chord change evident in the "song" movements of *Tarkus* nor of the intricate thematic episodes which play a major role in "Firth of Fifth." This, in turn, seemed to affect their choice of tempos. There are few alternations of tempos in *Shine On You;* much of the piece is characterized by a prevailing adagio in $\frac{3}{4}$ (indeed, the "fast" piece of *Wish You Were Here*, "Have a Cigar," would be considered "moderate" at best in most other contexts).

Second, modulations are much more infrequent in Pink Floyd's music than in the music of the bands mentioned above. The tonal plan of the *Wish You Were Here* LP is extremely straightforward. The first half of *Shine On You* is in G minor; "Welcome to the Machine" and "Have a Cigar" shift to E minor; "Wish You Were Here" shifts to G major (relative major of E minor and parallel major of G minor);

the second half of *Shine On You* returns in G minor. Within *Shine On You*, only parts five, seven, and nine contain short modulations from the tonic; the tonality of the three songs remains constant.

Another difference between the instrumental portions of *Wish You Were Here* and the other pieces discussed in this chapter is that Pink Floyd do not seem to think in terms of presenting distinctive, self-contained themes which are then developed and transformed in subsequent sections. Rather, in *Shine On You Crazy Diamond* the band seem to have developed three distinct strategies for creating large-scale instrumental structure. All three approaches are united by their avoidance of the principles of melodic repetition, development, and transformation.

The first method involves splicing together short melodic phrases—usually pentatonic in outline—over a drone until a long, winding melody has been created. The result is not a "tune" in the commonly understood sense of the word; there is relatively little repetition of individual phrases, and the phrase lengths often change, so there is no suggestion of question-answer phrase structure. This approach is evident in its "pure" form in part one of *Shine On You*. A smooth, slowly unfolding Moog melody is spun out over a sustained G-minor keyboard triad; occasional countermelodies, including a long-breathed string synthesizer line and a shorter, bell-like synthesizer motive, furtively dart in and out of the texture. The same structural approach is also evident in part six of *Shine On You*, but here the drone on G is "disguised" as a series of eight-bar rhythmic ostinatos in the bass guitar. However, Wright's Moog line often shows no regard for the four- and eight-bar groupings implied in the bass ostinato; its short, irregular motives often spill from one repetition of the ostinato pattern into the next, again with virtually no literal repetition of preceding phrases.

The second method of creating large-scale structure in *Shine On You Crazy Diamond* involves repeating somewhat lengthy chord progressions, over which new melodic material is constantly presented. This approach is most easily seen in parts two and nine of *Shine On You*. In part two, a twelve-bar chord progression is repeated twice (with an incomplete third repetition); each repetition presents an entirely new melodic idea, created here by Gilmour on electric guitar. In part nine, a sixteen-bar progression is repeated three times, each time with a totally new set of melodic ideas (realized by Wright on the Minimoog). Both movements suggest a theme-and-variations approach, except there is no real melodic theme of which later melodic ideas can be said to be variations. Rather, it is the chord cycles themselves which provide coherence.

The most impressive use of this approach, though, occurs in parts three and four of *Shine On You*. The structural foundation of these movements is a forty-eight-bar chord progression which begins with long blocks of tonic and subdominant harmony, and concludes with more active harmonic motion. In the third movement, the first repetition of this chord progression is overlaid by a mournful four-note guitar ostinato which Roger Waters has stated was crucial in generating the entire piece.[36] In the second repetition of the progression, the repetitive ostinato is in turn overlaid with a long-breathed electric guitar melody. In the best Pink Floyd fashion, Gilmour spins out his line by splicing together short pentatonic phrases of unequal length; there is little literal repetition of phrases, although certain pentatonic shapes (especially 1-7-5) recur periodically.

An interesting example of the band's talent for creating coherent large-scale structure can be seen at the end of part three of *Shine On You Crazy Diamond*. During the second repetition of the forty-eight-bar chord progression in part three, the last sixteen bars of the progression are replaced by a sixteen-bar segment of chords which is to play a major role in part five (the "song movement") of *Shine On You*. In this way, part three subtly foreshadows the musical substance of *Shine On You*'s song proper.

Another characteristic element of the Pink Floyd style which is especially evident in part three of *Shine On You* is the relative independence of the quasi-improvised melodic lines from the underlying chord progressions. In part three, David Gilmour's circular guitar lead is often extraordinarily independent of the repetitive four-note ostinato pattern, the sustained Hammond chords, and the bass line. As a result, the movement contains a number of examples of cross relations, or chromatic contradictions of a given scale degree within a chord. These cross relations stem from Gilmour's melodic use of a lowered seventh degree over a major dominant chord, which results in a triad that contains both raised and lowered thirds. The band must have been consciously aware of this aspect of their harmonic style: in part four of *Shine On You*, the two repetitions of the forty-eight-bar chord progression are modified from their earlier appearance in part three by virtue of the fact they now end with a dominant chord that contains both major and minor thirds (D-F♯-A-F♮). A similar use of cross relations can be found in some of the songs of *Dark Side of the Moon* ("Breathe"); Pink Floyd's characteristic use of cross relations helps to contribute to the somewhat doleful character of their predominantly minor-mode harmony.[37]

A final approach to large-scale instrumental structure can be found in the eighth movement of *Shine On You*. This section adopts a number of characteristics of contemporaneous jazz-rock fusion: a highly syncopated bass line, rhythmic comping on the Rhodes electric piano, a "funky" clavinet riff, and so on. The main difference is that there are no real chord changes: the bass line never budges from its eight-bar rhythmic ostinato on G. Over this static harmonic backing, parts are layered in one by one: guitar harmonics, the Rhodes, the funky clavinet, a short two-chord riff on guitar, and finally a spacey four-bar synthesizer theme. As new parts enter, earlier lines tend to fade into the sonic background. The result is a slowly evolving texture which points up pervasive, if probably indirect, points of contact between the music of Pink Floyd and the American minimalist style.

The structural dynamic of *Shine On You Crazy Diamond* is somewhat different from *Tarkus, Close to the Edge,* or "Firth of Fifth." These other pieces either open vigorously, or else (as in the case of *Close to the Edge*) explode into vigorous activity within the first sixty seconds of the opening; the structural outline of the remainder of these pieces is defined by a dialectic of tension and repose, by deliberately chosen juxtapositions of masculine and feminine sections. The structural dynamic of *Shine On You,* on the other hand, is defined by an almost continuous expansion of rhythmic, harmonic, timbral, and textural activity from the subdued, almost motionless part one to part five, the song proper, after which the piece temporarily breaks off in favor of the three independent songs. Tracing this process of expansion across parts one through five of *Shine On You* is both revealing and relatively simple.

As I mentioned above, part one of *Shine On You* is almost rhythmically motionless, harmonically static—based completely on a sustained G-minor triad—and dominated by several related "mellow" synthesizer colorings. The main focus of musical activity is the slowly unfolding Minimoog melody, characterized by long rhythmic values and a pentatonic outline; occasional countermelodies dart in and out, but the overall ambience is tranquil, even "cosmic."

Part two begins a process of expansion on a number of fronts. Most obviously, the electric guitar enters with the melody over sustained synthesizer chords, bringing a new sense of timbral variety. While there is not yet a definite sense of meter, the guitar line moves in shorter note values than the synthesizer line of the previous section, creating a sense of increased rhythmic motion. This sense of motion is furthered by the appearance of an elemental harmonic progression, involving the tonic, dominant, and subdominant chords, which is heard twice during the section.

The sense of increased motion apparent in part two is fully realized at the opening of part three, which represents the piece's first climax. The mournful four-note guitar ostinato which pervades the entire section is first heard against the backdrop of a stark G pedal point (on synthesizer). Upon the ostinato's fourth repetition, however, the rhythm section and organ enter, creating a definite beat for the first time: while the prevailing rhythmic pattern is not particularly muscular, the spaciness of what has preceded it gives it an aura of power. The entry of the Hammond with the rhythm section creates a new textural fullness as well, since it marks the first time in the piece that the four band members have been heard simultaneously. Furthermore, the introduction of the recurring forty-eight-bar chord progression which is to dominate parts three and four of the piece results in gradually increased harmonic activity. Upon the second repetition of this chord progression, textural activity is further increased, as a quasi-improvised guitar line is overlaid against the guitar ostinato, the sustained organ chords, and the accompaniment of the rhythm section. At the end of part three, the increased harmonic activity and the growing agitation of the guitar lead suggest that a new climax is being approached.

However, the beginning of part four—reached after a suspenseful pause on the dominant—proves to be a momentary point of repose instead. The guitar ostinato which pervaded part three is withdrawn from the texture, the lead guitar line is abandoned in favor of periodic rhythm chords in the sonic background, and a slower, smoother lead line is unfolded on a "mellow" synth setting. At the end of part four's first repetition of the forty-eight-bar progression, the band pauses uneasily on a dominant chord with clashing major and minor thirds—and then continues. The guitar resumes spinning out a melody on the second repetition of the forty-eight-bar progression, and the rhythmic motion again increases. Again there is a pause on the dissonant dominant chord; this time, however, the section passes on into the "song movement" of *Shine On You,* part five.

Shine On You's song proper represents the climax of the piece on a number of grounds: its greater harmonic motion (including a brief modulation via a G♭ major triad to B♭ major), its increase in textural density, and above all, the entrance for the first time of the human voice. Rather than alternating sixteen-bar verses with a refrain in the conventional pattern, brief eight-bar verses sung by Roger Waters are alternated with an eight-bar refrain ("Shine on you crazy diamond") sung by the band's three vocalists and two female backup singers. The compressed call-and-response pattern is reminiscent of black gospel music and generates considerable rhetorical power. Musical tension is retained and even increased right up to the end of the section. After the last vocal verse, sax soloist Dick Parry begins to lay out an angular solo over the song's chord changes;[38] the rhythm section's accompaniment shifts from quarter notes in $\frac{3}{4}$ to triplet eighth notes in $\frac{2}{4}$, creating the highest level of rhythmic energy yet heard on the album.[39] This new energy is only gradually dissipated by the emerging "machine sounds" which eventually swallow up the first half of *Shine On You* into the emerging "Welcome to the Machine," which concludes side one of the album.

The musical success of the first half of *Shine On You Crazy Diamond* stems from the band's ability to coherently manage dynamics, timbre, rhythm, and harmonic activity, so that the progression from the almost motionless opening to the energetic part five appears inevitable and pulls even the casual listener along. Unlike members of ELP, Yes, or Genesis, none of the members of Pink Floyd have ever publicly discussed studying traditional classical pieces or composers. However, there is probably some truth in Barry Miles's frequently repeated statement that the band's mastery of large-scale structure is at least partly a result of their backgrounds as architecture students at Regent Street Polytechnic.[40]

"Welcome to the Machine," which closes side one of the LP, is one of Pink Floyd's most haunting songs. The lyrics are more than just an attack on the recording industry; they are a reflection on the tendency of mass media to construct largely fictitious, unrealistic images of success. The song's protagonist is a young man who "bought a guitar to punish his ma." He hates school, but not to worry—

he knows he's "nobody's fool," and he's certain he'll find the proverbial pot of gold at the end of the rock-and-roll rainbow. But his dream, it turns out, is only an illusion that has been foisted upon him from outside:

> What did you dream? It's alright we told you what to dream.
> You dreamed of a big star. He played a mean guitar.
> He always ate in the steak bar. He loved to drive in his Jaguar.
> So welcome to the machine . . .

In the mid-1970s it was radical enough for a rock song to suggest that the rock-and-roll "dream" was illusory; to suggest the dream was an illusion foisted upon the young and the vulnerable by cynical, manipulative corporate executives (with the full cooperation of rock musicians and the other participants in the "machine") was unheard of. There is of course a certain irony in the fact that it took a millionaire rock star, Roger Waters, to make this observation, but the lyrics lose none of their effectiveness on account of this; part of their impact resides in the fact that while the protagonist could have been young Syd Barrett, he could just as easily have been a young Pink Floyd fan of the mid-1970s hoping to follow in his heroes' footsteps.

For the full impact of such bleak lyrics to be felt, a certain type of musical setting was required, and Pink Floyd delivered with music that amply justifies their reputations as "virtuosos of the studio." (One may perhaps find additional irony in the fact that the song's cry for some sort of human compassion in the midst of a hopelessly depersonalizing technocracy is being made by a band that was more dependent on technology for its very existence than virtually any other.) Most of the song consists of a relentless alternation between two chords, the E-minor tonic and a C-major seventh chord. Likewise, much of the haunting vocal line moves obsessively back and forth in the range of a third; it never exceeds the range of a perfect fifth.

If not handled carefully, a song based on such minimal harmonic and melodic resources could quickly become a study in banality. The Floyd avoid this fate by their attention to detail. First, there are the sound effects, which literally become the heart of the song. The song begins with a highly synthetic eighth-note pulse which suggests perhaps a distant train. Out of the sonic background emerge irregular buzzes, liquid "bursts," and other "industrial" sounds. Finally a quarter-note throb in the bass emerges to the forefront of the sonic mix, where it remains for the duration of the piece, serving as the song's mechanical "heartbeat." David Gilmour described the construction of the beginning of the song in these terms:

It's very much a made-up-in-the-studio thing which was all built up from a basic throbbing made on a VCS3, with a one repeat echo used so that each "boom" is followed by an echo repeat to give the throb. With a number like that, you don't start off with a regular concept of group structure or anything, and there's no backing track either. Really it is just a studio proposition where we're using tape for its own ends—a form of collage using sound.[41]

The same attention to sonic detail is evident when Gilmour enters on vocals. His voice is discreetly doubled an octave lower, giving the vocals a curiously "hollow," haunting quality; the ambience of bleakness is enhanced by the accompaniment, which features the relentless throb in the bass, irregular liquid "spurts" (synthesized white noise), and sudden bursts of synthetic string chords in the upper register of the mix. This extraordinarily subtle mixture of machine-like timbres, when combined with the restricted range of the vocal melody and the obsessively repeated chords,[42] evokes a hypnotic, trancelike ambience. When the refrain of the first verse ("so welcome to the machine") is reached, the band resorts to another masterstroke of subtle detail: Gilmour begins strumming his acoustic guitar. The sound of the acoustic instrument juxtaposed against the formidable wall of electronic timbres creates an air of indescribable vulnerability, and perfectly captures the personal/impersonal dichotomy of the lyrics.

The instrumental interlude which follows the first verse is in $\frac{3}{4}$ rather than $\frac{4}{4}$; since the same chords are now changing one beat sooner than they had during the vocals, an illusion of more urgent motion is created, though the tempo of the machine-like throb never varies. The interlude is a study in frustrated progress: three times a rising modal fragment (doubled by acoustic guitar and string synthesizer) appears to reach a climactic note, only to suddenly slide back to the starting point (via a glissando on Wright's Minimoog) and have to start the "climbing" process anew. Again, there are a number of sensitive details which help to contribute to the overall ambience, most notably Nick Mason's unobtrusive but effective timpani flourishes.

The final verse returns the music of the first verse with new lyrics, wherein the protagonist is told in no uncertain terms that he's been had. Following the "Welcome to the Machine" refrain, Wright commences a Minimoog cadenza over a harmonically static accompaniment. The Minimoog lead gradually fades into an obsessively repeated string synthesizer part; this in turn is overpowered by more machine noises, suggestive of a car engine. Suddenly the mechanical noise stops; a door slams. In the distance one hears the sound of a party. It would appear the protagonist has escaped the "machine," and has finally found an opportunity to experience genuine interaction with other people. However, as Roger Waters explains, even this is not really escape: "That [the party sounds which end side one of the LP] was put there because of the complete emptiness inherent in that way of behaving—celebrations, gatherings of people who drink and talk together. To me that epitomizes the lack of contact and real feelings between people."[43] In the end, even human socialization doesn't guarantee real human contact.

While "Have a Cigar," which opens side two, maintains the relentlessly bleak vision of side one, it also allows Waters some room for a few sardonic wisecracks about greed in the music industry. Contempt literally oozes out of his description of a record company executive who's so happy "he can hardly count," although the crass executive does stop his gloating over the proceeds long enough to enquire of the band, "Oh by the way, which one's Pink?"[44]

Musically, "Have a Cigar" plays much the same role on *Wish You Were Here* as "Money" does on *Dark Side of the Moon*. With both songs, sardonic lyrics are set in a relatively up-tempo R&B style, characterized by a recurring unison riff with a bluesy flatted fifth, jazzlike comping on the Rhodes electric piano, and some stinging guitar leads by Gilmour. A particularly interesting parallel is that each song provides the only forum on its respective album for the exploration of unusual meters; it's almost as if Waters at some level associated sarcastic, biting lyrics with unpredictable, off-balance metric schemes. In the case of "Have a Cigar," the refrain is set to a daunting pattern in which bars of five, four, two, and three alternate. This passage may be the most complex of its type in the band's output, and offers (for them) a relatively rare example of the kind of "show-offy" metrical virtuosity that was regularly associated with other progressive rock acts.

The transition from "Have a Cigar" to "Wish You Were Here" offers yet another example of the band's studio wizardry. "Have a Cigar" suddenly disappears into a thin, reedy transistor radio sound, which is then joined by a plainly recorded acoustic guitar. David Gilmour has stated that the effect was meant to suggest a fan playing along with his or her radio on acoustic guitar; only gradually is the stereo presence of "Wish You Were Here" asserted.

"Wish You Were Here" offers numerous contrasts with the rest of the album. First, it is the only song in a major key; as I mentioned earlier, its G-major tonality serves as a transition between the E minor of "Welcome to the Machine" and "Have a Cigar" and the G minor of the second half of *Shine On You Crazy Diamond*. Second, it is one of the band's more lyrical songs; Nicholas Schaffner has commented that it's "just about the only Floyd number you're ever likely to hear performed by street troubadours in places like New York's Washington Square Park."[45] It is also the most unabashedly acoustic part of the album; the acoustic guitar which opens the song is gradually joined by acoustic piano, sedate backing from the bass and drums, and even pedal steel guitar. This last instrument, perhaps in conjunction with the staunchly diatonic tonality (no traces of modality), gives the song a vaguely country-and-western feeling, which is certainly not a common ambience in the overall context of Pink Floyd's output. In short, "Wish You Were

Here" serves as the feminine foil of "Have a Cigar," and offers a moment of repose and relaxation before the recapitulation of the second half of *Shine On You.*

The sound of "wind" (synthesized white noise) gradually overpowers the close of "Wish You Were Here," preparing for the return of the second half of *Shine On You Crazy Diamond.* Part six of *Shine On You* slowly emerges out of the raging white noise "storm"; it begins with a relentless stream of eighth notes in the guitar and a fragmentary ostinato in the bass guitar. A slowly rising string synthesizer line enters over these ostinato patterns; eventually the smooth string line gives way to a more jagged, agitated Moog lead whose irregular phrases cut across the straightjacket-like regularity of the guitar and bass guitar ostinatos. As the Moog lead begins to emphasize movement between the tonic G and its flatted fifth, D$^\flat$, the mood turns more ominous. Suddenly, the band resorts to the same metric shift they had at the end of part five; the prevailing $\frac{3}{4}$ meter with straight-eight rhythmic accompaniment gives way to $\frac{2}{4}$ with triplet eighth notes, creating a new sense of urgent forward momentum. Gilmour enters with a highly distorted guitar lead characterized by a "razor-like" timbre; Wright continues spinning out a Moog line, so this section represents a new climax in terms of its rhythmic motion, its dense textural activity, and its "strident" tone colors. Eventually, the band reach a transitional passage in which the tempo broadens back out, the rhythmic motion slows, and the recapitulation of the song proper is prepared.

Part seven of *Shine On You* recalls the song proper, part five, with new lyrics. However, the song now functions differently. Upon its first appearance on side one of the album, the song represented the climax toward which the previous sections had been striving; now, after the rhythmic energy, textural density, and timbral stridency of part six, its second appearance functions more as a release of the previous section's pent-up tension. It also offers a final opportunity for Waters to summarize the piece's conceptual content: as the protagonist's withdrawal into madness plays itself out, there's little to do but "bask in the shadow of yesterday's triumph" and "sail on the steel breeze."

After the aggression of part six and the autumnal reflections of part seven, a final structural question is raised: Where does the music go next? The band's answer is to move further into the realm of fantasy and inner space, to symbolize musically the descent into madness and emotional/spiritual isolation suggested by the final lyrics of the previous section. In part eight of *Shine On You,* the band creates music that achieves this goal by drawing elements of jazz-rock fusion (a highly syncopated bass guitar line, brittle guitar riffing, jazzlike comping on the Rhodes) into a minimalist framework that emphasizes slowly mutating sonic soundscapes. The overall effect of the jazz-rock/minimalist fusion is not unlike the contemporaneous instrumental "space rock" of Daevid Allen's Gong; the use of "cosmic" tone colors such as "floating" electric guitar harmonics and "spacey" Moog lines further emphasizes the space rock connection.[46]

Having musically depicted the withdrawal of Syd Barrett (or of Everyman) into his own isolated world, the band cannot easily end *Shine On You* with part eight; a final commentary is needed. Part nine provides such a commentary and plays a roughly parallel role to the seventh movement ("Aquatarkus") of *Tarkus*. It lacks the marchlike quality of "Aquatarkus" and therefore cannot be described as a funeral march. However, its slow tempo, tonal instability, and doleful harmonic progressions (emphasizing, for instance, movement through G-minor, B$^\flat$-minor, and F-minor triads in the first six bars) give it the air of a lamentation. Furthermore, the return back to the synthesizer-dominated instrumentation and unassertive rhythms of part one of *Shine On You Crazy Diamond* suggest that symbolically, the music has come full circle. Ending with the solipsism of part eight could have been construed as a suggestion that perhaps madness isn't the worst fate one could suffer after all; the lamentational character of part nine assures that the band's commentary on the tragedy of the alienating forces of our times will not be misunderstood.

Postscript

In some ways, *Wish You Were Here* marked a watershed both in Pink Floyd's development and in the progress of progressive rock (no pun intended). There are still some "trippy" or surreal touches, evident not only in the music but also in Storm Thorgerson's cover art and in some of the verbal imagery (the "steel breeze," for instance). On the other hand, the whole hermetic approach which had marked *Tarkus, Close to the Edge,* and "Firth of Fifth" (not to mention Pink Floyd's earlier music) was clearly on the wane. The psychedelic era's conviction that music should contain hidden layers of meaning that a group of illuminati could search out was rapidly being replaced by the belief that the lyrics should relay a comprehensible message that would be readily apparent even to the casual listener, without the interference of a dense maze of verbal images and visual symbols.

As Schaffner suggested, *Wish You Were Here* is effective precisely because it strikes such a delicate balance between a richly developed musical style, suggestive, well-conceived cover art, and comprehensible but not (yet) overly prosaic lyrics. In his Pink Floyd biography, Schaffner goes on to argue that after *Wish You Were Here* the band's music became less distinctive and interesting in direct proportion to the degree that Roger Waters's conceptual obsessions were expressed more concretely and unambiguously. While ELP, Yes, and Genesis did not have to contend with the kind of open warfare that eventually took place between Waters and the other members of Pink Floyd, their music, too, shows similar tendencies in the late 1970s; the originality and creativity of the music (and even the cover art) decreased in direct proportion to the degree that lyrics become more comprehensible and musical style more accessible.

Of course, some critics would argue that this was a sign of growing "maturity," insomuch that the lyrics were now less "arcane" and more "down-to-earth." I would argue, though, that this trend can equally be viewed as a desire to simply take the easy way out, and to do whatever was necessary to appeal to the changing audience tastes of the late 1970s. The music of all four of these bands became more formulaic during the late 1970s, as they became increasingly willing to draw on warmed-over stadium rock (and eventually New Wave) styles. At least the decline in musical creativity and originality evident in Pink Floyd's music of the late 1970s and early 1980s was not accompanied by a loss of conceptual urgency; the other major progressive rock bands of the 1970s increasingly tended to adopt a bland, pop-friendly subject matter that suggested not only a musical, but a philosophical accomodation with the once-despised Establishment. In short, I would argue that the simplification of progressive rock that rapidly became evident after 1975 was a sign of complacency, and signaled a loss not only of the restless musical creativity of the late 1960s, but also of that period's spiritual urgency. I will return to this line of thought more fully in the final chapter.

Related Styles

There is going to be more and more trading of ideas in all areas of music. Different people will be meeting each other. Music is getting more like music, and it's getting harder and harder to categorize a piece of music.[1]

This remark—made by Joe Butler of the Lovin' Spoonful around 1970—suggests how arbitrary categorizations of popular music can be, especially popular music of the late 1960s and early 1970s. There was a general belief at that time that classical, jazz, folk, rock, and Eastern styles were all tributaries that were about to flow into a new, unified style; no less a figure than Karlheinz Stockhausen, perhaps the major avant-garde composer of his generation, spoke in terms of a universal music that was on the cusp of its emergence. Of course, such a style never did emerge; it was doomed by the fragmentation of the unified youth culture of 1966–1970 into a number of distinct subcultures. The record companies and rock journalists also contributed to the demise of this ideal with their insistence on classification and compartmentalization—the former for the purposes of targeting specific segments of the record-buying public with specific types of recorded product, the latter for ideological purposes.

In fact, the journalists and music industry executives did such a good job in creating the illusion (which later became the reality) of hardened subcategories of popular music, that it is very hard for people who encountered the music of the late 1960s and early 1970s after the fact to believe that Yes and Black Sabbath—or Pink Floyd and Paul Simon, or the Nice and Sammy Davis, Jr.—could have shared a stage. Yet they did, and for this reason in a study of progressive rock it would be very dangerous to ignore styles such as heavy metal, jazz-rock, and folk-rock that were once perceived to have a much closer relationship with each other than is now the case. In this chapter, then, I will examine the relationship of progressive rock with a number of genres that overlapped it to a certain degree; I believe comparisons of this type will illuminate the essential features of progressive rock even more clearly.

English Jazz-rock Fusion

The English jazz-rock movement arose during the late 1960s, at roughly the same time as the progressive rock movement; at this time the differences between the two styles were often nebulous. For instance, the term "jazz-rock" was applied to bands as diverse as Colosseum, a quintet fronted by virtuoso drummer Jon Hiseman that mixed jazz, rhythm-and-blues, and early progressive rock elements (one critic described their *Those Who Are about to Die Salute You* LP of 1969 as a conceptual link between John Coltrane and Procol Harum); Traffic, a group led by organist Steve Winwood that drew on jazz, soul, and folk elements; IF, a seven-piece ensemble that developed a big-band "jazz-pop" fusion analogous to the early music of American groups such as Chicago or Blood, Sweat, and Tears; and even King Crimson, whose "21st-century Schizoid Man" of 1969 was seminal in drawing elements of hard bop and free jazz into the mainstream of English rock. By the early 1970s, however, two distinct tributaries were developing in the English jazz-rock scene.

First, there was the heavy jazz-rock fusion pioneered by Mahavishnu Orchestra, a multinational band led by the extraordinary English guitarist John McLaughlin. Mahavishnu Orchestra's style of fusion (which is often what people automatically think of when "jazz-rock" is mentioned) is instrumental, highly electronic (based as it is on rock instrumentation), and is characterized by breakneck tempos and virtuoso soloing. This style became especially popular in the mid-1970s, and was represented in England by the music of Brand X, Colosseum II (another band led by Jon Hiseman, who may well have been the most formidable European drummer of his generation), Isotope, and the collaborations between English guitarist Jeff Beck and the Czech keyboardist and Mahavishnu alumnus Jan Hammer.

Parallel to the English fusion scene was the Canterbury school, purveyors of a more exclusively English jazz-rock style that grew out of the Canterbury underground of the late 1960s. While the seminal Canterbury band, the Wilde Flowers, never cut an album, it did contribute a number of members to the Canterbury scene's two most durable outfits, Soft Machine and Caravan; both bands released their first album at the height of the psychedelic era in the late 1960s, and remained active into the early 1980s. Soft Machine, who drew their name from William S. Burroughs's pornographic science fiction travelogue, were especially influential in establishing a peculiarly English instrumental jazz-rock approach. This style is best represented by their *Third* and *Fourth* LPs of 1970 and 1971, and blends together unusual structures, laid-back tempos, a "big band" sound emphasizing dense, complex arrangements, and an interest in avant-garde electronics that belies the legacy of psychedelia.

A number of later bands that formed outside of Canterbury have been labeled as "Canterbury bands" either because they were founded by a member of Soft Machine or Caravan, or because they were obviously influenced by one or both of these groups. Major exponents of the Canterbury style in this looser sense include Gong (another long-lasting band whose founder, Daevid Allen, was a member of the original lineup of Soft Machine); Matching Mole (founded by another Soft Machine alumnus, Robert Wyatt); Soft Heap (yet another Soft Machine spin-off); and Quiet Sun. Several bands in which keyboardists Dave Stewart and Alan Gowen played major roles, including Egg, Hatfield and the North, National Health, and Gilgamesh, have also frequently been considered representatives of the "Canterbury style."

I believe a major problem in the past coverage of the Canterbury bands is that writers have tended to imply that there is a "Canterbury style," when the early Canterbury bands in particular often sound quite different from each other. There were widely different levels of emphasis on singing and playing: for instance, while Soft Machine became a completely instrumental band early in their career, Caravan retained a strong interest in the pop song for the duration of their existence. Furthermore, while no one is likely to confuse the music of Yes, Genesis, or ELP with Soft Machine or Gong (an extraordinarily eclectic band that one critic described as a mixture of *Mystery Tour* Beatles, Bonzo Dog Band, Colosseum, King Crimson, and Frank Zappa's Mothers of Invention), the music of other early Canterbury bands is much closer to the progressive rock sound already discussed. For instance, Caravan's debut album represents a dreamy folk/rock/classical fusion that parallels the early music of Yes and Genesis. While the group increasingly incorporated jazz-rock elements into their later albums (especially their highly successful recordings of 1972 to 1974), their song-oriented output is decisively different than the instrumental jazz-rock of Soft Machine's mature recordings. Likewise, Egg's music suggests an intricate, more experimental alternative to the organ trio approach of the Nice or ELP.

It was only during the mid-1970s that a somewhat more easily recognizable "Canterbury style" emerged. A number of the Canterbury-influenced bands that appeared at this time—including Quiet Sun, Hatfield and the North, National Health, Gilgamesh, Soft Heap, and Bruford—created an eclectic, at times quirky, strain of predominantly instrumental fusion that draws (in different measures) on elements of hard fusion, progressive rock (especially its massive keyboard backdrops), and the legacy of Soft Machine and Caravan. It is this type of sound most critics refer to when discussing the Canterbury "style," and it must be admitted that by the mid-1970s even seminal Canterbury bands such as Soft Machine and

Gong had adopted this approach. Nonetheless, there remained exceptions. Henry Cow's first two albums are often cited as examples of Canterbury rock, but the extraordinarily dense, at times chaotic sound developed by this band, strongly permeated by free jazz and avant-garde classical music, is convoluted even by the standards of this admittedly complex style. (Henry Cow subsequently merged with another band, Slapp Happy, and proceeded to pioneer an even more complex, eccentric strain of progressive rock than Gentle Giant on albums such as *In Praise of Learning*.) Conversely, during the same period bands such as Ian Carr's Nucleus which are normally not considered Canterbury groups developed a sound which is quite similar to Soft Machine's music of the early 1970s.

Although the Canterbury sound became increasingly fusion-oriented during the mid-1970s, Canterbury musicians were often less than happy about being categorized as "jazz" players. During his time in Bruford, keyboardist Dave Stewart commented,

> To an American, the word "rock" means something slightly different. When I say rock, I mean beat music. Something that uses drums. People describe Bruford as jazz. To us, it's rock. We're always fighting against being classified as jazz. I hate being classified as a jazz musician. I'm happy to be a rock musician. That's what I've always been. I mean, I'm a *weird* rock musician.[2]

The music of English jazz-rock bands—whether of the Canterbury or fusion wings—does share a number of common features. There are two main approaches to instrumentation. First, there is the "big band" approach where several reed and brass players are augmented by a rock rhythm section and perhaps a guitarist: this approach is exemplified by IF's early albums, Soft Machine's *Third* and *Fourth* LPs, mid-period Caravan, Ian Carr's Nucleus, and especially Keith Tippett's Centipede Orchestra (which in fact contributed several members to Soft Machine's *Third* and *Fourth* albums). Second, there is the rock-based instrumentation popularized by Mahavishnu Orchestra consisting of guitar, keyboards, bass, and drums, with the optional inclusion of either a sax or an electric violin soloist. Most of the later Canterbury bands actually followed this approach. Structurally, many jazz-rock pieces alternate between one or more ritornello or "head" sections—precomposed passages that consist of intricate unison runs or well-rehearsed instrumental counterpoint—and lengthy improvised solos. These latter sections are usually anchored by a highly syncopated bass ostinato and a staccato chordal accompaniment supplied by either keyboards or guitar, over which the soloist lays out long, angular lead lines. When vocal material is present, it is often through-composed (that is, nonrepetitive), rather than being cast into the strophic format common to most popular songs. The drum parts, which heavily emphasize the snare, cymbals, and the high hat rather than the lower half of the kit, are hard-driving, yet intricate. Asymmetrical and shifting meters were part of the genre from quite early on;

former Soft Machine bassist Hugh Hopper notes that "Soft Machine's Mike Rat-ledge came up with elevens, thirteens, and fifteens in highly-arranged tunes such as "Slightly All the Time" and "Out-Bloody-Rageous" [both from the *Third* album of 1970]. One American musician commented on a Ratledge score, "You guys must be affiliated to Einstein!" (Indeed, Hopper's own "Facelift," also from the *Third* album, is largely in seven.)[3]

Hard fusion and Canterbury rock differed above all in the realms of tempo and texture. Breakneck tempos were the staple of hard fusion, while Soft Machine and their followers generally preferred more sedate tempos; the later Canterbury bands tended to alternate between the two approaches. Likewise, hard fusion tended to sacrifice complex arrangements in favor of virtuosic solos, while the Canterbury bands tended to emphasize sophisticated ensemble interplay and (especially in the late 1960s and early 1970s) avant-garde electronic episodes. This is not to say that the Canterbury school produced no virtuosos. The work of keyboardists Mike Ratledge, David Sinclair, and Dave Stewart can be profitably compared and con-trasted to that of the better-known progressive rock triumverate of Keith Emerson, Rick Wakeman, and Patrick Moraz. Ratledge's work as a soloist is especially rep-resentative; heavily influenced by the later modal style of John Coltrane, his solos combine "chromatic turns and tiny melodic motifs, his alternating fast runs and long-held notes."[4] The Canterbury scene produced a world-class guitarist of con-siderable harmonic sophistication in Allan Holdsworth, an extraordinary bass gui-tarist in Hugh Hopper, and several excellent reed players, of whom Elton Dean and Jimmy Hastings are especially notable.

English progressive rock is more intimately related to jazz-rock than to any other contemporaneous genre (with the possible exception of folk-rock), since the two shared so many common stylistic tendencies. Both genres placed much emphasis on long pieces, metrical virtuosity, and lengthy solos unfolded over a repeated ostinato pattern or chord progression. Both styles prized virtuoso soloing; if any-thing, the emphasis on instrumental virtuosity in jazz-rock was even greater than in progressive rock. Both were influenced from their infancy by jazz, although the jazz influence was much stronger upon jazz-rock, which at the same time showed few of the strong classical tendencies of progressive rock. Just as progressive rock's classical elements were often interjected by keyboardists, its jazz elements were usually most evident in the music of those groups that employed a woodwind specialist: King Crimson, Gentle Giant, Van der Graaf Generator, and Jethro Tull (for instance, many of the mannerisms of Ian Anderson's flute style resulted from his emulation of jazz flautist Roland Kirk).

However, certain jazz-derived tendencies permeated the entire progressive rock movement. The syncopated rhythmic patterns of progressive rock, often used to create a sense of urgent forward momentum, belie a jazz heritage; as I noted earlier, the rhythmic syntax of progressive rock can be considered a fusion between rhythmic patterning derived from jazz and other African-American styles and metric schemes derived from European musics. The jagged melodic passages played in unison by a progressive rock band's instrumentalists—often pentatonic in outline, with prominent flatted fifths and sevenths used as passing tones—represent another borrowing from jazz. An especially influential example of this kind of passage can be found in the Mingus-like instrumental middle section of King Crimson's "21st-century Schizoid Man." Finally, among the saxophonists of some progressive rock bands (King Crimson, Van der Graaf Generator, Henry Cow) there was a distinct enthusiasm for cutting loose at key structural junctures with a torrent of jagged atonal phrases that distinctly suggest the influence of the free jazz of the early 1960s (and particularly of Ornette Coleman). Allan Moore has suggested, not unreasonably, that in some progressive rock (he specifically singles out King Crimson and Van der Graaf Generator), "The unfamiliarity of free jazz and aspects of fantasy were combined to enhance the sense of strangeness . . . the recourse to such imagery is tied to a rather 'gothic' sense of impending doom."[5]

Because of the stylistic similarities between the two styles, many progressive rock musicians went on to work in the jazz-rock field, and vice versa. After the breakup of U.K.'s original lineup, drummer Bill Bruford went on to form his own eponymous fusion group, which released three albums in the late 1970s; Dave Stewart and Allan Holdsworth, both veterans of the Canterbury scene, played prominent roles in Bruford's group, which can perhaps be considered the last of the major Canterbury-influenced bands. The three solo albums of keyboardist Patrick Moraz (Refugee, Yes, the Moody Blues) released during the late 1970s also show a distinct fusion tendency. Phil Collins (Genesis) spent his free time during the late 1970s sitting in on drums for one of Britain's leading fusion bands, Brand X, while Pink Floyd's drummer, Nick Mason, produced an album for the Anglo-Gallic outfit Gong (Brian Davison, the Nice's ex-drummer, appeared briefly with this band as well). After leaving Curved Air, Darryl Way founded the more fusion-oriented Wolf; bassist/vocalist Mike Wedgwood left Curved Air to join Caravan. The crossover occasionally worked in the opposite direction. Bassist/vocalist Richard Sinclair joined Camel after the dissolution of Hatfield and the North, while Allan Holdsworth, who established his reputation as a preeminent jazz-rock guitarist with major Canterbury bands such as Soft Machine and Gong, was a founding member of U.K. and appeared on that band's first album.

Although the intersection between progressive rock and jazz-rock styles became more evident in the late 1970s—the first U.K. album in particular illustrates this tendency—the two genres were closely related from their infancies. Indeed, when Pink Floyd and Soft Machine appeared together at London's UFO Club in 1967, it was not at all obvious that the two bands would eventually develop along different stylistic paths. Even after 1970, when progressive rock and jazz-rock began to develop in clearly different directions, there was still a considerable overlap in the audience of the two styles: the major difference in this realm is that the jazz-rock bands in general, and the Canterbury groups in particular, did not generate the huge audiences of the leading progressive rock bands. The Canterbury groups continued to play clubs and small venues long after the major progressive rock bands had begun playing arenas and stadiums, and had few of the opportunities for trans-Atlantic tours afforded to the latter bands. As one might expect, the lavish stage shows of the major progressive rock bands were totally beyond the means of the Canterbury groups. The one possible exception might be Soft Machine during their early, psychedelic phase of the late 1960s, when they hired Mark Boyle, an innovator in light show design known for his swirling liquid effects. Soft Machine took Boyle's shows across the Channel to the developing Continental venues in France (where the band was especially popular) and other locales such as Amsterdam.

Because of the stylistic and audience overlap between progressive rock and jazz-rock, some popular music commentators have gone so far as to simply categorize the two genres as part of an overarching style, "progressive music," which takes in both the "symphonic" or "classical" progressive rock of ELP, Yes, Genesis, et al., and the more jazz-based "Canterbury progressive rock" of bands such as Soft Machine. Nonetheless, I believe the classification of progressive rock and British jazz-rock fusion as two distinct styles is justified, since there are a number of major differences between the two styles. Jazz-rock de-emphasizes lyrical melody to a degree unusual even in progressive rock; likewise, there is a density to Canterbury rock, in particular, that has no parallel in progressive rock (save perhaps the music of Gentle Giant). There is a difference in harmonic syntax between the two styles; the harmony of jazz-rock is more chromatic, richer, and features many more ninth, eleventh, and thirteenth chords (often with altered notes), whereas the harmony of progressive rock is more modal, more exclusively triadic, and generally more austere.[6]

Furthermore, unlike progressive rock, jazz-rock shows few specific influences of either the classical tradition or folk music. The symphonic tone colorings of the Mellotron are virtually nonexistent in jazz-rock, and the Hammond is seldom used as a substitute pipe organ; indeed, the rich, sustained chordal backdrops that are such an important part of the progressive rock keyboard style are not usually in evidence in jazz-rock. Keyboardists of the Canterbury bands often ran the Hammond organ through a fuzz box to evoke the sound of a distorted reed instrument (Mike Ratledge, David Sinclair) or electric guitar (Dave Stewart). The acoustic piano and guitar are featured less prominently in jazz-rock than progressive rock, and archaic instruments are seldom resorted to at all; on the other hand, instruments such as the bell-like Rhodes electric piano that are relatively unimportant to progressive rock play a major role in the jazz-rock sound.

These differences in instrumentation and tone color between the two genres have led to differences in structure as well. Since it is primarily electronic, jazz-rock seldom uses the juxtaposition of acoustic and electronic passages as a structural device. Even when jazz-rock bands do utilize programmatic forms such as the multimovement suite, the radical mood shifts and sharply drawn masculine/feminine contrasts that are such a defining feature of symphonic progressive rock are usually not present. It is for this reason that the music of the fusion and Canterbury bands seldom appears to bear a cosmic message in the manner of so much symphonic progressive rock.

Related to this last point is the fact that progressive rock and jazz-rock bands feature decisively different approaches to vocals and lyrics. Although a number of the Canterbury bands did utilize vocals in their earlier stages, jazz-rock was always more instrumentally biased than progressive rock; Soft Machine had become a purely instrumental outfit by 1971, Gong by the mid-1970s. Even when English jazz-rock bands did utilize vocalists, the intricate three- and four-part vocal arrangements that were so important to many leading English progressive rock bands seldom played a role; the high, sailing vocal arrangements of Caravan are somewhat atypical of the Canterbury school in this respect (indeed, of the major Canterbury bands, Caravan were probably stylistically the closest to the symphonic progressive rock sound). Some of the Canterbury groups (i.e., Hatfield and the North with their trio of sopranos, "the Northettes") tended to use vocals mainly for coloristic qualities; significantly, lyrics were seldom printed on the album sleeves of the major Canterbury groups.

Yet another differentiating factor involves the attitudes of the bands toward their lyrics. The rather playful, tongue-in-cheek, almost Dadaist lyrics of Soft Machine's Robert Wyatt, Caravan's Richard Sinclair, or Gong's Daevid Allen can be sharply contrasted with the deadly earnestness of the lyrics of Yes, ELP, Pink Floyd, King Crimson, and their peers. The playful streak that seemed to mark so much Canterbury rock is also evident in the titles; it is hard to imagine the major symphonic progressive groups composing pieces called "The Song of McGillicudie the Pusillanimous" (Egg), "(Big) John Wayne Socks Psychology on the Jaw" (Hatfield and the North), "Puffin" and "Huffin" (a two-part piece by Soft Machine), "Hold Grandad by the Nose" (from Caravan's suite *Nine Feet Under*), or "Mummy Was an Asteroid, Daddy Was a Small Non-Stick Kitchen Utensil" (Quiet Sun). This tendency toward whimsy, leavened by a satirical streak, probably reached its apogee in Gong's magnum opus *Radio Gnome Invisible,* a three-album cycle consisting of *Flying Teapot* (1972), *Angel's Egg* (1973), and *You* (1974). To be sure, on one level, at least, composer Daevid Allen had a serious purpose: the cycle's protagonist, Zero the Hero, is depicted in his attempts to attain cosmic consciousness in spite of the temptations of materialism, cheap sex, drugs, and religious programming. Nonetheless, it is hard to conceive of the symphonic progressive bands creating a concept piece in which the protagonist is greeted upon his arrival to the planet Gong by pot-head pixies who fly through space in tea-pot shaped UFOs! (Another Canterbury science-fiction epic leavened by a streak of whimsy, National Health's "Tenemos Roads," deals with ancient civilizations on the planet Mercury.) The use of this type of humor and gentle satire by the Canterbury bands—which owes something to the harder-edged and more incisive satire of Frank Zappa's Mothers of Invention—lends their music a certain sense of irony, which further contributes to the fact that even their longest, most complex pieces rarely appear to bear a cosmic message in the manner of so much symphonic progressive rock.

Many critics who found the high-mindedness of the major symphonic progressive bands insufferable rather enjoyed the more sedate, playful virtuosity of the Canterbury bands. Furthermore, there is no doubt that this style, with its dense textures, complex arrangements, arcane chord voicings, and attention to compositional artifice, was a connoiseur's music in the best sense of the word. English jazz-rock remained fresh two or three years longer than the symphonic progressive style; bands such as Brand X, National Health, and Bruford continued to release inventive, energetic recordings into the late 1970s and early 1980s, well after bands such as ELP, Yes, and Genesis had passed their creative peak. (In this vein, it is interesting to note that the original lineup of U.K. broke up because Bill Bruford and Allan Holdsworth wanted to take the band further in a jazz-rock direction, while John Wetton and Eddie Jobson wanted to return to a more traditional progressive rock framework.)[7] On the other hand, the music of bands like Yes, Genesis, and Pink Floyd contains certain key elements which jazz-rock largely lacked: hummable melodies, lush arrangements in which the "sweet" pairing of Mellotron (or subdued Hammond) and acoustic guitar play a major role, dramatic climaxes, and above all a strong emphasis on vocals. It was these elements that assured the commercial ascendency of progressive rock, and the lack thereof that consigned the vast majority of the Canterbury and fusion bands to cult status.

English Folk-rock

English folk-rock of the late 1960s and 1970s grew directly out of the folk music revival of the 1950s and 1960s. The guiding principles of the genre were twofold: to introduce electric instruments into the framework of traditional English folk music and (more rarely) other types of early music such as medieval and renaissance art music, and to produce a body of original music that reflected the heritage of folk song while drawing on contemporary instrumentation. The major proponents of the genre included the Incredible String Band, the Pentangle, Fairport Convention, Steeleye Span, the Strawbs, and Lindisfarne.

The most obvious connection between English folk-rock and English progressive rock is the juxtaposition of electric and acoustic instrumentation, although folk-rock groups never used electronics, especially electronic keyboards, to any-thing near the degree of contemporaneous progressive rock bands. Another con-nection between the two styles is the use of the electric/acoustic dichotomy as a means of variety, although this dichotomy is not often used structurally by folk-rock bands, nor does it seem to have the symbolic resonance in folk-rock that it does in progressive rock. Because of these similarities, even progressive rock bands that were influenced by folk and early music mainly on a subliminal level (Genesis, Yes, ELP) can sometimes sound similar to English folk-rock groups in their more meditative, pastoral acoustic passages.

A more specific relationship is evident between progressive rock bands that were directly influenced by art music of the English Middle Ages and Renaissance (mainly Jethro Tull and Gentle Giant) and English folk-rock groups that shared this interest such as Steeleye Span and Gryphon, a band that prominently featured krummhorns, recorders, harpsichords, and other archaic instruments. The influ-ence of medieval and renaissance music is evident not only in the use of archaic instruments, but also in the madrigal-like a capella vocal passages to which these groups sometimes resorted (i.e., the vocal arrangements of Jethro Tull's "Songs from the Woods," Gentle Giant's "On Reflection," and Steeleye Span's "Gau-dete").[8] Jethro Tull's Ian Anderson produced Steeleye Span's *Now We Are Six* LP; indeed, Anderson's reedy, nasal vocal delivery is far more suggestive of folk-rock vocal techniques than of the open, straight head tone favored by most other pro-gressive rock lead vocalists.[9] The strain of medievalist rock hinted at in some of the music of Steeleye Span, Gentle Giant, and especially Gryphon during the 1970s was further developed in the 1980s by bands such as Dead Can Dance.

Female singers featured much more prominently in the folk music revival of the early 1960s than in any genre of contemporaneous rock; one thinks immediately of Joan Baez, Judy Collins, and Mary Travers of Peter, Paul, and Mary. This trend continues with English folk-rock of the 1970s, which prominently featured so-pranos such as Sandy Denny (Fairport Convention), Jacqui McShee (the Pentan-gle), and Maddy Prior (Steeleye Span). There were of course a few well-known female singers in progressive rock as well, especially Renaissance's Annie Haslam, Curved Air's Sonja Kristina, and Henry Cow's Dagmar Krause (there is in fact a strong hint of folk-rock in much of Renaissance's music, created equally by Has-lam's clear, high soprano and by the band's largely acoustic instrumentation).

Nonetheless, progressive rock remained largely a male affair. It is perhaps ap-propriate at this time to speculate why this would have been so, since the pro-gressive rock style is based on masculine/feminine musical contrasts in a way that heavy metal and hard rock are not, and lacks the inherent sexism of these latter styles. There seems to be several interrelated reasons. First, the English rock culture of the 1960s and 1970s was largely a male affair. Women were present, but usually behind the scenes—as wives, girlfriends, or groupies (that is, sexual vassals for the musicians)—rather than as musicians, roadies, technicians, managers, engineers, or producers. This, in turn, would seem to stem from the fact that rock has a strong technological element, and technology has traditionally been considered the domain of men; women have been socially conditioned to steer clear of it, although in the past few years this seems to be changing.

Furthermore, as early as 1950 David Riesman pointed out that the audience for bebop and other more arcane forms of jazz that involve a considerable amount of virtuosity and complexity was overwhelmingly male.[10] While the major progressive rock bands may have had somewhat more of a female audience than this—especially those that emphasized vocal harmony and contained more of a pop element—the general pattern of virtuosic music being a largely male affair seems to have held. (Interestingly, John Wetton has described progressive rock's fondness for virtuosic metric shifts as being "rather like acne; it flourishes when you are immature, and bursts out with testosterone . . . but soon you will grow out of it.")[11] Playing an instrument yourself seems to be a prerequisite for a deep appreciation of virtuosity; since in rock playing an instrument usually involves an acquaintance with technology, it becomes easier to see why progressive rock's following was largely male, and also why there were extraordinarily few female instrumentalists of note in rock during the 1960s and 1970s. (Mireille Bauer, mallet percussionist for the late 1970s incarnation of Gong, is one of the few female instrumentalists I am aware of that made it to core-member status in a band.) It appears to me that there may have been more female audience participation in the early days of progressive rock, before it moved out of clubs and small venues into arenas and stadiums; however, I have no hard statistical data to back this assertion up, and I must leave it at the level of a hypothesis.[12]

English Heavy Metal

At first it might seem that two styles could not be any more different than progressive rock and heavy metal. The apparent simplicity of heavy metal (although as Rob Walser has pointed out in his recent study, this simplicity is often more apparent than real) stands in stark contrast to the surface complexity of progressive rock. The subject matter of the two styles' lyrics is totally different; as I suggested earlier, progressive rock developed the Apollonian aspect of counter-cultural thinking, heavy metal the Dionysian aspect. The Aquarian optimism of at least some progressive rock bands is in sharp contrast to the nihilism of heavy metal bands such as Black Sabbath. The two styles originated in different geographical regions of England; progressive rock arose in southeast England, heavy metal in the industrial heartland (especially around Birmingham). Furthermore, English progressive rock musicians were usually of middle-class, even upper-middle-class background; while heavy metal musicians were often of working-class origin; this was a point Chris Welch developed at considerable length in his biography of Black Sabbath.[13]

That most incorrigible of heavy metal icons, Ozzy Osbourne, probably spoke for a good number of heavy metal fans in his assessment of progressive rock:

> I just can't stand to see a band on stage trying to baffle the audience. I've been to the Marquee and seen groups and they're just playing bollocks man, complete and utter rubbish. And the kids, you can see them looking and thinking, "Wow man, I don't dig this, but it must be good." . . . If you can stamp your feet to it and nod your head, it's good as far as I'm concerned. It's good old rock'n'roll and God bless it man because that's what it's all about for me.[14]

There was certainly less overlap between progressive rock and heavy metal audiences in England than was the case for the genres discussed earlier, at least in part because the distinctions in class and geographical origin mentioned above suggest that the styles appealed to rather different taste publics. There was, however, a considerably greater overlap among American audiences—both styles were very popular in the Midwest—with results that will be discussed more fully in the next chapters.

Because of these differences, one might suspect that the two styles shared no common ground; in the case of Black Sabbath, the English heavy metal band that exerted the most long-term influence on the development of the genre, this assumption is largely true.[15] However, there are connections between progressive rock and the other two major English heavy metal bands of the 1970s, Deep Purple and Led Zeppelin, which deserve further exploration.

Deep Purple began as a psychedelic band that during the late 1960s showed considerable affinity to the style of Cream and Hendrix. With the release of *Concerto for Orchestra* (performed by the band in conjunction with the London Symphony Orchestra) in 1970, composed by the band's organist Jon Lord, it appeared as if the group were about to enter the same territory as the Nice and Pink Floyd, who had also released albums containing a multimovement suite for rock band and orchestra in 1970. However, with their *Machine Head* album of 1971 Deep Purple appropriated the major elements of the "classic" heavy metal sound which had recently been pioneered by Led Zeppelin and Black Sabbath. One encounters the familiar loud, distorted guitars (Lord also ran his Hammond organ through a fuzz box to suggest the sound of an electric guitar); repetitive rhythm guitar riffs, two- or four-bar melodic/rhythmic formulas (often consisting of so-called "power chords," open fourths or fifths, rather than full triads) in between and sometimes during vocal verses; and very simple metric schemes, almost always in four. Most characteristically of all, there is the shudderingly powerful beat, iterated by the bass guitar and bass drum, that shows few traces of the boogie or shuffle rhythms that had characterized the music of earlier hard rock bands such as the Rolling Stones.[16] Later albums by the band showed an increasingly tenuous connection with the progressive rock style. However, during the early 1970s bands such as Argent and Uriah Heep carried on the progressive rock/heavy metal fusion suggested in Deep Purple's early music, combining hard rock's heavy beat and prominent guitar riffs with progressive rock's rich vocal arrangements and "churchy" Hammond organ parts. Argent in particular, spearheaded by Rod Argent's virtuosic flourishes on the Hammond, often came very close to the "classic" progressive rock sound on their later albums such as *Nexus* (1974) and *Circus* (1975). The main difference between Argent and bands such as Yes or Genesis is that Argent maintained a much closer link to the British blues-rock tradition of the 1960s.

Of the three major English heavy metal bands of the 1970s, it is the connection between Led Zeppelin and progressive rock that is the most complex—and ultimately the most interesting. Although this band is generally credited with founding the heavy metal style, throughout their existence they produced a body of music that cannot be categorized as "classic" heavy metal in either style or substance. Thus the band's two best-known songs, "Stairway to Heaven" and "Kashmir," are lengthy epics which address the topic of the spiritual quest, a subject that was of great importance to progressive rock but of no special interest to heavy metal. Two other well-known songs by Led Zeppelin, "The Battle of Evermore" and "Achilles' Last Stand," treat the mythological subject matter so beloved by progressive rock musicians. The prominent use of acoustic instruments in some of their songs ("The Battle of Evermore," for instance, is entirely acoustic) falls outside heavy metal conventions and suggests English folk-rock. The structural approach of "Stairway" and several other songs, in which electric instruments and ultimately the rhythm section are gradually layered in over an acoustic background to create a grandiose climax, is also far more reminiscent of progressive rock than heavy metal. Finally, the intricate metrical schemes of certain songs (the alternations of $\frac{5}{8}$ and $\frac{6}{8}$ in "Four Sticks," the daunting shifts between bars of five, four, and two in "Black Dog") suggest a progressive rock influence. As will be seen, during the late 1970s a whole new genre—stadium rock, or corporate rock, as it was often derisively called—resulted from the fusion of stylistic tendencies derived from progressive rock with ideas drawn from Led Zeppelin's "eclectic" heavy metal. (On the other hand, the "hard core" heavy metal bands of the late 1970s such as Iron Maiden, Judas Priest, and AC/DC drew much more exclusively on Black Sabbath's "primitivist" strain of heavy metal.)

Minimalism

Minimalism is probably the most significant style of art music to emerge during the second half of the twentieth century. It emerged at roughly the same time as psychedelic music, during the mid-1960s. Its originators were young composers who were consciously rebelling against the complexity and icy abstractness of contemporary avant-garde styles such as the total serialism of the 1950s or the aleatoric (chance) music of the 1960s. As a style, minimalism is characterized by the use of ostinato networks—that is, several interlocking melodic patterns, usually modal—that are repeated over and over again with gradual, undramatic changes. The resulting harmonic progressions are simple and essentially consonant; there are few cadences. The rhythmic patterns are usually highly charged and energetic, reflecting the influence of African-American styles, especially jazz. An even clearer nod in the direction of African-American music was the increased unwillingness of a composer like Terry Riley to notate his music, and the correspondingly increased reliance on improvisation. The major minimalist composers—Steve Reich, Philip Glass, Terry Riley, LaMonte Young—undertook a systematic study of specific world musics, especially Indian classical music. Not surprisingly, the overall structural conception of their pieces, which are often very long, emphasize ideals more generally associated with Eastern than with Western musics—gradual, undramatic change, and an emphasis on musical elements such as overtones that normally go unnoticed in music where harmonic and melodic changes occur more quickly.

Progressive rock audiences often overlapped with audiences for American minimalism, which has had by far the largest audience of any art music style originating in the second half of the twentieth century;[17] it is perhaps surprising, then, that the two styles have not interpenetrated more than they have. There are isolated progressive rock passages that bear an almost uncanny resemblance to contemporaneous minimalist pieces. The opening of Van der Graaf Generator's "Lost" (1970) resembles the busy, woodwind-dominated ostinato networks often used by Philip Glass in his music of the 1970s; the superimposed ostinato patterns and asymmetrical meters of ELP's "Infinite Space" (1971) suggest a slowed-down version of Steve Reich's *Octet* (1978).

For the most part, however, the two styles remained clearly separated. Both styles were monumental, but minimalism was above all a meditative music, a music that focused narrowly on a deep channel of experience; the greatest achievement of the minimalists was to create structural approaches that successfully capture psychedelia's acid-induced sense of timelessness.[18] While progressive rock did of course prominently feature meditative passages as well, the foundation of the style rests on sudden shifts between acoustic and electric instrumentation, between rock- and classically-oriented rhythmic conceptions, between simple/consonant and complex/dissonant harmonies. In short, progressive rock was a dramatic (and an eclectic) style in a sense minimalism never set out to be.

A more intimate connection can be seen between the electronic minimalism of Terry Riley and the English jazz-rock of the Canterbury school. Daevid Allen, who was involved in early incarnations of both Soft Machine and Gong, worked with Riley in Paris in the mid-1960s, and introduced Riley's use of tape loops and electronic drones to other members of the early Canterbury school. Quite frequently, these bands juxtapose meditative minimalist passages with more straight-ahead jazz-rock sections: for instance, the opening of Soft Machine's "Out-Bloody-Rageous" (1970), with its plethora of rhythmically charged electronic organ ostinati that writhe and overlap each other in ever-changing patterns, is strongly reminiscent of Riley's almost contemporaneous *Rainbow in Curved Air*. Riley's influence remains discernible in mid-period Soft Machine (i.e., "French Lesson" from Soft Machine's *Seventh*), and is also apparent in the work of various Soft Machine alumni (Hugh Hopper's *1984*) and in the spacey synthesizer passages of Gong during their early 1970s incarnation ("A Sprinkling of Clouds" from *You*).

The musicians who did the most in establishing a rapport between minimalism and progressive rock were Brian Eno and Robert Fripp. Their two collaborative albums, *No Pussyfooting* (1972) and *Evening Star* (1975), largely created minimalist rock. Significantly, Fripp's work in this context had little discernible influence on the 1970s incarnation of King Crimson, even though he was involved in the two projects simultaneously. In these two albums, Eno drew on the tape loop technique developed by Terry Riley and Steve Reich: short melodic fragments and drones (for the most part played by Fripp on electric guitar) are looped over each other continuously, so that even as some patterns disappear into the aural background, new ones are introduced. The overall result is the same kind of slowly evolving soundscape that is apparent in the music of the minimalists. After King Crimson broke up in 1974, Fripp undertook a solo tour in which he performed this kind of music, which he dubbed "Frippertronics."

Another group that deserves mention in this context is Jade Warrior. This band started out as another English progressive rock group in the mold of King Crimson, but already on their *Last Autumn's Dream* LP of 1972 certain tracks ("Obedience") suggest a rock minimalism analogous to Fripp's and Eno's. By the mid-1970s the music of this band had become almost entirely instrumental; by frequently de-emphasizing the rhythm section and drawing minimalist, ethnic (especially Chinese), and cool jazz sources into a progressive rock framework, Jade Warrior created a distinctive sound—sometimes acoustic, sometimes electric—that presages the New Age style of the 1980s by nearly a decade. The music of Jade Warrior, Mike Oldfield (whose Terry Riley–influenced *Tubular Bells* LP of 1973 was a surprise hit, reaching number three in the U.S. charts), and the seminal German group Popol Vuh (named after the Mayan sacred text) points up the consistent, if often tangential relationship between progressive rock, minimalism, and New Age styles. It is significant that two well-known progressive rock keyboardists, Rick Wakeman of Yes and Eddie Jobson of U.K., went on to become prominent New Age performers during the 1980s after their groups broke up.

Avant-garde Electronic Music

I have pointed out that there was a great deal of interest in electronic music among the practicioners of psychedelic music of the 1966–1970 period. It is not surprising, then, that much interest was generated in the electronic art music of the 1950s of composers such as Edgar Varèse (who was lionized by American guitarist/bandleader Frank Zappa) and Karlheinz Stockhausen (who appeared on the cover of the Beatles' *Sergeant Pepper* album, and whose *Gesang der Jünglinge* of 1956 remains a classic of early electronic music).

More than any other form of twentieth-century music, the electronic music of composers such as Varèse and Stockhausen has exemplified the term "avant-garde," with traditional musical elements such as melody, harmony, and even rhythm being abandoned in favor of sound's purely coloristic qualities. Electronic music of this sort—which may be constructed from both electronically generated sounds and electronically altered natural sounds—is characterized by pulsating, buzzing, and wooshing noises which would not be considered "musical" by any traditional standards. This sonic material is often superimposed to create complex sound "collages" in which several layers or planes of seemingly unrelated sonic events are unfolded simultaneously.

The band that most fully explored this avant-garde electronic heritage was Pink Floyd. The group's organist, Rick Wright, in particular acknowledged the influence of Stockhausen;[19] the band's early use of quadrophonic sound in their concerts suggests a conscious emulation of the attempt to surround an audience with sound undertaken by Varèse, whose landmark *Poème électronique* was presented through four hundred loudspeakers at the 1958 Brussels World Fair. However, progressive rock was at its essence too much of a dramatic idiom to be overly influenced by the abstractness of experimental electronic music, and even at the height of the psychedelic era Pink Floyd carefully alternated experimental electronic passages with a largely acoustic, modal ballad style. After *Atom Heart Mother* (1970), which integrated their electronic experimentation into the framework of symphonic rock, Pink Floyd pursued electronic effects less and less for experimental reasons, but used them more sparingly, often to further emphasize the thematic content of their songs (thus the machine-like effects of "Welcome to the Machine," the jingling cash registers at the opening of "Money," the chiming of clocks at the beginning of "Time"). Several of the early Canterbury bands, especially Soft Machine, Matching Mole, and Egg, also evinced a strong interest in avant-garde electronics, even if not quite to the degree of Pink Floyd. Like Pink Floyd, though, these bands gradually abandoned their electronic experimentation during the early 1970s, as the Canterbury style grew increasingly close to mainstream fusion.

Perhaps the most surprising aspect of the mass appearance of synthesizers among progressive rock bands during the early 1970s is that they were used mainly as a souped-up organ or as an orchestral substitute. The most adventurous electronic experimentation in English rock music had already taken place by 1970, before the mass availability of synthesizers; as suggested above, after synthesizers did become common, electronic effects were used increasingly sparingly, and usually to emphasize the thematic content of a piece. After 1970, electronic experimentation was taken up in earnest mainly by German electronic rock bands such as Tangerine Dream and Kraftwerk; these groups entirely dispensed with both acoustic instruments and with the rock rhythm section of bass guitar and drums, with all members playing synthesizers. Tangerine Dream's sound, in particular, often comes very close to that of electronic "art" music; the "rock" element is supplied above all by the band's characteristic use of sequencers to create throbbing, repetitive bass lines.

Indeed, the 1970s witnessed the confluence of a number of sources into a style that eventually came to be termed electronic New Age or simply electronic music. In music of this type one encounters the influence of minimalism (both the rhythmically charged minimalism of the Riley/Reich school and the more motionless, atmospheric minimalism of the Eno/Fripp collaborations); the abstract sound collages of early pioneers of electronic music such as Varèse, Stockhausen, and Pierre Henry; and on occasion certain devices drawn from progressive rock, such as complex metrical episodes, sudden shifts in mood, and gradual buildups to huge climaxes. Tangerine Dream and its various alumni, often referred to collectively as the "Berlin school," were especially notable proponents of this style; at their peak during the mid-1970s on albums like *Rubycon* (1975), Tangerine Dream pioneered a sound that was at once meditative and intense, pastoral and futuristic. Other notable practicioners of this style during the 1970s included the Greek synthesist Vangelis (a.k.a. Evangelos Papathanassiou) and the French synthesist Jean-Michel Jarre, whose music fused elements of the progressive rock style with the more atmospheric and cosmic electronics of the Berlin school, and two lesser-known French keyboardists/guitarists, Didier Bocquet and Richard Pinhas (the latter's *Iceland* of 1979 is an especially fine example of the style). In the 1980s and 1990s new figures such as Steve Roach have become prominent purveyors of the electronic style, which in recent years has often been termed "electronic New Age"; a number of veterans of the 1970s scene have remained active in this field as well.

Brian Eno has remained an especially important figure, pioneering a style in pieces such as *Music for Airports, Discreet Music,* and *Thursday Afternoon* which he has labeled "ambient music." Eno's ambient music is often created for particular times and situations; his intention is that these pieces should function as tapestries, large-scale, nonintrusive atmospheres which lend a consistent mood to the environments in which they are heard. The ambient style is even-textured, spacious, and contemplative; several musical events appear and recur more or less regularly, but in ever-changing permutations. Eno's ambient music, at once tranquil and extraordinarily subtle, suggests that the development of a plethora of related electronic instrumental styles is far from being played out.

Postscript

What stands out in an examination of progressive rock's relationship with contemporaneous musical styles is above all its eclecticism: there was probably no other musical style during the 1970s that drew on so many diverse sources. This, in turn, gave progressive rock one of the most diverse audiences of any 1970s style. Listeners with an interest in contemporary "art music" styles such as minimalism and avant-garde electronic music were often drawn to progressive rock, even if they had little interest in other rock styles. Likewise, jazz enthusiasts who disdained hard rock were often drawn to progressive rock because of its obvious parallels with fusion; during the mid-1970s Keith Emerson repeatedly placed near the top of *Downbeat*'s yearly poll for best organist, even though the journal's readership was overwhelmingly jazz-oriented (furthermore, Emerson's influence on fusion keyboardists such as Chick Corea at this time was undeniable). Heavy metal audiences seldom listened to folk-rock, and vice versa; there were sizable segments of both audiences, however, who showed more than a passing interest in progressive rock. In this sense, then, progressive rock was not only musically, but also sociologically, at the nexus of popular music culture between the early and mid-1970s. This is a point I will examine at greater length in the next chapter, when I explore the sociology of progressive rock.

A Sociology of Progressive Rock

The leading lights of Pink Floyd never could (or did) pretend to be "working-class heroes." Their backgrounds were strictly white-collar, their parents downright distinguished.[1]

In terms of their social backgrounds, the members of Pink Floyd were fairly representative of English progressive rock musicians as a whole. Progressive rock was never a working-class style, and progressive rock musicians never set out to be working-class heroes. To the contrary, progressive rock—especially in its early stages—was the vital expression of a bohemian, middle-class intelligentsia. By considering the contribution of the colleges, universities, and the Anglican Church to the formation of progressive rock, I will show how the style perfectly reflects its origins in an intellectual, southeastern English youth-based subculture; as I will argue, it could have hardly developed elsewhere. Nonetheless, English progressive rock would have achieved only a fraction of its ultimate success had it not found massive commercial acceptance in the United States. A substantial portion of this chapter is therefore spent examining the reception of progressive rock not only by its original audience, English hippies, but also by the large, youth-based American taste public which made the style a substantial commercial phenomenon between the early and mid-1970s. I will also consider the social significance of progressive rock's classical/rock fusion by examining its compositional methods, which unite African-American music's allowance for spontaneity and individual expression with European classical music's potential for large-scale organization and expansion.

The Musicians

Most popular music studies tend to be more sociologically than musicologically oriented, and to categorize and describe particular styles largely through a demographic assessment of its audiences. I do not question the validity of this approach, and indeed I draw on it myself. I believe it is an important tool in determining the social significance of a given musical style, and it has been a key element in many major studies of popular music as subcultural expression. However, I feel that too often the backgrounds of the musicians themselves tend to be ignored; I suspect this stems from the premise (which I feel is mistaken) underlying many sociological studies of popular music that musicians are merely passive conduits of social tensions. Therefore, before I examine the reception of progressive rock by its English and American audiences, I will undertake a demographic assessment of the musicians themselves. I believe this is particularly important because during the style's formative period, the musicians and their audience shared a common social background. Illuminating progressive rock's social origins—its emergence in southern England, its ties with solidly middle-class institutions such as the universities and the Anglican Church—will go a long way in clarifying its ultimate cultural significance.

In his seminal study *Albion's Seed: Four British Folkways in America,* David Hackett Fischer recognizes four distinct cultural regions in England. The first, the east of England, stretches from Norfolk south to Essex and includes eastern Cambridgeshire and Lincolnshire. The second, the south of England, takes in the area from Kent west to Dorset and north to Warwickshire. The third area, the north Midlands, includes a broad belt of territory from Cheshire and Derbyshire north through Yorkshire. The fourth area, the Border Region, takes in England's northernmost counties along the Scottish border.

Progressive rock has been a phenomenon mainly of southern England. Most of the major progressive rock bands of the 1970s formed here (as did the bulk of the prominent neo-progressive bands of the 1980s); many major progressive rock musicians were born in this region (for the most part between 1942 and 1950), and even those who were born in other regions of the United Kingdom were often raised here. The members of bands such as Yes and Genesis hail largely from the London/Kent/Surrey area; King Crimson and Gentle Giant are south-coast bands, hailing from Bournemouth and Portsmouth, respectively; Pink Floyd has contained members from both London and the ancient university town of Cambridge; the entire Canterbury school originated in one of England's most venerable and historic cities, in the county of Kent. Of the major progressive rock bands of the late 1960s and 1970s, only the Moody Blues (based in Birmingham in the industrial Midlands) and Jethro Tull (formed in Blackpool on the northwest coast) came from outside of southeast England.

Even those bands formed outside this area, however, ended up in London and its environs, since this was the hub of the English counterculture during the late 1960s; many of these groups launched their careers from a few specific clubs in London such as the UFO Club, the Middle Earth, and the Marquee that were important countercultural haunts during this period. Thus in 1967 one could hear

Pink Floyd, Soft Machine, and Procol Harum play at the UFO Club; during the same year Pink Floyd and the Nice regularly played at the Marquee, the same club that Yes played at throughout 1969.[2] Of course, many of the bands that played at these clubs folded before they achieved real commercial success; however, even these bands often contained musicians that eventually landed in better-known progressive rock groups. For instance, The Crazy World of Arthur Brown, a group that frequently performed at the UFO Club in 1967, included drummer Carl Palmer, later of ELP; the band Tomorrow, which performed at the same club at the same time, included Steve Howe, later of Yes. By the end of the 1960s, certain clubs outside of London became important countercultural haunts as well; for instance, in 1969 and 1970 one could see a number of bands that later achieved prominence as part of progressive rock's "second wave"—King Crimson, Van der Graaf Generator, Genesis, Renaissance—perform at the Friars Club in Aylesbury, near Oxford.

Even in the late 1960s, clubs were not the only possible performance site for the early progressive rock bands. Many of these bands also performed at somewhat larger venues in London such as the Royal Albert Hall, the Rainbow Theater, and the Lyceum, a converted ballroom. Open-air festivals featuring a number of acts could also be an important means of recognition; ELP were catapulted to stardom as a result of their performance at the Isle of Wight Festival in August 1970, while the free concerts at Hyde Park, begun in 1968, brought sudden prominence to King Crimson and Jethro Tull.[3] Both the midsized venues and the open-air festivals remained viable performance forums throughout the 1970s. However, after 1970 the club circuit rapidly declined in importance as a feasible revenue-generating source; the major progressive rock bands moved into arena and stadiums (increasingly in the United States rather than Britain), and the rift between the musicians and the subcultural milieu from which they originated began to widen.

Remarkably few musicians from outside of England participated in the English progressive rock movement during its heyday. The only major participant in the English progressive rock scene born in Continental Europe was Swiss keyboardist Patrick Moraz, and virtually no American musicians participated in the English scene until the late 1970s. Significantly, Moraz lasted for only one album with Yes; some of his bandmates believed that as a foreigner, he really didn't grasp the essence of their music.[4]

Indeed, it is likely that one of the reasons English progressive rock developed such a definite sonic code is that these musicians almost seem to have formed a guild among themselves. Many of them played in at least two major progressive rock bands; some played in three or four, while Bill Bruford played in five (Yes, King Crimson, National Health, Genesis, and U.K.), not counting his own eponymous fusion band of the late 1970s. Bandmembers frequently sat in as guest artists on other groups' albums as well; for instance, Jon Anderson of Yes sang on part of King Crimson's *Lizard*, and King Crimson's Robert Fripp sat in as guest guitarist on Van der Graaf Generator's *H to He Who Am the Only One* and *Pawn Hearts*. It was also very common for progressive rock musicians to sit in on each other's solo albums. The Canterbury rock scene represented, if anything, an even tighter "guild" than the symphonic progressive rock scene, although (as was seen in chapter 6) there was a good deal of interaction between the musicians of these two "schools."

Why did progressive rock develop in southern England rather than another part of Britain or, for that matter, the United States? I submit that the answer can be found in the peculiar cultural, historical, and social background of this region. First of all, it is fair to say that the south and east of England are more professional and white-collar, while central and northern England are more working-class and blue-collar.[5] Obviously, a style like progressive rock, with its references not only to classical music but also to the art and literature of high culture, was not going to spring from a working-class environ. Its emergence depended on a subculture of highly educated young people.

Furthermore, there are at least two cultural factors at work in southern England which made it a logical birthplace of progressive rock. As Fischer points out in *Albion's Seed*, this region has historically been the most staunchly Anglican of any part of England, and the region of England where distinctions between the social classes have been the most overt.[6] As I will show below, the long shadow cast by the Anglican Church in this region had a very real impact on the development of progressive rock as a musical style. So, too, did the traditional class distinctions of this region, which dictated a strong exposure to high culture in the educations of middle-class youth. The most important education institution for earlier English rock musicians (e.g., members of the Beatles, the Rolling Stones, the Who) had been the art school, an institution designed to help working-class students escape a working-class future.[7] Few progressive rock musicians attended art school; few needed to. To the contrary, it is rather astonishing how many of these bands were formed at institutions of higher learning.

Throughout the late 1960s and early 1970s, college and university campuses were just as important as clubs in serving as a creative cauldron for English progressive rock. Van der Graaf Generator formed at Manchester University; Henry Cow coalesced at Cambridge University; Pink Floyd was formed by a group of architectural students at Regent Street Polytechnic; Genesis came together at the exclusive Charterhouse public school; and Robert Fripp and John Wetton, who later cofounded the influential 1972–1974 lineup of King Crimson, met at Bournemouth College. Ian McDonald illuminates the highly literate nature of the late 1960s Canterbury underground:

> It's all pretty idyllic in retrospect: visiting each other's houses (but mostly congregating at the fifteen-room Georgian mansion owned by Robert [Wyatt's] mother) to play the new jazz albums—Mingus, Coleman, Monk and Taylor—

and to enthuse over contemporary mainstreamers (Luigi Nono, Stockhausen), painters (Mark Rothko, Jackson Pollock), and writers (Burroughs, and the Beats).[8]

Of course, there are a few progressive rock musicians who do hail from working-class backgrounds: Yes's Jon Anderson, progressive rock's master of cosmic soliloquy, was raised in a coal-mining town in northern England. The bulk of progressive rock musicians, however, came from families in which some sort of post-secondary education was to be expected. Few of these musicians actually completed their college or university educations, though; as members of the counterculture, they believed that pursuing a career as a rock musician was a far more authentic and ultimately "honorable" option than entering the nine-to-five world of "straight" society. Thus, in addition to all the bands mentioned above whose members never graduated, Bill Bruford dropped out of Leeds University; Tony Banks (Genesis) abandoned Sussex University; Tony Kaye and Rick Wakeman (keyboardists in different incarnations of Yes) dropped out of the Royal Academy of Music at different stages of their programs, as did Francis Monkman (Curved Air); Steve Hillage (Gong) fled Kent University after a year; and Matthew Fisher (Procol Harum) left the Guildhall School of Music. However, a few actually did graduate. Kerry Minnear of Gentle Giant received a degree in composition from the Royal Academy of Music; Karl Jenkins (Soft Machine) received a Bachelor of Music Degree from University College, Cardiff; Patrick Moraz took a degree in economics from Geneva University; and Mike Ratledge took an honors degree in philosophy and psychology from Oxford University.

There is no doubt that the educational backgrounds of English progressive rock musicians as a group go a long way in explaining their familiarity with the European classical repertoire, without which progressive rock would not have developed. They would have become acquainted with the music both by virtue of their class background—classical music has always played a more important role in the lives of European middle classes than that of their American counterparts—and because of the considerable training in classical music they often received. Even those that did not go on to music schools often studied privately for a number of years, sometimes with well-known teachers. As Greg Lake of ELP once commented, it was as natural for these musicians to draw on their European classical heritage as it was for American popular musicians to draw on their native blues, jazz, and gospel heritage.[9]

To be sure, English rock musicians had a profound respect for African-American jazz and blues musicians. Dick Heckstall-Smith (saxophonist for the Graham Bond Organization and later for the seminal jazz-rock outfit Colosseum) stated that English popular musicians of the 1960s "wished above all to *be* black; as a result, they took the only road open to them and tried to play black music. . . . Throughout my life as a jazz musician I've had people—mostly white, come to think of it, but not always—come up to me and pay the compliment of saying I play like a black. . . . Mostly I take it as it's meant, as a simple, high compliment.[10]

Nonetheless, the Rolling Stones were probably the last major English band of the 1960s that did not self-consciously strive to draw something of their own cultural heritage into their music. For those musicians who by virtue of upbringing and class background had become familiar with classical music, the classical/rock fusion of the progressive rock style made perfect cultural sense. Thus John Wetton has remarked,

> I'm basically European, and my background comes from classical music, which is itself very geometric. I think where we're lucky in Britain is that we stand between the two continents: we have the sort of American R&B blues music influence and we have a couple of thousand years of classical music on the other side as well. And that's where the Beatles came in—they just melted the two into one. They took American R&B, which is very plain and simple, and put European melodies and harmonies on top of it. And it's fantastic. All the late 60s bands really came in the wake of the Beatles. They just extended what the Beatles had been doing: Pink Floyd, Yes, Genesis, you name it. They were a little bit heavier, but the taste was that of the American audience.[11]

Keith Emerson makes a similar point in acknowledging the influence of both African-American and European sources on his music:

> British rock-and-roll was created out of American black soul music, and the Beatles were the first to use that for their style. My interests too, at the very beginning, revolved around listening to a lot of Blue Note recordings, Miles Davis. I decided to use the European influence, but using the jazz mentality of improvisation to try to enhance these pieces.[12]

Another powerful cultural agent in the formation of the progressive rock style was the Anglican Church. I believe if one wants to understand why the progressive rock style arose in England rather than the United States, one need look no farther than the obvious influence the Anglican choral tradition exerted on the genre. Many progressive rock musicians attended the Anglican Church as youths; quite a few of them served as church musicians. John Wetton states that his first musical experience was assisting his elder brother, a choirmaster and organist.[13] Chris Squire, Yes's bassist and backing vocalist, was a choirboy in the St. Andrew's Cathedral Choir under the direction of Barry Rose;[14] Peter Gabriel, lead singer of Genesis until 1975, was also a choirboy during his teens.[15] After his arrival in England, Patrick Moraz worked as an organist for a church in the Bournemouth area.[16] Mike Ratledge of Soft Machine studied organ with the organist of the Canterbury Cathedral.[17] Robert Fripp of King Crimson often cites Anglican choral music, specifically the anthems of the seventeenth-century composer Orlando Gibbons, as a major influence;[18] Keith Emerson has also alluded to an Anglican background in interviews.[19] Although Peter Hammill is more unusual in that he hails from a Catholic rather than an Anglican background (he attended a Jesuit public school as a youth), he also has admitted to being influenced by the choral music of English renaissance masters such as Thomas Tallis, who composed music for both the Anglican and Catholic churches.[20]

Jim Curtis has gone so far as to say that English progressive rock represents a "secularization" of Anglican (and maybe Catholic) church music in much the same way that American rhythm-and-blues secularizes black gospel music.[21] While this supposition may push matters just a bit—it is not likely that the worldview of English progressive rock musicians was shaped by the Anglican Church to the degree that black and white Pentecostal churches shaped the worldview of American R&B musicians[22]—there is no doubt that the Anglican liturgical experience made a profound and lasting impression on a number of future progressive rock musicians. Chris Squire comments that "the actual understanding of, and spiritual feeling towards, music that I got from that [i.e., serving as a choirboy at St. Andrew's] is something that's stayed with me."[23] Peter Gabriel comments that "hymns used to be the only musical moment at Charterhouse. . . . [T]he organ in Chapel was magnificent and the playing was great . . . excellent. Everyone would stand up and scream their heads off. It would be as moving as a Negro spiritual. It was really emotional, and people would come out of Chapel feeling like they were on top of the world."[24] Peter Hammill has also admitted to being influenced by the Church's sense of ritual.[25] It is not at all unreasonable to suppose that some of the most notable aspects of the progressive rock sound—modal harmony, the emphasis on "pipe organish" sonorities and quasi-choral vocal arrangements, the fondness for pure head tones and tempered singing—stem at least in part from the influence of Anglican Church music.

James Lincoln Collier, in his survey of the history of jazz, notes a pattern whereby a genre of popular music is created by working-class black musicians, eventually reaches a certain level of respectability among white society, and then attracts the attention of middle-class, college-educated musicians. These musicians, in turn, self-consciously attempt to integrate the structural and timbral resources of the European classical tradition into the music—hence the "symphonic jazz" of Stan Kenton and Woody Herman during the 1940s and the cool jazz of Dave Brubeck, Lennie Tristano, and the Modern Jazz Quartet during the 1950s.[26] If progressive rock is viewed as part of the overall history of rock music, it can be seen as fulfilling a very similar role to cool jazz in terms of its intellectualization and "classicalization" of rock.

Furthermore, the more "intellectual" jazz styles played a subcultural function very similar to the role that progressive rock came to play a number of years later. As David Riesman points out, the subculture that surrounded the more complex jazz styles consisted mostly of educated white males who held more liberal than average social views, looked on the Establishment-approved pop culture with disdain, and rallied behind the hermetic, exclusionary element of their music as a symbol of resistance against the Establishment.[27] The parallels here with the later hippie and post-hippie subcultures surrounding progressive rock are striking, and certainly not coincidental.

One might conceivably wonder whether future styles of popular music will also undergo this type of "classicalization." I am inclined to answer no. Classical music has been undergoing a steady decline in popularity since the early 1960s. The attempts by educated jazz musicians during the 1940s and 1950s to fuse jazz with classical music—and thus effect a fusion between their parents' high culture and the popular culture of their day—took place at a time when the classical tradition still retained its full power as a symbol of high culture. Even when progressive rock musicians began their experiments with fusing rock and classical motifs in the late 1960s, classical music still held a considerable cultural resonance. In the more than twenty-five years since the advent of psychedelia, however, I believe that classical music has slipped so precipitously in popularity that it retains little of the cultural resonance it held even in the late 1960s. I suspect the intellectualization of future forms of popular music will take some form other than fusion with the European classical tradition.

The Fans

It is with a certain amount of trepidation that I undertake this section. It is not just that I am not a professional sociologist; I believe it is nearly twenty years too late to do a statistically accurate demographic study of progressive rock fans. One would have to interview a representative pool of fans, and I am not convinced that this can any longer be done; the members of current fan clubs of Yes, ELP, Genesis, Pink Floyd, etc., are almost certainly atypical of the average record-buying or concert-attending fan of twenty years ago. Likewise, it is difficult if not impossible to determine (or even approximate) what percentage of these bands' current audiences are new (or relatively new—say, the last ten years), and what percentage are throwbacks to the 1970–1976 period. In this sense, I must say up front that I do not think a totally accurate ethnographic survey of the progressive rock fan circa 1970–1976 is possible. Nonetheless, I do have some observations which I believe will cast some light on the subject.

First of all, I must reemphasize something I have said several times: between 1966 and approximately 1970 or 1971 I believe that in important respects the musicians and the audiences for progressive rock were alike. During this period, progressive rock was still the music of a regionally distinct subculture that was essentially homogeneous in terms of its members' ages and class origins. Like the musicians, the audience was young (under thirty); it was centered above all in southeastern England; its socioeconomic background was solidly middle-class; and it shared the musicians' general educational backgrounds, and thus their familiarity with the art, literature, and music of high culture. The only major difference between audience and performers at this time involved gender: while the audience seems to have had a roughly equal female-male ratio, the performers were overwhelmingly male.

Not only was this audience similar to the musicians demographically; it rubbed shoulders with the musicians in an intimate way at the clubs and slightly larger venues which provided the forum for progressive rock in its formative stages. The musicians were "one of them," even if the musicians happened to be the ones on stage (it is useful to remember, though, that when the "Spontaneous Underground" series was introduced at London's Marquee Club in 1966, there was no performer/audience distinction). Only the huge open-air festivals of the late 1960s offered any intimation that a huge audience/performer divide might be in the offing. Otherwise, it was perfectly reasonable for an audience member in 1968 to assume that he or she might personally meet the members of Pink Floyd, Procol Harum, the Nice, or Soft Machine.

When the English hippies were not taking in their favorite bands in the clubs, they could often be found engaged in another activity of great importance to them: listening in rapt attention to their favorite albums in someone's apartment, often while smoking marijuana. Paul Willis heavily emphasized the importance of this activity to the hippies in his seminal ethnographic study of the English counterculture, *Profane Culture*.[28] Such listening activity seems to have usually taken place in small groups, and one is again reminded of the place music played in another middle-class "drop out" subculture, that of the nineteenth-century Romantics.

Something that emerges very potently in Willis's study is that the English hippies were a music-based subculture in the truest sense of the word. That is, for these audiences listening to records and listening to live music was not usually an accompaniment for dancing or other activities; it *was* the primary activity, and the music often served as a springboard for whatever conversation took place. As Robert Wyatt points out, there is no doubt that the audiences' fondness for hallucinogens and resulting listening habits exerted a profound impact on the musical development of progressive rock, by encouraging musicians to unfold ideas over a much longer timespan than would have been possible in pre-countercultural popular music:

> One of the biggest influences [on Soft Machine during the late 1960s] was the atmosphere at [the] UFO [Club]. In keeping with the general ersatz orientalism of the social set-up you'd have an audience sitting down. . . . Just the atmosphere

created by an audience sitting down was very inducive to playing, as in Indian classical music, a long gentle droning introduction to a tune. It's quite impossible if you've got a room full of beer-swigging people standing up waiting for action, it's very hard starting with a drone. But if you've got a floor full of people, even the few that are listening, they're quite happy to wait for a half hour for the first tune to get off the ground. So that was a wonderful influence, or a terrible one according to your taste, but it was an influence on what the musicians played.[29]

It is because of the obvious connections between the music and its social role that it is so easy to draw a number of clear homologies—which I presented in chapter 2—between the hippie subculture and early progressive rock.

The years 1970–1972 brought a series of important and permanent changes to this situation, however. First, a host of the major progressive rock bands broke in the United States. The States had (and have) a much larger potential audience than Britain; this not only makes for the possibility of concert tours on a greatly increased scale, it also creates a hugely expanded record-buying public. Not surprisingly, the record companies realized that the most profitable route was seeing to it that bands such as ELP, Yes, Pink Floyd, Jethro Tull, and the Moody Blues released an album approximately once a year, and followed it up with a lengthy promotional tour of the States.

This new pattern had two major effects. First, it effectively removed the major British progressive rock bands from the regional subculture in which they had originated; they often went for months (occasionally even years, in the case of Pink Floyd or Led Zeppelin) without performing in Britain. Second, it obsolesced the club circuit, since the promoters discovered to their delight that these bands could easily fill North American arenas and stadiums. As a result, the intimate performer/audience relationship of the club days became a thing of the past; at really large venues fans were hard pressed to even see the performers, and by 1974 the average fan maintained no illusions about rubbing shoulders with Keith Emerson, Robert Fripp, or Roger Waters. The huge performer/audience dichotomy which was such a central facet of the rock scene during the 1970s had become an established fact.

Several interesting questions are thus raised. First, why did English progressive rock do so well in the States? Lester Bangs, Dave Marsh, and others have argued that it was all record company hype,[30] but while hype may sustain a performer for a year or two, it does not enable musicians to repeatedly reach the top ten (or even number one) in the album charts over a five-, six-, or even seven-year period in the manner of the major progressive rock bands. So we must assume that there was a body of fans in the United States to whom this music mattered very much. But who were they, and what did they share in common with the British fan of the 1966–1970 period?

First, I think there were definite regional identities to the progressive rock taste public in the United States. (I will no longer use the term "subculture," as I think that by and large progressive rock ceased to be a subcultural style once it made the move from Britain to the States and from clubs to stadiums). Progressive rock did not do equally well in all parts of the country; it seemed to be especially popular in the Midwest, in the Northeast and Mid-Atlantic regions, and to a lesser extent on the West coast. I base this observation on three premises. First, American progressive rock bands of the early 1970s—who at the time were often unknown outside of a very limited area, and whose work is only now being reissued on specialty labels—most often came from these regions. Second, the American stadium rock style, which essentially involves a progressive rock/heavy metal fusion, emerged out of the Northeast, the Midwest, and the West coast during the mid-1970s. (I will deal with these two factors in greater detail in the next chapter.)

Finally, in examining popularity polls of a regional (as opposed to a national) nature from the 1970s, the popularity of progressive rock in the Midwest, in particular, is clear. For instance, a poll administered in Detroit as late as 1978 by WWWW, then a major rock station, asked listeners to identify their favorite songs, from which the station compiled a list of the top 106 (WWWW was 106 FM; the 106 songs were then played on July 4, 1978). ELP placed entries at positions 20, 36, and 53; Yes at 9 and 33; Pink Floyd at 21 and 35; the Moody Blues at 12 and 28; and Jethro Tull at 13 and 101. It is interesting to note that these five bands totaled nine of the top 50 positions, a not unimpressive number. It is also significant that Led Zeppelin's two most overtly progressive epics, "Stairway to Heaven" and "Kashmir," placed at positions 1 and 5, respectively. While one could certainly extrapolate too many generalizations from one local poll, I think the popularity of the English progressive rock style in these regions—particularly the Midwest—cannot be doubted.

The next question, then, is why would listeners in these regions find progressive rock appealing? This is a question I feel I can answer with some confidence. When one examines the work of the major progressive rock bands, one notices, besides the references to high culture, an implicit British nationalism. This is evident not only in the obvious debt of progressive rock as a musical style to English folk song, Anglican choral music, and the music of English nationalist composers such as Holst and Vaughan Williams, but also in the medievalism of the cover art and subject matter and the recurrent references to English folklore. One sees these elements at one level or another in Genesis, Yes, King Crimson, Gentle Giant, Jethro Tull, the Moody Blues, even Led Zeppelin. A remark by D. W. Meinig might offer a key to understanding why progressive rock was especially well received in these three regions. Jim Curtis quotes him as saying that "America has identified herself with three symbolic landscapes—the New England village, the Midwestern Main Street memorialized at Disneyland (which opened July 17, 1955), and the California suburbs."[31] Curtis goes on to remark that "none of these landscapes can accomodate anyone except affluent White Anglo-Saxon Protestants; the blacks, Jews, Eastern Europeans, and hillbillies who have created so much of American popular culture, destroy the coherence of these places."[32]

I do not wish to be sidetracked by the ideological ramifications of this last remark, other than to posit that there are and always have been plenty of less-than-affluent WASPs in New England villages and on Midwestern main streets. Nonetheless, I think there is no doubt that these are the most WASPish regions of the United States; the British legacy to the Northeast and Midwest, in particular, needs no further comment. It is not surprising, then, that the nationalist element of English progressive rock was much more sympathetically received in these regions than, for instance, in the Southeast. In a sense, I suspect progressive rock's British nationalism provided a kind of surrogate ethnic identity to its young white audience at a time when (for the first time in American history) the question of what it means to be a white person in America was coming under scrutiny,[33] just as its flights of fantasy and mysticism and its quasi-liturgical live shows provided its audiences—many of whom had lapsed from mainline Christian denominations—a surrogate religion. In turn, the nationalist elements of British progressive rock probably also contributed to the lack of interest the style held for blacks, hispanics, and most of the southeastern United States, where the white population had always defined itself as a culture distinct from the WASP/northern mainstream.

One might wonder why American audiences would have responded to the references to high culture in progressive rock which were, initially at least, grounded in a highly educated English subculture. I would suggest that American audiences had already been acclimated to references to high culture in popular music during the late 1960s by Bob Dylan, Paul Simon, and Jim Morrison. Granted, these musicians drew on the literature of high culture, not the music; but one can assume that audiences who had been exposed to ideas drawn from everyone from Emily Dickinson (Simon's "For Emily, Wherever I May Find Her") to Antonin Artaud (the Doors' "Break On Through," which also seems to refer to Huxley's *Doors of Perception*) to Marshall McLuhan (Dylan's *Highway 61 Revisited*) would not find musical references to Bach, Musorgsky, or Aaron Copland especially heavy-going.

As Landon Jones pointed out in his book *Great Expectations*, the baby boomer generation from which progressive rock drew its audience was the most educated in American history:

> What we would later call the generation gap was at first an education gap. Eighty-five percent of the baby boomers born from 1947 to 1951 completed high school, compared to only 38% of their parents. More than half of them had gone to college, a proportion unthinkable in their parents' era. The baby boom generation will always seem different from other generations if only because no generation, before it or after it, produced so many college graduates.[34]

Jim Curtis has remarked that "the American kids who were going to college in such huge numbers didn't necessarily learn to love Beethoven . . . [but] they lost some of their defensiveness about high culture."[35] Even if they didn't learn to love Musorgsky or Stravinsky, either, they were willing to give them a listen when performed by ELP or Yes; as much as the critics such as Lester Bangs hated it, there seems little doubt that albums such as ELP's *Pictures at an Exhibition* that contained arrangements of well-known classical pieces spurred at least some listeners to explore the originals. Not only was the college-educated segment of progressive rock's American taste public sympathetic to (or at least tolerant of) progressive rock's references to the music of high culture; it was also essentially sympathetic to the hippie ideology which progressive rock promulgated (although, as Jim Curtis points out, the fear of totalitarianism which pervades so much British rock of the 1970s was probably a bit more foreign to American audiences).[36]

Paradoxically, however, there is also no doubt that progressive rock's American taste public had a greater proportion of blue-collar listeners than did the English hippie subculture from which the style originated. This segment of the progressive rock taste public often enjoyed heavy metal, hard rock, and progressive rock equally, and made no essential distinctions between the styles (although many of them probably preferred the harder-rocking progressive bands such as ELP and King Crimson to the mellower sounds of Genesis or Renaissance). These listeners had little interest in (or perhaps even awareness of) progressive rock's classical quotations and references to high culture; they probably could not have explained exactly what the lyrics of *Karn Evil 9, Close to the Edge,* or *Thick as a Brick* were getting at, and probably had relatively little sympathy for the more twee elements of the style.[37] However, there were two elements of the style that this segment of the progressive rock taste public enjoyed very much. The first was virtuosity. As I noted in chapter 2, in both progressive rock and heavy metal the soloist takes on the role of Romantic hero, the fearless individualist whose virtuoso exploits allow for a symbolic escape from social constraints. At heavy metal concerts, in particular, audience members often participated in the lead guitarist's virtuosity vicariously, by accompanying their hero on "air guitar." To this segment of the progressive rock taste public, it made no difference whatsoever whether Keith Emerson's virtuosity stemmed from J. S. Bach or T-Bone Walker; the fact of his virtuosity was enough.

A second element which was important to this segment of progressive rock's taste public was visual spectacle. As I commented in chapter 3, the major progressive rock bands found that once they made the move from clubs to arenas some sort of visual props were necessary to retain the audience's attention. Simply standing on stage and playing works well enough for an audience of 500 to 1,000, but becomes problematic in front of an audience of 50,000 in which members in the back of the stadium can barely see the performers. Thus there arose a whole set of increasingly audacious technical props: laser lights, dry ice fog, catapulting pianos, self-destructing modular synthesizers, crashing airplanes, floating pigs, and so on. It seems to me that this kind of stage show is both peculiarly American (in that the parallels with Disneyland, etc., are obvious) and very much a product of the early 1970s, when general economic prosperity made spectacle on this scale a viable proposition. At any rate, this kind of stage show could be found in other rock styles of the 1970s as well, albeit not often on the same scale.

It seems certain that the album-oriented radio (AOR) format which many FM stations adopted between the early and mid-1970s played a major role in the formation of progressive rock's American taste public at that time. This kind of format replaced the free-form "underground" FM rock radio of the late 1960s with a continuous selection of "classic" rock cuts from the Beatles/Dylan era on into the 1970s; it thus brought together the format of top forty AM radio with the music that had been played on the free-form stations. The styles from the early 1970s which AOR featured most prominently were progressive rock, heavy metal, hard rock, and to a certain degree the singer/songwriter genre of James Taylor, Elton John, and similar performers (although this latter style was even more prevalent on AM radio). Through AOR progressive rock became an important part of a young, largely male American taste public for whom attending concerts of the leading heavy metal, hard rock, and progressive rock bands was an important activity. I also suspect that through AOR the fans of the singer/songwriter acts, which were much more likely to be female and perhaps more college-oriented, were induced to buy progressive rock albums, even if they weren't as likely to attend the concerts. Listening to albums in small groups and intimate settings was undoubtedly an activity that American progressive rock audiences of the 1970s inherited from their English hippie predecessors, although AOR radio reemphasized the importance of the rock single and, paradoxically, marked the apotheosis of the album as rock's primary medium.

It seems likely that progressive rock probably was at the nexus of some subcultural activity, especially on college campuses (Will Straw has suggested that through the mid-1970s it played an important role in certain college subcultures in which fantasy games such as dungeons and dragons featured heavily).[38] For the most part, though, progressive rock's success in the States during the 1970s seems to have been the result of its adoption by a large youth-based taste public with fairly catholic tastes. To be sure, there were undoubtedly some heavy metal fans who found progressive rock too arty, some progressive rock fans who found heavy metal too simplistic (these would have frequently gravitated toward fusion instead), and some singer/songwriter aficionados who disliked both styles. For the most part, though, I think AOR went a long way in creating a youth-oriented taste public in the United States during the 1970s for which all these styles had varying degrees of relevance.

Having charted the rise of America's progressive rock taste public, what of its decline? While I think the rise of punk rock in 1976–1977 brought the musicians themselves to the realization that an era was passing, the fact is that punk was never popular in the United States, while progressive rock remained popular in the States (especially among conservative Midwestern audiences) into the late 1970s. I think there was a whole host of other factors at work in the dissolution of the progressive rock taste public during the late 1970s. One could cite the stagnation of AOR, the changed economic conditions (particularly the high inflation) which made the genre's massive stage shows more problematic, the stagnation of progressive rock itself as a musical style, the rise of commercially viable postpunk styles such as New Wave, and the rise of a new musical technology which was perhaps not ideally suited to progressive rock. Perhaps above all, though, loomed the general demise between circa 1976 and circa 1981 of the whole hippie ethos which had been such a driving force to the genre. I will discuss this matter in greater detail in the final chapter.

Subverting High Culture: Notation versus Improvisation

There has been a notable trend in post-1980 textbooks on twentieth-century art music to devote some space to progressive rock—usually in the same chapter as minimalism—as an example of a late-twentieth-century classical/popular fusion.[39] So far as this trend shows a growing awareness on the part of musicologists of music outside the narrowly circumscribed area of "art" or "serious" music, it is healthy. It is an especially good sign in that it signals a new realization that only through the continuous interaction between "art" and "popular" styles can a classical music culture remain healthy and vigorous rather than becoming ingrown and jejune.

Nonetheless, it is a mistake to regard progressive rock as classical music. To be sure, progressive rock has been fascinated with high culture, and has drawn on many compositional techniques associated with the classical music tradition. However, it also subverted many of high culture's most fundamental tenets. Nowhere is this more evident than in progressive rock's compositional methods. In its attitudes toward notation and the act of composition itself, progressive rock is radically different from classical music; it is in these realms that progressive rock most clearly shows its debt to the legacy of the African-American musical tradition.

Perhaps the most characteristic aspect of the Western art music tradition is its immense reliance on notation. While it is true that a certain amount of limited improvisation formerly played a greater role in this tradition than is now the case, the overall thrust of this music's history involves nearly a millennium of seeking ever-more precise ways of notating a composer's intentions—first in terms of pitch, then in terms of rhythm, then tone colors (through the specification of which instruments or voice types are required for a specific part), and finally dynamics, articulation, phrasing, and tempo. (The earlier the notation, the more likely it is that realizing elements other than pitch and rhythm will involve a certain amount of guesswork for modern performers.) The musical score is the source of Western art music's most unique contribution to world music culture: the idea of the objective existence of a piece of music. In other words, the score renders the composer's ideas precisely enough that even if the performer is geographically or chronologically removed from the composer, he or she is able to render the composer's directions with confidence that the resulting sounds will roughly correspond to the composer's intention. Because of notation, in the European art music tradition the piece exists separate from its conception, separate from any single performance, and is ultimately capable of outliving its composer.

The advantage of this system—the incredible amount of control it gives the composer over every detail of his or her creation—also is responsible for its most negative quality, a tendency to deny performer and listener alike a vital role in shaping a piece. This tendency has been pointed out by a number of commentators in the latter half of our century, as the primacy of notated music over nonnotated music has increasingly come into question. Robert Fripp once wryly noted that in a symphonic performance "the only person who is expressing himself is the composer, with the conductor as chief of police and the musicians as sequencers."[40] Henry Pleasants, the first writer to seriously question the absolute value that Western musical culture has placed in notation, states that

> Given such constraints as these [i.e., the score as a kind of sacred text], it is a tribute to the Serious musician's skills, diligence, and patience, sometimes even to his intelligence, that he is not a duller fellow than he is, especially the orchestral musician, playing more or less the same notes in more or less the same way under the daily supervision of a variety of opiniated conductors year in and year out.[41]

African-American music, on the other hand—be it jazz, blues, R&B, or rock—does not rely on notation, even though it may be notated in a limited way, as in the lead sheets of jazz, which show chord progressions and important thematic material, while leaving other elements open for individual interpretation. The blues, in particular, is a genre in which a piece does not—indeed, cannot—exist separately from its performance. The blues performer draws on specific harmonic, melodic, and rhythmic formulae to produce something new each time; differences between one performance and the next result not only from the performer's whim, but also from his or her ever-changing interaction with the audience. The blues, jazz, and other African-American forms thus allow performers and listeners alike a chance to share in the creative experience. This is in direct opposition to classical music, which allows the performer relatively limited self-expression, and the listener none. For the listener, especially, classical music is very much like the Western cultural tradition at large: one either takes it or leaves it.

In most African-American musical styles, to be sure, there are certain features of an individual piece that will not change from performance to performance. In jazz, for instance, a piece's chord progressions will remain constant, as will the "head" (i.e., the main theme that recurs periodically throughout the performance of the piece). However, the recurring chord progression serves as the basis of a series of melodic improvisations, each of which will (ideally) be different (certain chord types may also be substituted for other chord types). Two performances of the same piece may also be in a different key and tempo, and may use different instrumentation; more subtle musical elements such as dynamics and phrasing are also bound to change from performance to performance. The popular song is even more constant from performance to performance, but even here the accompaniment may be varied in terms of chord voicings, instrumentation, tempo, and rhythmic contour each time it is rendered anew. In short, the tendency in African-American music has been to give the performer a much greater role in the re-creation of a given piece. The performer is, in essence, a co-creator, and the give-and-take between performer and audience allows the audience a creative role as well.

Like other forms of rock, progressive rock is not a notated music; although notated versions of the music have appeared, these were put together after the music's creation, often by people from outside the bands. Rather, the recording is the primary repository of the sonic text, and even progressive rock musicians such as Keith Emerson who are able to notate music fluently tend to resort to notation only in collaboration with classical ensembles.

In this sense, then, progressive rock is squarely within the tradition of African-American music. On the other hand, the complexity of much progressive rock has tended to discourage wholesale improvisation, and the tendency since the late 1960s has been for a band's live performance to reproduce its studio recordings.[42] Once a band has arrived at a finished arrangement of a particular piece, they tend to stick to it closely, and many sections are repeated almost note-for-note from performance to performance. Improvisation has usually been limited to particular sections in which a keyboardist, guitarist, or some other instrumentalist improvises a lead line over a repeated bass ostinato and/or chord progression; even such "improvised" sections can often be remarkably similar from performance to performance.

Indeed, although free-form improvisation did have some champions within the progressive rock community (most notably King Crimson's Robert Fripp), by and large progressive rock musicians showed a marked mistrust toward this type of music-making, and rock musicians with a burning interest in improvisation usually gravitated to jazz-rock instead. Kerry Minnear (Gentle Giant) reflected a common attitude when he commented that "free form is not something that I have a great deal of interest in—not free form from the word go, where something might happen or might not. When it does it's great, but it seems a waste to sit for three-quarters of an hour waiting for five minutes' worth of something that really works."[43]

David Gilmour, commenting on Pink Floyd's origins as a largely improvisational band during the psychedelic era, states that when "exploring live in front of an audience, the way we did in the '60s and very early '70s, you make as many mistakes as you get things right. A lot of it was awful."[44] Keith Emerson has spoken of the importance of having "landmarks" which are repeated from solo to solo, saying "these landmarks help to keep the audience in touch, because you might be getting too far off the subject. It gives some method of association."[45] The breakup of the original lineup of U.K. was precipitated at least in part by the very different attitudes held by Allan Holdsworth and the rest of the band toward improvisation. Keyboardist Eddie Jobson complained that "Allan won't commit himself to playing specific parts. He's more into freeform. He just likes to improvise everything he does all the time."[46] Holdsworth, who was much more influenced by the jazz ideal of continuous improvisation than U.K.'s other members, fumed that "one of the silly things that U.K. wanted me to do . . . [was] to play the same solos. I said, 'sorry, no can do.' Once a solo is done, try something else. In fact I really get worried if my live solos sound like the ones on the records."[47] The clashing viewpoints of Jobson and Holdsworth underline the tension that exists in progressive rock between the African-American legacy of improvisation and spontaneity and the European ideal of re-creating a piece in essentially the same way from performance to performance.

Because of the relatively limited role of improvisation in much progressive rock, when a progressive rock piece is notated, the listener can usually relate the resulting score to recordings and/or performances of the piece, provided that the piece has been notated adequately and important sections have not been excised (which are by no means uncommon problems in notated versions of progressive rock). However, notated versions of progressive rock (or virtually any other genre of popular music from the mid-1960s on, for that matter) are woefully inadequate in indicating tone color. Existing systems of notation simply have no way of conveying the complex electronic tone colors that are used. For instance, two guitarists playing the same type of electric guitar will sound completely different if they use different effects devices (i.e., a chorus unit as opposed to a flanger); even if they use the same devices, they will sound different if they use different amplification systems. Classical notation, designed to convey the tone colors of standardized acoustic instruments for which there are no appreciable tone color variances, simply has no way of dealing with these subtleties. Furthermore, there is no good way, using traditional notation, of capturing the subtle changes in vocal coloring that popular singers often make from phrase to phrase, or the glissandi and portamenti frequently resorted to by guitarists (less often electronic keyboardists). Popular musicians, who usually do not like to have their freedom of expression limited by fully notated scores, are aware of these problems as well; it is yet another reason why so few of them consider the mastery of classical notation to be an essential skill.

The lack of dependence on notation leads the progressive rock musician to take a somewhat different view of what a "composition" is all about than his classical counterpart. This tendency is furthered by the fact that while the conventions of classical music dictate that a single person be responsible for all the musical aspects of a given piece, pieces by many rock bands—and progressive rock is no exception—tend to be cowritten by several, or perhaps all, of a group's members. Many progressive rock bands were more or less democratic, with members having roughly equal creative control, and pieces were pieced together by combining different members' ideas.[48] Robert Fripp describes how this collaborative process worked in the genesis of King Crimson's "21st-century Schizoid Man": "The first few notes—Daaa-da-da-daa-daa-daaa—were by Greg Lake, the rest of the introduction was Ian McDonald's idea, I came up with the riff at the beginning of the instrumental section, and Michael Giles suggested we all play in unison in the very fast section towards the end of the instrumental."[49]

A similar process can be seen at work in the creation of Pink Floyd's lengthy "Echoes." As the band's drummer, Nick Mason, has commented,

> We booked a studio for January [1971], and throughout January we went in and played, anytime that anyone had any sort of rough idea for something we would put it down. . . . [B]y the end of January we listened back and we'd got thirty-six different bits and pieces that sometimes cross-related and sometimes didn't. "Echoes" was made up from that.[50]

Mason's description reveals the degree to which the studio had become an essential compositional device in popular music by the late 1960s, taking on the role that a composer's sketchbooks had played in an earlier, pre-electronic era. He also points up the way that bands went about forging a "group sound" that drew on the idiosyncrasies of several individuals, yet was greater than the sum of its parts.

"Schizoid Man" and "Echoes" are examples of an approach wherein several musicians contribute freshly conceived musical ideas that are fashioned into a large-scale piece. At other times, the musicians would dismember unused pieces they had already written, fusing the best thematic ideas from several sources together to create something new. Dan Hedges notes that the chorus of Yes's *Close to the Edge*

Was lifted from a song of the same name [guitarist] Steve Howe had put together a few years earlier, "Partially about the longest day of the year." Howe says, "when [lead vocalist] Jon [Anderson] and I got together to write, we'd each contribute different parts, and that chorus fit best with Jon's song, "Total Mass Retain." . . . [W]hen you're writing for Yes, the whole integrity of holding on to these things disappears. If the lick fits, you use it."[51]

In bands where everyone had a roughly equal creative input, arguments about the final shape of a composition could be bitter, and often no one was completely satisfied with the eventual outcome. Drummer Bill Bruford described his experience with U.K. as follows:

> Trying to make the album *U.K.* was a little like four writers all trying to write the same novel simultaneously, with only the barest common understanding of the plot. Writers two and three have a good handle on the middle of the book, assuming writer one, who doesn't seem to like anything so far, doesn't object. Meanwhile writer four, who likes the title, will only accept writers two and three's view of the middle, so long as his denouement is accepted verbatim. This method of music making was, and is, laborious, exhausting, and expensive.[52]

It was not uncommon for musicians to leave bands which they felt were short-shifting their ideas. One of the reasons that Peter Gabriel gave for leaving Genesis was that "I believe the use of sound and visual images can be developed to do much more than we have done. But on a large scale it needs one clear and coherent direction, which our pseudo-democratic committee system could not provide."[53]

It is not surprising, then, that in order to avoid these problems some bands either were never democratic from the beginning, or eventually allowed one member to exert primary compositional control. Even here, however, the composer did not control every detail of the composition in the manner of a classical composer. Rather, he would be responsible for chord progressions, vocal melodic lines, and other important thematic material, yet would expect instrumentalists to invent their own parts within the suggested framework. Eric Tamm points out that although Robert Fripp has become King Crimson's primary composer by the time of the *Lizard* LP of 1970, "Everyone who played on the record had some part in the music's creation, since Fripp did not, Zappa-like, write out every last note and nuance of expression, but rather strove to elicit from given players the type of semi-improvised passages he deemed fitting for a given piece."[54]

Keith Emerson of ELP describes the origin of his "Abaddon's Bolero" in similar terms:

> I had picked out this little melody that I liked, and I put it down on tape. After listening to it several times I began to put down overdubs, and it struck me that

this was the perfect thing for the kind of piece which begins at nothing and grows to everything. I took it in to Greg [Lake] and Carl [Palmer] and we played through it several times. I told them what I had in mind, so we just started with me playing the melody on a little flute sound that was programmed into the synthesizer. Each time we repeated the theme, I added something, Greg added something, and Carl added more sound on his drums. . . . [W]e just kept on building the sound, and almost instinctively knew when the piece had reached its peak. I looked at Greg and Carl, and we cut off exactly together.[55]

Yet another similar description of the compositional process is given by Kerry Minnear, one of the principal songwriters of Gentle Giant:

If I've written it [a song], I'll give out the guitar part to Gary Green as I hear it, the bass part to Ray [Shulman], try to get the right feel on the drums from John Weathers, and the vocal we leave until last. It's normally a question of reproducing what the inspiration was. After a few plays though, they start adding their own little quirks to what I've given them, so we end up with something slightly different than I intended. But that's good because we're a group and not an orchestra.[56]

What, then, is the ultimate social significance of progressive rock's compositional procedures? I certainly do not agree with Robert Walser's view that the real goal of the style's classical/rock fusion is "to refer to a prestigious discourse and thus to bask in reflected glory."[57] I think this remark is, for Walser at least, an uncharacteristically uncritical repetition of the "accepted" critical stance that any fusion of popular and classical styles is by definition "sterile," "inauthentic," and "elitist." I will examine the assumptions behind this view in the next chapter; for now I will momentarily address the relative merits of the view itself. John Street gives a fairly standard exposé of it in his *Rebel Rock*;[58] he derides the music for its "elitism" and "traditionalism," and makes the standard accusation that the musicians sought the approbation of the "elite." The weakness of this argument is twofold. First, the "elite" are never precisely identified; nor is it explained why Keith Emerson, Robert Fripp, or Peter Gabriel would seek their approbation. (Does Street really believe the "elite"—assuming he means academics—enthused over the manner in which Emerson stuck knives in his Hammond?) Second, and more problematically, Street's assessment shows no awareness of the obvious relationship between progressive rock as a musical style and the counterculture as a social/ spiritual/aesthetic movement. He attempts to argue that the style did not rise *from* the counterculture, but rather was imposed *upon* the counterculture by an unholy alliance of musicians, record company executives, and academics (never mind that the implicit "conspiracy element" of this argument strains the credulity of even the most gullible).[59]

Just three examples highlighting how progressive rock as a musical style clearly did arise from the concerns and worldviews of the counterculture will have to suffice here. First, Street shows no awareness of the fact that the hippies' new, hallucinogen-induced perception of time demanded much longer, more involved formal approaches than had been traditional in earlier pop music styles; did not classical forms offer a logical model from which countercultural musicians could work? Second, he complains that "progressive music encouraged even more passivity from its audiences than the much-derided pop, where it was expected that audiences would dance or listen with only half an ear."[60] Again, Street begs the question of what constitutes "passivity." To the counterculture, with their emphasis on the exploration of "inner space," dancing was more "passive" than listening intently to music to the accompaniment of a light show, since the first involves merely the body, while the second engages the mind. (Street must realize it was not for nothing the hippies called their music "head music"; this is an issue Paul Willis engages in considerable depth in his *Profane Culture.*)

Finally, Street seems profoundly unaware of the degree to which both drug-taking and listening to music became ritualistic activities for the hippies. In an effort to create some sort of social and metaphysical depth in what seemed to them a hopelessly sterile and artificial world, is it particularly surprising that the hippies would reach back into their cultural past and draw on "traditional" elements from folk and religious music? While I understand that some will continue to cling to the position outlined by Street, I think it is high time to point out that the "elitist" and "traditionalist" elements of progressive rock are open to interpretation on multiple levels, not only to the one-dimensional interpretations they have frequently been given by past commentators.

My own interpretation of progressive rock's social function is, therefore, very different than Street's. I would suggest that in its approaches to musical composition, progressive rock serves as a forum in which a number of cultural opposites are reconciled: high and low culture, European and African-American creative ideals. In the best progressive rock, one senses the tension that results from attempting to balance these values. When either the intellectualization of classical music or the unbridled energy of rock get the upper hand, the tension vanishes and the music loses its power, becoming either middle-brow classical music or flaccid, unenergetic rock.

However, at its best progressive rock is bona fide third-stream music. To be sure, it is possible to see the appropriation of classical instrumentation by progressive rock musicians as merely a superficial veneer of classical elements over a rock/pop framework. On the other hand, the formal approaches of progressive rock intermingle manners of creating and organizing musical material drawn from two distinct musical traditions. Progressive rock is thoroughly grounded in African-American musical concepts such as group composition, improvisation (or at least the performer's right to realize certain aspects of a piece differently in each performance), and a general lack of reliance on notation. At the same time, however, progressive rock musicians thoroughly absorbed the essence of European programmatic forms such as the song cycle and the multimovement suite, and this point cannot be overstated.

Andrew Chester has argued that the main musical difference between European and African-American musics lies in the realm of structure.[61] He describes classical music as "extensional," with basic musical atoms being combined through space and time to form huge, complex structures. He describes African-American forms such as the blues, on the other hand, as "intensional": "The basic musical units . . . are not combined through space and time as simple elements into complex structures. The simple entity is that constituted by the parameters of melody, harmony, and beat, while the complex is built up by modulation of the basic notes, and by inflection of the basic beat."[62] Although progressive rock was still in its embryonic stage when Chester formulated his extensional/intensional dichotomy in 1970, he already recognized that the music of the most sophisticated psychedelic bands (he cites, for instance, Jefferson Airplane and the original Soft Machine) relied more on "extensional" than on "intensional" methods. As the progressive rock style matured, its debt to the structural methods of classical music became ever more pronounced.

There is no doubt, then, that at one level progressive rock musicians celebrate their middle-class heritage by appropriating the music of high culture. Just as important, though, is the way they subvert many of high culture's central tenets, especially through their absorption of African-American musical concepts. In the end, progressive rock brings forth a new totality, never before heard in either rock or classical music; herein lies its ultimate success, and the source of its musical and social vitality during the late 1960s and early 1970s.

The Critical Reception of Progressive Rock

Not all rock critics reacted to progressive rock as scathingly as Lester Bangs who said of ELP: "These guys amount to war criminals."[1] However, this kind of invective was hurled against the major bands frequently enough that at this point in our study it is time to address a matter that has up to now been dealt with only indirectly: the critical reception of progressive rock. To address this topic adequately, though, a brief outline of the history of rock journalism is necessary.

Prior to the mid-1960s, pop music journals were essentially fanzines, issued under the auspices of record companies. These papers listed concert and record release dates, showed recent chart positions, and printed short "features," usually brief biographies of the latest chart sensations that included details such as eye color and favorite food. However, the rise of the counterculture in the 1960s created a group of readers who frankly despised the values of the traditional entertainment industry. They wanted journals that would provide historical and cultural perspectives of the music that was covered, that would develop critical positions and standards, and that would tie the music in with the ideological struggles of the counterculture. As a result, the late 1960s witnessed the rise of an underground press devoted to psychedelic music and the hippie lifestyle, including American publications such as *Rolling Stone* (founded 1967), *Crawdaddy, Creem,* and *Circus,* and the British *Zig-Zag.* Furthermore, England's two leading pop music journals of the pre-counterculture era, the *New Music Express* and *Melody Maker,* adopted many aspects of the underground journals at this time as well.

Rock journalists tended to treat the major figures of the 1966–1970 period with an almost uniform respect; there was a general consensus between journalists and audiences as to what constituted "good" music. The Beatles and Bob Dylan became semilegendary figures in their own time; a rung below demigod status, but still highly respected, were the Rolling Stones, the Who, the Yardbirds, Cream, Hendrix, Procol Harum, the Doors, and Jefferson Airplane. It was only with the fragmentation of a largely unified youth counterculture after 1970, and the subsequent emergence of several distinct rock styles, that rock critics and rock audiences went their separate ways. Heavy metal was one of the new genres that the critics disliked; progressive rock was another.

As I pointed out earlier in this study, there was always a strong element of "art for art's sake" in progressive rock that rubbed critics the wrong way. This tendency manifested itself in a number of ways—in the style's frequent appeal to virtuosity, in its eclecticism and its delight in mixing different stylistic sources, and in its pervasive references to the music of high culture. Nowhere was the appeal to high culture of the past by English progressive rock bands more evident than in their frequent arrangements of and quotations from classical music. One band in particular, ELP, became famous (or notorious, depending on one's point of view) for their electronic reinterpretations of nineteenth- and early-twentieth-century symphonic music. One entire LP by the group, *Pictures at an Exhibition,* was devoted to an electronic reinterpretation of Musorgsky's well-known piano piece (later orchestrated by Maurice Ravel) of 1874. The band's debut album contains arrangements of Bartók's *Allegro barbaro* and the fifth movement of Janáček's *Sinfonietta,* retitled "The Barbarian" and "Knife-Edge," respectively. Later albums contain arrangements of works by Aaron Copland (*Hoedown* and *Fanfare for the Common Man*), Alberto Ginastera (the fourth movement of his Piano Concerto No. 1, retitled "Toccata" by the band), and Joaquín Rodrigo's "Canario" (from his *Fantasia para un gentilhombre*). It must be noted that the band's heavy emphasis on arrangements of classical music was something of a two-edged sword: although it did draw much critical attention (not all of it favorable), it also served to draw attention away from their more genuinely creative, original works.

Other progressive rock bands arranged or quoted from classical music more sparingly. Yes opened their concerts with an excerpt from Stravinsky's *Firebird;* the first incarnation of King Crimson performed Holst's "Mars" (from *The Planets*) live, while the Electric Light Orchestra arranged Grieg's "In the Hall of the Mountain King" (from *Peer Gynt*). Jethro Tull's "Bouree" was based on a piece by J. S. Bach, as was Egg's "Fugue in D minor" (drawn from the famous Toccata and Fugue in D minor for organ) and the main melodic idea of Procol Harum's "A Whiter Shade of Pale."[2] Many progressive rock bands clearly saw themselves in the role of bringing high culture to the masses, and approached this task with an almost missionary zeal. Thus Carl Palmer of ELP remarked to an indignant Lester Bangs that "we hope if anything we're encouraging the kids to listen to music that has more quality."[3] The liner notes of Gentle Giant's *Acquiring the Taste* LP informs the listener that "it is our goal to expand the frontiers of contemporary popular music at the risk of being very unpopular. . . . From the outset we have abandoned all preconceived thoughts on blatant commercialism. Instead we hope to give you something far more substantial and fulfilling."[4] Likewise, Jethro Tull's self-written "review" of their album *Thick as a Brick* comments that "taken on the whole however this is a fine disc and a good example of the current pop scene attempting to break out of its vulgarisms and sometimes downright obscene derivative hogwash."[5]

To many rock critics, especially those associated with *Rolling Stone* and *Creem*, progressive rock's aesthetic stance was anathema, nothing short of heresy. First of all, the critics resented the insinuation that progressive rock's appropriation of the classical tradition somehow "expanded the frontiers of popular music," enabled the pop scene to "break out of its vulgarism," or "encouraged kids to listen to music that has more quality." They found this viewpoint elitist and a betrayal of rock's populist origins. I would not necessarily defend the viewpoint expressed by Palmer, Gentle Giant, or Jethro Tull, insomuch as I do not believe that drawing "classical" influences into pop music will necessarily make for music that "has more quality." However, I also believe that such references to high culture will not necessarily lead to pop music that is more "inauthentic" or "sterile," either. Furthermore, far too much emphasis has been put on remarks such as these in past assessments of progressive rock. As we have already seen, progressive rock musicians drew on symphonic music and the Anglican/Catholic choral tradition because it was part of their cultural heritage as middle-class Europeans, and it made perfect sense for them to do so. As Jim Curtis has remarked, "In the sixties the major British groups had adapted American popular music with startling results, but such adaptations could continue only so long. No group could repeat the Stones' awesome assimilation of black blues, and no group needed to."[6] Many progressive rock musicians never went out of their way to draw attention to the "classical" elements of their music. Even ELP, considered by many critics to be the most overweening progressive rock band of all, did not bother to note that two of the songs on their first album were based on material derived from pieces by Bartók and Janáček until lawsuits filed by the composers' heirs forced them to do so.[7]

Besides disliking the perceived suggestion that progressive rock's appeal to high culture lent it "superiority," the critics asserted that the style's eclecticism and appropriation of devices associated with classical music removed it too far from rock's roots in rhythm-and-blues. Dave Marsh, in speaking of the body of twentieth-century popular music as a whole, stated, "What's really marginal [to the history of popular music] is the progressive rock that has produced great albums and few if any hit singles, while dominating critical discussion. . . . [P]rogressive rock sounds dessicated to me because it's so thoroughly divorced from the taproot of rock and roll: rhythm and blues."[8] Lester Bangs, in his vitriolic write-up of ELP for *Creem*, charged the band with what he considered the greatest "crime" of all: "The insidious befoulment of all that was gutter pure in rock."[9] Even the style's heavy reliance on instrumental music was looked upon with great suspicion:

Robert Christgau speaks condescendingly of Robert Fripp's "rare if impractical gift for instrumental composition in a rock context."[10]

If the critics didn't like the musical style of progressive rock, they didn't like its conceptual content either, demonstrating a great disdain for its epic subject matter, its fractured, surrealistic verse, and above all its lack of irony and self-conscious hipness. What Robert Christgau liked least about King Crimson's *Lizard* LP, for instance, was that "neither Gordon Haskell nor (keep off the weeds) Jon Anderson delivers Pete Sinfield's overwrought lyrics with the sarcasm they deserve."[11]

What is one to make of statements of this type? First, it is clear that the rock critics cast themselves as populists. Bill Bruford, discussing critics' attacks on Yes's *Fragile* LP of 1971, noted that the critics, "Suspicious of 'slick, academy-trained' musicians . . . felt that music like this indicated an attempt to purloin their favorite three-chord folk music and turn it into High Art."[12] Clearly, the critics felt that "good" music was music that hewed closely to the legacy of rock's "golden age," from the mid-1950s through the late 1960s. Such music should be primarily vocal, not instrumental. It should be technically simple and maintain clear ties with R&B traditions. Above all, it should concentrate on short songs and on singles rather than emphasizing long, extended compositions and the album as a unit.

Furthermore, "good" music, in the critics' estimation, would not take itself too seriously. Ideally, it would be dance music, rather than music meant to be listened to for its own sake. If it did fall into the latter category, the lyrics were expected to acknowledge rock's past, and to show a certain amount of self-conscious irony. Will Straw notes that "the consistent high regard for singers such as Bruce Springsteen, Emmylou Harris, and Tom Waits, for performers like Lou Reed, who played self-consciously with rock and roll imagery, stands out in a rereading of *Rolling Stone* from this period" (i.e., the early to mid-1970s).[13] Progressive rock lyrics, which grappled with metaphysics and spun out complex narratives, were considered "pretentious" and "overly serious" and were lambasted for lacking any sense of irony. In fact, what the critics meant, but seldom said, was that progressive rock's lyrics dealt with subject matter that rock (or at least their idealized version of it) could not adequately address. As Dave Marsh said, listeners who want to grapple with these types of topics are "better off listening to classical (or anyway, 'serious') music."[14]

Anyone who is familiar with rock music of the era 1954–1964 knows that its musical syntax and its topical material is limited, and not subject to infinite development. Furthermore, it is ridiculous to expect musicians who lived through the turmoil of the late 1960s to have the same innocent, carefree attitudes toward their music as did the pre-counterculture rockers. Nonetheless, the "populist" credo of critics such as Dave Marsh has led to an insistence that rock is most valid when it shows direct, lineal descent from rhythm-and-blues.

However, in an extremely perceptive section of his *Rock: The Primary Text*, Allan

Moore has convincingly demonstrated that the critics' assumptions concerning the blues tradition—and their attempts to measure the relative value of other musics based on criteria derived from that tradition—are not without serious difficulties. As I have already noted, one of the major problems the Marsh/Frith/Bangs/Christgau school had with progressive rock was its relative lack of "black" influence. As Moore rightly points out, the basic premise behind this line of thought is the belief that black music is "authentic" and "natural" in a way that white music is not: "It [the critical stance of Marsh and his peers] entails the assumption that blacks in the southern USA lived in a state of mindless primitivism, in which they expressed themselves through music 'naturally,' without the intervening of any musical 'theory'; hence the black sense of rhythm being 'natural' and 'unmediated.' "[15] After pointing out that the blues are just as "theoretical" as any classical style one would care to mention (insomuch as the style is governed by a set of demonstrable, recurring principles), Moore goes on to note,

> The "mouldy fig" attitude is as alive as ever. Small (1987) considers the value of black music to lie in its subversive nature, which accrues to it because it is spontaneous, immediate, and "close to nature." Frith talks dangerously of black music being "felt," perhaps implying that white music tends to be "thought," and therefore that blacks are incapable of thought. Even more recently Wicke has insisted that the blues were "a pure expression of genuine experience."[16]

What emerges most urgently from Moore's analysis is that since the critics' equation of the blues tradition and "authenticity" is inherently flawed by a series of overly simplistic assumptions, their criticism of styles such as progressive rock as "unnatural" and "inauthentic" cannot be accepted at face value.

One can suspect that a strong motivating factor behind the critics' dislike of progressive rock stemmed from a territorial imperative. There was much hope in the late 1960s and early 1970s that classical, jazz, and rock musics were tributaries that were about to flow into a new megastyle. For instance, David Ernst stated that

> The desire [of progressive rock and jazz-rock performers] to create large compositional structures is due at least in part to these performers' musical training. It can be considered another step toward the fulfillment of Stockhausen's ideal of a universal music. All musical styles are gradually being amalgamated into a single framework, so that categorization of music as classical, jazz, rock, and folk, has begun to lose its significance.[17]

The prospect of rock transmutating into a new style with classical overtones would certainly have made the critics uncomfortable, since it would have compromised the "authenticity" of their beloved low culture style by drawing on elements associated with high culture and the dreaded bourgeois. Of course, I have already drawn attention to the highly questionable nature of the critics' notion of "authenticity"; furthermore, their stance showed little historical awareness of the degree to which earlier African-American styles such as ragtime and jazz resulted from a high culture/low culture fusion.[18] Nonetheless, the critics often went out of their way to attack any kind of fusion attempt: as Lester Bangs said, "Everyone knows that Classical-Rock (alternating with Jazz) Fusions never really work."[19] To the critics' consternation, though, many musicians and a large segment of the listening public (through the late 1970s, at any rate) consistently disagreed.

The rock critics' dislike of progressive rock also showed a territorial imperative in that it not only was based on a "populist" (and hence anti–high culture) stance, but also was implicitly anti-European. English performers were respected only insomuch as they hewed closely to the conventions established by American performers. When European musicians began appropriating too many clearly European musical conventions, the critics cried foul. A frequent charge was that European performers were "colder" and had less "heart" than their American counterparts: thus Robert Christgau remarks about King Crimson's live album *USA* that "the excitement generated is more Wagner than Little Richard—this record is a case study in the Europeanness of English heavy metal."[20] Clearly, the critics' anti-European and anti–high culture biases are closely related.

As Will Straw and especially Deena Weinstein have pointed out, however, the "populist" stance of these critics is often rather hypocritical.[21] If progressive rock was too complex, too grandiose, too ambitious, too concerned with art for art's sake, then one would have thought that heavy metal—certainly a populist strain of rock if ever there was one—would receive the critics' approbation. To the contrary, however, the critics attacked heavy metal with the same fury with which they attacked progressive rock, often illogically reversing their arguments. The seminal English heavy metal band Black Sabbath was described by one critic as having the "sophistication of four Cro-Magnon hunters who've stumbled on a rock band's equipment."[22] Another critic described heavy metal as "music made by slack-jawed, alpaca-haired, bulbous-inseamed imbeciles in jackboots and leather chrome *for* slack-jawed, alpaca-haired, downy-mustachioed imbeciles in cheap, too-large T-shirts with pictures of comic-book Armageddon ironed on the front."[23] One notes in these criticisms a complete abandonment of the populist stance with which progressive rock was critiqued. As Jim Curtis noted, "Like art rock, heavy metal often displeased the critics. They often thought that art rock was too pretentious, but that heavy metal was too unpretentious."[24] While populism was the club with which the critics beat progressive rock, the same critics' critique of heavy metal reveals that their "populism" was not particularly heartfelt; there were deeper reasons for their dislike of the style.

Indeed, one might do well to ask what trait is shared by heavy metal and progressive rock, which on the surface appear to be so very different; I would submit that the answer is that both styles display a disinterest in—and often a mistrust of—direct political action. As I have already argued, heavy metal represents a Dionysian extension of countercultural values—pursuit of fleshly pleasure is seen as the answer to life's problems—while progressive rock represents an Apollonian extension of countercultural values, emphasizing an inner spiritual quest and the search for some sort of deeper metaphysical truth. Neither style put much stake in direct political action. As a result of their drug use, many hippies believed that the material world was essentially unreal, and that attempts to change this exterior world via political revolution were ultimately useless—one's energies were best spent on seeking inner transformation. Rock critics, however, viewed both styles as escapist and asocial; to superimpose a concept of the 1990s back into the 1970s, neither progressive rock nor heavy metal were politically correct.[25] The role of rock, critics asserted, was in "channeling righteous anger into intelligent political action."[26] Deena Weinstein noted that "rock criticism has always defined the meaning of music in only one way: the ability, or anyways the desire, to shake up the world."[27]

Of course, as I pointed out in chapter 4, progressive rock contains some highly penetrating religious/humanistic critiques of industrial society. While many of these are somewhat oblique, couched as they are in surrealistic and fantastic imagery, at least some (i.e., later Pink Floyd) are quite straightforward. Since few of the major critics ever made any real attempts to gain anything more than the most superficial familiarity with progressive rock, however, their overriding impression of the genre was "escapist," and when they attack progressive rock on a musical basis, they are often really attacking its perceived apolitical nature. For instance, Simon Frith makes the highly arguable claim that "disco is a much richer musical genre than progressive rock."[28] On what basis? It is very difficult to see how one could successfully argue that disco is a richer musical genre than progressive rock in terms of harmonic and thematic variety or structural and metric interest. Frith offers no evidence to support this claim, and seems unable even to suggest the criteria upon which such a claim might be based.[29]

One might ask, then, why Frith chose disco in particular as a style against which to measure the relative worth (or lack thereof) of progressive rock. I would suggest the reason is that disco is a style associated with the politically disadvantaged; Robert Fripp called it "a political movement that votes with its feet. It started out as the expression of two disadvantaged communities . . . the gays and the blacks."[30] To a rock critic such as Frith, then, who views "good" music and music which reacts against social repression as one and the same, disco is indeed a "much richer musical genre than progressive rock."

However, Frith himself has admitted there are two ways to assess the value of music: one can use an anti-culturalist response, "valuing music for its effects on and relationships with an audience rather than for its creator's intentions or skills," or one may take a "culturalist approach, wherein music's value lies in the technique and complexity of the 'text' itself."[31] I am fully convinced that during the late 1970s Frith's radical "anti-culturalism," with its emphasis that notes only have meanings as they unfold in specific communities, was a useful antidote to the equally radical positivism of traditional musicology. However, I think it is only fair to point out that Frith's utter dismissal of the "culturalist" position would seem to stem at least in part from the fact that as a trained sociologist with no musicological background, it is much easier for him to assume that the "text" is just a cipher that passively reflects social tensions and lacks any internal dynamic; this relieves him of the responsibility of addressing the "text" on its own terms.[32] Furthermore, even if one acknowledges the validity of their anti-culturalist stance, critics such as Frith, Marsh, Bangs, and Christgau still tend to make far too many dubious assumptions to which the popular music culture as a whole is expected to give a priori approval, for example, that only the music of repressed minorities or "politically conscious" music is capable of exerting any real social power. Deena Weinstein makes the poignant observation that

> The progressive critics assume that they are speaking to and for a community with shared standards. When rock criticism came into being that was a fair assumption; indeed, the critics helped to inform an audience that was willing to learn. After the 1960s, however, rock music began to diversify and fragment. The counterculture dissolved and was replaced by a multitude of taste publics and several music-based subcultures. It was no longer fair for critics to assume a community with shared standards to which they could contribute enlightenment.[33]

It is my belief that the whole neo-Marxist idea of "politically conscious" popular music—in the sense of music that "channels righteous anger into intelligent political action" or gives audiences "the desire to shake up the world"—is for the most part a myth perpetrated by rock critics. This becomes especially evident in the following *Rolling Stone* interview with Mick Jagger:[34]

> *Chet Flippo*   Mick, did it ever seem to you that ten or eleven years ago rock and roll was a powerful social force, and that since then it's been slowly defanged or coopted?
>
> *Mick Jagger*   (shaking his head) No. That was obviously a false notion.
>
> *Chet Flippo*   But, for example, "Street Fighting Man" *was* a rallying point, politically.
>
> *Mick Jagger*   (shrugs) Yeah, but that was during that radical Viet Nam time. It was merely *then*. You've always got to have good tunes if you're marching. But the tunes *don't make the march*. Basically, rock and roll isn't protest, and never was. It's *not* political. . . . The whole rebellion in rock and roll was about not being able to make noise

at night and not being able to play that rock and roll so loud and boogie-woogie and not being able to use the car and all that.[34]

In his *Rebel Rock: The Politics of Popular Music,* John Street is quite explicit as to what degree pop music can actually be "political":

> Popular music's interplay between everyday common sense and imagination makes it a wholly inappropriate vehicle for accompanying political manifestos or inspiring collective actions. It is not, however, politically inconsequential. Pop's inability to change the world is compensated for by its ability to articulate and alter our perceptions of that world, and perhaps more importantly, to give a glimpse of other better worlds.[35]

Using this definition as a yardstick, Pink Floyd's "apolitical" *Dark Side of the Moon* is actually a much more politically effective album than *The Wall,* although the latter was generally accepted by critics as the band's first truly "socially conscious" album. *Dark Side of the Moon* imaginatively involves the audience in its depiction of the human condition, and encourages them to think through the ramifications for themselves. On the other hand, *The Wall* too often simply lectures the audience and tells them what to think. Roger Waters admits as much himself in a startlingly frank assessment of the cinematic version of *The Wall:*

> It seemed to start bashing you over the head in the first ten minutes, and it didn't stop until it was over; there was no quiet time. . . . I wasn't interested in the Pink character [the movie's and song cycle's protagonist]; I didn't feel any empathy for him at all . . . about his concerns about the totalitarian nature of the iconography of rock n' roll. . . . And if I go to the cinema and I don't care for any of the characters, it's a bad film.[36]

It is my belief that the politically conscious "anti-culturalist" wing of the counterculture, which seems to have taken in so many of the leading rock critics, represented only a minority of the counterculture as a whole. I maintain my earlier assertion that the counterculture was mainly a spiritual/religious/humanistic, rather than a political, movement. The massive commercial success of so many of the major progressive rock bands in the early to mid-1970s demonstrates that a sizable portion of the counterculture and its post-hippie extension felt that these groups spoke to and for them; I believe the parallel fragmentation of the counterculture as a distinct subculture and progressive rock as a commercially viable style during the mid-1970s proves my assertion even further. Significantly, the bands that the rock critics attacked most harshly were precisely those groups that were most successful during the early to mid-1970s: ELP, Yes, Pink Floyd, Jethro Tull, and the Moody Blues. Bands that remained cult attractions (especially King Crimson) were treated with considerably greater respect.

It is here, I think, that the lack of consistency in the critics' assessment of progressive rock becomes especially apparent. The critics' suspicion of commercially successful acts would seem to stem once again from their understanding of "authenticity." If, as the critics saw it, the lack of an explicit political stance and an overreliance on high culture were two sure routes to artistic compromise, massive commercial success was another (by the late 1970s the Marsh-Bangs-Frith-Christgau line of criticism had become notorious for its rejection of all but the most obscure punk/New Wave bands). However, the critics never satisfactorily explained how earlier critical darlings such as the Beatles, the Stones, and Dylan were able to retain their "authenticity" while selling tens of millions of records. In short, "authenticity" became a mythic quality that the critics constantly redefined, a title they bestowed on the acts they liked and withheld from the acts they didn't. Interestingly, the critics' frequently expressed suspicion of commercial success bears a surprisingly close resemblance to many academic musicologists' contempt of "commercial music," in that both suppose that a musical style (or an individual performer) is somehow automatically contaminated by mass popularity. Robert Walser has justifiably rejected this kind of romanticized elitism in his *Running with the Devil:*

> I see the "popular" as an important site of social contestation and formation, and I find unconvincing the common assumption that culture which exists either at the margins of society [as the rock critics would have it] or among a prestigious elite [as the academics have maintained] is necessarily more important, interesting, complex, or profound than the culture of a popular mainstream.[37]

Nevertheless, the antipathy of the *Rolling Stone/Creem* wing of critics toward the major progressive rock bands is as powerful today as it ever was. Jimmy Guteman (a former *Rolling Stone* staffer) and Owen O'Donnell in their *The Fifty Worst Rock'n'Roll Records of All Time* are very careful to include albums by ELP, Yes, Jethro Tull, and the Moody Blues.[38] Pink Floyd are represented here via a solo album by the band's ex-bassist and lyricist, Roger Waters.

To be sure, the fact that the critics consistently refused to acknowledge any meaningful role that progressive rock may have played in the lives of its audience does not mean they were totally incorrect in their assessment of the style's more negative qualities. As I have mentioned repeatedly, the relationship of the major progressive rock bands with their fans (and, for that matter, the demographics of the progressive rock taste public) underwent a profound shift during the early 1970s, as the major bands made the move from clubs and smaller venues to stadiums and arenas (not to mention from Britain to the United States). There is no doubt that as these bands lost the opportunity to enjoy a symbiotic relationship with a distinct regional subculture, they increasingly called upon virtuosity, visual spectacle, and a certain sense of imperial remoteness to cement (and then hold)

their large American fan base. To the degree that this is true, one could say progressive rock's love of spectacle was self-indulgent, its fondness for virtuosity and
technical pyrotechnics exhibitionistic, and its penchant for fantasy a form of self-
absorption. But were these qualities not a hallmark of the 1970s as a whole? This
period was not, after all, labeled the "Me Generation" for nothing. One can see
the same tendencies in such diverse seventies styles as heavy metal, glam-rock (here
I would lump a whole spectrum of acts from David Bowie to Alice Cooper to
Queen and Elton John), and disco, which did eliminate the glaring performer/
audience dichotomy evident in the other styles, but which also raised self-
absorption,[39] love of spectacle, and exhibitionism to the status of quasi-religious
precepts.

In closing, then, it is fairly obvious that the critics' disdain of progressive rock
tells us more about themselves than it does about the style which they so often
demonized. Above all, the critics' likes and dislikes must be understood against
the background of the neo-Marxist view of music that they embraced, the belief
that a musical style was valid in direct proportion to the degree it challenged social
conventions and the existing political order. It was this stance, not the "anti-
culturalism" expounded by Frith, that was the true bedrock of the critics' convictions. As a result, the anti-culturalist criteria he and others expounded were always
selectively applied; the critics valued music "for its effect on and relationships with
an audience" only when the audience in question was socially-disadvantaged, or
when the music in question directly confronted the Establishment. When these
conditions did not exist in a musical style, the critics showed markedly less interest
in matters of reception. Progressive rock, like heavy metal, was not a style of the
oppressed; again like heavy metal, it did not make the sort of direct challenge to
the Establishment that the critics desired; and worst of all, it drew upon elements
of high culture, which the despised bourgeois had always used as a badge of superiority. Is it any wonder that the critics disliked it?

The fact is, however, that the neo-Marxist view of music championed by Bangs,
Marsh, Christgau, Frith, et al. was foreign to a large segment of the American rock
audience of the 1970s. Bands such as ELP, Yes, and the Moody Blues—or Black
Sabbath, Deep Purple, and Rush—did well no matter what the critics said. The
more self-righteous and venomous reviews often had the opposite of the intended
effect, motivating fans to circle the wagons of their beleaguered heroes. Indeed,
the complete one-sidedness of such reviews tended to destroy the credibility of the
reviewer in the eyes of the fans, who perceived the critic as having fallen prey to
exactly the same kind of arrogance and self-importance that he denounced the
musicians for. Ultimately, burdened down by an overly rigid ideology, these critics
give us at best a very distorted picture of progressive rock as a social force, and
they have virtually nothing useful to say about progressive rock as a musical style.
They abandoned what should have been their primary duty: coming to grips with

how the progressive rock style reflected the interests, concerns, and identity of its sizable taste public, and judging individual progressive rock bands according to how imaginatively and coherently they communicated the style to their fans. The fact that the critical consensus was never seriously challenged until Allan Moore's *Rock: The Primary Text* (1993) is significant: it suggests that we are only now reaching a place where we can reexamine the cultural history of the 1970s from a clearer, more objective vantage point.

Progressive Rock After 1976

(King Crimson) ceased to exist in September 1974, which was when all English bands in that genre should have ceased to exist. But since the rock'n'roll dinosaur likes anything which has gone before, most of them are still churning away, repeating what they did years ago without going off in any new direction.[1]

The history of progressive rock since 1976 can be divided into two distinct periods. The period from 1976 to 1981 or 1982 was marked by the fragmentation of the genre into simpler, more commercially mainstream subgenres such as American stadium rock and British symphonic pop, as well as a noticeable decline in the creativity of the major progressive rock bands. It was also during this period—which witnessed a strong reaction against the counterculture's aesthetic sensibilities—that progressive rock lost its mainstream commercial viability. The period from the early 1980s on has witnessed three major tendencies. The first involves the major bands of the 1960s and 1970s; most have continued to achieve at least some measure of commercial success, but their challenge has been to avoid crass commercialization on the one hand and an endless restatement of past triumphs on the other. Second, the early 1980s witnessed the rise of the neo-progressive movement, first in England, then elsewhere, as a younger group of bands sought to bring a more contemporary sensibility to the "classic" idiom of the 1970s. Finally, a number of new bands have cultivated what might be termed a post-progressive style, following up on the implications of King Crimson's landmark *Discipline* LP of 1981 and introducing entirely new elements (drawn especially from minimalism and various ethnic musics) into the genre.

Fragmentation and Decline—1976 to 1981

In the summer of 1976, punk rock exploded out of the working-class sections of London like a pent-up howl of rage. The impact of this event on the history of popular music in general—and on progressive rock in particular—was enormous. As I suggested in the opening chapter, the counterculture had already entered a period of fragmentation by the early 1970s; punk rock delivered a deathblow to the series of assumptions which had sustained it. Punk countered the counterculture's largely discredited message of optimism and brotherhood with a chilling nihilism; the message underlying the Sex Pistols' *God Save the Queen* was hard to ignore, however one might feel about it. There was of course a strong element of class antagonism involved—punks were largely of working-class origin, while the counterculture had largely been a middle-class phenomenon. There was also a generational cleavage at work in punk; in retrospect, punk can probably be viewed as the musical coming-of-age of the vanguard of Generation X. The punks saw little concrete progress resulting from the hippies' credo of peace, love, and understanding; instead, they saw the counterculture as having fallen victim to exactly the kind of self-indulgent materialism and hypocrisy that the hippies themselves had once so vehemently denounced.

British rock stars of the late 1960s and early 1970s, perhaps the most obvious symbols of the counterculture, were attacked by the punks with special vehemence; progressive rock made an especially inviting target. The elaborate stage shows of bands such as ELP, Pink Floyd, and Yes were seen as examples of blatant materialism and self-indulgence, while progressive rock lyrics were seen as escapist because of their constant emphasis on fantasy imagery. The style's tendency toward instrumental and metrical virtuosity was viewed as elitist, and its fondness for lengthy, monumental forms was seen as part of a futile attempt to gain the approbation of high culture. Of course, rock critics such as Lester Bangs and Dave Marsh had already said this; the punk rockers went a step further, though, by actually creating a style that addressed these concerns. In a sense, punk rock can be interpreted as a populist critique of progressive rock. Songs are short, the musical syntax is very simple, if not primitive, lyrics are direct, often offensively so, and the lack of ability to play one's instrument with any degree of skill was regarded as an emblem of authenticity and hence a positive sign.

Perhaps even more ominous to the future of progressive rock was the meteoric rise of disco between 1976 and 1978. The significance of disco did not reside in its richness as a musical style; the music of the major disco performers—from Donna Summers, Cerrone, and the Bee Gees to Sylvester and the Village People— now sounds uniformly dated. But this was precisely the point. Like punk, disco was not about innovation by an artistic elite; it was about participation by the average fan. Indeed, disco went farther than punk rock in this regard; since the performers were not present in the discotheque, the real performers were the dancers, and in this sense everyone had their chance at "stardom." Furthermore, by insisting on music as a mere accompaniment for dancing, disco returned popular music to its utilitarian pre-countercultural role, and implicitly denied the aura of prophetic revelation which the hippies had assigned to their music. Clearly, disco and punk rock, different as they were, struck at the very heart of the social assumptions that had given rise to progressive rock.

To be sure, progressive rock had already begun to cut its ties with its subcultural moorings by the early 1970s, when major progressive rock groups abandoned the clubs of England in order to perform the stadium/arena circuit. Nonetheless, the taste public that had patronized progressive rock during the early and mid-1970s was in many ways just as much a product of countercultural worldviews and assumptions as the musicians themselves. However, the late 1970s and particularly the early 1980s witnessed the rise of a younger taste public—coinciding with the coming-of-age of the vanguard of Generation X—for whom the ideals and assumptions of the counterculture appeared outdated, even hopelessly quaint. Since it had not been a genuinely subcultural style since the early 1970s, progressive rock had no core audience to fall back on when its taste public dissolved. Bands could pack it in—and a number did—or they could swallow the notions of authenticity which had been accepted without question since the early days of the counterculture, alter the style and substance of their music as necessary, and ride the currents of the new pop mainstream. The bands which survived the cataclysm took the latter route.

A comparison between progressive rock and heavy metal in this realm is instructive. By the early 1970s, heavy metal had already become the nexus of a distinct subculture whose values were often very different from, sometimes even diametrically opposed to, those of the counterculture. Thus the unique subculture associated with heavy metal withstood the dissolution of the counterculture during the early to mid-1970s, and as a result, heavy metal continues to exist as a commercially viable idiom, plied by musicians young enough to be the sons (much more rarely, the daughters) of the musicians who pioneered the genre. To be sure, a second generation of progressive rock bands have emerged during the 1980s and even into the 1990s. Because any subcultures surrounding this music are so much more fragmentary and less unified than the metal subculture, however, progressive rock as a living, developing idiom has been unable to maintain mainstream commercial viability, although the "classic" progressive rock bands continue to sell millions of records. Needless to say, none of the newer progressive rock bands have achieved the commercial success of their metal counterparts such as Metallica.

The cul-de-sac reached by progressive rock during the second half of the 1970s was the result not only of sociological pressures, but of purely musical difficulties as well. As long as it was to remain classified as rock music, the progressive rock style had to maintain some sort of discernible beat and an at least marginally comprehensible melodic/harmonic syntax. Yet, by the mid-1970s bands such as King Crimson and Gentle Giant had pushed the metric, harmonic, and thematic complexity of progressive rock to the limits of its commercial viability. Furthermore, by the middle of the decade the symphonic string and brass sounds of the Mellotron, the cathedral-like ambience of the Hammond, and the rich, quasi-choral vocal arrangements that characterized the genre had largely been mined out, and were beginning to become manneristic. Finally, by the mid-1970s progressive rock's monumental formal approaches had been pushed beyond reasonable bounds; pieces such as Yes's four-movement magnum opus *Tales from Topographic Oceans*, nearly an hour-and-a-half long, strained both audience concentration and the musicians' structural resourcefulness beyond the breaking point.[2]

In short, progressive rock musicians of the mid-1970s found themselves in a very similar situation to composers in the Western classical tradition in the years following World War I, wondering where to go next with a musical style whose potentialities had largely been exhausted. As with their classical counterparts earlier in the century, progressive rock musicians had three choices: to continue the move toward complexity until the conventions of the existing style were broken, to make minor adjustments to the existing style, or to subject the existing style to considerable simplification.[3]

A few bands such as Henry Cow, a band that did its most representative work in the mid-1970s, continued the trend toward complexity even though it meant introducing elements outside of the code of progressive rock and indeed rock in general. In any given Henry Cow piece one is likely to encounter furious atonal instrumental passages with no discernible melodic contour or key center, impossibly complex shifting meters alternating with freely ametric sections with no definable beat or regularly recurring rhythms, and jagged, *sprechstimme*-like vocal lines that blur the line between song and speech. The band's music was part and parcel of an idealistic socialist worldview; as the band's drummer, Chris Cutler, explained, "We had to make what amounted to political decisions about the organization of the group and its relations to the commercial structures, and this was bound to be reflected in the music too."[4] Henry Cow's music was highly eclectic even by the standards of progressive rock; "Living in the Heart of the Beast," from the *In Praise of Learning* LP, for instance, opens with an atonal, highly distorted electric guitar solo, but closes (nearly fifteen minutes later) with a stately modal march that would not have been out of place on an ELP or Procol Harum album. In their best music, Henry Cow's eclecticism works; however, the group complexified the progressive rock style beyond the point of commercial viability (their strident socialist lyrics didn't help their sales potential, either), and in fact are often more reminiscent of an avant-garde performance ensemble than a rock band. As one might expect, they remained a cult phenomenon, almost unknown outside of England and a few centers in continental Europe.

A second possibility for progressive rock bands emerging in the mid- to late 1970s was to continue to work in the general stylistic framework of the genre. The problem here was that it was difficult for bands that made this choice not to sound quite similar to already-established progressive rock groups. U.K. were probably the most successful progressive rock band to emerge in the late 1970s, and they did manage to leave an individual imprint on the style (especially in terms of drawing it closer to contemporary fusion) without, however, contributing any essential new characteristics. Significantly, U.K. were a "supergroup," consisting of musicians such as Bill Bruford, John Wetton, Eddie Jobson (Curved Air), and Allan Holdsworth (Soft Machine, Gong) who had already garnered significant reputations elsewhere. Of the "second wave" groups surveyed in chapter 1, only one band, ELP, were a supergroup in this manner. The general difficulty faced by new progressive rock talent after the mid-1970s in achieving any kind of mainstream commercial success—or even in finding any kind of numerically significant audience—indicates the degree to which the taste public surrounding progressive rock fragmented as the ideals of the counterculture lost their hold.

Most progressive rock bands followed the third possible route—simplification. As early as 1972, King Crimson began to dispense with many of the rich tone colors drawn from classical music—the symphonic colorings of the Mellotron, the rich vocal harmonizations, the ornate acoustic passages—in favor of a more austere timbral palette dominated by distorted guitar and bass guitar. A similar tendency is evident in Van der Graaf Generator's trio of mid-1970s albums: *Godbluff, Still Life*, and *World Record*. On the other hand, in terms of harmonic and metric syntax and formal approach, the music of these groups remained as complex as ever; King Crimson's harmonic syntax reached a new degree of sophistication in their three great albums of 1973 and 1974, *Lark's Tongue in Aspic, Starless and Bible Black*, and *Red*. In the late 1970s, however, most of the established progressive rock bands simplified virtually every aspect of their music significantly, not so much in direct response to punk rock—which never did achieve mass popularity in the United States—but rather in response to American stadium rock and British symphonic pop, two mid-1970s styles that, ironically, drew much from progressive rock.

Indeed, in this study progressive rock has been viewed as an exclusively English phenomenon; the role of Continental Europe and the United States in the development of the idiom has been seen largely as one of providing English progressive rock bands with a huge taste public. Progressive rock penetrated Continental Europe more rapidly than the United States; a number of English progressive rock bands made major inroads into the European market long before they achieved success in the States, and by the early 1970s the progressive rock style had spread throughout much of Western Europe. As early as 1971 the Dutch progressive rock band Focus, spearheaded by the daunting instrumental attack of guitarist Jan Akkerman and organist/flautist Thijs van Leer, were garnering significant attention as a major exponent of the style. The early 1970s saw the rise of other well-known European progressive rock bands such as the Italian outfits Banco del Mutuo Soccorso (later known as Banco), PFM (Premiata Forneria Marconi), Museo

Rosenbach, Acqua Fragile, Celeste, and Il Balletto di Bronzo; the French bands Ange, Mona Lisa, Atoll, and Pulsar; the Spanish groups Granada and Triana; the German bands Triumvirat, Eloy, and Grobschnitt; and the Finnish group Wigwam.

These bands had relatively little interaction with their English counterparts, although the established British bands did sometimes play the role of "mentors" to Continental (mainly Italian) bands that attempted to break into the English-speaking market. For instance, English-language versions of PFM's and Banco's albums were distributed on ELP's now-defunct Manticore label; King Crimson lyricist Peter Sinfield assisted members of PFM in translating their lyrics into English, while Peter Hammill rendered a similar service to the Italian band Le Orme. Significantly, while the major English progressive rock bands were popular throughout Europe and North America, few Continental European bands were able to break through the English or American markets with any degree of success (Focus and to a lesser extent the major Italian bands that were willing to do English-language versions of their albums were exceptions). Indeed, although Continental Europe produced some very accomplished progressive rock bands, most of these groups are stylistically indebted to one or more of the major English bands;[5] it is in fact possible to write a coherent history of progressive rock as a style by focusing entirely on English progressive rock bands.

The main contribution of Continental bands was to bring national characteristics to bear upon the idiom. For instance, the Spanish band Triana introduced a strong element of flamenco into their music. A number of Scandinavian bands such as Samla Mammas Manna introduced a healthy dose of national folk styles into their take on the progressive rock idiom. German progressive rock groups such as Eloy and Grobschnitt evinced an interest in further developing Pink Floyd's late-1960s "space rock" sound, with a nod in the direction of the more abstract soundscapes of contemporaneous German electronic bands such as Kraftwerk and Tangerine Dream. Italian bands introduced an emphasis on lyricism, vocal effusiveness, and melodrama that often differentiates them from their English colleagues. While those attuned to the relative reserve of much English progressive rock may find some Italian progressive rock (i.e., Il Balletto di Bronzo's acclaimed *YS* album) unnecessarily melodramatic, even slightly vulgar, those who find English progressive rock somewhat "cold" and "lacking in heart" (i.e., certain American critics) may well prefer the Italian equivalent.

The one Continental European progressive rock band that forged a genuinely new path was the French outfit Magma. Like Henry Cow, Magma consistently introduced elements from outside the code of rock at large into their music. The band's mature style was indebted not only to the earlier twentieth-century masters that English progressive rock bands regularly drew from (Bartók, Stravinsky, Holst), but also to the music of Carl Orff (especially his choral writing), the postwar avant-garde, black gospel music, and the free jazz of the 1960s (John Coltrane, Sun

Ra). Magma were greatly admired for their distinctive bass sound; they employed two bassists, who played "air bass" and "earth bass," respectively (to quote the band's own terminology). Many of the groups that followed Magma developed this bass sound further through the introduction of low, dark acoustic instruments such as trombones, bassoons, and cellos. The group's strongly individual personality resulted from extramusical factors as well; leader Christian Vander developed a synthetic language, Kobaian, for the group's lyrics, which consistently express a peculiar, science-fiction-tinged apocalyptic viewpoint involving intergalactic warfare, battles between demons and wizards, and the like. During the 1970s it was said that hard-core members of the band's European cult following were able to converse in Kobaian.

Unlike Henry Cow, which largely remained an isolated phenomenon in England,[6] Magma actually founded a new and distinct genre—which has alternately been termed "neoclassical" (not to be confused with the interwar neoclassicism of Stravinsky, Hindemith, or French composers such as Milhaud), "experimental classical," "chamber progressive rock," or "modern classical rock." This style has been plied by a number of bands that emerged during the late 1970s such as the Belgian Univers Zero and the French bands Art Zoyd and Shub Niggurath. These groups continued to develop Magma's general musical direction and their apocalyptic motifs, as is evidenced in a number of their album titles: Univers Zero's *Ceux de dehors* and Art Zoyd's *Generation sans futur* are representative samples (indeed, the group Shub Niggurath drew its name from a short story by the American gothic horror writer H. P. Lovecraft). The music of these bands is best described as a fusion of the harmonic practices of Bartók and Stravinsky with the sonorous resources of post–World War II avant-garde composers such as Krzysztof Penderecki (i.e., the "bands of sound" which he utilizes in his *Threnody to the Victims of Hiroshima*) and the rhythmic and timbral sensibilities of rock. While never achieving mainstream commercial viability, this style became the focus of a loyal and dedicated cult following, especially in France and the Low Countries.

Progressive rock took root in the United States more slowly; bands such as Yes and Pink Floyd that were already well known in Britain did not achieve a major breakthrough in the American market until 1971 and 1972. Throughout the early to mid-1970s, English progressive rock was especially popular in the Midwest, the Northeast, and to a lesser degree the West Coast; that is, precisely the same areas as English heavy metal. The penetration of the United States by English progressive rock did not result in the rise of a group of commercially successful bands that purveyed a stylistically "pure" progressive rock. To the contrary, "genuine" American progressive rock bands of the early to mid-1970s remained cult attractions even in the United States, with followings confined to a limited geographical area, usually in either the Midwest (Atlantis Philharmonic in Cleveland, Ethos in Fort Wayne, Starcastle in Champaign-Urbana, October in Detroit, Easter Island in Louisville) or the Mid-Atlantic coast (Happy the Man and However in Washington, D.C., Cathedral in New York, Fireballet in New Jersey). Only a few American progressive rock bands of the 1970s came from outside of these two regions (Babylon, from the Tampa–Saint Petersburg area of Florida, probably being the most important exception). As Will Straw points out, the chief importance of the simultaneous penetration of the United States by English progressive rock and heavy metal styles was that "the distinction between heavy metal and progressive rock audiences began to weaken. . . . American groups that combined features of these two forms achieved considerable success (Boston, Kansas, Styx, etc.). and this hybrid sound came to be characteristic of album-oriented rock radio."[7]

"Stadium rock"—as the style purveyed by Kansas, Boston, and Styx (as well as Rush, Toto, Journey, R.E.O. Speedwagon, Foreigner, Heart, and a host of other bands) came to be known—became enormously popular in the United States between 1976 and the early 1980s. This style largely avoids the epic forms and the more complex rhythmic, harmonic, and textural techniques of progressive rock, as well as the more abrasive and strident elements of heavy metal. Thus the stadium rock style simultaneously commercialized the two genres and initiated the fragmentation of the progressive rock style.

Stadium rock bands especially admired progressive rock's virtuosity, and lengthy solos became a part of stadium rock as well. Indeed, certain stylistic elements of progressive rock were used over and over again by these bands until they were reduced to clichés: toccata-like organ and synthesizer solos, sudden juxtapositions of acoustic and electric sections, and three- or four-part vocal arrangements dominated by high tenors. (On the other hand, the screaming guitar leads, chordal riffing, and deep bass lines that dominated the genre owed more to heavy metal, especially Led Zeppelin.) Album cover designs drew upon the same science fiction, fantasy, and surreal motifs that had long been current in progressive rock; this is especially evident in the mid- to late-1970s album covers of Styx, Boston, Rush, and Kansas, the North American stadium rock bands that were stylistically closest to progressive rock. (In all fairness, some of the music from Kansas's first five albums and much of Rush's output from 1976 to 1981 can be said to represent unique variants of the progressive rock style—often suggestive of unusually sophisticated heavy metal in the case of Rush, or a progressive rock/southern rock fusion in the case of Kansas.)[8] A number of the stadium rock bands tended to treat favorite progressive rock themes—the spiritual quest, apocalyptic motifs, fantasy narratives—in an ever-more formulaic manner; Styx's "Come Sail Away" and "Lord of the Rings" are especially noteworthy examples of this tendency. Those stadium rock bands closer in conception to heavy metal (Journey, Foreigner) often ignored progressive rock themes entirely, instead celebrating the same subject matter that had animated so much heavy metal and hard rock of the early 1970s: sex, drugs, and rock-and-roll. While the musicianship of the best stadium rock bands was often excellent, and the production of their albums often superior, these qualities did not compensate for the frequent dearth of creativity and the corporate standardization that characterized much of this music. To its many detractors, the appearance of stadium rock marked the record companies' triumph in establishing full control over rock as product.

British symphonic pop, another genre that can be viewed as a progressive rock splinter, arose at virtually the same time as American stadium rock. The musicians who plied this style—of which the Electric Light Orchestra, Supertramp, 10 cc, the Alan Parsons Project, and Al Stewart are best known—drew not so much on progressive rock's tradition of virtuosity and monumentality (the prime attraction of the progressive rock idiom to American stadium rockers), but rather on its quasi-symphonic fullness. This style puts far less emphasis on instrumental solos than does stadium rock and largely avoids the elements of that genre most closely associated with heavy metal: screaming electric guitar leads, heavy bass lines, and a forceful beat. Instead, it relies on straightforward song-writing, rich vocal arrangements, and a quasi-orchestral fullness (for instance, in addition to a keyboardist, ELO employed two cellists and a violinist). While there was some use of surrealism and cosmic motifs (especially on the Alan Parsons Project's *Tales of Mystery and Imagination* of 1976 and *I Robot* of 1977, two of the more interesting albums to emerge from the genre), these groups were above all singles bands, and the subject matter of British symphonic pop was often frankly romantic and sentimental in the tradition of the popular music mainstream. Topics of romance and personal relationships were the rule, other subjects the exception.

Faced with competition on both sides of the Atlantic from two genres that had drawn heavily from progressive rock even while simplifying key elements of the genre, most progressive rock bands felt they had little choice but to simplify their own music if they were to remain commercially competitive. When bands proved reluctant to simplify their approach, record companies, who did not relish the prospects of seeing groups that regularly sold a million records lose their audience, were not adverse to arm-twisting (ELP's disappointing *Love Beach* of 1978 is one of the more regrettable examples of a progressive rock band being talked into experimenting with a more "mainstream" pop style against their own better judgment).[9] Some bands drew on the soft-rock stylizations of British symphonic pop: this approach is evident in Genesis's *Then There Were Three*, ELP's *Love Beach*, Renaissance's *A Song for All Seasons*, and the Moody Blues' *Octave* (all released in 1978). Other bands adopted a heavier, harder-edged sound reminiscent of American stadium rock: one can observe this tendency in Gentle Giant's *The Missing Piece* and Pink Floyd's *Animals* (both 1977), Yes's *Drama* (1980), and Jethro Tull's *A* (1980) and especially their *Broadsword and the Beast* (1982).

Both tendencies involved a simplification of the progressive rock style on virtually every level. Harmonic syntax was narrowed to a straightforward modality, shifting and asymmetric meters were used less and less frequently, and lengthy programmatic forms largely fell out of favor after 1979. To be sure, a number of English progressive bands managed to produce late-period masterpieces during the mid- to late 1970s. ELP's "Pirates," Yes's "Awaken" (both from 1977), and some of the material from Jethro Tull's *Songs from the Wood* and *Heavy Horses* (1977 and 1978, respectively) must be counted among the finest material these bands put forth during their careers; furthermore, the two fine U.K. studio albums, *U.K.* and *Danger Money*, were released in 1978 and 1979, respectively. However, Pink Floyd's *The Wall* (1979) seems more indicative of the direction progressive rock was taking during the late 1970s. Although the album certainly represents lyricist Roger Waters's most audacious conceptual undertaking (whether *The Wall* is more successful on a conceptual level than *Dark Side of the Moon* is open for debate—I am inclined to think not), there is a marked decline in musical creativity and sophistication. This situation was mirrored in most of the albums released by major progressive rock bands at the close of the decade.

Indeed, by the late 1970s it had become clear that for a number of interrelated styles that had originated out of the counterculture's creative cauldron during the late 1960s—not only progressive rock but jazz-rock and folk-rock as well—a golden age had passed. It is no surprise, then, that a number of important progressive rock bands folded on a permanent basis at this time. Van der Graaf Generator, perhaps the finest British progressive rock band that failed to break the American market, released a final studio album in 1977 (*The Quiet Zone*) that showed a prescient awareness of New Wave tendencies, issued their final album (*Vital: Van der Graaf Live*) in 1978, and then broke up. Gentle Giant folded in 1980 after the release of their *Civilian* LP made it clear that the change toward a simpler, harder-rocking style had been to no commercial avail. After existing less than three years, U.K. dissolved following the release of a live album in 1979; one can only guess what level of success they might have achieved if they had released their first album in 1975 rather than 1978.

Even massively successful acts such as ELP, Pink Floyd, and Yes went on hiatus during the early 1980s. ELP released no studio albums between *Love Beach* and the *Emerson, Lake and Powell* LP of 1986, when Cozy Powell replaced Carl Palmer on drums; indeed, Emerson, Lake, and Palmer were not to record together again until the *Black Moon* album of 1992. Pink Floyd did not release a new studio album between 1979 and 1983, and then appeared to break up permanently until their dramatic reformation without Roger Waters in 1987. After their transitional and less-than-satisfying *Drama* (1980), Yes went on hiatus until 1983, when the release of their *90125* LP marked the emergence of a new, more commercially oriented incarnation of the band. Of the major progressive rock bands of the 1970s, only Jethro Tull and Genesis continued to release albums unabated through the early 1980s. Genesis, more than any other major progressive rock band of the 1970s, has cut its ties with the progressive rock legacy; a gradual but consistent development toward a straight-ahead pop approach can be heard over three albums of the early 1980s, *Duke* (1980), *Abacab* (1981), and *Genesis* (1983), culminating with the *Invisible Touch* LP of 1986.

Perhaps the single most defining moment in the dissolution of the "classic" progressive rock style of the 1970s was the emergence of the supergroup Asia in 1982. Formed from the wreckage of a number of progressive rock's greatest bands, many believed that Asia, which consisted of John Wetton (King Crimson, U.K.), Steve Howe (Yes), Geoff Downes (Yes), and Carl Palmer (ELP) would usher in a brave new era of progressive rock, and bring about a renaissance of the style. To the contrary, however, their debut album, recorded in 1981, demonstrated the degree to which progressive rock, American stadium rock, and English symphonic pop had coalesced into a single style which could simply be termed "commercial rock." This is not to deny the tunefulness of the material, the arranging and production excellence of the record, or the technique of the players. It should be noted, however, that the restless musical creativity which had so characterized progressive rock during its heyday was no longer apparent; stylistically, Asia is far more akin to Journey, Boston, Styx, or Kansas circa 1978 than to Yes, Genesis, ELP, or King Crimson circa 1972.

Even more significant is the change in philosophical emphasis that is apparent between the music of Asia and that of its progressive rock predecessors. In its heyday, progressive rock had engaged its audience in a search for metaphysical depth, for spiritual authenticity, for a way around the depersonalizing tendencies of modern society. If there was one theme that consistently threaded its way through the best progressive rock of the early 1970s, it was the recovery of lost spirituality. It is only against the backdrop of this pursuit that Asia's bland, pop-radio friendly subject matter takes on its full significance: it signaled that for the post-hippie extension of the counterculture which had followed progressive rock throughout the 1970s, the idealistic impulses of the 1960s had finally run their course. The dream—or the illusion, if you will—of individual and global enlightenment was over.

1981 and beyond, Part I: The Major Bands

The years 1980 to 1983 witnessed an enormous change in the popular music scene, comparable in scope to the psychedelic revolution of the mid- to late 1960s. While the shifts in the cultural landscape which I discussed above were a major factor in this transformation, changes in the record industry and in music technology also played a role. These shifts, then, deserve at least brief consideration.

The musicians who recorded their first albums in the late 1960s entered the recording industry at an extremely fortuitous time. The period of 1965 to 1970 was one of "turbulence" for the record industry. It was struggling to absorb a strange new style, rock;[10] record company executives were often unsure as to what would sell, and how to best market records for specific record-buying publics. This situation encouraged a healthy competition among the larger labels, as well as musical experimentation on the part of musicians. The economic vitality of the late 1960s and early 1970s made such experimentation a commercially viable proposition for large and midsized record labels alike. As a result, musicians had unprecedented leverage with the record companies in terms of what they were allowed to release; they were often encouraged in their eclecticism and experimentation by sympathetic record company figures.[11] Furthermore, they were given a control of the recorded product in terms of production, graphics and album cover art, packaging, etc., that earlier popular musicians could have only dreamed about.

The early to mid-1970s, however, witnessed a reversal of many of these trends. An almost monopolistic situation developed in which six major record companies controlled much of the market. Competition, and with it experimentation, gradually ceased to exist under these conditions. As record company executives became ever more selective in their means of targeting specific record-buying publics, eclecticism and experimentation became commercially abhorrent. The major labels lost interest in signing any artist that could not be conveniently pigeonholed into an existing style; a parallel trend became evident in the radio programming of this time as well with the rise of the AOR (album-oriented radio) format. By the mid-1970s Dave Stewart had noticed these changed conditions while attempting to get a recording contract for his band National Health:

> After countless refusals and rejections from other companies, things reached a head when Virgin Records, a company who had to some extent built their reputation on progressive music and with whom we had close ties, turned us down. . . . What Virgin had rightly divined, of course, was that this band had *musicians* in it, and by some unspoken inter-record company edict that persists to the present day, had decreed that musicians were bad news, and bands which sported them were *not to be signed*. Far better to sign up some good-looking front person who's not particularly interested in music (like the record company) and replace the band, if there is one, with session players or *machines*. Then you can get down to the real business of making a *hit record* without all that music stuff getting in the way.[12]

Not surprisingly, during this period even major bands began to lose a certain amount of leverage to the record companies over matters they had once controlled. By the early 1980s it was becoming rarer for bands to produce their own albums without the "assistance" of a producer hired by the record companies; in some cases bands stopped producing their own albums entirely. Likewise, during the

1980s record company executives exerted a greater say in matters such as album cover art and packaging which had been more or less the exclusive domain of the musicians during progressive rock's heyday. Indeed, it is no exaggeration to say that if the progressive rock style had not emerged when it did, the commercial conditions would have never existed for it to emerge at all.

These changes in social function and in the dynamics of the recording industry were accompanied by the digital revolution of the early 1980s, which wrought huge changes in the technology of electronic musical instruments. The early 1980s witnessed the rise of sequencers, which enable a musician to program a part into a synthesizer (perhaps a part that he or she cannot play in real time) and to re-create the part by merely activating a memory button. This capability obsolesced, to a certain degree at least, the cult of instrumental virtuosity which had been such a hallmark of progressive rock; it was now no longer a given, even in live performances (much less recordings), whether musicians were actually playing the parts they appeared to be playing. Also becoming common during this period were synthetic drum machines, which reproduce preprogrammed drum parts, and may be used to replace a live drummer. A whole genre of synthesizer rock arose in which the drum kit was eliminated entirely in favor of sequenced drums, and this tendency was not without impact even among the "classic" progressive rock bands. For instance, Jethro Tull dispensed with a regular drummer on their *Under Wraps* LP of 1984, with group leader Ian Anderson handling the drum programming and using studio drummers only as needed. This period also witnessed the rise of samplers, which allow one to prerecord a sound, store it in a synthesizer's memory, and reproduce it at will: effects that were previously available only in the studio now became possible to re-create in live situations.

Above all, the early 1980s were marked by the emergence of MIDI (Musical Instrument Digital Interface). Synthesizers with MIDI capability can be linked together; one keyboard can be used to control an entire setup of synthesizers, and more important, characteristic preset sounds from two or more synthesizers can be mixed together to create yet different sounds. The replacement of analog by digital equipment after 1980 meant that many of these capabilities (sequencers, samplers, MIDI, etc.) could be used in conjunction; specific sounds which on analog synthesizers had formerly been obtainable only through a painstaking manipulation of a whole series of knobs and/or patchcords could now be created, stored, and retrieved by simply pressing a button. But while digital technology made retrieving and reproducing specific parts easier than ever, it often required an expert to harness the full capabilities of MIDI; in the 1980s, synthesizer programmers became as important to bands as the engineer and the producer.

Not surprisingly, changes in record industry dynamics and in music technology during the early 1980s were accompanied by equally radical shifts in musical style. In hindsight, the stadium rock of the late 1970s and early 1980s can be seen as the final playing out of a "classic" rock style that can be traced back to Bob Dylan, the Beatles, the Rolling Stones, the Who, and a few other seminal performers of the mid-1960s. Of the two radical styles of the late 1970s which brought rock's "classic" period to a close, punk rock never achieved any real commercial viability, and was important after 1980 mainly as a cult style; likewise, disco's dissolution was almost as sudden as its rise. However, out of the ashes of these two styles arose New Wave, which was to be the predominant rock style of the early 1980s. The major New Wave acts came out of England (the Police, Elvis Costello, Thomas Dolby), New York City (the Talking Heads, Blondie), and occasionally other areas of the States (the Cars from Boston, Devo from Akron, Ohio). Stylistically, they ranged from a clear punk background (Costello) to a strong disco sensibility (Blondie). New Wave pared off the rough edges of punk—especially the latter's fiercely distorted guitars—and drew on the punchy bass lines, synthetic tone colors, and ceaselessly repeated rhythmic patterns of disco. While New Wave was metrically, harmonically, and structurally simpler than progressive rock, it was innovative in different realms, especially in texture, timbre, and production techniques. The intricately layered textures of the two most inventive New Wave bands, the Police and the Talking Heads, seem to have stemmed at least in part from their interest in the burgeoning world music scene: the Police drew from reggae and Middle Eastern styles, while the Talking Heads were clearly interested in African music. Since the New Wave bands emerged at the junction when digital technology was beginning to replace the older analog equipment, it is perhaps not surprising that these groups initially used the new equipment with greater confidence than did the established progressive rock bands. The Police exerted a powerful influence on Genesis, Yes, and Rush during the early 1980s; the highly linear textures of King Crimson's 1980s incarnation clearly owed something to the Talking Heads.

One unforeseen result of the enormous impact of the new technology on virtually all styles of popular music has been a further "leveling off" of formerly distinct genres. As I mentioned above, the progressive rock bands that adopted the new equipment during the early 1980s were often put in the unfamiliar position of being followers rather than innovators; at its worst, their music of this period could sound uncomfortably derivative of the major New Wave performers. As the established progressive rock bands adopted the new equipment, they often abandoned just those analog keyboards (the Hammond, the Mellotron, and later analog string synthesizers) that had been responsible for the genre's distinctive, classically influenced sound. Even more significantly, in the rush to appropriate all the newly available digital technology, acoustic instruments disappeared entirely, or almost entirely, from the music of the major progressive rock bands during the early to mid-1980s. This trend is evident in every Genesis album issued since 1980, in Yes's *90125* (1983) and *Big Generator* (1987), and in Pink Floyd's *A Momentary Lapse of Reason* (1987). Even Jethro Tull, one of the most aggressively acoustic progressive rock bands of the 1970s, tended to favor a surprisingly electronic sound during the 1980s (especially on their *Under Wraps* LP of 1984). Replacing the distinctive tone colors of the Mellotron, the Hammond, and acoustic instruments were a set of timbral resources common to all types of popular music of the 1980s: washes of synthetic strings, sudden bursts of synthetic brass, bell-like or chimelike chordal backdrops, metallic-sounding sequenced ostinato patterns, throbbing synthetic bass lines, and the unmistakable synthetic resonance of drum machines or electronic drums. Even when acoustic instruments have been used, it has almost always been with a wash of synthetic tone colors in the background.

There is of course nothing wrong with the new digital sounds per se; indeed, one can only expect musicians to experiment with new timbral resources as they become available. Nonetheless, I believe that the elimination (or at least severe de-emphasis) of acoustic instruments in some ways destroys the soul of progressive rock. Dan Hedges once remarked that "While Yes had always sweated overtime to be precise and technologically adventurous, there was always that underlying flavor of something older in their music. They were a modern electric band, but their influences and subtle colorings stretched back over the centuries—something that always came through on their albums."[13] This remark, which recalls yet again the importance of the acoustic versus electronic dichotomy to the genre, can be applied to progressive rock of the 1970s as a whole. Eliminating the acoustic element of progressive rock eliminated the capacity for creating the dramatic contrasts that was one of the style's most distinctive features, and has tended to make it increasingly indistinguishable from other commercial rock styles.

Tone color is not the only element of the major bands' output during the 1980s that was impacted by the new currents. If there was one lasting legacy of the disco revolution, it was its reinstatement of rock's pre-countercultural function as dance music. In New Wave, this legacy receives its clearest stylistic expression in the frequent predominance of a single rhythmic pattern (not to mention a single tempo) throughout an entire song. On the other hand, the "classic" progressive rock style, with its dramatic contrasts, was characterized by frequent shifts in tempo and in rhythmic character (as well as specific rhythmic patterns) from one section of a composition to the next. The adaptation by a number of major progressive rock bands of New Wave tendencies during the early 1980s gave their music of this period a rhythmic character that was radically different from their music of the 1970s. At least some of the music of Yes ("Owner of a Lonely Heart"), Genesis ("Invisible Touch"), and others during the 1980s suggests the dance rhythms of techno-pop and other New Wave–derived styles.

The abandonment of the "classic" progressive rock style of the 1970s by the established progressive rock bands was most evident from the late 1970s to the mid-1980s. It was at this time that the reaction against the aesthetic values of the 1970s was at its peak, and the established bands had to make at least some concessions to the tastes of a new generation of teenagers if they were to remain part of the popular music mainstream (as opposed to becoming a nostalgic "cult" attraction for an aging hippie subculture).[14] Long, multisectional pieces or song cycles were, of course, a legacy of countercultural sensibilities. As a result, epic forms of this type largely disappeared from the music of established progressive groups after 1980. Such forms became not only culturally anachronistic, but musically unnecessary during this period as well, since bands were no longer utilizing the juxtapositions of electric and acoustic tone colors or of different rhythmic approaches which had made the forms desirable in the first place. Not surprisingly, the epic subject matter that had animated progressive rock of the 1970s—cosmic narratives, spiritual quests, apocalyptic scenarios—fell out of favor as well. Subject matter turned to more mundane topics such as romance and personal relationships, as well as to socially conscious lyrics that reflect the political coming-of-age of certain elements of the countercultural agenda (environmentalism, attempts to address problems of urban decay, advocacy of the homeless, etc.). Occasionally these bands did deal with more "cosmic" or "philosophical" conceptions during the early and mid-1980s, but they seldom (if ever) achieved the epic sweep of their best material from the 1970s, which had so perfectly meshed with the contemporary zeitgeist. The grandly charted flow of ideas, the gradual buildups from soft acoustic murmurs to apocalyptic electronic climaxes, the sense of the transcendental that characterized pieces such as *Supper's Ready, Close to the Edge,* and *Karn Evil 9* are lost. At the same time, their more socially conscious lyrics of the 1980s often seem a bit rote and formulaic; at their worst, they come off as politically correct in a bad (that is to say, a calculated) sense.

Surrealism disappeared almost entirely from the lyrics and even the cover art of the major bands during this period. One sees in the simple, abstract, geometrical designs of album covers such as Yes's *90125* and *Big Generator,* Genesis's *Abacab, Genesis,* or *Invisible Touch,* Emerson, Lake and Powell's eponymous album, and the three King Crimson albums of the early 1980s a strong reflection of contemporaneous New Wave tendencies. The abandonment of surrealism suggests again the degree to which these bands had become divorced from the hippie subculture in which they originated.

Other elements of progressive rock that had stemmed from countercultural sensibilities were the emphasis on unusual metric and harmonic schemes and on instrumental virtuosity. As noted above, the cult of instrumental virtuosity which had so defined progressive rock during the 1970s was dealt a heavy blow with the mass appearance of sequencers in the 1980s, since it was now possible for someone with no keyboard skill to program a sequenced part that even a Keith Emerson or a Rick Wakeman could never hope to play. As a result, lengthy solos do not play a major role in the music of most of the major progressive rock bands during the 1980s. Asymmetric and shifting meters disappeared almost entirely from the music of some bands (i.e., Genesis) and were used less often and more unobtrusively by other bands. Harmonic progressions and textures are much simpler; less emphasis is placed on the notes themselves, on thematic relationships or contrapuntal configurations, and much more emphasis is placed on mixing different electronic timbres, that is, on tone color for its own sake. (Reverb plays an especially critical role in this; in the 1980s reverb was often used to "bleed" different parts together and eliminate registral "holes" in the overall mix.) The de-emphasis of virtuosity and lessening of the music's metric and harmonic sophistication did increase its accessibility; however, it also lessened the music's sense of tension, excitement, and distinciveness.

Of course, one could argue that for too long Western musicians have ignored the limitless possibilities of sound itself (as opposed to the relationships between sounds created in rhythm, melody, and harmony), and that experimentation with tone color for its own sake is long overdue. I would not disagree. I would point out, though, that even as the major progressive rock bands have forsaken the rhythmic, harmonic, and melodic interest of their earlier music during the 1980s and 1990s, they have tended to work from a limited palette of commercially acceptable timbres. They have shown relatively little of the sensitivity toward the new possibilities of electronic tone colors that is evident, for instance, in the contemporaneous music of Brian Eno (to further illustrate this point, one may wish to compare Genesis's music of the 1980s with the contemporaneous music of their ex-lead singer, Peter Gabriel).

In all fairness, the late 1980s witnessed something of an anti–anti-progressive movement among at least some of the major bands of the 1970s. In 1988, Jon Anderson left the 1980s incarnation of Yes and rejoined with most of Yes's legendary *Close to the Edge* lineup. The resulting band, Anderson, Bruford, Wakeman and Howe, released an eponymous album in 1989 that reintroduced the longer, multisectional pieces, epic subject matter, and surrealistic verse that Yes had abandoned after 1980. The *Emerson, Lake and Powell* LP of 1986 sounds closer to the classic ELP sound than anything the group did during the late 1970s; side one of the album, in particular, reasserted the group's penchant for monumental structural conceptions and also prominently reintroduced the sound of the Hammond organ. On the other hand, much of the *Three* album of 1987, done by Emerson, Palmer, and California singer-songwriter Robert Berry, hearkens back to the worst moments of *Love Beach*. Pink Floyd's *Momentary Lapse of Reason* (1987) intentionally reasserts the longer pieces, more keyboard-oriented timbres, and richer, more complex textures that the band felt were lost when Roger Waters took unilateral control of the group during the late 1970s.

From our perspective in the mid-1990s, it appears the work of the major progressive rock bands may be undergoing yet another shift in emphasis. From the late 1970s to the mid-1980s, these bands tended to react against the "classic" progressive rock style of the 1970s in favor of a more mainstream pop style. The driving motivation among many of these groups during the late 1980s and early 1990s appeared to be a desire to integrate some of the key elements of the classic progressive rock style into the new commercial realities and the changed musical technology. On releases such as Pink Floyd's *The Division Bell*, Yes's *Talk* (featuring the *90125* lineup), and Emerson, Lake and Palmer's *In the Hot Seat* (all 1994), the bands seem to have entered yet a new phase. In addition to attempting to draw the "classic" style of the 1970s into a more contemporary framework, they also seem interested in coming to terms with the legacy of their more pop-inspired work of the late 1970s and early 1980s.

It is here, perhaps, that the predicament of these bands becomes especially clear. Progressive rock was founded on the belief, derived from high culture, that rock as a style was capable of development and evolution through systematically expanding its harmonic, metric, and structural resources. By the mid-1970s, however, progressive rock had reached the point where harmony, meter, and structure had been developed to their limits. As Allan Moore notes, "A style can only "progress" to the point at which it has all the possible materials available for use. Thereafter, these elements can only be juggled with to produce new, different, but not "better" styles. After this point, styles change, but do not develop."[15] Moore goes on to compare Genesis's *Foxtrot* (1972) with their *Invisible Touch* (1986) and Gentle Giant's *Octopus* (1972) with their *Civilian* (1980) in order to illustrate this point. He notes that

> These [comparisons] clearly point to changes of style, and, with Genesis and Gentle Giant, away from features that seemed to betoken a strong measure of originality. . . . [T]he greater accessibility gained by Genesis and Gentle Giant [in their later albums] could be construed as maturing (in terms of their becoming less "obscure" and thus more "relevant") but could equally be seen as a loss of vitality and settling for the easy way out.[16]

Therefore, while a number of these bands have produced individual gems during the 1980s and 1990s (Yes's "Miracle of Life," Anderson, Bruford, Wakeman and Howe's "The Order of the Universe," the entire first side of the *Emerson, Lake and Powell* LP), it has by now become clear that the original progressive rock bands will not surpass their best music of the 1970s in either style, substance, or cultural resonance. In many ways the most formidable obstacle these bands have faced— whether they have chosen to hew fairly closely to the legacy of the 1970s or to renounce this legacy—is an overriding sense of historical self-consciousness. Many decisions made by these bands during the 1980s seem to reflect more than anything else a reaction to (or against) their work of the past. In a sense, they have become victims of the success of their original goal of developing a style that would expand the musical resources of rock to the furthest possible limits.

1981 and beyond, Part II: The Neo-Progressive Movement

In discussing the stylistic history of rock, Allan Moore notes that:

Although within rock there will be a time before which a style cannot appear, there is not necessarily a time after which it can no longer have a place . . . the extension through historical time so prized by art music aficionados is thus also an attribute of rock.[17]

It is the impulse alluded to in the first half of this quote that has been the driving force behind the neo-progressive revival: the belief that if a style of music (that is, the progressive rock of the 1970s) was vital and meaningful when it first appeared, there was no reason it cannot remain vital and meaningful even when the set of cultural conditions which originally gave rise to it are no longer in force.

Of course, the very fact that musicians and audiences become aware that the cultural conditions which gave rise to a music have changed—or, to put it another way, that "an era has passed"—gives rise to a particular set of problems. As Moore notes, for a music to still be found useful to listeners, "Either the cultural attributes that enabled the formation of the music must still be prevalent, or the music is being used to serve a new function, that of the re-creation of those attitudes in a spirit of nostalgia."[18]

Clearly, the neo-progressive style of the 1980s and beyond falls into the second category outlined by Moore. There is an element of self-conscious reference by the neo-progressive bands to the music of an earlier "golden age" which has no parallel in the music of the original generation of progressive rock bands. As many commentators have noted, there is danger in any such situation. It is true that an attitude of nostalgia for an earlier "golden age" may sometimes produce something genuinely new, as, for instance, the emergence of Italian opera around 1600 out of an attempt to revive ancient Greek drama (although a key element here is that Italian baroque musicians had no idea what Greek music actually sounded like, and had to create from scratch a style which they believed would approximate it). However, it is equally possible that attempting to keep a style alive in a state of pristine, unchanging "perfection" (not only by acknowledging a canon of "masterpieces," but also insisting that the value of new music rests on how closely it mirrors the "masterpieces") may be a sign of a kind of cultural paralysis, a refusal to acknowledge the realities of one's current cultural situation. One may be drawn to a style in this case not because of what it now means, or even because of what it once meant, but because of the magical aura it possesses by the very fact that it once meant something. Since I think it likely that there is at least some element of this attitude present in the neo-progressive revival of the 1980s, I believe it is only honest to admit it explicitly.[19]

On the other hand, one of the chief virtues of the neo-progressive bands of the

1980s is that while they have managed to bring a more contemporary sensibility to the "classic" progressive rock style of the 1970s, they have not been embarrassed to draw on elements that the "classic" bands have in recent years often self-consciously avoided in a (largely misguided) effort to prove their contemporaneousness. For instance, in the most representative neo-progressive rock one often encounters analog and acoustic tone colors, surrealistic and (occasionally) psychedelic visual and verbal motifs, and more ambitious thematic conceptions. The neo-progressive movement, which began in England during the early 1980s, has been spearheaded by a younger group of musicians, most of whom were born in the late 1950s and early 1960s. The major English neo-progressive bands include Marillion, IQ, Pendragon, Twelfth Night, Pallas, Ark, and Solstice. Most of these bands released their first album between 1983 and 1985; a number of them are still active, although some have broken up.

Some interesting parallels between the major neo-progressive bands and the "second wave" bands that emerged in the late 1960s and early 1970s can be established. Keith Goodwin and Tony Stratton-Smith, two figures who played very important roles in the 1970s progressive scene, were instrumental in the neo-progressive revival as well. Goodwin, who served as publicist for such major acts as Yes, Gentle Giant, Argent, and Black Sabbath during the 1970s, discovered Marillion in the early 1980s playing "in small clubs to very sparse audiences." He says,

> I sensed the guys had the drive and talent to go all the way. So I took them under my wing. . . . [A]ll sorts of people in the music industry warned me that I'd be banging my head against a brick wall—"prog rock" was washed up, the music was desperately unfashionable, and Marillion stood no chance. But I knew differently, so I ignored the critics and forged ahead. Slowly, I convinced the British music press to take note, and by the time Marillion cut their first maxi-single for EMI, we had created a big waiting public for the product. "Market Square Heroes" climbed into the charts—and the rest is history![20]

Goodwin eventually represented most of the major neo-progressive acts of the 1980s, including Pallas, Twelfth Night, Pendragon, IQ, Solstice, and Quasar.

Stratton-Smith, as founder of the Charisma label in the late 1960s, signed a number of the great bands of the 1970s, including the Nice, Genesis, Van der Graaf Generator, and the folk-rock act Lindisfarne; Charisma eventually became the most powerful and prestigious of the independent labels that specialized in progressive rock. Stratton-Smith had hoped to sign Marillion; he was unable to match EMI's offer, but as a gesture of appreciation the band published their music through Charisma, as did Pendragon.[21] Charisma had in fact been poised to offer Twelfth Night a recording contract in 1985, but went broke first (Virgin, which bought out Charisma, eventually signed the group). Thus Goodwin and Stratton-Smith, who died in 1987, served as mentor figures for two generations of progressive rock bands. Marillion's *Clutching at Straws* LP, released shortly after Stratton-Smith's death, was dedicated to his memory, as was Keith Emerson's "On My Way Home" from the *Three* album.

Another interesting parallel between the progressive rock scenes of the 1970s and 1980s involves the importance of specific clubs to both movements. The Friars' Club in Aylesbury, which had featured a number of prominent progressive rock bands during the late 1960s, served as the launching pad for Marillion's rise to success in the early 1980s. Even more important is London's Marquee club, which played the same seminal role for the emerging neo-progressive movement that it had played in the emergence of the original progressive rock movement in the late 1960s. The Marquee has been a frequent focal point for performances by Marillion, IQ, Pendragon, Ark, and Solstice since the early 1980s; Twelfth Night was something of an unofficial house band during the mid-1980s. Nick Barrett of Pendragon has commented that "The Marquee was the focal point of the [neo-] progressive bands' rise; it was nearly always packed when the progressive bands played there, and had an incredible atmosphere. It was painted black and had no air conditioning. There was no other venue like it!"[22]

Although the neo-progressive movement was somewhat more geographically diffuse than the earlier progressive rock movement in its origin, a surprising number of major neo-progressive bands came out of a cluster of adjoining counties in south-central England. Marillion was formed in the Aylesbury area, near Oxford; Pendragon came out of Gloucestershire; IQ hailed from Southampton, in Hampshire; and Twelfth Night coalesced in Reading, Berkshire. There were, of course, exceptions: Pallas formed in Glasgow, Scotland, while Haze (one of the very first neo-progressive bands) formed in the late 1970s in Sheffield in the industrial midlands.

Nonetheless, like the original progressive rock movement, the neo-progressive movement was above all a phenomenon of southeast England, centered in London. The main difference is that unlike so many of the major bands of the 1970s, the major neo-progressive bands originated outside the London/Kent/Surrey area. As with the progressive movement of the 1970s, the neo-progressive revival was especially popular in college and university settings. A few of the major neo-progressive bands were formed at institutions of higher learning, such as Twelfth Night at Reading University. One also notes the references to high culture in the names of these groups: Pendragon (originally Zeus Pendragon) and Pallas are derived from Greek mythology, Marillion from J. R. R. Tolkien's *The Silmarillion*, Twelfth Night from Shakespeare's play of the same name. It does appear that in terms of the social backgrounds of both musicians and fans, the neo-progressive movement of the 1980s may have been less exclusively middle-class than the earlier movement.

These demographic similarities between the original progressive rock movement and the neo-progressive revival are eclipsed in importance by the changed social and economic conditions between the late 1960s and the mid-1980s. These changes left the neo-progressive bands with a hard, uphill struggle; nowhere is this more evident than in the difficulty these bands have faced in generating a mass audience.

As I have suggested throughout this book, the move of the "classic" progressive rock bands from clubs to arenas during the early 1970s reflects the manner in which the progressive rock style was ceasing to be the music of a narrowly defined hippie (or post-hippie) subculture, and was achieving mainstream acceptance among the mass youth culture at large. By the time that bands such as Yes, ELP, Pink Floyd, Jethro Tull, and the Moody Blues were garnering top ten albums in 1971, 1972, and 1973, there was no question that they had a huge contingent of fans that stood at the periphery of the hippie subculture, fans that the "real" hippies would have considered poseurs or philistines. As the counterculture unraveled between the early and mid-1970s, progressive rock audiences came to resemble a taste public ever more and a genuine subculture less and less. Will Straw sees the rise of North American stadium rock in the mid-1970s as signaling both the mainstream acceptance of progressive rock in the United States and the end of progressive rock–based subcultures, although he suggests that for a while it may have remained part of a "nerd" subculture centered around science-fiction literature and fantasy games such as dungeons and dragons.[23]

By the time the neo-progressive bands had arrived on the scene in the early 1980s, the counterculture was a distant memory, as was the distinct subculture that had once surrounded progressive rock; the taste public that had followed the genre during its period of mass popularity in the mid-1970s had dissolved long ago. A new, much younger cult audience did emerge around the neo-progressive bands at this time. However, it never came remotely close to numerically rivaling the audiences of the major bands of the 1970s, nor did it successfully cross the Atlantic, which automatically precluded the level of success experienced by the bands of the 1970s.

Rather, the progressive rock subculture as it was redefined during the 1980s consists largely of audiophiles who are concerned with the music itself, rather than with allegiance to a specific lifestyle (one could perhaps describe it as a very specialized taste public). Members of this taste public communicate via underground journals and keep abreast of new music via mail order catalogs which specialize in contemporary progressive rock releases on small, independent labels, rereleases of obscure recordings from the late 1960s and 1970s (again, often issued by independent labels specializing in progressive rock), and collectible LPs from the 1960s and 1970s. As a result, the progressive rock taste public of today (which consists both of new converts of the 1980s and 1990s and those who discovered the genre during, or shortly after, its golden age of the early to mid-1970s) is more geographically dispersed than it was even during the height of the progressive rock movement during the 1970s, now spreading across Europe, North America, some parts of South America, and Japan. Conversely, however, it is much more thinly spread out than it was during its heyday.

This has meant, in effect, that progressive rock bands emerging after 1980 have often had considerable difficulty finding numerically significant audiences in any one location outside of a few isolated centers in England and on the Continent. Philip Halper comments that "only one of the second generation of [English] progressive bands has enjoyed any substantial success: Marillion. Bands such as IQ, Pallas, Pendragon, Twelfth Night, Ark, etc., whilst having a very loyal cult-following, remain virtually unheard of, very rarely playing to audiences in excess of 1000 and often considerably less."[24] This situation has caught many of the English neo-progressive bands in a vicious cycle. On the one hand, to really capture a mass audience, these bands require a record company to throw its full financial weight behind them. At the same time, however, the major record companies have become increasingly reluctant to sign a band that is felt to be incapable of immediately generating a mass audience.

Under these circumstances, it is perhaps surprising that as many neo-progressive bands were offered contracts with major labels as was the case. If it were not for Keith Goodwin, Tony Stratton-Smith and Charisma, EMI/Capitol (which signed Marillion, Pendragon, and Pallas), Tommy Vance (whose "Friday Rock Show" catapaulted Marillion into national prominence in 1981, and later featured Pallas, Pendragon, IQ, and Solstice), and a few other sympathetic figures, the number would certainly have been less. Only one neo-progressive band, Marillion, has achieved genuine international commercial success, yet even Marillion has never had a top forty album in the United States, although their *Fugazi* (1984) hit number five and their *Misplaced Childhood* (1985) hit number one in Britain. A number of these bands that did receive major-label contracts lost them during the late 1980s, and some have broken up as a result. For instance, Hans Rochat wryly notes that in 1987 "Twelfth Night expired from a lack of commercial nourishment."[25] The band had previously managed to have several albums released on small, independent labels, but they only managed to have one album put out by a major label (Virgin) before their contract was canceled. Michiel van de Ven suggests that two of IQ's original members departed in 1985 as a result of the band's financial difficulties.[26] The original lineup of Solstice, one of the more promising neo-progressive bands of the 1980s, released just one album before disappearing.

A number of the British neo-progressive bands commercialized their sound at the end of the 1980s (much as the original progressive bands had a decade earlier) in order to stave off complete commercial collapse. Other neo-progressive bands have recorded for private labels, which are sold through progressive rock speciality catalogs or at the (rare) record stores that specialize in progressive music (it has already become very difficult to obtain recordings of British neo-progressive bands other than Marillion in the United States). Recording on private labels has allowed these bands to pursue their musical vision without compromise, but it also means that mass distribution will always be out of reach, that they will give relatively few concerts, which will usually be local affairs, and that bandmembers will often have to work a second job, rather than pursue their career as a bandmember full-time. Most frustratingly, it means that fans of the established progressive rock bands, who certainly constitute a potential audience, will usually never hear the music. As Philip Halper notes, "It is not as if fans of the established progressive bands have heard IQ, Pallas, etc., and didn't like them. It is that they not only haven't heard them, but haven't even heard of them."[27]

The Neo-progressive Style

The British neo-progressive style is perhaps even easier to define than the progressive rock style of the 1970s. The primary reason is that so many of these bands—Marillion, IQ, Pendragon, Pallas—used one specific source, midperiod Genesis (i.e. 1973–1977) as a starting point. (This is not to repeat the common accusation that these bands sound "just like Genesis," or to deny that they each manage to forge a distinct variant of this sound.) Solstice, who pursued the folk/classical/soft jazz fusion of Renaissance, is one exception. Other bands, such as Twelfth Night and Ark, have exploited a harder-edged, more riff-oriented sound that seems to owe something to the example of North American stadium rock.

The timbral soundscape favored by these bands typically features the lead singer (again, usually a tenor) backed by heavily chorused electric guitar arpeggios and spongy synthetic string chords. In harder-rocking passages neo-progressive guitarists utilize more distorted, fuzzed settings and lay out riffs (often rhythmically doubled by the bass) that suggest an American stadium rock influence. Discreet touches of analog synth voicings (especially the Minimoog) and even acoustic instruments (especially six- and twelve-string guitars) are resorted to frequently enough, although the overall sound of these bands is more digital and electronic than the progressive rock of the 1970s.

Rather little use is made of vocal harmonizations; the Moody Blues/Yes/Gentle Giant legacy of intricate vocal arrangements seems to have fallen into disuse. Only one really distinctive singer, Marillion's former lead singer Fish (aka Derek Dick), has emerged from the neo-progressive movement. It is thus perhaps not surprising that instrumental interludes, sometimes rather lengthy, play an important role in English neo-progressive music. Such interludes tend to feature guitar or keyboard solos, usually with simple chordal backing, more often than thematic ensemble interplay. The keyboard solos tend to be strongly reminiscent of Tony Banks's work with Genesis during the 1970s, both in terms of the arpeggiation of straightforward modal or diatonic chord progressions, and in terms of the digital approximations of Banks's ARP Pro-Soloist sound that many of the neo-progressive keyboardists seem to favor. The lyrical modal guitar leads of a number of these guitarists are often reminiscent of the work of Genesis's ex-guitarist Steve Hackett; a number of Hackett's mannerisms, such as his use of vibrato and portamento, are also adopted. Some of the stylistic quirks of Yes's Steve Howe are drawn upon as well (especially the rapidly arpeggiated passagework that these players resort to in more frenzied leads); in fact, the interplay between guitar arpeggios and backing synth chords in the quieter passages of these groups tends to be rather reminiscent of mid-period Yes.

Asymmetrical and shifting meters have, to a certain degree, remained part of the neo-progressive style. Meters of five and seven are not uncommon; more arcane asymmetrical meters are occasionally resorted to as well. For instance, much of IQ's "Fascination" is in thirteen, while fifteen figures prominently in Twelfth Night's "The Poet Sniffs a Flower" and Solstice's "Brave New World."

Just as the neo-progressive bands have proved less embarrassed to draw on key elements of progressive rock's sonic legacy than have the established bands themselves during the 1980s, they have also proved less self-conscious about drawing on progressive rock's legacy of surrealism and epic statement, often handling these elements with an interesting contemporary twist. The legacy of surrealism is especially evident in the cover art of these groups. Patrick Woodroffe's cover art for Pallas's *The Sentinel* is reminiscent of the very best of Roger Dean's fantasy/mythic landscapes, as is Simon Williams's cover art for Pendragon's *The World*. Artist Mark Wilkinson's association with Marillion recalls the collaboration between Paul Whitehead and Genesis during the early 1970s; Wilkinson's alternately droll and violent imagery is especially reminiscent of Whitehead's peculiar strain of surrealism. Some of the neo-progressive bands actually bypassed the surreal visual style of the early 1970s in favor of the out-and-out psychedelic style of the late 1960s; the cover art of Solstice's *Silent Dance* and Ark's *The Dreams of Mr. Jones* are good examples of this tendency. The Ark cover reveals a strong expressionistic tinge as well; a similar expressionistic tendency is also evident in the covers of IQ's *Tales from the Lush Attic* and *The Wake* and Twelfth Night's *Fact and Fiction* (painted, interestingly enough, by the band's lead singers, Peter Nicholls and Geoff Mann, respectively).

Besides drawing more freely on visual surrealism than the major bands had been wont to do in the 1980s, the neo-progressive bands have also been more willing to tackle large-scale concepts. Marillion's *Misplaced Childhood* and *Clutching at Straws* are both concept albums; the separate songs of *Clutching at Straws* each represent the views of a different patron at a bar, and serve as a forum for exploring the forces that drive people to drink and (by extension) to desperation. *Clutching at Straws* illustrates the difference between sensibilities in the 1970s and 1980s;

while it is an epic composition in its own way, it is doubtful that the major bands of the 1970s would have considered the underlying concept worthy of epic treatment. Thus one of the contributions of at least some of the neo-progressive bands has been to show the epic possibilities of more mundane subject matter. The music of Marillion, in particular, often contains a verismo (that is, a "true-to-life") element; the band's lyricist Fish has commented that "We've got non-stick frying pans, wonderful new drugs for cancer, micro-chip technology . . . and yet we've still got slums in Liverpool and Glasgow and everyone ignores them."[28]

On the other hand, many of these bands have drawn upon subject matter more directly associated with the legacy of the 1970s. Pallas's *The Sentinel* calls to mind the apocalyptic motifs of earlier progressive rock with a storyline that chronicles the fall of Atlantis and the progress of the computer ("The Sentinel") which that civilization left behind. IQ's *The Wake* represents an album-long extension of the supernatural thriller tradition of the 1970s. Twelfth Night's *Fact and Fiction* alternates between ominous meditations on the increasingly totalitarian nature of contemporary society ("We Are Sane") that recall Roger Waters's misanthropic work of the late 1970s, and tortured existentialist soliloquies ("Creepshow") that call to mind the work of Peter Hammill with Van der Graaf Generator. Yet another extension of seventies themes can be seen in the lyrics of Solstice's *Silent Dance* LP, which are strongly reminiscent of the pre–New Age nature mysticism of Yes's Jon Anderson.

At its best, the English neo-progressive rock of the 1980s has rivaled—and in some cases surpassed—the contemporaneous work of the "classic" bands. Comparing the neo-progressive style with the best progressive rock of the 1970s, however, is another matter. The textures favored by the neo-progressive bands are usually quite simple (one could be uncharitable and say simplistic): there is little of the sophisticated linear interplay that characterized so much of the progressive rock of the 1970s. The harmonic syntax of the neo-progressive style is usually relatively simple; harmonic progressions tend to repeat in shorter blocks, too. While there is some metric irregularity in the British neo-progressive style, the standard rock beat plays a prominent role, and the complex shifting metric episodes so common to progressive rock of the 1970s are seldom in evidence.

Furthermore, there is little of the sense of musical architecture that marked the best progressive rock of the 1970s. This situation goes beyond the fact that the neo-progressive bands mostly abandoned large-scale forms such as the multimovement suite. Even the most musically inventive neo-progressive bands (IQ, Pendragon, Marillion), who have regularly shown themselves capable of creating interesting musical ideas, seldom show the same talent for convincingly developing, extending, and varying thematic material as did the major bands of the seventies. Rather, they are usually content to juxtapose two or three unrelated musical ideas, which are then subjected to fairly literal repetition.[29] In their best music, the "classic" bands created an effective tension by balancing unpredictable phrase structures and harmonic progressions (which generated suspense) with repetition, usually nonliteral, of key melodic and rhythmic ideas from section to section. By comparison, verse/refrain structures are more predictable, two-chord-per-bar chord changes more pervasive, and musical relations between successive sections are more arbitrary in the "neo-prog" style. As a result, the opportunity to build up suspense over a period of time is diminished, and the sense of musical breadth and expansiveness evident in the multimovement suites of ELP, Yes, Genesis, Van der Graaf Generator, and others is largely lacking.

By the late 1980s, even as a number of the bands that had spearheaded the British neo-progressive movement began to falter, the neo-progressive movement had spread elsewhere, and bands began using sources other than mid-period Genesis and Yes as starting points. For instance, the music of the American neo-progressive bands Mastermind and Ancient Vision suggests the influence of ELP and Jethro Tull, respectively. The music of the Japanese neo-progressive band Bi Kyo Ran draws from *Red*-era King Crimson, while the albums of another Japanese band of this period, Kenso, are indebted to the Canterbury school. The work of the Mexican neo-progressive group Iconoclasta suggests the heritage of Italian bands such as PFM and Banco.

The debut album of the Swedish band Änglagård, *Hybris* (1992), is particularly deft in its seamless appropriation of the most characteristic stylistic features of early Genesis, Yes, *Red*-era King Crimson (the unusual root movements) and Italian bands such as Banco and Museo Rosenbach (the three- or four-part counterpoint in rhythmic unison). Änglagård proved to be a major success at the first annual Progfest, held at UCLA's Royce Hall in 1993;[30] fans seemed to particularly appreciate the band's staunchly analog soundscapes, which avoid digital synthesizers in favor of the Mellotron and Hammond. Their second release, *Epilog* (1994), is in some ways an even more impressive achievement. Here the band welds dense textures, hairpin metric shifts, and alternately lyrical and angular melodic impulses into a sound that is highly individual despite its traditionalism. More than nearly any other neo-progressive band, the work of Änglagård can be profitably compared and contrasted with the post-progressive bands discussed in the next section. To be sure, the music of Änglagård is ultimately less innovative than the music of bands such as Djam Karet or Edhels. On the other hand, these latter bands have been less successful in forging a unified, organic, instantly recognizable style than Änglagård. Furthermore, unlike so many of their neo-progressive peers, Änglagård have retained much of the metric, textural, and structural sophistication that was a hallmark of progressive rock of 1970–1976.

The unusually traditionalistic approach of Änglagård is by no means dominant in the neo-progressive rock of the 1990s. Even the music of bands that appeared in the late 1970s has been drawn on by emerging neo-progressive groups looking to establish some semblance of individual identity. For instance, the work of Citadel suggests an extension of Rush's late 1970s style; Kalaban (like Citadel, an American band) apparently have modeled their music after that of U.K. and Kansas.

When one listens to the music of the best neo-progressive bands, one is continuously surprised at how much mileage these bands have been able to draw from what is by now an essentially conservative style. Nonetheless, the possibilities for continued neo-progressive reinterpretation of the "classic" 1970s style are not infinite, and it seems likely that the neo-progressive movement will soon reach its zenith—if it has not already. In the long run, the most promising course for the genre is the eclectic, or post-progressive, approach inaugurated by King Crimson with their *Discipline* LP of 1981, although this path will ultimately lead to a considerable transmutation of the progressive rock style.

1981 and beyond, Part III: King Crimson's *Discipline* and the Post-progressive Style

It is ironic that while King Crimson's erstwhile leader Robert Fripp has been outspoken in his reluctance to be associated with the progressive rock movement of the 1970s,[31] no other progressive rock musician has grappled so persistently with the question of what precisely constitutes genuinely "progressive" music. For Fripp, "progressive rock" was not so much a definitive style as an attitude; the progressive rock of the 1970s had been "progressive" only as long as it pushed the stylistic and conceptual boundaries of rock outwards through the appropriation of procedures (as opposed to surface details) from classical music and jazz. Once progressive rock ceased to cover new ground, but became a set of conventions to be repeated and imitated, the genre had, in Fripp's view, ceased to be "progressive" at all. Thus it was that in 1974—when progressive rock was at the very height of its commercial success—Fripp unilaterally broke up King Crimson, even though the group had just released *Red,* which many consider to be their finest album. He was concerned that from a purely musical perspective, the 1970s progressive rock style had already reached its zenith, telling Irwin Stambler, "The band ceased to exist in September 1974, which was when all English bands in that genre should have ceased to exist. But since the rock'n' roll dinosaur likes anything which has gone before, most of them are still churning away, repeating what they did years ago without going off in any new direction."[32] At the time, many critics scoffed; in hindsight, however, Fripp's grasp of the situation proved accurate, and most critics now concede that virtually every major English progressive rock band recorded their best album between 1971 and 1975.

Fripp's concern with the progressive rock scene went beyond the stylistic direction of the music. As I have pointed out a number of times, the move by major progressive rock bands from playing clubs and small venues to playing stadiums and arenas effectively divorced the bands from the subcultural milieu in which they originated, and created a situation where a meaningful symbiotic relationship with the audience was increasingly difficult. This situation could have only a detrimental effect on the music itself in the long run. Fripp was the first progressive rock performer to publicly express concern about this situation, and he set forth his views about the necessity for genuine audience-performer interaction (if the music was to remain valid, at any rate) in an extraordinarily articulate manner:

> In 1974 I left King Crimson for a number of reasons; on a professional level this was largely a result of the decreasing possibility for any real contact between audience and performers. This seemed to me to be caused by three main factors: firstly, the escalation in the size of rock events; secondly, the general acceptance of rock music as spectator sport; thirdly, the vampiric relationship between audience and performer.[33]

After King Crimson's breakup, Fripp left the music business entirely for a period, going into reclusion and becoming a disciple of J. G. Bennett (whose philosophy was in turn strongly influenced by the Russian mystic G. I. Gurdjieff). In 1977 Fripp moved from England to New York and began to reenter the music scene, first as a producer, then as a solo performer. Fripp's performances, which he dubbed "Frippertronics," involved a kind of improvised minimalism based on the meditative, almost arhythmic soundscapes pioneered in his collaborations with Brian Eno during the early 1970s. Fripp was determined in his Frippertronics concerts to avoid the mistakes which he felt were destroying the vitality of the rock music scene:

> Amongst other aims Frippertronics seeks to counter these three trends to idiocy [huge concerts, rock as a spectator sport, and the "vampiric" performer/audience relationship] by suggesting three steps to participation in an intelligent world: firstly, by limiting the size of the event to between 10 and 250; secondly, by inviting the audience to listen actively which places listeners in a position of equal responsibility with the performer; thirdly, by declining to humor each other's mutual pretensions, egocentricities, and conceits. In an appropriate situation with active listening and abandoning attempts to imprison the event on tape or film, it is quite possible that something remarkable may happen.[34]

This approach worked so well for Fripp in his solo performances that he maintained it when he fronted a New Wave dance band called The League of Gentlemen, and finally when he reformed King Crimson in early 1981 with former drummer Bill Bruford and new members Tony Levin (bass, Chapman stick) and Adrian Belew (guitar, vocals). Fripp originally planned to call the group Discipline. However, he eventually decided to name the band King Crimson, explaining that "any thought-form which attracts interest becomes partly iconic and since the group "ceased to exist" in 1974 interest has continued. At the beginning of rehearsals during the first week of April [1981], I recognized this potential hovering behind the band, an available energy if we chose to plug in."[35] Using the name of a legendary band of the 1970s meant that the group could have played larger venues if they chose. However, Fripp maintained his determination that the music itself could remain healthy only if the audiences remained small enough for each individual in attendance to feel that his or her presence could in some way make a difference in the performance itself—thus recreating the ambience of progressive rock's earliest days in small English clubs.

Fripp was not only determined that the reformed King Crimson would not fall into the same trap of playing huge venues that had befallen the band in its previous incarnation; on a musical level, he was also determined to achieve something genuinely new within a progressive rock framework. Specifically, Fripp wished to avoid returning to those aspects of the progressive rock style that had been mined out during the 1970s. In his view, the entire concept of the classical/jazz/folk/rock fusion represented by progressive rock during the 1970s had been developed to its logical conclusion and subsequently exhausted. The progressive rock of the 1980s, if it were to remain "progressive" in the sense of covering new ground, would need to be nourished by new sources. Thus, the classical tone colors and lengthy programmatic forms of the 1970s played no role in the new King Crimson. Instead, minimalism rather belatedly became an important influence for King Crimson during the 1980s (as I said earlier, it is somewhat surprising that mid-1970s Crimson betrays so little minimalist influence, considering that Fripp had already begun working on his groundbreaking minimalist rock collaborations with Brian Eno). The band drew both from the almost motionless, largely arhythmic rock minimalism of the Fripp/Eno collaborations and Frippertronics and from the rhythmically charged ostinato networks of the Reich/Glass/Riley school.

Another important source for the band was the newly burgeoning field of world music, particularly Javanese music. To be sure, Fripp was not the first progressive rock performer to draw on world music traditions. Patrick Moraz featured Brazilian percussionists prominently on his solo albums of the late 1970s, while Genesis's ex-lead vocalist Peter Gabriel also began to work with various ethnic styles rather extensively in his solo recordings of the early 1980s. Nevertheless, King Crimson's exploration of Javanese music was particularly intense and involved the most important element of all true fusion attempts—not merely borrowing surface details, but appropriating procedures and modes of approach. Thus Bill Bruford notes that "Fripp's search for an escape from the individual egotism of Western musicians had led him east to Java, and there was much talk of a style of playing demanding in communal rather than individual virtuosity and social rather than individualistic skills."[36] These two influences, minimalism and Javanese music, meshed to encourage a style decidedly "progressive" (in the sense of expanding the stylistic and conceptual boundaries of rock), yet decisively different from progressive rock of the 1970s.

King Crimson recorded a greater proportion of instrumental music than any of their major progressive rock colleagues in the 1980s; indeed, even in the "songs" many of Adrian Belew's vocal lines seem to be added as an afterthought, and the "vocals" of pieces like "Indiscipline" and "Thela Hun Ginjeet" are actually spoken recitations. Nonetheless, there are remarkably few instances of virtuosic solos. Bruford's description of the *Discipline* album's title cut gives considerable insight into the group's style:

> The tune itself is undemonstrative but nevertheless extremely intricate. To the casual observer, nothing seems to be happening, but the more committed listener would hopefully find among the "elaborate heterophonic interweaving" that "state of music" to which we aspire. Because all four players had a virtually endless stream of sixteenth notes with varying accents, the piece required great concentration in performance in order that all parts locked tightly and exactly. Then it was light, airy, and flowing.[37]

Often, while the individual lines are simple, the texture as a whole can be exceedingly complex. In "Thela Hun Ginjeet," for instance, parts in $\frac{7}{8}$ and $\frac{4}{4}$ constantly move in and out of phase with each other, although the casual listener is aware only of a somewhat nervous, off-balance effect. "Discipline" is in $\frac{17}{4}$, an extremely complex asymmetrical meter; however, as Bruford points out, there are steady streams of sixteenth notes in all parts at a constant tempo, and one has to listen carefully to note the asymmetrical meter at all.

Unlike progressive rock of the 1970s, but very much like minimalism and Javanese music, King Crimson's work of the 1980s is usually not dramatic, and for the most part lacks a sense of climax and resolution. Rather, the music exists in long, static blocks, and change, so much as it occurs, is gradual and almost imperceptible. Nonetheless, a surprising number of moods are suggested through the use of varied tempos, timbral approaches, and rhythmic patternings. The wildly lurching "Indiscipline" and somewhat more controlled "Thela Hun Ginjeet," both rapid pieces dominated by fiercely distorted guitar parts (suggestive at times of mid-1970s King Crimson pieces such as "Fracture" or "Red"), create a mood of menace and danger. On the other hand, "The Sheltering Sky," a much slower piece featuring Bruford's unobtrusive slit drum part, Belew's gentle guitar ostinati, and Fripp's surprisingly warm guitar synthesizer leads, is tranquil, meditative, and almost suggests a richly developed New Age style. "Discipline" is somewhat evocative of the more sophisticated New Wave dance styles (especially the highly linear music of the Talking Heads) with its constant tempo, rather neutral electronic timbres,

and endless streams of sixteenth notes. Yet another facet of the group's music is evident in gentle ballads such as "Matte Kudesai" (one of the few pieces in which the vocal line is independent of the instrumental accompaniment in a really convincing manner). Other pieces, such as the eerie "Requiem" and "Industry," suggest yet other sources—the bleak grandeur of solo Frippertronics, free jazz of the 1960s (the furious atonal and ametric instrumental outbursts), and experimental electronic music (the strange metallic timbres produced by Bruford's electronic drums, one of the first such sets in rock).

The 1980s incarnation of King Crimson lasted for three years (1981 to 1984) and produced three albums, *Discipline* (1981), *Beat* (1982), and *Three of a Perfect Pair* (1984). In 1984, feeling that King Crimson was once again beginning to repeat itself, Fripp broke up the band. He then went on to other projects, most notably serving as administrator and principal instructor of the American Society for Continuous Education's Guitar Craft Courses at Claymont Court near Charles Town, West Virginia.[38] By 1992 Fripp was speaking of reforming King Crimson in the near future;[39] this intention was realized in 1994 with the release of *Vroom*, in which the 1980s lineup is joined by Trey Gunn (stick) and Pat Mastelotto (percussion). Unlike the *Crimson King-*, *Red-*, and *Discipline*-era lineups, the *Vroom* lineup—which has since released *Thrak* (1995), a more polished presentation of *Vroom*'s essentially live-in-the-studio tracks, and *B'boom* (1995), a live album—does not produce any groundbreaking innovations. Rather, the emphasis seems to be on further developing directions initially explored by the mid-1970s and 1980s incarnations of the band (the title track of *Vroom*, in particular, suggests a 1990s reinterpretation of "Red").

The three albums of the 1980s, on the other hand, contain some highly innovative music, but I cannot help feeling that they are more important for what is suggested than what is actually accomplished (perhaps justifying the further development of 1980s tendencies evident in *Vroom*). Certainly, King Crimson could have explored a number of realms that were either largely or completely ignored in these albums. One wishes at times for a more convincing fusion of electronic and acoustic resources (the tone colors of these albums are overwhelmingly electronic), a more thoroughgoing blend of instrumental and vocal resources, or a warmer, more lyrical ambience (not only is the music undramatic, at times it skirts dangerously close to the passionless and over-cerebralized).

However, such criticisms may ultimately be misguided. It seems to me that *Discipline*, in particular, was more about creating a blueprint upon which future explorations could draw than it was about presenting a finished, mature style. The lesson of the 1980s incarnation of King Crimson is that progressive rock is ultimately more an attitude than a specific style; that there are viable choices for established and emerging progressive rock bands other than being buffeted by the currents of mainstream pop or endlessly repeating the tried-and-true formulas of the "classic" progressive style; and most important for future progressive music musicians, that a whole world of musical influences beckons. I happen to largely agree with Fripp that the 1970s version of progressive rock—that is, the classical/jazz/folk/rock fusion—has largely played itself out. While some of the more inventive neo-progressive bands of the 1980s managed to get surprising mileage out of the "classic" 1970s idiom, one cannot foresee this situation continuing indefinitely under even the most optimistic conditions.

On the other hand, rock has proven to be an extraordinarily elastic music, and there is no need for it to be straightjacketed within the confines of commercially "acceptable" limits. The phenomenon of world music is burgeoning so rapidly that it is almost impossible for a given musician or group to thoroughly explore more than a few sources. King Crimson effectively absorbed the inner workings of one particular source, Javanese music, then applied the distilled lessons in a rock context. Furthermore, as King Crimson demonstrated, there are other sources—minimalism, above all the resources of electronic experimental music—that are by no means exhausted. In closing this book, I will examine the work of three bands—one American, one French, and one English—that have sought to enrich and expand the legacy of English progressive rock with other sources such as world music, minimalism, electronic experimentation, and thus might be said to be purveyors of an emerging contemporary "post-progressive" style.

Post-progressive Music of the 1980s and beyond

The emphasis on younger bands in this final section does not mean that there are no major progressive rock figures from the 1970s other than Fripp and King Crimson that have gone on to do work that could be termed "post-progressive." Certainly Peter Gabriel's solo albums of the 1980s have been continuously innovative, expanding the framework of the pop song through the appropriation of elements drawn from various ethnic styles, minimalism (Gabriel has evinced a special admiration for the music of Steve Reich), and a discreet use of electronic experimentation. Likewise, Bill Bruford's Earthworks, a band consisting of young British jazz musicians, released three adventurous albums between 1987 and 1991 in which ethnic styles and electronic experimentation (especially with Simmons electronic drums) are explored in a jazz/fusion context. Peter Hammill's solo work of the 1980s was consistently innovative and interesting; a particular milestone in his career was the release of *The Fall of the House of Usher* in 1991, a musical setting of Poe's classic tale that he had begun planning nearly twenty years before. Some of his albums such as *Skin* (1986) contain contributions from all the Van der Graaf core members, although the resulting music is very different. Many of the musicians who had been part of the Canterbury scene during the 1970s remain active in a variety of stimulating projects, ranging from the state-of-the-art electronic fusion of Allan Holdsworth or Phil Miller to the quirky, ethnic-tinged folk/pop of Robert Wyatt to the carefully crafted techno-pop of Dave Stewart and Barbara Gaskin. All of these musicians have created music that is progressive and explores new directions (especially in terms of drawing on ethnic styles and electronic experimentation), and is not too closely bound to their trail-blazing work of the 1970s.

Nonetheless, some of the most exciting post-progressive music of the 1980s and beyond has been created by a new, younger group of musicians. Choosing just three bands to discuss in this final section has been difficult, and doubtless I have had to ignore many bands whose contributions to progressive music may even-tually prove important. I have chosen these three bands—one American (Djam Karet), one French (Edhels), and one English (Ozric Tentacles)—because each illustrates a different facet of the post-progressive style. To be sure, there are a number of similarities between the groups. All three bands drew inspiration from major English progressive rock bands of the 1970s: Djam Karet from the alternating electronic/experimental and acoustic/pastoral passages of King Crimson and Pink Floyd; Edhels from the symphonic progressive rock of Yes, Genesis, and ELP; and Ozric Tentacles from the early 1970s psychedelic fusion of Gong. At the same time, however, these bands are not neo-progressive. Not only do they bring a contem-porary sensibility to the "classic" 1970s idiom, they introduce a number of entirely new elements such as minimalism, electronic experimentation, and various ethnic styles into their music as well. In this sense, then, all of these bands carry on in one way or another the post-progressive rock revolution initiated by King Crimson with their *Discipline* LP.

One will note that all three bands are almost entirely instrumental (there are a few fairly inconsequential vocal parts on later Ozric Tentacles albums). As I have suggested, vocals and lyrics have posed a fairly major problem for the neo-progressive movement. The progressive rock idiom of the 1970s became so closely associated with a specific type of subject matter that abandonment of this subject matter in favor of more "commonplace" subject matter risked the charge of com-mercialization, while adherence to it risked the appearance of mindlessly copying earlier groups. Furthermore, when a band follows the latter route, they must be aware that the lyrical subject matter most favored by progressive rock bands of the 1970s does not always have the same cultural relevance today. Even vocal arrange-ments have been problematic; rich vocal arrangements are often unduly reminis-cent of the Moody Blues/Yes/Gentle Giant/Caravan tradition, while a general avoidance of vocal harmonies tends to make the music sound overly spare by comparison. Instrumental bands such as Djam Karet, Edhels, and Ozric Tentacles have been able to avoid these difficulties in a way that groups with vocalists cannot.

Of the bands discussed here, Djam Karet is the most directly influenced by

Discipline-era King Crimson. However, other influences are evident as well: early to mid-period Pink Floyd (i.e., through *Wish You Were Here*), the trailblazing rock minimalism of the Fripp/Eno collaborations, and various ethnic styles (perhaps mediated through Peter Gabriel's ethnic-pop LPs such as *Peter Gabriel 3* and *Security*). There are also discreet touches of the melancholy acoustic guitar episodes that were so characteristic of English progressive rock during its earlier stages. As Chuck Oken, the band's long-time drummer, has commented,

> In the nineties, we have a generation of progressive musicians who have grown up with the old progressive music and who are simultaneously drawing musical influences from that history along with the musics of the world and the times currently surrounding them. With the music of Djam Karet this creates a fusion of the old and the new as our inspiration draws itself from King Crimson and Pink Floyd to traditional ethnic music, "trance music," and rock as explored in the nineties. The new progressives will draw from the well of inspiration of the past as well as the musical rivers of the times in creating a new direction for the future of progressive music.[40]

Djam Karet were founded in 1984, hailing from Claremont (east of Los Angeles), California. Even the band's instrumentation of two guitarists, bass, and percussion suggests the influence of King Crimson, since the presence of two guitarists in a single band was very rare in English progressive rock prior to the release of the *Discipline* album. However, sonic variety is provided by the fact that all the band's members double on synthesizers as well. Following the path of many progressive bands during the 1980s who have released their music privately, Djam Karet issued two cassette-only releases during the mid-1980s, *No Commercial Potential* (1985) and *The Ritual Continues* (1987, since released on CD). The band released their first CD, *Reflections from the Firepool*, in 1989; two different but complementary CDs, the atmospheric *Suspension and Displacement* and the blistering *Burning the Hard City*, were released in 1991, followed by *Collaborator* (1994).

The two CDs of 1991 illustrate especially well the dichotomy that exists in the band's music between a heavier post-progressive rock style and a sophisticated, highly accomplished electronic/minimalist/New Age approach. The band's minimalism is influenced above all by the brooding, largely arhythmic tone paintings of the Fripp/Eno collaborations; "Dark Clouds, No Rain," the first cut of the *Suspension and Displacement* CD, offers an especially good example of the band's more atmospheric side. The piece begins with a low, foghorn-like drone on B (evocative of the opening of "The Heavenly Music Corporation" from Fripp and Eno's *No Pussyfooting* album), over which higher drones on A (which phases in and out) and D♯ are gradually superimposed. These three notes form the sonic basis of the entire piece. However, variety is provided by a seemingly infinite parade of musical fragments—bell-like effects, short flute-like motives, segments of descending modal scale fragments in the guitars, ethnic percussion—which appear momentarily and then disappear, sometimes to reappear later, sometimes to vanish entirely. At the end of the piece, this other material fades out, leaving the opening three notes; the tritone A-D♯ is especially emphasized, creating a tense, unstable atmosphere which characterizes the whole piece to a degree. Like Eno and Fripp, Djam Karet often use the layering of particular intervals to create a piece's mood: stable intervals such as perfect fifths create a peaceful mood, while unstable intervals such as tritones and minor seconds create a more tense, unstable atmosphere.

Occasionally they emphasize a minimalist style more akin to the rhythmically charged minimalism of the Reich/Glass school. For instance, much of "A City with Two Tales" is dominated by a synthesized metallic ostinato pattern in $\frac{13}{8}$, over which the guitarists layer drones and more clearly melodic solo lines. Metallic ostinato patterns of this sort—which seem to suggest an ethnic source, perhaps the Indonesian gamelan—are much favored by the band and also occur in "The Red Monk," "Run Cerberus Run," and "Reflections from the Firepool." "Djam Karet" is, in fact, an Indonesian/Malay term meaning "elastic time."

This minimalist strain in the band's music is counterbalanced by a heavier rock approach that almost suggests a post-industrial blues-rock style (for example, the opening of "At the Mountains of Madness"). Occasionally, the band draw on this style to cover genuinely new ground: there is nothing in English progressive rock of the 1970s (or even on the *Discipline* LP) that quite prepares one for the dissonant, tortured guitar counterpoint in "Fall of the Monkeywalk," backed by a spare, powerful bass line and menacing "jungle" drumming.

At times they do draw on touches more characteristic of English progressive rock of the 1970s. The melancholy modal acoustic guitar episodes that the band frequently utilize (the close of "Reflections from the Firepool," "Consider Figure Three," and "Severed Moon") are especially evocative of David Gilmour's work with Pink Floyd and the acoustic guitar episodes of the early incarnations of King Crimson and Genesis. The toccata-like Hammond organ figuration that opens "Run Cerberus Run," meanwhile, can be traced back through late 1970s stadium rock (i.e., Boston's "Foreplay/Long Time") to the work of progressive rock keyboardists of the 1970s. Occasionally the band draws on a digital approximation of the Mellotron's string setting, as in the modal "string" chords superimposed over the acoustic guitar line at the close of "Consider Figure Three."

There are few bands active today capable of creating richly developed, interesting textural configurations as consistently as Djam Karet. The band's greatest strength is undoubtedly their ability to layer electronic drones, fragmentary melodic lines, quasi-ethnic drum patterns, and other sonic material—such as a doctor's medical lecture in "Consider Figure Three," which is gradually subjected to digital delay until a tape-loop-like effect is suggested—to create atmospheric, brooding, richly developed textures that change from moment to moment. If there is one criticism to be lodged against the band, it is that they have yet to completely bridge the gap between their minimalist/New Age and hard rock styles to create a metastyle that draws on both stylistic tributaries, yet is greater than either.

This dichotomy is most apparent in the simultaneous release of *Burning the Hard City* and *Suspension and Displacement* in 1991, but it is also apparent in the extremely sectional construction of many of the pieces on *Reflections from the Firepool*. While progressive rock of the 1970s was certainly sectional, the musicians were also careful to unite the different sections via thematic transformation, dynamics, or rhythm. On the other hand, one searches the three or four sections which invariably constitute the various pieces from *Reflections* in vain for some sort of unifying thread. This is a tendency I already noted in the British neo-progressive style of the 1980s, and may well reflect an unfamiliarity on the part of younger musicians with the classical models on which the first generation of progressive rock bands based so many of their lengthy pieces. Indeed, for me, *Suspension and Displacement* is the most satisfying of the group's releases—despite the fact that it is the most removed stylistically from English progressive rock of the 1970s—because by and large musical ideas are extended and developed convincingly throughout the course of the entire piece. *Collaborator* (1994) further explores and refines the ambient soundscapes pioneered on *Suspension*. This release, which is enriched by contributions from a number of sympathetic musicians (including Walter Holland, Kit Watkins, and Steve Roach), offers several tantalizing suggestions of a fusion of Djam Karet's "heavy" progressive rock and "cosmic" ambient tendencies. One suspects that as the band continues to develop the different facets of their style, they will draw them closer together and unite them more confidently on subsequent releases.

Edhels are a French band that were formed by Marc Ceccotti in 1981 out of the wreckage of an earlier band, Royal Flush. Like the English neo-progressive group Marillion, the members of Edhels drew their name (which means elf) from Tolkien's novel *Silmarillion*. Like Djam Karet, the band initially had great difficulty in attracting the attention of a major record company (despite staging a number of live performances in southern France) and decided to release their first album, *Oriental Christmas* (1985), privately. This album brought the group to the attention of the French Musea label, which rereleased it and has since released two other albums by the band, *Still Dream* (1988) and *Astro-Logical* (1991).[41]

The first two albums are essentially exquisitely polished examples of instrumental neo-progressive rock, combining something of ELP's rhythmic energy and dramatic, stabbing chord progressions with the lyrical sensitivity and polished sonorities of early Genesis. The lyricism of this music is rare even by the standards of progressive rock of the 1970s; its extraordinarily refined timbral palette suggests a typical Gallic sensitivity to tone color.

More than virtually any of their leading British neo-progressive contemporaries,

Edhels have achieved a sound that is at once digital and contemporary, and yet is faithful to models of the 1970s. There are two major reasons. First, the textures preferred by the band usually involve a rich linear interplay of the different lines; there is none of the marshmallowy washes of digital electronics that has characterized the work of many of the major English progressive rock bands (such as Genesis or *90125*-era Yes) during the 1980s. Second, while the keyboard voicings are clearly digital, they are based on some of the most important progressive rock tone colors of the 1970s. One hears echoes of the pipe organ ("Capitaine Armoire"), the Yamaha GX-1 polyphonic synthesizer (the quasi-brass fanfares of "Christie Feline Girl"), the Mellotron string setting ("Annibal's Trip") and choral setting ("Butterfly Child"). Acoustic six- and twelve-string guitars are drawn on to recall the more pastoral moments of early progressive rock, while the band's digital piano sound is both highly distinctive and easily recognizable.

In comparison to their British neo-progressive contemporaries and even to the English progressive rock bands of the 1970s, a surprisingly high percentage of material in any given Edhels piece involves thematic ensemble interplay, and the relative scarcity of lengthy solos over a repeated chord progression or bass ostinato is refreshing. Nonetheless, the band is capable of virtuosity as well; the trade-off between eight-bar guitar and synth leads in "Heart Trip" is almost reminiscent of the exchange of brief lead lines cultivated between John McLaughlin and Jan Hammer in the early days of Mahavishnu Orchestra. The band is also capable of a sophisticated metric approach, as in the $\frac{13}{8}$ episodes of "Heart Trip" and the complex $\frac{19}{8}$ fanfare theme (consisting of alternating bars of four, five, four, and six) of "Christie Feline Girl."

With the release of their third album, *Astro-Logical*, in 1991, Edhels entered post-progressive stylistic territory. The primary new influence seems to have been contemporary electronic music. There is a new tendency toward the use of ostinato networks; melodic material is less lyrical, more fragmentary, and on occasion even atonal. The tone colors most closely associated with traditional progressive rock (pipe organ, acoustic guitar, etc.) largely disappear, to be replaced by more "cosmic" and explicitly synthetic tone colors.

One admires the band's willingness to take major musical risks, as well as the album's conceptual ambitions: the twelve pieces are meant to be musical depictions of the twelve signs of the zodiac. On the other hand, one misses the lyricism of their earlier material. Furthermore, the highly sectionalized structure of many of the pieces on *Astro-Logical* often creates the impression of several short sections that have been cobbled together to form longer pieces: the structural interrelationships evident in the longer pieces of the band's first two albums are largely lacking. Hopefully, as the group continues to work within this expanded post-progressive framework, they will achieve a more convincing synthesis of these newer stylistic elements with their characteristic lyricism and timbral refinement.

Marc Ceccotti's assessment of their most recent album suggests that the band is indeed approaching such a synthesis: "*Astro-Logical* opens on a new musical landscape; it's not a milestone, it's a key. In the future we will use this key but also we will use precedent keys and probably a new one; I think there are other keys in *M.A.S.C.*" (Ceccotti's first solo album, released in 1993).[42] Edhels certainly remain one of the most promising of the emerging post-progressive bands.

Ozric Tentacles very possibly represent the most intriguing success story among the emerging progressive rock groups of the 1980s and 1990s. This is at least in part because of their success in generating a hardcore cult following in front of whom they regularly perform live, a rare achievement for a post-1980 progressive band of any kind. Ozric Tentacles emerged from the mid-1980s British psychedelic festival circuit, becoming especially closely associated with the now-banned Stonehenge Free Festival and with Deptford's late Crypt Club (located, curiously enough, underneath an active Catholic church). One sees a strong parallel between Ozric Tentacles and the psychedelic bands of the late 1960s on a number of levels. Both served as the nexus of a psychedelic subculture devoted to consciousness expansion; both depended on playing small clubs and loosely organized jam sessions; and above all, both created music not for a mass audience mediated through the record industry, but directly for the subculture of which they were a part.

The band's dependence on the record industry was so slight, in fact, that their first six recordings were privately recorded cassettes that were sold at their concerts, at headshops, and by various underground mail order enterprises: *Erpsongs* (1985), *Tantric Obstacles, Live Ethereal Cereal,* and *There Is Nothing* (all 1986), *Sliding Gliding World* (1988), and *The Bits between the Bits* (1989). (The best material from these cassettes was issued by Dovetail Records on a two-CD set, *Afterswish,* in 1991.) It was only in 1990 that the band's first album, *Pungent Effulgent,* appeared on Dovetail Records; this release was followed by *Erpland, Strangeitude,* and *Live Underslunky.* In 1993 Ozric Tentacles scored their first release on a major label (IRS) with *Jurassic Shift,* which has since been followed by *Arborescence* (1994) and *Become the Other* (1996).

Ozric Tentacles have at various times contained (simultaneously) two guitarists, two keyboardists, two percussionists, and a bass player. The core of the band during its formative years, however, was the Wynne brothers, Ed (guitar), and Roly (bass), and keyboardist Joie Hinton, who met the Wynnes at the Stonehenge Free Festival of 1983. All three shared an interest in ethnic music, especially East Asian; Hinton visited India in 1983, and Ed Wynne spent three months in Thailand in 1987.

Ethnic music has thus been a constant factor in much of Ozric Tentacles's music. This influence is reflected in the frequent use of "Eastern" modes with two augmented seconds, in the use of Asian string instruments (a number of which are used in soloistic contexts on "Secret Names"), in the almost constant presence of ethnic percussion, and in the occasional use of the synthesizer to suggest the metallic, bell-like sonorities of the Javanese gamelan ("Chinatype," "Mae Hong Song"). However, despite the strong ethnic flavor of Ozric Tentacles' music, the band is rooted above all in the psychedelic jazz-rock style of the late 1960s and early 1970s, as represented by Daevid Allen's Gong (especially their *You* LP) and perhaps to a lesser extent by early to mid-period Soft Machine.

The jazz-rock influence is suggested by a number of stylistic tendencies apparent in the music of the Ozrics. One hears it in the generally fast tempos, which seldom vary from beginning to end (although there are some "cosmic," essentially a-rhythmic, synthesizer preludes and postludes); in the use of one or more syncopated, highly energized bass guitar ostinato patterns as the structural foundation of a piece; in the adherence to a style of drumming that heavily emphasizes the high hat, which is often opened and closed on every beat; and in the general harmonic syntax. Asymmetric meters, especially in five ("Travelling the Great Circle") and seven ("Guzzard," "Thrashing Breath Texture"), are heard fairly often. Ed Wynne's guitar work seems to owe a particularly strong debt to Steve Hillage, Gong's lead guitarist during the mid-1970s, especially in some of Wynne's heavier, more fusion-oriented playing ("Guzzard").

On the other hand, there is an undeniable psychedelic element to the Ozrics' music as well, and this is largely a result of the synthesizer work, which suggests both Tim Blake's playing with Gong and Mike Ratledge's and Karl Jenkins's more ethereal keyboard passages in mid-period Soft Machine. There is a decided preference for analog equipment, with spacey, heavily chorused string-like or electronic organ–like settings, filter sweeps, and glissandi especially common. Another psychedelic element is the use of delicate guitar and even bass guitar harmonics as a coloristic element; an important ostinato pattern in "Sacred Turf," for instance, consists entirely of guitar harmonics. The continued use of analog equipment is, from my point of view, completely valid: the full potential of a number of very sophisticated analog synthesizers that appeared in the late 1970s such as the Sequential Circuits Prophet-10 or the Roland Jupiter was never fully explored before the digital revolution caused all analog equipment to fall out of favor during the early 1980s.

The Ozrics also show their allegiance to the early 1970s psychedelic fusion style through their preference for clearly layered, essentially linear textures, rather than the synthetic washes of much digitally recorded music of the 1980s in which individual lines are often nearly impossible to detect. In much of the Ozrics' music, the constant factors are the bass guitar ostinato and the drum part, which often repeat one or more four- or eight-bar rhythmic patterns throughout much of the piece, and a keyboard and/or guitar ostinato, which serves a harmonic/melodic function. Variety is created by introducing and then withdrawing other parts (a second keyboard or guitar ostinato, a second percussion part, instrumental solos) at various junctures. This approach is evident in a number of the band's very best pieces such as the ethereal "Floating Seeds," in which a single bass pattern is utilized throughout much of the piece, and variety is achieved through ever-changing textural formations and timbral combinations.

If the music of Djam Karet represents an extension of Fripp and Eno's atmospheric, largely arhythmic rock minimalism, then the music of Ozric Tentacles suggests an extension of the rhythmically energized, linear minimalism of the Reich/Riley/Glass school as mediated through the psychedelic Canterbury rock of Gong and Soft Machine. In particular, one can draw a straight line of influence from Riley's electronic organ music of the mid- to late 1960s (*A Rainbow in Curved Air*) through the spacey electronic keyboard passages of Soft Machine ("French Lesson," the opening section of "Out-Bloody-Rageous") and Gong ("A Sprinkling of Clouds") on into similarly cosmic pieces of Ozric Tentacles ("Velmwend," "Floating Seeds," the opening of "Symmetricum").

There is no doubt the music of Ozric Tentacles is very different from King Crimson's *Discipline* and is also very different from the music of the other post-progressive bands discussed here. Nonetheless, it represents the same general fusion of minimalist, ethnic, and electronic sources within a progressive rock framework, although the Ozrics have drawn subtly on certain post-1980 pop music styles such as rave that other post-progressive bands have not. Because of both the high quality of the music itself and because of the thriving subculture that surrounds the band, Ozric Tentacles may very possibly be regarded eventually as the most important new progressive band to emerge during the 1980s.

Postlude

Whither progressive rock? In terms of its modest revival during the later 1980s and 1990s, I suspect each of the trends discussed in the final chapter will continue to play out over the next few years. On the strength of album sales, musical influence, and pure longevity, the six major progressive rock acts of the 1970s are Pink Floyd, Jethro Tull, Yes, Genesis, ELP, and King Crimson; all six were active at some point between 1992 and 1994, and will probably remain active, at least sporadically, for the foreseeable future. At this point, none of these bands is really "progressive" in the cutting-edge, 1970s sense of the word; even King Crimson, with their *Vroom* (1994), have begun a process of self-quotation. Rather, the bands have become cultural, musical, and business institutions that remain alive because, to various degrees and in various ways, they fulfill a need among an aging taste public. These bands supply this need not so much by their new releases as by the very fact of their continued existence. Their fans are by and large drawn to them not because of what their new music means, but because their continued existence lends them an almost iconic status. They generate an almost "magical" aura by the fact their music once meant something special to a large contingent of people.

However, in order to endure long enough to attain this iconic stature, these bands have had to make adjustments of varying degrees to the progressive rock style of the era 1970–1976. This in turn fueled the neo-progressive movement of the 1980s and 1990s: the belief that if a style was valid when it first appeared, it should remain valid indefinitely, and therefore should need no alteration. On the one hand, I am afraid there is a certain cultural reactivism in this view, so I think it is safe to assume that the fan base for this music will remain somewhat limited. On the other hand, the emergence of a band like Änglagård, with members hardly over twenty at the time of their first release (*Hybris*) in 1992, suggests that within limits this fan base may very well be self-perpetuating for some time to come. It is an open question, though, whether the neo-progressive movement can long avoid musical stagnation—especially when so many of its adherents refuse to countenance the introduction of any influences outside of the "classic" Yes/Genesis/ELP lineage into the neo-progressive style.

From a purely musical vantage point, I believe it is the post-progressive style pioneered on King Crimson's *Discipline* LP and pursued by later bands such as Djam Karet, Ozric Tentacles, and Edhels that has the most potential for genuine musical development. Whether this music will ever become the vehicle of genuine subcultural self-expression, however, is another question. There is an outside possibility that a fusion of "classic" progressive rock influences with contemporary rock styles could provide such an opportunity. *Nine to Five* (1995), the debut release of Death Organ (yet another band that has emerged from Sweden's burgeoning progressive music scene of the early 1990s) suggests once again that progressive rock is a more elastic and adaptable idiom than its critics would admit. *Nine to Five* offers an unlikely yet surprisingly coherent mixture of death metal (growling "monster" vocals) and alternative rock (virtuosic speech-song and trebly bass lines reminiscent of Primus) with intricate metric shifts and scorching Hammond organ solos that recall ELP and Egg at their heaviest. In listening to Death Organ, it is hard to avoid the conclusion that a full-fledged fusion of 1970s stylistic roots with 1990s sensibilities is eminently practicable.

On the other hand, in studying the rise of musical styles it is also important to remember that composers or elite musicians don't create musical styles; people do. No matter how musically promising a style may appear, its cultural power will ultimately depend on the degree to which it fulfills the role of self-definition among a group of people and not on its potential for purely musical development.

It seems to me, then, that it is unlikely that the rise of bands like Ozric Tentacles or Death Organ signals the beginning of a new cycle in which progressive music will again capture a mass audience and exert a powerful cultural influence. It seems more likely that such bands are part of a final playing out of a cycle that began over a quarter of a century ago, and that rock as a whole is slowly losing its cultural vitality. The power of rock, after all, stemmed from the power of the cultural revolution that spawned it, a cultural revolution the likes of which we have seen only one other time this century—in the early 1920s, with the birth of the jazz age. I suspect that only when the next cultural revolution ushers in new modes of thinking will conditions again exist for a music of cultural power and aesthetic substance to be a viable commercial proposition. Such music will almost certainly represent an entirely new form, and not an extension of rock.

Listeners who are committed to the indefinite perpetuation of the progressive rock style (or any other specific style) may find this prospect disturbing, although it seems to me such a view would be mistaken. To be sure, I believe that music of the past has many things to say to us; nevertheless, I think it is a grave error to insist that music of the present conform to a style that came out of a cultural context that is now extinct. Thus, I see no point in bewailing that the golden age of progressive rock (or of rock itself) is over. I cannot help believe that the remarkable thing is not that the golden age of progressive rock and its ancillary styles did not last longer; but rather that the special convergence of cultural, aesthetic, and commercial conditions—without which the genre could have never emerged—occurred in the first place.

In the end, I suspect that the attempts of progressive rock's most ardent supporters to keep it alive in a state of unchanging, pristine "perfection" distorts, to a certain degree at least, one of the major reasons for progressive rock's importance: its role as a mirror through which the cultural history of the 1970s can be viewed. Through it one can see all the weaknesses of that decade: the self-absorption, the self-indulgence, the love of spectacle on a scale that can often only be termed vulgar. However, through progressive rock one can also see the strengths of that period—strengths which keep drawing many listeners back to the music despite the best efforts of the critics.

Above all, progressive rock, like the period which gave rise to it, was optimistic. The whole underlying goal of progressive rock—to draw together rock, classical, jazz, folk, and avant-garde styles into a new metastyle that would supersede them all—is inherently optimistic. So too is the attempt to bridge the gulf between high and low culture, which I consider progressive rock's worthiest ambition: by creating a style of music that combined technical innovation and sophistication with mass appeal, progressive rock musicians achieved a goal that avant-garde composers could only dream of. The heroic scale on which so much progressive rock unfolds also suggests an abiding optimism; as do the epic conflicts and the grapplings with the Infinite and otherworldly which dominate so much progressive rock. It is also possible to see in the "uncommercial" nature of progressive rock a reminder of a time when the music industry was more tolerant of experimentation and individual expression, and less concerned with standardization and compartmentalization.

At its best, progressive rock engaged its listeners in a quest for spiritual authenticity. Sometimes its earnestness could lapse into a rather sophomoric naïveté. However, even at its most naive it was never wide-eyed or saccharine, while even at its bleakest, it never gave way to bitterness, cynicism, or self-pity.[1] In short, I suspect that progressive rock has retained its attraction for many of its older followers—and has even drawn some younger ones—because it encapsulates an optimism, a confidence, and perhaps even an innocence that is a refreshing antidote to the cynicism and pessimism of more recent times.

Appendix
Discographies and Personnel Listings of Major English Proto-Progressive, Symphonic Progressive, and Canterbury Bands

What follows is a discography/family tree of the major English proto-progressive, symphonic progressive, and Canterbury bands. My approach is obviously indebted to Peter Frame's, but my charts are not meant to replace his, nor do they convey exactly the same information. In terms of the discography, I have attempted to give a complete account of studio albums, live albums released during a band's lifetime, and recognized compilations. I do not list bootlegs or unofficial compilations; I do not pretend to give a complete account of EPs or of the posthumous live releases that have proliferated over the last few years. In terms of the lineup listings, I have not, in the manner of Frame, attempted to describe a band's complete history. I do not list pre-debut LP lineups if they differ from the lineup of the first LP, nor have I listed lineups of a band which toured together but never cut an album. I have in virtually all cases used the albums as my guide in determining personnel lists. Dates refer to the year an album was released, which may differ from the year that the actual recording sessions took place.

I have attempted to make my charts more specific than Frame's in certain realms. Underneath each album, I list important sidemen when relevant. Furthermore, I have attempted to be specific about which instruments specific musicians played, again referring to album credits whenever possible. "Pianos" signifies acoustic and electric pianos (either Rhodes or Clavinet), while "piano" signifies the acoustic instrument only; "el. piano" is used to designate the use of only the electric instrument. Likewise, "guitars" signifies the use of both electric and acoustic guitars, while "guitar" signifies the electric instrument only. When a musician only utilizes the acoustic guitar, this is signified by "ac. guitar." "Synthesizers" takes in any of the analog solid-state keyboard equipment of the 1970s; the Mellotron is listed separately. Since MIDI and digital sampling have effectively rendered past distinctions between different keyboard instruments obsolete (in that one can now mix, say, a piano sound, a Hammond organ sound, and a Mellotron-like sound together and play it in real time from one controlling instrument), with post-1980 lineups I have abandoned any attempts to separately list specific keyboard instruments, instead using the generic term "keyboards." "Drums" signifies both the kit and any percussion objects a drummer might use. "Bass" signifies bass guitar; the upright bass is listed as such. Finally, I have listed only instruments that a given musician played with a fair amount of regularity; Keith Emerson's use of the zoukra on one cut of ELP's *Trilogy* LP or Michael Rutherford's use of electric sitar on one cut of Genesis's *Selling England by the Pound* LP were not, in my view, sufficient cause to list these instruments among those that these musicians regularly played.

Bands appear in one of three categories: proto-progressive, symphonic progressive, or Canterbury bands. Within each category, bands are introduced chronologically, based on the year their debut LP was released. When two or more bands released their debut albums in the same year, they are introduced alphabetically. Short-lived bands that are obviously offshoots of longer-lasting bands (such as Refugee from the Nice or U.K. from King Crimson) are listed immediately below the "parent" band.

The Moody Blues

Lineup 1
DENNY LAINE guitar, vocals
CLINT WARWICK bass
MICHAEL PINDER piano
RAY THOMAS harmonica, vocals
GRAEME EDGE drums

Album
1. *The Magnificent Moodies* (1965)

Lineup 2
JUSTIN HAYWARD guitars, sitar, piano, lead
   and backing vocals
JOHN LODGE bass, ac. guitar, lead and backing
   vocals
MICHAEL PINDER piano, Mellotron, organ,
   harpsichord, lead and backing vocals
RAY THOMAS flutes, lead and backing vocals
GRAEME EDGE drums

Albums
2. *Days of Future Passed* (1968)
   [Guest: London Festival Orchestra]
3. *In Search of the Lost Chord* (1968)
4. *On the Threshold of a Dream* (1969)
5. *To Our Children's Children's Children*
   (1969)
6. *A Question of Balance* (1970)
7. *Every Good Boy Deserves Favour* (1971)
8. *Seventh Sojourn* (1972)
9. *This Is the Moody Blues* (1974)
   [Contains music from albums 2–8]
10. *Caught Live + 5* (1977)
   [Contains live performances of music
   from albums 2–5 and outtakes]
11. *Octave* (1978)

Lineup 3
JUSTIN HAYWARD guitars, lead and backing
   vocals
JOHN LODGE bass, lead and backing vocals
PATRICK MORAZ keyboards
RAY THOMAS flutes, lead and backing vocals
GRAEME EDGE drums

Albums
12. *Long Distance Voyager* (1981)
13. *The Present* (1983)
14. *Voices in the Sky: Best of the Moody Blues*
   (1985)
15. *The Other Side of Life* (1986)
16. *Sur la Mer* (1988)
17. *Legend of a Band* (1989)
   [Greatest hits compilation]

Lineup 4
JUSTIN HAYWARD guitars, lead and backing
   vocals
JOHN LODGE bass, lead and backing vocals
RAY THOMAS flutes, lead and backing vocals
GRAEME EDGE drums

Albums
18. *Keys of the Kingdom* (1991)
19. *The Moody Blues: A Night at Red Rocks
   with the Colorado Symphony Orchestra*
   (1993)
20. *Time Traveller* (1994)
   [Retrospective CD set containing music by
   all previous lineups]

Pink Floyd

Lineup 1
SYD BARRETT guitar, lead vocals
ROGER WATERS bass, backing vocals
RICHARD WRIGHT organ, piano
NICK MASON drums

Album
1. *The Piper at the Gates of Dawn* (1967)

Lineup 2
DAVID GILMOUR guitars, VCS3, lead and
   backing vocals
ROGER WATERS bass, VCS3, tape effects, lead
   and backing vocals

RICHARD WRIGHT organ, pianos, synthesizers,
   VCS3, backing vocals
NICK MASON drums, tape effects

Albums
2. *A Saucerful of Secrets* (1968)
   [Guest: Syd Barrett, guitar, vocals]
3. *More* [soundtrack] (1969)
4. *Ummagumma* (1969)
   [Live album with some newly-recorded
   tracks]
5. *Atom Heart Mother* (1970)
   [Guests: Ron Geesin, conductor, the John
   Aldiss Choir]

Pink Floyd (cont.)

6. *Relics* (1971)
   [Outtakes by first lineup]
7. *Meddle* (1971)
8. *Obscured by the Clouds* [soundtrack] (1972)
9. *The Dark Side of the Moon* (1973)
   [Guests: Dick Parry, saxes, Clare Torrey, Doris Troy, Leslie Duncan, Liza Strike, Barrie Saint John, backing vocals]
10. *A Nice Pair* (1973)
    [Reissue of albums 1–2]
11. *Wish You Were Here* (1975)
    [Guests: Dick Parry, saxes, Roy Harper, lead vocal, Venetta Fields, Carlena Williams, backing vocals]
12. *Animals* (1977)
13. *The Wall* (1979)
    [Guests: Toni Tennille, Bruce Johnston, Joe Chemay, John Joyce, the Islington Green School students, backing vocals]
14. *A Collection of Great Dance Songs* (1981)
    [Greatest hits package]

Lineup 3

DAVID GILMOUR guitars, vocals
ROGER WATERS bass, vocals
NICK MASON drums

Albums

15. *The Final Cut* (1983)
    [Guests: Andy Newmark, drums, Michael Kamen, Andy Brown, keyboards, Raphael Ravenscroft, saxophone, Ray Cooper, percussion]
16. *Works*
    [Features outtakes and music from albums 2, 4, 6, 7, 8, 9]

Lineup 4

DAVID GILMOUR guitars, bass, keyboards, sequencers, vocals
RICHARD WRIGHT keyboards, vocals
NICK MASON drums, sound effects

Albums

17. *A Momentary Lapse of Reason* (1987)
    [Guests: Bob Ezrin, Jon Carin, Pat Leonard, Bill Payne, keyboards, Jim Keltner, Carmine Appice, drums, Steve Forman, percussion, Tom Scott, Scott Page, John Haliwell, saxes, Tony Levin, bass and stick, Michael Landau, guitar, Darlene Koldenhaven, Carmen Twillie, Phyllis Saint James, Donnie Gerard, backing vocals]
18. *The Delicate Sound of Thunder* (1988)
    [Live recordings from *Momentary Lapse* tour]
19. *The Division Bell* (1994)
    [Guests: Jon Carin, keyboards, Guy Pratt, bass, Gary Wallis, percussion, Tim Renwick, guitars, Dick Parry, saxes, Bob Ezrin, keyboards and percussion, Sam Brown, Durga McBroom, Carol Kenyon, Jackie Sheridan, Rebecca Leight-White, backing vocals]
20. *Pulse* (1995)
    [Live recordings from *Division Bell* tour]
21. *Us and Them: Symphonic Pink Floyd* (1995)
    [Guest: London Philharmonic Orchestra]

Procol Harum

Lineup 1

GARY BROOKER piano, lead and backing vocals
MATTHEW FISHER organ, lead and backing vocals
ROBIN TROWER guitars, lead and backing vocals
DAVE KNIGHTS bass
B. J. WILSON drums
KEITH REID words

Albums

1. *Procol Harum* (1967)
2. *Shine of Brightly* (1968)
3. *A Salty Dog* (1969)

Lineup 2

GARY BROOKER piano, lead vocals
CHRIS COPPING bass, organ
ROBIN TROWER guitars, lead and backing vocals
B. J. WILSON drums
KEITH REID words

Albums

4. *Home* (1970)
5. *Broken Barricades* (1971)

Lineup 3

GARY BROOKER piano, vocals
CHRIS COPPING organ
DAVE BALL guitars

Procol Harum (cont.)

ALAN CARTWRIGHT bass
B. J. WILSON drums
KEITH REID words

Album

6. *Live in Concert With the Edmonton Symphony Orchestra* (1972)

Lineup 4

GARY BROOKER piano, lead vocals
CHRIS COPPING organ
MICK GRABHAM guitar
ALAN CARTWRIGHT bass
B. J. WILSON drums
KEITH REID words

Albums

7. *Grand Hotel* (1973)
8. *Exotic Birds and Fruit* (1974)
9. *Procol's Ninth* (1975)
10. *The Best of* (1975)
    [Contains music by lineups 1–3]

Lineup 5

GARY BROOKER piano, vocals
CHRIS COPPING bass
MICK GRABHAM guitar
PETE SOLLEY organ
B. J. WILSON drums
KEITH REID words

Albums

11. *Something Magic* (1977)
12. *Classics* (1987)
    [Contains music by lineups 1–3]

Lineup 6

GARY BROOKER piano, vocals
MATTHEW FISHER organ
ROBIN TROWER guitars
KEITH REID words

Album

13. *The Prodigal Stranger* (1991)
    [Guests: Dave Bronze, bass, Mark Brzezicki, drums]

Lineup 7

GARY BROOKER piano, organ, harpsichord, accordion, vocals
GEOFF WHITEHORN guitars
DAVE BRONZE bass
MARK BRZEZICKI drums

Album

14. *The Long Goodbye: Symphonic Music of Procol Harum* (1995)
    [Guests: London Symphony Orchestra, London Philharmonic Orchestra, James Galway, flute, Robin Trower, guitar, Matthew Fisher, organ]

The Nice

Lineup 1

KEITH EMERSON organ, piano
DAVID O'LIST guitar
LEE JACKSON bass, vocals
BRIAN DAVISON drums

Album

1. *The Thoughts of Emerlist Davjack* (1968)

Lineup 2

KEITH EMERSON organ, piano
LEE JACKSON bass, cello, vocals
BRIAN DAVISON drums

Albums

2. *Ars Longa Vita Brevis* (1968)
3. *The Nice* (1969)
4. *Five Bridges* (1970)
   [Guest: London Sinfonia]
5. *Elegy* (1971)

Posthumous Albums

6. *From Autumn to Spring* (1973)
   [Contains material from album 1 and previously unreleased material by first lineup]
7. *Keith Emerson With The Nice* (1973)
   [Repackages *Five Bridges*, *Elegy*]

Refugee

PATRICK MORAZ organ, pianos, synthesizers, Mellotron
LEE JACKSON bass, cello, vocals
BRIAN DAVISON drums

Album

1. *Refugee* (1974)

Jethro Tull

Lineup 1
IAN ANDERSON flute, piano, lead vocals
MICK ABRAHAM guitars, backing vocals
GLENN CORNICK bass
CLIVE BUNKER drums

Album
1. *This Was* (1968)

Lineup 2
IAN ANDERSON flute, mandolin, piano, organ,
    ac. guitar, vocals
MARTIN BARRE guitar
GLENN CORNICK bass
CLIVE BUNKER drums

Albums
2. *Stand Up* (1969)
3. *Benefit* (1970)
    [Guest: John Evan, piano and organ]

Lineup 3
IAN ANDERSON flute, ac. guitar, lead vocals
MARTIN BARRE guitar, recorder
JOHN EVAN piano, organ, Mellotron
JEFFREY HAMMOND-HAMMOND bass,
    recorder, backing vocals
CLIVE BUNKER drums

Album
4. *Aqualung* (1971)

Lineup 4
IAN ANDERSON flute, saxes, ac. guitar, vocals
MARTIN BARRE guitar, lute
JOHN EVAN piano, organ, harpsichord,
    synthesizers
JEFFREY HAMMOND-HAMMOND bass
BARRIEMORE BARLOW drums

Albums
5. *Thick as a Brick* (1972)
6. *Living in the Past* (1972)
    [Contains music from albums 1–4, previ-
    ously unreleased material]
7. *A Passion Play* (1973)
8. *War Child* (1974)
9. *Minstrel in the Galley* (1975)

Lineup 5
IAN ANDERSON flute, mandolin, ac. guitar,
    lead vocals
MARTIN BARRE guitar, lute

JOHN EVAN piano, organ, synthesizers
DAVID PALMER portative pipe organ,
    synthesizers
JOHN GLASCOCK bass, backing vocals
BARRIEMORE BARLOW drums

Albums
10. *M.U.: Best Of* (1976)
    [Contains music by lineups 2–4]
11. *Too Old to Rock 'n' Roll* (1976)
    [Guest: Maddy Prior, vocal]
12. *Songs from the Wood* (1977)
13. *Repeat: Best Of, Volume II* (1977)
    [Contains music by lineups 2–4]
14. *Heavy Horses* (1978)
    [Guest: Darryl Way, violin]
15. *Bursting Out: Jethro Tull Live* (1978)
16. *Stormwatch* (1979)

Lineup 6
IAN ANDERSON flute, vocals
MARTIN BARRE guitar
EDDIE JOBSON keyboards, electric violin
DAVE PEGG bass
MARK CRANEY drums

Album
17. *A* (1980)

Lineup 7
IAN ANDERSON flute, vocals
MARTIN BARRE guitar
PETER-JOHN VETTESE keyboards
DAVE PEGG bass
GERRY CONWAY drums

Album
18. *The Broadsword and the Beast* (1982)

Lineup 8
IAN ANDERSON flute, ac. guitar, electric drum
    programming, vocals
MARTIN BARRE guitar
PETER-JOHN VETTESE keyboards
DAVE PEGG bass

Albums
19. *Under Wraps* (1984)
20. *Original Masters* (1985)
    [Contains music by lineups 3–5]

Lineup 9
IAN ANDERSON flute, ac. guitar, keyboards,
    electric drum programming, vocals

Jethro Tull (cont.)

MARTIN BARRE guitars
DAVE PEGG bass

Albums
21. *Crest of a Knave* (1987)
    [Guests: Gerry Conway and Doane Perry, drums, Ric Sanders, violin]
22. *Twenty Years of Jethro Tull* (1988)
    [Retrospective CD set includes previously unreleased material]

Lineup 10
IAN ANDERSON flute, ac. guitar, vocals
MARTIN BARRE guitar
MARTIN ALLCOCK keyboards
DAVE PEGG bass
DOANE PERRY drums

Album
23. *Rock Island* (1989)

Lineup 11
IAN ANDERSON flute, ac. guitar, vocals
MARTIN BARRE guitar
ANDY GIDDINGS keyboards
DAVE PEGG bass
DOANE PERRY drums

Album
24. *Catfish Rising* (1991)

Lineup 12
IAN ANDERSON flute, ac. guitar, vocals
MARTIN BARRE ac. guitar
DAVE PEGG double bass
DAVE MATTACKS percussion

Albums
25. *A Little Light Music* (1992)
    [Live and "unplugged"]
26. *Nightcap: Unreleased Masters 1973–91* (1993)
    [Contains music by fourth and subsequent lineups]
27. *The Best of Jethro Tull: The 25th Anniversary Collection* (1993)
    [Updated retrospective collection]

Lineup 13
IAN ANDERSON flutes, ac. guitar, vocals
MARTIN BARRE guitar
ANDY GIDDINGS keyboards
DAVE PEGG bass
STEVE BAILEY bass
DOANE PERRY drums

Album
28. *Roots to Branches* (1995)

Genesis

Lineup 1
PETER GABRIEL flute, lead vocals
TONY BANKS piano, organ, backing vocals
ANTHONY PHILLIPS guitars, backing vocals
MICHAEL RUTHERFORD bass, guitars, backing vocals
JOHN SILVER drums

Album
1. *From Genesis to Revelation* (1969)

Lineup 2
PETER GABRIEL flute, lead vocals
TONY BANKS piano, organ, backing vocals
ANTHONY PHILLIPS guitars, backing vocals
MICHAEL RUTHERFORD bass, guitars, backing vocals
JOHN MAYHEW drums

Album
2. *Trespass* (1970)

Lineup 3
PETER GABRIEL flute, lead vocals
TONY BANKS piano, organ, Mellotron, synthesizers, ac. guitar, backing vocals
STEVE HACKETT guitars
MICHAEL RUTHERFORD bass, bass pedals, guitars
PHIL COLLINS drums, backing vocals

Albums
3. *Nursery Cryme* (1971)
4. *Foxtrot* (1972)
5. *Genesis Live* (1973)
6. *Selling England by the Pound* (1973)
7. *The Lamb Lies Down on Broadway* (1974)
   [Guest: Brian Eno, electronics]

Genesis (cont.)

Lineup 4

TONY BANKS pianos, organ, Mellotron, synthesizers, backing vocals
STEVE HACKETT guitars
MICHAEL RUTHERFORD bass, bass pedals, guitars, backing vocals
PHIL COLLINS drums, lead vocals

Albums

8. *A Trick of the Tail* (1976)
9. *Wind and Wutherinng* (1976)
10. *Seconds Out* (1977)
   [Live recordings. Guests: Bill Bruford and Chester Thompson, drums]

Lineup 5

TONY BANKS keyboards, backing vocals
MICHAEL RUTHERFORD bass, guitars, backing vocals
PHIL COLLINS drums, lead vocals

Albums

11. *... And Then There Were Three* (1978)
12. *Duke* (1980)
13. *ABACAB* (1981)
14. *Three Sides Live* (1982)
   [Guests: Chester Thompson, drums, Darryl Stuermer, guitars]
15. *Genesis* (1983)
16. *Invisible Touch* (1986)
17. *We Can't Dance* (1991)
18. *The Way We Walk: The Shorts* (1992)
   [Live recordings emphasizing more pop-oriented material of the 1980s. Guests: Chester Thompson, drums, Darryl Stuermer, guitars]
19. *The Way We Walk: The Longs* (1993)
   [Live recordings emphasizing earlier, more extended material. Guests: Chester Thompson, drums, Darryl Stuermer, guitars]

King Crimson

Lineup 1

ROBERT FRIPP guitars
IAN MCDONALD woodwinds, Mellotron, backing vocals
GREG LAKE bass, lead vocals
MICHAEL GILES drums, backing vocals
PETER SINFIELD words, illumination

Album

1. *In the Court of the Crimson King* (1969)

Lineup 2

ROBERT FRIPP guitars, Mellotron, devices
MEL COLLINS woodwinds
GREG LAKE lead vocals
MICHAEL GILES drums
PETER SINFIELD words
PETER GILES bass
KEITH TIPPETT piano

Album

2. *In the Wake of Poseidon* (1970)
   [Guest: Gordon Haskell, lead vocal]

Lineup 3

ROBERT FRIPP guitars, Mellotron, devices
MEL COLLINS woodwinds
GORDON HASKELL bass, vocals
ANDY MCCULLOCH drums
PETER SINFIELD words, pictures

Album

3. *Lizard* (1971)
   [Guests: Keith Tippett, piano, Jon Anderson, lead vocal, Robin Miller, double reeds, Mark Charig and Nick Evans, brass]

Lineup 4

ROBERT FRIPP guitars, Mellotron, devices
MEL COLLINS woodwinds, backing vocals
BOZ BURRELL bass, lead vocals
IAN WALLACE drums, backing vocals
PETER SINFIELD words, pictures

Albums

4. *Islands* (1971)
   [Guests: Keith Tippett, piano, Robin Miller, oboe, Mark Charig, cornet]
5. *Earthbound* (1972)
   [*Islands* lineup live]

Lineup 5

ROBERT FRIPP guitars, Mellotron, devices
DAVID CROSS violin, viola, Mellotron
JOHN WETTON bass, vocals
BILL BRUFORD drums

King Crimson (cont.)

Albums
6. *Larks' Tongue in Aspic (1973)*
   [Guest: Jamie Muir, percussion]
7. *Starless and Bible Black* (1974)
8. *Red* (1974)
   [Guests: Ian McDonald and Mel Collins, saxes, Robin Miller, oboe, Mark Charig, cornet]
9. *USA* (1975)
   [*Starless* lineup live. Guest: Eddie Jobson, violin, piano]
10. *The Young Person's Guide to King Crimson* (1976)
    [Compilation; contains music from albums 1–4, 6–8]

14. *The Abbreviated King Crimson: Heartbeat* (1991)
    [Greatest hits package]
15. *The Compact King Crimson* (1991)
    [Contains music from albums 1, 11–13]
16. *Frame by Frame: the Essential King Crimson* (1991)
    [Retrospective CD set containing music by all previous lineups and previously unreleased live material]
17. *The Great Deceiver: Live 1973–74* (1992)
    [Previously unreleased live material by *Starless* lineup]
18. *The Concise King Crimson* (1993)
    [Alternate greatest hits package]

Lineup 6
ROBERT FRIPP guitars, devices
ADRIAN BELEW guitars, lead vocals
TONY LEVIN bass, stick, backing vocals
BILL BRUFORD drums, electronic drums

Albums
11. *Discipline* (1981)
12. *Beat* (1982)
13. *Three of a Perfect Pair* (1984)

Lineup 7
ROBERT FRIPP guitar
ADRIAN BELEW guitar, vocals
TREY GUNN stick
TONY LEVIN bass, stick
PAT MASTELOTTO drums, electronic drums
BILL BRUFORD drums, electronic drums

Albums
19. *Vroom* (1994)
20. *Thrak* (1995)
21. *B'Boom* (1995)
    [*Vroom/Thrak* lineup live in Argentina]

U.K.

Lineup 1
EDDIE JOBSON synthesizers, organ, pianos, violin, backing vocals
JOHN WETTON bass, lead vocals
BILL BRUFORD drums
ALLAN HOLDSWORTH guitars

Album
1. *U.K.* (1978)

Lineup 2
EDDIE JOBSON synthesizers, organ, pianos, violin, backing vocals
JOHN WETTON bass, lead vocals
TERRY BOZZIO drums, backing vocals

Albums
2. *Danger Money* (1979)
3. *Night After Night: U.K. Live* (1979)
   [*Danger Money* lineup in concert]

Renaissance

Lineup 1
KEITH RELF guitars, harmonica, vocals
JANE RELF vocals
JOHN HAWKEN piano, harpsichord
LOUIS CENNAMO bass
JIM MCCARTY drums, vocals

Albums
1. *Renaissance* (1969)
2. *Illusion* (1970)
   [Note: this lineup later regrouped and recorded under the aegis of Illusion.]

Renaissance (cont.)

Lineup 2
ANNIE HASLAM lead vocals
JOHN TOUT piano, organ, string synthesizer, backing vocals
ROB HENDRY guitars, mandolin, backing vocals
JON CAMP bass, backing vocals
TERRENCE SULLIVAN drums

Album
3. *Prologue* (1972)
[Guest: Francis Monkman, VCS3]

Lineup 3
ANNIE HASLAM lead vocals
JOHN TOUT piano, harpsichord, celeste, string synthesizer, organ, backing vocals
MICHAEL DUNFORD guitars, backing vocals
JON CAMP bass, bass pedals, guitars, lead and backing vocals
TERRY SULLIVAN drums, backing vocals
BETTY THATCHER words

Albums
4. *Ashes are Burning* (1973)
   [Guest: Andy Powell, guitar]
5. *Turn of the Cards* (1974)
6. *Scheherazade* (1975)
   [Guests: unspecified members of the London Symphony Orchestra]
7. *Live at Carnegie Hall* (1976)
8. *Novella* (1977)
9. *A Song for all Seasons* (1978)
10. *Azure d'Or* (1979)

Lineup 4
ANNIE HASLAM lead vocals
JON CAMP bass, guitar, lead and backing vocals
MICHAEL DUNFORD guitars

Album
11. *Camera Camera* (1981)
    [Guests: Peter Gosling, keyboards, Peter Barron, drums, Betty Thatcher, words]
12. *Time-Line* (1983)
    [Guests: Peter Gosling and Nick Magnus, keyboards, Peter Barron and Ian Mosley, drums]

Posthumous Albums
13. *Tales of 1000 Nights, Volume I* (1990)
14. *Tales of 1000 Nights, Volume II* (1990)
    [Albums 12–13 constitute a retrospective CD set spanning albums 2–11]
15. *Da Capo—the Story of Renaissance* (1995)
    [Alternate retrospective CD set containing some previously unreleased material]
Note: In 1995 two competing "Renaissance" bands released new albums. Renaissance's *The Other Woman* featured vocalist Stephanie Adlington interpreting songs by the band's long-time songwriting team of Betty Thatcher (words) and Michael Dunford (music). Annie Haslam's Renaissance released *Blessing in Disguise*, highlighting Haslam's vocals and songs by Tony Visconti. Haslam, Dunford, and Thatcher were the only members of the 1972–1983 period involved in these projects.

Van Der Graaf Generator

Lineup 1
PETER HAMMILL ac. guitar, vocals
HUGH BANTON organ
KEITH ELLIS bass
GUY EVANS drums

Album
1. *The Aerosol Grey Machine* (1969)

Lineup 2
PETER HAMMILL ac. guitar, piano, lead vocals
HUGH BANTON organ, piano, bass, backing vocals
DAVID JACKSON saxes, flutes, devices, backing vocals

NIC POTTER bass
GUY EVANS drums

Albums
2. *The Least We Can Do Is Wave to Each Other* (1970)
3. *H to He Who Am the Only One* (1970)
   [Guest: Robert Fripp, guitar]

Lineup 3
PETER HAMMILL guitars, pianos, lead vocals
HUGH BANTON organ, piano, Mellotron, bass pedals, bass guitar, backing vocals

Van Der Graaf Generator (cont.)

DAVID JACKSON saxes, flutes, devices, backing vocals
GUY EVANS drums

Albums
4. *Pawn Hearts* (1971)
   [Guest: Robert Fripp, guitar]
5. *Godbluff* (1975)
6. *Still Life* (1976)
7. *World Record* (1976)

Van Der Graaf

PETER HAMMILL guitars, piano, vocals
GRAHAM SMITH violin
NIC POTTER bass
GUY EVANS drums

Albums
8. *The Quiet Zone* (1977)
9. *Vital: Van der Graaf Live* (1978)
   [Guests: David Jackson, saxes; Charles Dickie, cello, synthesizers, electric piano]

Posthumous Albums
10. *Repeat Performance* (1980)
    [Contains music from albums 2–4 and singles]

11. *Time Vaults* (1982)
    [Previously unreleased material from post-*Pawn Hearts*, pre-*Godbluff* era]
12. *First Generation* (1987)
    [Contains music from albums 2–4 and B-sides]
13. *Second Generation* (1987)
    [Contains music from albums 5–8]
14. *I Prophesy Disaster* (1993)
    [Contains music from albums 1–9, singles]

Yes

Lineup 1
PETER BANKS guitar
CHRIS SQUIRE bass, backing vocals
TONY KAYE organ, piano
BILL BRUFORD drums
JON ANDERSON lead vocals

Albums
1. *Yes* (1969)
2. *Time and a Word* (1970)

Lineup 2
STEVE HOWE guitars, vachalia, backing vocals
CHRIS SQUIRE bass, backing vocals
TONY KAYE organ, piano
BILL BRUFORD drums
JON ANDERSON lead vocals

Album
3. *The Yes Album* (1971)
   [Guest: Colin Goldring, recorders]

Lineup 3
STEVE HOWE guitars, backing vocals
CHRIS SQUIRE bass, backing vocals

RICK WAKEMAN organ, pianos, Moog, Mellotron
BILL BRUFORD drums
JON ANDERSON lead vocals

Albums
4. *Fragile* (1971)
5. *Close to the Edge* (1972)

Lineup 4
STEVE HOWE guitars, backing vocals
CHRIS SQUIRE bass, backing vocals
RICK WAKEMAN organ, pianos, synthesizers, Mellotron
ALAN WHITE drums
JON ANDERSON lead vocals

Albums
6. *Yessongs* (1973)
   [Live performances from *Close to the Edge* tour. Guest: Bill Bruford, drums]
7. *Tales from Topographic Oceans* (1973)
8. *Relayer* (1974)
   [Guest: Patrick Moraz, keyboards; Rick Wakeman did not appear on this album.]

Yes (cont.)

9. *Yesterdays* (1975)
   [Contains music from albums 1–2 and previously unreleased material by third lineup]
10. *Going for the One* (1977)
11. *Tormato* (1978)

Lineup 5
STEVE HOWE guitars, backing vocals
CHRIS SQUIRE bass, backing vocals
GEOFF DOWNES keyboards
ALAN WHITE drums
TREVOR HORN lead vocals

Albums
12. *Drama* (1980)
13. *Yesshows* (1980)
    [Live performances, mostly by fourth lineup]
14. *Classic Yes* (1982)
    [Compilation, contains music by lineups 2–4]

Lineup 6
TREVOR RABIN guitars, backing vocals
CHRIS SQUIRE bass, backing vocals
TONY KAYE keyboards
ALAN WHITE drums
JON ANDERSON lead vocals

Albums
15. *90125* (1983)
16. *9012Live: The Solos* (1986)
17. *Big Generator* (1987)

Lineup 7 (Recorded and toured as "Anderson, Bruford, Wakeman and Howe")
JON ANDERSON lead vocals
BILL BRUFORD drums, electronic drums
RICK WAKEMAN keyboards
STEVE HOWE guitar

Album
18. *Anderson, Bruford, Wakeman and Howe* (1989)
    [Guests: Tony Levin, bass, stick, and backing vocals, Matt Clifford, keyboards and backing vocals, Milton McDonald, rhythm guitar, the Oxford Circus Singers, the J.M.C. Singers, Emerald Community Singers]

Lineup 8
TREVOR RABIN guitars, backing vocals
CHRIS SQUIRE bass, backing vocals
TONY KAYE keyboards
ALAN WHITE drums
JON ANDERSON lead vocals
BILL BRUFORD drums, electronic drums
RICK WAKEMAN keyboards
STEVE HOWE guitars

Albums
19. *Union* (1991)
    [Guests: Tony Levin, bass and stick, Jim Crichton, Jonathan Elias, and Alex Lasarenko, keyboards, Jerry Bennett and Allan Schwartzberg, percussion, Richard Baker, Gary Barlough, Jerry Bennett, Jim Crichton, Jonathan Elias, Sherman Foote, Brian Foraker, Chris Fosdick, Rory Kaplan, Alex Lasarenko, and Steve Porcaro, synthesizers, Jimmy Haun, guitar, Deborah Anderson, Jonathan Elias, Gary Falcone, Tommy Funderburk, Ian Lloyd, Michael Sherwood, Danny Vaughn, and Pauline Cheng, backing vocals]
20. *Yesyears* (1991)
    [Retrospective CD set containing music by all previous lineups, including previously unreleased material]
21. *Yesstory* (1992)
    [Alternate retrospective CD set]
22. *The Best of Yes* (1993)
    [Updated greatest hits compilation]
23. *Symphonic Music of Yes* (1993)
    [Anderson, Bruford, Howe and the London Philharmonic]
24. *An Evening of Yes Music Plus* (1994)
    [Anderson, Bruford, Wakeman and Howe live]

Lineup 9
TREVOR RABIN guitars, backing vocals
CHRIS SQUIRE bass, backing vocals
TONY KAYE keyboards
ALAN WHITE drums
JON ANDERSON lead vocals

Album
25. *Talk* (1994)

Curved Air

Lineup 1
SONJA (LINWOOD) KRISTINA lead vocals
DARRYL WAY violin, pianos, backing vocals
FRANCIS MONKMAN guitar, organ, piano,
   VCS3, Mellotron, harpsichord
ROBERT MARTIN bass
FLORIAN PILKINGTON-MIKSA drums

Album
   1. *Air Conditioning* (1970)

Lineup 2
SONJA KRISTINA lead vocals
DARRYL WAY violin, pianos, backing vocals
FRANCIS MONKMAN guitar, organ, pianos,
   VCS3, Mellotron, harpsichord
IAN EYRE bass
FLORIAN PILKINGTON-MIKSA drums

Album
   2. *Second Album* (1971)

Lineup 3
SONJA KRISTINA lead vocals, ac. guitar
DARRYL WAY violin, pianos
FRANCIS MONKMAN guitar, organ, piano,
   synthesizers, Mellotron
MIKE WEDGWOOD bass, backing vocals
FLORIAN PILKINGTON-MIKSA drums

Album
   3. *Phantasmagoria* (1972)
     [Guest: Frank Ricotti, xylophone and
     vibes]

Lineup 4
SONJA KRISTINA lead vocals
EDDIE JOBSON violin, pianos, organ,
   Mellotron, VCS3
KIRBY guitar, backing vocals
MIKE WEDGWOOD bass, backing vocals
JIM RUSSELL drums

Album
   4. *Aircut* (1973)

Lineup 5
SONJA KRISTINA lead vocals
DARRYL WAY violin, el. piano, backing vocals
FRANCIS MONKMAN guitar, organ,
   synthesizers
PHIL KOHN bass
FLORIAN PILKINGTON-MIKSA drums

Album
   5. *Live* (1975)

Lineup 6
SONJA KRISTINA vocals
DARRYL WAY violin, el. piano
MICK JACQUES guitar
TONY REEVES bass, keyboards
STEWART COPELAND drums

Albums
   6. *Midnight Wire* (1975)
   7. *Airborne* (1976)
   8. *Best of* (1976)
     [Contains music by lineups 1–3]

Posthumous Album
   9. *Love Child* (1990)
     [Previously unreleased music recorded in
     1973 by *Aircut* lineup]

Darryl Way's Wolf

Lineup 1
DARRYL WAY violin, viola, el. piano
JOHN ETHERIDGE guitars
DEK MESSECAR bass, vocals
IAN MOSLEY drums

Albums
   1. *Canis Lupus* (1973)
   2. *Saturation Point* (1973)

Lineup 2
DARRYL WAY violin, el. piano, synthesizers
JOHN ETHERIDGE guitars
DEK MESSECAR bass, backing vocals
IAN MOSLEY drums
JOHN HODGKINSON lead vocals

Albums
   3. *Night Music* (1974)
   4. *Darryl Way's Wolf* (1974)
     [Compilation]

Emerson, Lake and Palmer

KEITH EMERSON organ, piano, synthesizers
GREG LAKE bass, guitars, vocals
CARL PALMER drums

Albums

1. *Emerson, Lake and Palmer* (1970)
2. *Tarkus* (1971)
3. *Pictures at an Exhibition* (1972)
4. *Trilogy* (1972)
5. *Brain Salad Surgery* (1973)
   [Guest: Peter Sinfield, words]
6. *Welcome Back My Friends to the Show That Never Ends* (1974)
   [Triple live album recorded during 1973–1974 world tour]
7. *Works Volume 1* (1977)
   [Guests: London Philharmonic Orchestra, Orchestra de l'Opera de Paris, Peter Sinfield, words]
8. *Works Volume 2* (1977)
   [Guests: London Philharmonic Orchestra, Peter Sinfield, words]
9. *Love Beach* (1978)
   [Guest: Peter Sinfield, words]
10. *In Concert* (1979)
    [Rereleased in 1993 with additional tracks as *Works Live*]
11. *The Best of* (1980)
12. *Black Moon* (1992)
13. *The Atlantic Years* (1992)
    [Compilation containing tracks from albums 1–9]
14. *Live at the Royal Albert Hall* (1993)
    [Recorded live during the *Black Moon* tour]
15. *Return of the Manticore* (1993)
    [Retrospective CD set containing music from albums 1–10 and 12, newly-recorded material, and previously unreleased material]
16. *The Best of Emerson, Lake and Palmer* (1994)
    [Updated greatest hits compilation]
17. *In the Hot Seat* (1994)

Emerson, Lake and Powell

KEITH EMERSON keyboards
GREG LAKE bass, vocals
COZY POWELL drums

Album

1. *Emerson, Lake and Powell* (1986)

Three

KEITH EMERSON keyboards
ROBERT BERRY bass, guitar, vocals
CARL PALMER drums

Album

1. *To the Power of Three* (1988)

Gentle Giant

Lineup 1

DEREK SHULMAN lead and backing vocals
RAY SHULMAN bass, violin, ac. guitar, backing vocals
PHIL SHULMAN saxes, trumpet, recorder, lead and backing vocals
KERRY MINNEAR organ, pianos, synthesizers, Mellotron, vibraphone, cello, lead and backing vocals
GARY GREEN guitars
MARTIN SMITH drums

Albums

1. *Gentle Giant* (1970)
2. *Acquiring the Taste* (1971)

Lineup 2

DEREK SHULMAN lead and backing vocals
RAY SHULMAN bass, violin, ac. guitar, backing vocals
PHIL SHULMAN saxes, trumpet, recorder, lead and backing vocals
KERRY MINNEAR organ, pianos, synthesizers, Mellotron, vibraphone, cello, lead and backing vocals
GARY GREEN guitars
MALCOLM MORTIMORE drums

Album

3. *Three Friends* (1972)

Gentle Giant (cont.)

Lineup 3
DEREK SHULMAN saxes, lead and backing vocals
RAY SHULMAN bass, violin, ac. guitar, backing vocals
PHIL SHULMAN saxes, trumpet, lead and backing vocals
KERRY MINNEAR organ, pianos, synthesizers, vibraphone, cello, lead and backing vocals
GARY GREEN guitars
JOHN WEATHERS drums, xylophone

Album
4. *Octopus* (1973)

Lineup 4
DEREK SHULMAN saxes, lead and backing vocals
RAY SHULMAN bass, violin, ac. guitar, backing vocals

KERRY MINNEAR organ, pianos, synthesizers, vibraphone, cello, lead and backing vocals
GARY GREEN guitars
JOHN WEATHERS drums, xylophone, vibraphone, backing vocals

Albums
5. *In a Glass House* (1973)
6. *The Power and the Glory* (1974)
7. *Free Hand* (1975)
8. *Giant Steps: the First Five Years* (1975) [Contains music from albums 1–6 and outtakes]
9. *Interview* (1976)
10. *Playing the Fool: Gentle Giant Live* (1977)
11. *Pretentious* (1977) [Contains music from albums 1–6]
12. *The Missing Piece* (1977)
13. *Giant for a Day* (1978)
14. *Civilian* (1980)

Jade Warrior

Lineup 1
TONY DUHIG guitars
GLYN HAVARD bass, ac. guitar, vocals
JON FIELD flutes, percussion

Albums
1. *Jade Warrior* (1970)
2. *Released* (1971) [Guests: Dave Connors, reeds, Allan Price, drums]
3. *Last Autumn's Dream* (1972) [Guests: Allan Price, drums, David Duhig, guitar]

Lineup 2
TONY DUHIG guitars, bass, keyboards
JON FIELD flutes, percussion, keyboards

Albums
4. *Floating World* (1974) [Guests: David Duhig, guitar, Orpington Junior Girls Choir]
5. *Waves* (1975) [Guests: Graham Morgan, drums, Steve Winwood, Moog, el. piano, David Duhig, guitar]
6. *Kites* (1976) [Guests: Graham Morgan, drums, Fred Frith, violin]

7. *Way of the Sun* (1978) [Guests: Graham Morgan, drums, Gowan Turnbull, reeds]
8. *Reflections* (1980) [Compilation of material from albums 4–7]
9. *Horizen* (1984) [Guests: David Duhig, guitar, Gowan Turnbull, reeds, Pro Musica of London chorus]

Lineup 3
JON FIELD flutes, electronic wind instrument, percussion, vocalese
COLIN HENSON guitars, keyboards, vocalese
DAVE STURT bass, percussion, keyboards, vocalese

Albums
10. *Breathing the Storm* (1992) [Dedicated to the memory of Tony Duhig, 1943–1991]
11. *Distant Echoes* (1993) [Guests: David Cross, Andy Aitchison, electric violins, Gowan Turnbull, Theo Travis, reeds, Russell Roberts, drums]
12. *Elements* (1995) [Repackages albums 4–7]

Camel

Lineup 1

ANDY LATIMER guitars, flute, vocals
PETER BARDENS pianos, organ, synthesizers
DOUG FERGUSON bass
ANDY WARD drums

Albums

1. *Camel* (1973)
2. *Mirage* (1974)
3. *The Snow Goose* (1975)
4. *Moonmadness* (1976)

Lineup 2

ANDY LATIMER guitars, flutes, vocals
PETER BARDENS pianos, organ, synthesizers
RICHARD SINCLAIR bass, vocals
MEL COLLINS saxes
ANDY WARD drums

Albums

5. *Rain Dances* (1977)
6. *A Live Record* (1978)
   [Guests: London Symphony Orchestra]
7. *Breathless* (1978)

Lineup 3

ANDY LATIMER guitars, flutes, vocals
JAN SCHELHAAS keyboards
KIT WATKINS keyboards
COLIN BASS bass, vocals
ANDY WARD drums

Album

8. *I Can See Your House From Here* (1979)
   [Guests: Mel Collins, saxes, Phil Collins,
   drums]

Lineup 4

ANDY LATIMER guitars, flutes, vocals
DUNCAN MACKAY keyboards
MEL COLLINS woodwinds
COLIN BASS bass, vocals
ANDY WARD drums

Albums

9. *Nude* (1981)
   [Guests: Jan Schelhaas, piano, Chris
   Green, cello, Gaspar Lawal, percussion,
   Herbie Flowers, tuba]

10. *Chameleon: The Best of Camel* (1981)
    [Compilation containing music from al-
    bums 2–5, 7–9]

Lineup 5

ANDY LATIMER guitars, keyboards, vocals
CHRIS RAINBOW vocals
ANTHONY PHILLIPS ac. guitar, keyboards,
   marimba
DAVID PATON bass, vocals
GRAHAM JARVIS drums

Album

11. *The Single Factor* (1982)
    [Guests: Peter Bardens, keyboards, Francis
    Monkman and Duncan Mackay, synthe-
    sizers, Simon Phillips, drums]

Lineup 6

ANDY LATIMER guitars, piano, flute, vocals
CHRIS RAINBOW vocals
HAYDEN BENDALL keyboards
TOM SCHERPENZEEL keyboards
MEL COLLINS saxes
DAVID PATON bass
PAUL BURGESS drums

Albums

12. *Stationary Traveller* (1984)
13. *Pressure Points: Live* (1984)
14. *Echoes* (1991)
    [Alternate compilation set with some un-
    released material]

Lineup 7

ANDY LATIMER guitars, keyboards, flute,
   vocals
TOM SCHERPENZEEL keyboards
MICKEY SIMMONS keyboards
COLIN BASS bass, vocals
PAUL BURGESS drums

Albums

15. *Dust and Dreams* (1992)
16. *On the Road 1972* (1993)
    [Lineup 1 in concert]
17. *On the Road 1982* (1994)
    [*Single Factor* lineup in concert]
18. *Never Let Go* (1994)
    [*Dust and Dreams* lineup in concert]

Soft Machine

Lineup 1
ROBERT WYATT drums, vocals
KEVIN AYERS bass, vocals
MIKE RATLEDGE organ, piano

Album
1. *Soft Machine* (1968)

Lineup 2
ROBERT WYATT drums, vocals
HUGH HOPPER bass
MIKE RATLEDGE organ, piano

Album
2. *Volume Two* (1969)

Lineup 3
ROBERT WYATT drums, vocals
HUGH HOPPER bass
MIKE RATLEDGE organ, pianos
ELTON DEAN alto sax, saxello

Albums
3. *Third* (1970)
   [Guests: Rab Spall, violin, Lyn Dobson, flute, Jimmy Hastings, woodwinds, Nick Evans, trombone]
4. *Fourth* (1971)
   [Guests: Jimmy Hastings, woodwinds, Nick Evans, trombone, Mark Charig, cornet, Alan Skidmore, tenor sax, Roy Babbington, double bass]

Lineup 4
JOHN MARSHALL drums
HUGH HOPPER bass
MIKE RATLEDGE organ, el. piano
ELTON DEAN alto sax, saxello

Album
5. *Five* (1972)
   [Guests: Phil Howard, drums, Roy Babbington, double bass]

Lineup 5
JOHN MARSHALL drums
HUGH HOPPER bass, devices
MIKE RATLEDGE organ, pianos
KARL JENKINS oboe, saxes, el. piano

Album
6. *Six* (1972)

Lineup 6
JOHN MARSHALL drums
ROY BABBINGTON bass, double bass
MIKE RATLEDGE organ, el. piano, synthesizers
KARL JENKINS oboe, saxes, el. piano

Album
7. *Seven* (1973)

Lineup 7
JOHN MARSHALL drums
ROY BABBINGTON bass, double bass
MIKE RATLEDGE organ, pianos, synthesizers
KARL JENKINS oboe, saxes, pianos
ALLAN HOLDSWORTH guitars

Album
8. *Bundles* (1975)

Lineup 8
JOHN MARSHALL drums
ROY BABBINGTON bass
ALAN WAKEMAN saxes
KARL JENKINS pianos, synthesizers
JOHN ETHERIDGE guitars

Albums
9. *Softs* (1976)
   [Guest: Mike Ratledge, synthesizers]
10. *Rubber Riff* (1976)
11. *Triple Echo* (1977)
   [Compilation containing music from albums 1–9 and previously unreleased material]

Lineup 9
JOHN MARSHALL drums
STEVE COOK bass
RIC SANDERS violin
KARL JENKINS pianos, synthesizers
JOHN ETHERIDGE guitars

Album
12. *Alive and Well, Recorded in Paris* (1978)

Lineup 10
JOHN MARSHALL drums
JACK BRUCE bass
DICK MORRISEY saxes
KARL JENKINS keyboards
RAY WARLEIGH flutes
ALLAN HOLDSWORTH guitars

Soft Machine (cont.)

Album
13. *Land of Cockayne* (1981)
    [Guests: Alan Parker, guitars, John Taylor, keyboards, John G. Perry, Stu Calver, Tony Rivers, vocals]

Posthumous Album
14. *Live at the Proms 1970* (1988)
    [*Third* lineup in concert]

Caravan

Lineup 1
RICHARD SINCLAIR bass, ac. guitar, lead and backing vocals
PYE HASTINGS guitars, lead and backing vocals
DAVID SINCLAIR organ, piano, backing vocals
RICHARD COUGHLAN drums

Albums
1. *Caravan* (1969)
   [Guest: Jimmy Hastings, flute]
2. *If I Could Do It All Over Again, I'd Do It All Over You* (1970)
   [Guest: Jimmy Hastings, saxes and flutes]
3. *In the Land of Grey and Pink* (1971)
   [Guest: Jimmy Hastings, saxes and flutes]

Lineup 2
RICHARD SINCLAIR bass, lead and backing vocals
PYE HASTINGS guitars, lead and backing, vocals
STEVE MILLER pianos, organ, el. harpsichord
RICHARD COUGHLAN drums

Album
4. *Waterloo Lilly* (1972)
   [Guests: Jimmy Hastings, saxes and flutes, Lol Coxhill, saxes]

Lineup 3
JOHN G. PERRY bass, lead and backing vocals
PYE HASTINGS guitars, lead and backing vocals
DAVID SINCLAIR organ, pianos, synthesizers
GEOFF RICHARDSON viola
RICHARD COUGHLAN drums

Albums
5. *For Girls Who Grow Plump in the Night* (1973)
   [Guest: Jimmy Hastings, flutes]
6. *Caravan and the New Symphonia* (1974)
   [Guests: Jimmy Hastings, flutes, the New Symphonia conducted by Martyn Ford]

Lineup 4
MIKE WEDGEWOOD bass, lead and backing vocals
PYE HASTINGS guitars, lead and backing vocals
DAVID SINCLAIR organ, pianos, synthesizers
GEOFF RICHARDSON viola, guitars, flute
RICHARD COUGHLAN drums

Albums
7. *Cunning Stunts* (1975)
8. *Canterbury Tales* (1976)
   [Compilation of albums 1–6]

Lineup 5
MIKE WEDGWOOD bass, lead and backing vocals
PYE HASTINGS guitars, lead and backing vocals
JAN SCHELHAAS organ, pianos, synthesizers
GEOFF RICHARDSON viola, flute, guitars
RICHARD COUGHLAN drums

Album
9. *Blind Dog at Saint Dunstan's* (1976)

Lineup 6
DEK MESSECAR bass, lead and backing vocals
PYE HASTINGS guitars, lead and backing vocals
JAN SCHELHAAS organ, pianos, synthesizers
GEOFF RICHARDSON viola, flute, guitars
RICHARD COUGHLAN drums

Albums
10. *Better By Far* (1977)
11. *The Best of Caravan* (1978)
    [Greatest hits compilation]

Lineup 7
DEK MESSECAR bass, lead and backing vocals
PYE HASTINGS guitars, lead and backing vocals
DAVID SINCLAIR keyboards
GEOFF RICHARDSON viola, flute, backing vocals
RICHARD COUGHLAN drums

Caravan (cont.)

Albums
12. *The Album* (1980)
13. *The Best of Caravan Live* (1980)

Lineup 8
RICHARD SINCLAIR bass, lead and backing vocals
PYE HASTINGS guitars, lead and backing vocals
DAVID SINCLAIR keyboards
RICHARD COUGHLAN drums

Album
14. *Back to Front* (1982)
[Guest: Mel Collins, saxes]

Lineup 9
JIM LEVERTON bass
PYE HASTINGS guitars, vocals
DAVID SINCLAIR keyboards
GEOFF RICHARDSON viola, woodwinds, vocals
RICHARD COUGHLAN drums

Album
15. *The Battle of Hastings* (1995)
[Guest: Jimmy Hastings, saxes and flutes]

Richard Sinclair's Caravan Of Dreams

RICHARD SINCLAIR bass, vocals
DAVID SINCLAIR keyboards
RICK BIDDULPH bass
ANDY WARD drums

Albums
1. *Richard Sinclair's Caravan of Dreams* (1992)

[Guests: Jimmy Hastings, saxes and flutes, Michael Heupel, flutes, Allan Clarke, harmonica]
2. *An Evening of Magic* (1993)
[Live performance]

Egg

DAVE STEWART organ, pianos
MONT CAMPBELL bass, French horn, vocals
CLIVE BROOKS drums

Albums
1. *Egg* (1969)
2. *The Polite Force* (1970)
3. *The Civil Surface* (1974)

[Guests: Steve Hillage, guitar, Barbara Gaskin, Amanda Parsons, Ann Rosenthal, vocals]
[Note: In 1969 the Egg lineup recorded an album with guitarist Steve Hillage. Because of contractual problems, the group billed themselves as "Arzachel" rather than "Egg." The resulting *Arzachel* LP appeared in 1970.]

Hatfield And The North

DAVE STEWART organ, pianos
RICHARD SINCLAIR bass, vocals
PHIL MILLER guitars
PIP PYLE drums

Albums
1. *Hatfield and the North* (1973)
[Guests: Robert Wyatt, vocal, the Northettes (Barbara Gaskin, Amanda Parsons, Ann Rosenthal), backing vocals]

2. *The Rotters' Club* (1975)
[Guests: the Northettes, backing vocals, Jimmy Hastings, flutes and saxes, Mont Campbell, French horn]
3. *Afters* (1980)
[Posthumous album with previously unreleased tracks]

Gilgamesh

Lineup 1
ALAN GOWEN pianos, Moog
JEFF CLYNE bass
PHIL LEE guitar
MICHAEL TRAVIS drums

Album
1. *Gilgamesh* (1975)

Lineup 2
ALAN GOWEN pianos, Moog
HUGH HOPPER bass
PHIL LEE guitar
TREVOR TOMKINS drums

Album
2. *Another Fine Tune You've Got Me Into* (1978)

National Health

Lineup 1
DAVE STEWART organ, pianos
NEIL MURRAY bass
PHIL MILLER guitar
PIP PYLE drums

Album
1. *National Health* (1978)
[Guests: Alan Gowen, Moog and pianos, Amanda Parsons, vocals, Jimmy Hastings, flute, and John Mitchell, percussion. Mont Campbell (bass) and Bill Bruford (drums) were pre first-LP members.]

Lineup 2
DAVE STEWART organ, pianos, synthesizers
JOHN GREAVES bass, vocals
PHIL MILLER guitar
PIP PYLE drums

Albums
2. *Of Queues and Cures* (1978)
[Guests: Georgie Born, cello, Jimmy Hastings, woodwinds]
3. *D.S. al Coda* (1982)
[Guests: Jimmy Hastings, woodwinds, Elton Dean, saxello, Ted Emmett and Annie Whitehead, brass, Richard Sinclair, Amanda Parsons, and Barbara Gaskin, vocals]
4. *National Health Complete* (1990)
[Repackages albums 1–3]
5. *National Health: Missing Pieces* (1994)
[Contains previously unreleased music by pre-first LP lineup, including Bruford, Campbell, Gowen, and Amanda Parsons]

Bruford

Lineup 1
BILL BRUFORD drums, mallet percussion
JEFF BERLIN bass
DAVE STEWART organ, pianos, synthesizers
ALLAN HOLDSWORTH guitars

Albums
1. *Feels Good to Me* (1977)
[Guests: Annette Peacock, vocals, Kenny Wheeler, flugelhorn]
2. *One of a Kind* (1979)

Lineup 2
BILL BRUFORD drums
JEFF BERLIN bass, vocals
DAVE STEWART organ, pianos, synthesizers
JOHN CLARK guitar

Albums
3. *The Bruford Tapes* (1979)
[Lineup 2 live in concert]
4. *Gradually Going Tornado* (1980)
[Guests: Georgie Born, cello, Barbara Gaskin and Amanda Parsons, vocals]

Gong

The history of Gong is so convoluted that a complete discography and an album-by-album listing of lineups is not practical. The band was founded in France by Daevid Allen, previously a founding member of Soft Machine; Gong's best-known music was released on the British label Virgin between 1973 and 1978, and features both English and French musicians. The first six albums are as follows:

1. *Magick Brother* (1970)
2. *Camembert Electrique* (1971)
3. *Continental Circus* (1971)
4. *The Flying Teapot* (1972)
5. *Angels' Egg* (1973)
6. *You* (1974)

Albums 4–6 constisute Allen's magnum opus, a three-album concept cycle entitled "Radio Gnome Invisible." Allen's principal sidemen during this period included Steve Hillage (guitar), Tim Blake (synthesizers), Mike Howlett (bass), Didier Malherbe (woodwinds), Pierre Moerlen (drums), and Gilli Smyth (who was responsible for the sultry "space whispers"). Allen himself contributed vocals and rhythm guitar work.

During the mid-1970s Allen left the band; Pierre Moerlen, who assumed leadership, led the band in the direction of mallet percussion-dominated heavy jazz fusion. Albums released by the Moerlen-led incarnation of Gong include:

7. *Shamal* (1975)
8. *Gazeuse* [released in the United States as *Expresso*] (1976)

9. *Expresso II* (1977)
10. *Downwind* (1979)
11. *Time is the Key* (1979)
12. *Pierre Moerlen's Gong Live* (1979)
13. *Leave it Open* (1981)
14. *Breakthrough* (1986)
15. *Second Wind* (1988)

Moerlen's principal sidemen included Hansford Rowe (bass), Allan Holdsworth (guitars), Benoit Moerlen and Mireille Bauer (mallet percussion), and Didier Malherbe (woodwinds on albums 7–8).

Allen has remained active as a solo artist, and some of his releases have been under the name "Gong." For instance, in 1978 Allen's group Planet Gong released *Floating Anarchy*; in 1980 his band New York Gong released *About Time*; later Allen releases have also been under "Gong" auspices from time to time. Another Gong splinter, "Mother Gong" (led by "space whisperer" Gilli Smyth) released *Fairy Tales* in 1979 and *Robot Woman 1, 2,* and *3* in the early 1980s. The 1977 *Gong est mort* LP is a collaboration between the Moerlen- and Allen-led factions of Gong. Nearly the entire *You*-era band assembled at the Forum in London on October 9, 1994, for a 25th Anniversary reunion concert. A live recording of this show, *The Birthday Party*, was released in 1995, and features Daevid Allen, Gilli Smyth, Tim Blake, Mike Howlett, and Didier Malherbe. Steffi Sharpstrings (guitar) replaced Steve Hillage, while Pip Pyle (drums) subbed for Pierre Moerlen.

Matching Mole

Lineup 1

ROBERT WYATT drums, Mellotron, vocals
DAVID SINCLAIR organ, piano
PHIL MILLER guitar
BILL MCCORMICK bass

Album

1. *Matching Mole* (1971)
   [Guest: Dave McRae, el. piano]

Lineup 2

ROBERT WYATT drums, vocals
DAVE MCRAE pianos, organ
PHIL MILLER guitar
BILL MCCORMICK bass

Album

2. *Little Red Record* (1972)
   [Guest: Brian Eno, VCS3]

Quiet Sun

CHARLES HAYWARD drums, lead vocals
DAVE JARRETT pianos, organ, VCS3
PHIL MANZANERA guitar, el. piano
BILL MCCORMICK bass, backing vocals

Album

1. *Mainstream* (1975)
   [Guest: Brian Eno, electronics]

Soft Heap

Lineup 1
HUGH HOPPER bass
ELTON DEAN alto sax, saxello
ALAN GOWEN pianos, Moog
PIP PYLE drums

Album
1. *Soft Heap* (1979)
[Guests: Radu Malfatti, Marc Charig, brass]

Lineup 2
JOHN GREAVES bass
ELTON DEAN saxes
MARK HEWINS guitars
PIP PYLE drums

Album
2. *A Veritable Centaur* (1995)
[Material recorded in 1982, 1988]

Henry Cow

Lineup 1
FRED FRITH guitars, violin, viola, piano
TIM HODGKINSON organ, piano, alto sax, clarinet
GEOFF LEIGH woodwinds
JOHN GREAVES bass, piano, vocals
CHRIS CUTLER drums

Album
1. *Legend* (1973)
[Guest: Lindsey Cooper, woodwinds]

Lineup 2
FRED FRITH guitars, violin, viola, piano
TIM HODGKINSON organ, piano, alto sax, clarinet
LINDSEY COOPER woodwinds
JOHN GREAVES bass, piano
CHRIS CUTLER drums

Album
2. *Unrest* (1974)

Lineup 3
FRED FRITH guitar, violin, piano
TIM HODGKINSON organ, clarinet, piano
LINDSEY COOPER double reeds
JOHN GREAVES bass, piano
CHRIS CUTLER drums

DAGMAR KRAUSE vocals
ANTHONY MOORE piano, electronics
PETER BLEGVAD guitar, clarinet

Albums
3. *Desperate Straights* (1975)
4. *In Praise of Learning* (1975)

Lineup 4
FRED FRITH violin, guitar, piano
TIM HODGKINSON organ, piano, clarinet
LINDSEY COOPER double reeds
JOHN GREAVES bass, piano
CHRIS CUTLER drums
DAGMAR KRAUSE vocals

Album
5. *Concerts* (1976)

Lineup 5
FRED FRITH guitar, violin, piano
TIM HODGKINSON organ, piano, clarinet
LINDSEY COOPER double reeds
GEORGIE BORN cello
CHRIS CUTLER drums
ANNEMARIE ROELOFS trombone

Album
6. *Western Culture* (1978)

Art Bears

Lineup 1
FRED FRITH guitar, violin, piano
TIM HODGKINSON organ, piano, clarinet
LINDSEY COOPER double reeds
GEORGIE BORN cello
CHRIS CUTLER drums
DAGMAR KRAUSE vocals

Album
1. *Hopes and Fears* (1978)

Lineup 2
FRED FRITH guitar, violin, piano
CHRIS CUTLER drums
DAGMAR KRAUSE vocals

Albums
2. *Winter Songs* (1979)
3. *The World As It Is Today* (1981)

Notes

Prelude

1. Henry Pleasants, *Serious Music—And All That Jazz* (New York: Simon and Schuster, 1969).

2. Christopher Small, *Music of the Common Tongue: Survival and Celebration in Afro-American Music* (New York: Riverrun Press, 1988).

3. See Lawrence Levine's *Highbrow/Lowbrow: The Emergence of Cultural Hierarchy in America* (Cambridge, Mass.: Harvard University Press, 1988), especially "The Sacralization of Culture," 83–168. Levine's line of argument is similar to Pleasants's and Small's. He demonstrates that sharply drawn qualitative divisions between "popular" and "serious" music are largely an invention of the late nineteenth and early twentieth centuries, rather than being an eternal condition of culture; that before 1900 operatic and even symphonic audiences engaged in spontaneous displays of approval and disapproval, and were active participants in, rather than mute spectators of, a performance; and that eighteenth- and nineteenth-century opera, in particular, offered a forum in which upper-, middle-, and even lower-class men and women could come together in shared appreciation. In short, Levine demonstrates that in the later eighteenth and nineteenth centuries opera (and to a lesser extent, perhaps, symphonic music) *was* popular culture. Because he writes more dispassionately and documents his arguments more copiously than Pleasants or Small, many readers will probably find his line of argument more convincing than theirs. The only real weakness I find in Levine's book is his pervasive lack of awareness of twentieth-century popular music culture. He argues (p. 195) that athletics plays the role in modern society that opera and Shakespeare's dramas played in the nineteenth century, not seeming aware that the rich audience/performer interaction he discovered in nineteenth-century opera is alive and well in jazz, rock, gospel, country-and-western, and other styles of contemporary popular music.

4. William Weber, *Music and the Middle Class* (New York: Holmes and Meier, 1975). Weber's basic premise is that the nineteenth-century classical music scene in London, Paris, and Vienna (the three cities he researched) served as a forum through which the competing social aims of the upper and middle classes could be mediated. He argues that the newly empowered middle class sought cultural legitimacy, while the

older elites who were losing their grip on political and economic authority sought continued hegemony by dictating the terms of cultural legitimacy. Considering musicology's longstanding disinterest in (even hostility toward) sociological enquiry, it is perhaps not surprising to learn that Weber is a historian, not a musicologist.

5. Roger Rideout, "The German Model in Music Curricula," *College Music Symposium* 30 (fall 1990), 109.

6. Igor Stravinsky, *An Autobiography* (New York: Norton, 1962).

7. Milton Babbitt, "Who Cares If You Listen?" High Fidelity Magazine 8/2 (1958), 38–40.

8. Deryck Cooke, *The Language of Music* (London: Oxford University Press, 1959).

9. Jim Curtis, *Rock Eras: Interpretations of Music and Society, 1954–1984* (Bowling Green, Ohio: Bowling Green State University Popular Press, 1987), 232.

10. Allan Moore, *Rock: The Primary Text; Developing a Musicology of Rock* (Buckingham, Eng.: Open University Press, 1993), 103.

Introduction

1. For those who want a more strictly analytical approach, there are a few possible sources. One might wish to consult Blair Pethel's D.M.A. paper, "Keith Emerson: The Emergence and Growth of Style" (Johns Hopkins University, 1987), or Eric Tamm's two books, *Brian Eno: His Music and the Vertical Color of Sound* and *Robert Fripp: From King Crimson to Guitar Craft.* The tenth chapter of my Ph.D. dissertation, "An Analytical Survey and Comparative Study of the Music of Ralph Vaughan Williams and Gustav Holst, c. 1910–35," views the harmonic and metric practices of progressive rock as part of a twentieth-century "English style" that can be traced back to the music of Vaughan Williams and Holst. I expand this idea further in my article " 'The Spirit of Albion' in 20th-century English Popular Music: Vaughan Williams, Holst, and the Progressive Rock Movement," which appears in *Music Review* 53 (May 1992). Nors Josephson's "Bach Meets Liszt: Traditional Formal Structures and Performance Practices in Progressive Rock," *Musical Quarterly* 76 (spring 1992) attempts, sometimes too literally, to link progressive rock's structural approaches to specific baroque and Classic period forms. The most comprehensive technical analysis of progressive rock, however, appears in chapter 5 of Allan Moore's *Rock: The Primary Text; Developing a Musicology of Rock* (Buckingham, Eng.: Open University Press, 1993). Moore's analyses are particularly interesting because he sees progressive rock as occupying a pivotal position in rock's stylistic evolution.

2. Paul Willis, *Profane Culture* (London: Routledge and Kegan Paul, 1978).

3. Ibid., 191.

4. Dick Hebdige, "Style as Homology and Signifying Practice," in *On Record,* ed. Simon Frith and Andrew Goodwin (New York: Pantheon Books, 1990), 56.

5. Dick Hebdige, *Subculture: The Meaning of Style* (London: Methuen, 1979).

6. Stuart Hall and Tony Jefferson, eds., *Resistance Through Rituals: Youth Subcultures in Post-war Britain* (London: Hutchinson, 1976).

7. Will Straw, "Characterizing Rock Music Culture: The Case of Heavy Metal," in *On Record*, ed. Frith and Goodwin, 97–110.

8. Deena Weinstein, *Heavy Metal: A Cultural Sociology* (New York: Macmillan, 1991).

9. Curtis, *Rock Eras*.

10. When Curtis speaks of the covenant, he refers to the Puritan ideal of America as a city "built on a hill" to exemplify an alternative way of living to the sinful and corrupt Old World. In the Puritan's view, America has a covenant with both God and mankind, since others are watching us, and we have the power of influencing them for good or for ill.

11. Ed Ward, Geoffrey Stokes, and Ken Tucker, *Rock of Ages: The Rolling Stone History of Rock & Roll* (New York: Summit Books, 1986).

12. Davin Seay and Mary Neely, *Stairway to Heaven: The Spiritual Roots of Rock'n'Roll* (New York: Ballantine Books, 1986).

13. Neil Rosenberg, ed., *Transforming Tradition: Folk Music Revivals Examined* (Champaign, Ill.: University of Illinois Press, 1993).

14. Robert Walser, *Running with the Devil: Power, Gender, and Madness in Heavy Metal Music* (Hanover, N.H.: Wesleyan University Press, 1993).

15. Moore, *Rock: The Primary Text*.

16. Ibid., 6.

17. For instance, in the final chapter of his book Moore compares earlier and later recordings of Gentle Giant and Genesis (see p. 183). Since he largely divorces stylistic development from social context, he is left merely stating the obvious: the earlier recordings show an originality and creativity that the later ones do not. What is missing is an equally comprehensive discussion of the social, cultural, and economic factors that brought this state of affairs to pass.

18. John Shepherd, *Music as Social Text* (Cambridge, U.K.: Polity Press, 1991).

19. Simon Frith and Angela McRobbie, "Rock and Sexuality," in *On Record*, ed. Frith and Goodwin, 371-89.

20. Angela McRobbie, "Settling Accounts with Subcultures: A Feminist Critique," in *On Record*, ed. Frith and Goodwin, 66-80. The subject of gender in music has received much attention in recent years. The most influential work is Susan McClary's *Feminine Endings: Music, Gender, and Sexuality* (Minneapolis: University of Minnesota Press, 1991). For a concise summary of objections to McClary's positions, see Elizabeth Sayrs, "Deconstructing McClary: Narrative, Feminine Sexuality, and Feminism in Susan McClary's *Feminine Endings*," *College Music Symposium* 33/34 (1993/1994), 40-55.

21. Roland Barthes, in his *S/Z* (London: Jonathan Cape, 1975), differentiates between "writerly" texts that absorb the spectator, and "readerly" texts that do not allow the spectator in to complete the meaning. African-American popular music is "writerly"; European classical music is "readerly." See Shepherd, *Music as Social Text*, 163.

22. Readers desiring demographic information (birthdates and birthplaces of band members, complete discographies of bands) are advised to consult *The Rolling Stone Encyclopedia of Rock and Roll,* ed. Jon Parales and Patricia Romanowski (New York: Summit Books, 1983), a very complete source for the rock music scene through the early 1980s. An excellent general discography is Terry Hounsome's *New Rock Record* (New York: Facts on File Publications, 1981, 1983), which gives complete discographies for hundreds of groups and individuals, and lists all musicians who played on a given album. Three English progressive rock bands have been particularly well served by biographies: Yes (Dan Hedges's *Yes: The Authorized Biography* and Tim Morse's *Yes Stories*), Genesis (Armando Gallo's *Genesis: I Know What I Like* and Dave Bowler's *Genesis: A Biography*), and Pink Floyd (Miles's *Pink Floyd: A Visual Documentary,* the late Nicholas Schaffner's *Saucerful of Secrets: The Pink Floyd Odyssey,* and Chris Welch's *Pink Floyd: Learning How To Fly*). Both the Hedges and the Gallo books are out of print. Eric Tamm's study of the music of Robert Fripp also functions as a King Crimson biography to a certain degree. Mike King's *Wrong Movements: A Robert Wyatt History,* besides offering a comprehensive overview of Wyatt's career, also offers a thorough description of Soft Machine's history through the early 1970s (when Wyatt left the group) and serves as a fine introduction to the so-called "Canterbury scene" that included Soft Machine, Caravan, Matching Mole, Quiet Sun, and a number of other like-minded bands. David Shaw-Parker's interesting if somewhat offbeat *The Lemming Chronicles* is simultaneously an autobiography, a "critical appreciation" of the music of Peter Hammill and Van der Graaf Generator, and a meditation on the nature of hero worship and fandom in contemporary Western society.

Chapter 1

1. Mick Dillingham, "Van der Graaf Generator: The David Jackson Interview, Part One," *Ptolemaic Terrascope* 2 (May 1991), 6.

2. Harvey Pekar, "From Rock to ???—A Searching Look at the Pop Explosion," *Downbeat* 35 (May 2, 1968), 20.

3. The Beatles' lead guitarist, George Harrison, began using the sitar as early as 1966; his one song-writing contribution to the *Sergeant Pepper* album of 1967, "Within You, without You," prominently features both sitar and tabla (an Indian drum). By 1968, the sitar could also be heard on the Moody Blues' album *In Search of the Lost Chord* and on Procol Harum's multimovement suite *In Held twas in I* (from the *Shine on Brightly* LP). Even bands that didn't adopt Indian instruments often experimented with raga-like modes during this period. Thus on the live version of "Set the Controls for the Heart of the Sun" (from the *Ummagumma* LP of 1969) Pink Floyd's keyboardist Rick Wright treats the organ very much as a sitar in his solos, which are monophonic, highly ornamental, and utilize a scale with two augmented seconds (i.e., A-B♭-C♯-D-

E-F-G$\sharp$-A). By 1970, with the fragmentation of psychedelia, interest in Indian music waned considerably among English rock musicians.

4. The Beatles, of course, came out of Liverpool in northwest England. As I demonstrate in chapter 7, progressive rock was very much a phenomenon of southeast England. Most English progressive rock musicians began their careers in or around London, where the electric blues revival of the early to mid-1960s generated much more interest than the "Merseybeat" sound of the Beatles. The one early progressive rock band that has an obvious stylistic affinity with the early to mid-period Beatles is the Moody Blues; significantly, this band originated in Birmingham, not London (one of the Moody Blues' early members, Denny Laine, who left the group before their landmark *Days of Future Passed* LP, went on to work with Paul McCartney after the breakup of the Beatles).

5. In all fairness, this claim has been made for other LPs as well. I have heard arguments that the Kink's *Face to Face* (1966) and even Johnny Cash's *Ride This Train* (1960) should be considered the first pop concept album.

6. A startling anticipation of the mature progressive rock style can, however, be heard in the music of a little-known Bay-area band of the psychedelic era, It's a Beautiful Day, whose eponymous debut album appeared in 1969. This band seems to have especially anticipated the style of Curved Air (a result of David Laflamme's violin work) and Renaissance (on account of the music's generally pastoral ambience, Linda Laflamme's synthless multikeyboard setup, and the general prominence of female vocals). Linda Laflamme, incidentally, played a much greater role in this band than any female instrumentatlist was ever to play in any of the major (or even semimajor) English progressive rock bands.

7. Bill Bruford, correspondence with the author, July 4, 1993.

8. For Schuller's latest pronouncement on the ramifications of the term "third stream," see Gunther Schuller, "The Influence of Jazz on the History and Development of Concert Music," in *New Perspectives on Jazz*, ed. David Baker (Washington: Smithsonian Institute Press, 1990), 13–14.

9. See *The Rolling Stone Encyclopedia of Rock and Roll*, 447–48.

10. *The Marshall Cavendish Encyclopedia of Popular Music* (New York: Marshall Cavendish, 1990), vol. 14, 1563.

11. Simon Frith, *The Sociology of Rock* (London: Constable, 1978), 121.

12. For more specific information, consult Joel Whitburn's *Top Pop Album Tracks, 1955–1992* (New York: Billboard Publications, 1993). As a general rule of thumb, the albums of the major English progressive rock bands charted even higher on the British charts than on American charts. Of the progressive rock bands that never quite achieved megastar status, King Crimson had two top forty albums in the U.S. charts (their first album, charting at 28, was their best-seller), while neither Peter Gabriel–era Genesis nor Gentle Giant ever had a top forty album in the

United States (Gentle Giant's best-seller, *Free Hand*, topped out at 48, while Genesis's final two albums with Gabriel, *Selling England by the Pound* and *The Lamb Lies down on Broadway*, charted at 70 and 41, respectively.)

13. A number of major progressive rock bands (Yes, Genesis) became popular in Continental Europe long before achieving renown in the States; other bands that never broke through the American market at all weve very successful in Europe. A primary example here is Van der Graaf Generator. This band was hugely popular in Italy; their *Pawn Hearts* rode the top of the Italian charts for twelve weeks in 1972, and the band played for audiences of up to 40,000 over the course of several tours in that country. However, their only North American tour, in 1976, was cut short only one show into the U.S. segment (they had previously managed to play several shows in Canada) when their record company withdrew all financial support. As a result, the band never achieved more than a small cult following in the United States.

Chapter 2

1. Keith Emerson, quoted in "Emerson," 14.

2. As Christopher Small, Robert Walser, Lawrence Levine, and others have pointed out, the "classical tradition" is essentially a late-nineteenth- and twentieth-century phenomenon (see especially Small's *Music of the Common Tongue*, 359–63). I use the term throughout the book for the sake of convenience.

3. The Moody Blues' *Days of Future Passed* was recorded in late 1967 in collaboration with the London Festival Orchestra. Other major rock band/symphony orchestra collaborations include the Nice's *Five Bridges* (recorded with the London Sinfonia in late 1969), Deep Purple's *Concerto for Group and Orchestra* (recorded in 1970 with the Royal Philharmonic Orchestra under the direction of Malcolm Arnold), Procol Harum's *Live with the Edmonton Symphony Orchestra* (1972), Renaissance's *Scheherazade* (recorded with members of the London Symphony Orchestra in 1975), and ELP's "Pirates" (recorded with the Orchestra de l'Opera de Paris). The orchestras featured on Yes's *Time and a Word* and Pink Floyd's *Atom Heart Mother* (both 1970) were pickup groups assembled in the studio.

4. A number of factors conspired to prevent most of these collaborations from being completely successful. First, rock musicians' conception of rhythm, governed by the explicit beat laid out by the rhythm section, is very different from the implicit beat set forth by the orchestral conductor; it proved very difficult to combine rock bands and symphony orchestras without compromising either the energetic beat characteristic of rock or the flexible rhythmic style inherent to classical music. As a result, in most rock/symphonic collaborations there was a tendency to alternate orchestral passages with sections for rock band in a rather stereotypical tutti/soli approach. ELP's "Pirates" of 1977, composed late in the "classic" progressive rock era, probably represents the

most satisfactory blending of the two forces; transitions between sections featuring rock band and orchestral passages are much more seamless in this particular work than in most "symphonic rock."

A second problem inherent in collaborations of this type is that the rock musicians often tried much too hard to squeeze their formal, timbral, and harmonic ideas into "approved" classical molds. A perfect example is Keith Emerson's Piano Concerto No. 1, recorded with the London Symphony Orchestra (on ELP's *Works, Vol. 1* LP of 1977). While adequately orchestrated, the work has little of the timbral interest of ELP's best pieces, which show a virtuoso handling of the electronic tone colors available in the early 1970s (e.g., "Abaddon's Bolero"). Furthermore, the harmonic and melodic material of the piano concerto seem all too "polite" compared to the pungent sonorities of pieces such as *Tarkus.* Finally, the piano concerto's formal plan, which adheres all too faithfully to classical formal conventions (first movement in sonata-allegro form, etc.), comes off as forced and awkward when compared to the far more natural, sectionalized formal contours of pieces such as *Tarkus* and *Karn Evil 9.* This general tendency toward "overpoliteness" is apparent in most collaborations between rock bands and symphony orchestras (i.e., Paul McCartney's *Liverpool Oratorio*).

5. An electric instrument transduces a mechanical phenomenon into an electronic signal, usually via a pickup. An electronic instrument produces sound by purely electronic means. In this book, I usually use the two terms interchangeably, contrasting the tone colors of electric/electronic instruments (i.e., electric guitar, electronic keyboards) with the tone colors of acoustic instruments (i.e., acoustic guitar, piano, flute, etc.).

6. *Marshall Cavendish Encyclopedia of Popular Music,* vol. 14, 1562.

7. Ibid.

8. Tony Bacon, ed., *Rock Hardware* (New York: Harmony Books, 1981), 90. The instruments of choice were usually Hammond B3 and C3 models. More rarely, Farfisa's Professional model was used (especially by Rick Wright of Pink Floyd).

9. Transcribed from "Emerson, Lake & Palmer: Welcome back—A Musical Biography," Strand Home Video 8121, 1992.

10. A number of prominent progressive rock keyboardists, notably Keith Emerson, already owned custom-built polyphonic synthesizers by this time. For more on Emerson's role in developing the instrument that eventually became the Polymoog, see Dominic Milano, "Keith Emerson," *Contemporary Keyboard* 3 (October 1977), 28.

11. Thus Pink Floyd's *Ummagumma* album of 1969, virtually a catalog of late 1960s electronic experimentation, represents the band's apotheosis as exponents of psychedelia; in *Atom Heart Mother* of 1970, recorded with a symphony orchestra and a concert choir and laid out in the form of a multimovement suite, one can already see the band adopting the stylistic conventions that would eventually define progressive rock.

12. *Marshall Cavendish Encyclopedia of popular Music,* vol. 14, 1562.

13. Steve Hackett, quoted in Steve Rosen, "From England's Genesis, Here's Steve Hackett," *Guitar Player* 10 (October 1976), 46.

14. Chris Squire, quoted in Leonard Ferris, " 'Yes' Bassist Chris Squire," *Guitar Player* 7 (July 1973), 42.

15. Bill Bruford, *When in Doubt, Roll!* (Cedar Grove, N.J.: Modern Drummer Publications, 1988), 30.

16. See, e.g., Susan McClary and Robert Walser's "Start Making Sense! Musicology Wrestles with Rock," and Roland Barthes's "The Grain of the Voice," in *On Record*, ed. Frith and Goodwin, 277–92 and 293–300.

17. I refer a number of times during the course of this book to the obvious parallels between nineteenth-century Romanticism and rock music of the late 1960s. Nonetheless, while I am confident that the Romantic movement did exert a certain amount of direct influence on the hippies, I believe Robert Pattison's *The Triumph of Vulgarity: Rock Music in the Mirror of Romanticism* (New York: Oxford University Press, 1987), may overstate the level of direct influence. On the other hand, I find his argument that a watered-down version of nineteenth-century pantheism pervades rock's attitudes towards politics, religion, and history extremely convincing.

18. Tony Banks, quoted in Dominic Milano, "Tony Banks," *Contemporary Keyboard* 4 (July 1978), 26. Incidentally, it is not my intention during this section to say that only goal-oriented music or music that develops organically over a lengthy stretch of time is "good" music. I do believe that most successful large-scale instrumental music strikes some kind of balance between contrast and repetition, and between the need for both tension and relaxation. I suspect the reason that twelve-tone and later serial music has not done well outside of academic circles is that it makes so few concessions to the principles of repetition and the relaxation of tension. Ultimately, however, individual listeners must decide for themselves what works. In the case of progressive rock, I can only say that the musical material usually seems to require coherent long-range development, and seems to suffer when such is not forthcoming.

19. This tension is especially evident in "Rondo," the band's epic arrangement of Dave Brubeck's *Blue Rondo à la Turk*. It should be added that while Emerson was the Hammond's foremost champion during the late 1960s—he was often referred to as "the Hendrix of the organ"—he was not the first. Graham Bond and Brian Auger both played important roles in introducing the Hammond into British R & B during the mid-1960s.

20. Palmer was tutored by jazz great Buddy Rich and studied with noted classical percussionist James Blades at the Royal Academy of Music. Bruford has performed with the New Percussion Group of Amsterdam.

21. As might be expected, the live version of a given piece is often considerably longer than the studio version, with one or more lengthy solos being responsible for the extra length.

22. However, I take strong exception to the mindlessly repeated assertions of some critics that the genre is worthless simply because of the emphasis placed on virtuosity and soloing; for a particularly blatant exposé of this theory, see Jimmy Guteman and

Owen O'Donnell, *The 50 Worst Rock'n'Roll Records of All Time* (New York: Citadel Press, 1991), 8. When have jazz or the blues been categorically dismissed on the same premise?

23. Brubeck's two most influential albums in this regard are *Time out* (1960) and *Time Further out* (1961), both recorded with his legendary Quartet (Brubeck, Paul Desmond, Eugene Wright, Joe Morello).

24. Rick Wright, quoted in Miles, *Pink Floyd: A Visual Documentary* (New York: Omnibus, 1980), November 19, 1966. Miles arranged his material chronologically and used dates rather than page numbers.

25. Keith Emerson, quoted in Milano, "Keith Emerson," *Contemporary Keyboard* 3, 30.

26. For instance, the simultaneous juxtaposition of parts in seven and four at the close of ELP's *Three Fates,* of five and four in Yes's "Relayer," or of $\frac{9}{8}$ and $\frac{4}{4}$ in Egg's "Germ Patrol."

27. Geddy Lee, quoted in Tom Mulhern, "Geddy Lee of Rush, Rock's Leading Bassist," *Guitar Player* 20 (April 1986), 86.

28. Curtis, *Rock Eras,* 130.

29. Shepherd, *Music as Social Text,* chapter 6, "Functional Tonality: A Basis for Musical Hegemony," 96–127.

30. Robert Wyatt, quoted in Mac Randall, "Musician Forum: Robert Wyatt Meets Bill Nelson," *Musician Magazine* (August 1992), 39.

31. Hedges, *Yes: The Authorized Biography,* 67.

32. Tamm, *Fripp,* 183.

33. Dominic Milano, "Kerry Minnear; Keyboardist/Composer for Gentle Giant," *Contemporary Keyboard* 2 (May/June 1976), 8.

34. Dominic Milano, "Dave Stewart: Poll-winning British Keyboardist," *Contemporary Keyboard* 6 (January 1980), 27.

35. "The Barbarian" on ELP's eponymous debut album of 1970 is an arrangement of Bartók's *Allegro barbaro;* "Knife's Edge" from the same album freely borrows material from the final movement of Janáček's *Sinfonietta;* the Nice's album *Ars Longa Vita Brevis* (1968) contains an arrangement of the "Intermezzo" from Sibelius's *Karelia Suite* (the band's *Five Bridges* LP of 1970 contains a much more rousing live rendition of this piece).

36. EG/Virgin's four-CD retrospective package of music by King Crimson, *Frame by Frame: The Essential King Crimson,* contains a previously unreleased live performance of "Mars" dating from 1969.

37. Pethel, "Emerson," 69.

38. Gary Brooker, quoted in Steve Rosen, "Gary Brooker, Rock Piano Mainstay with Procol Harum," *Contemporary Keyboard* 4 (July 1978), 48.

39. Tony Banks, quoted in Dominic Milano, "Tony Banks and the Evolution of Genesis," *Keyboard* 10 (November 1984), 46.

40. Keith Emerson, "Howard Jones," *Keyboard* 15 (August 1989), 85.

Chapter 3

1. Tom Mulhern, "Robert Fripp on the Discipline of Craft and Art," *Guitar Player* 20 (January 1986), 100.

2. It is true that a hit single was a key element in catapulting a band to megastar status. It is doubtful that ELP, Yes, Pink Floyd, and Jethro Tull would have become huge concert draws without notable singles (ELP's "Lucky Man," Yes's "Roundabout," Pink Floyd's "Time" and "Money," Jethro Tull's "Aqualung") that received enough radio airplay to bring them to the attention of the American rock public at large. On the other hand, many of these bands issued top ten albums that received virtually no radio airplay in the States (ELP's *Tarkus,* Yes's *Tales from Topographic Oceans,* Pink Floyd's *Animals,* Jethro Tull's *A Passion Play*). Furthermore, bands such as King Crimson, Gentle Giant, and Peter Gabriel-era Genesis that never had a hit single in the United States were able to mount successful (if somewhat less ambitious) North American tours.

3. Adam Smith, *The Powers of Mind* (New York: Random House, 1975), 46.

4. Donald Lehmkuhl, Dominy Hamilton, and Carla Capalbo, *Roger Dean: Views* (London: Dragon's Dream, 1975), 100.

5. Whitehead also did the cover art for Genesis's *Trespass* (1970) and for Van der Graaf Generator's *H to He Who Am the Only One* (1970) and *Pawn Hearts* (1971). The cover for the latter album, which features a number of individuals encased in translucent capsules floating in outer space, is almost as strange as the two Genesis covers. Both Genesis and Van der Graaf Generator were signed by Tony Stratton-Smith to Charisma records; Whitehead thus served as the label's unofficial "house artist" during the early 1970s. As for the manor house on the cover of *Nursery Cryme* being based on Coxhill, see Armando Gallo, *Genesis: I Know What I Like* (Los Angeles: D.I.Y. Press, 1980), 151.

6. Miles, *Pink Floyd: A Visual Documentary,* November 19, 1966.

7. Nicholas Schaffner, *Saucerful of Secrets: The Pink Floyd Odyssey* (New York: Harmony Books, 1991), 33.

8. This information is gleaned both from the band's concert booklet for the fateful *Works* tour of 1977–1978 and from my own attendance of one of ELP's last concerts before their fourteen-year hiatus, at Detroit's (now defunct) Olympia on March 4, 1978.

9. Miles, *Pink Floyd,* May 18–19, 1973.

10. Ibid., November 4, 1973.

11. Lehmkuhl et al., *Roger Dean,* 122.

12. Roger Dean, quoted in Ibid.

13. Tamm, *Robert Fripp,* 58.

14. Clem Gorman, *Backstage Rock* (London: Pan Books, 1978), 91.

15. Emerson gives a very complete description of the genesis of his stage show in an interview with Dominic Milano in *Contemporary Keyboard* 3 (October 1977), 24.

16. See Brian Harrigan and Malcolm Dune, *Encyclopedia Metallica* (London: Bobcat Books, n.d.), 13.

17. David Shumway, "Rock and Roll as Cultural Practice," in *Present Tense: Rock & Roll and Culture*, ed. Anthony DeCurtis (Durham: Duke University Press, 1992), 117–35.

18. Ibid., 129.

19. Paul Willis, "The Cultural Meaning of Drug Use," in *Resistance through Rituals: Youth Subcultures in Post-war Britain*, ed. Hall and Jefferson, 106.

20. Stephen Davis, *Hammer of the Gods: The Led Zeppelin Saga* (New York: Ballantine Books, 1985), 237. I must admit that I did not fully appreciate the aptness of Burroughs's comparison until I had the opportunity to hear the Master Musicians of Jajouka live at Humboldt State University in October 1995.

21. Hedges, *Yes*, 68.

22. Robert Fripp, quoted in Tamm, *Fripp*, 64.

23. Aldous Huxley, *The Doors of Perception and Heaven and Hell* (New York: Harper Colophon, 1963), 165.

24. Rick Wakeman, quoted in Curtis, *Rock Eras*, 279–80.

25. Record review of ELP's *Works Volume 1*, *Downbeat* 44 (October 6, 1977), 28–29.

Chapter 4

1. Davin Seay with Mary Neeley, *Stairway to Heaven: The Spiritual Roots of Rock'n'Roll* (New York: Ballantine Books, 1986), 211.

2. Hedges, *Yes*, 67–68.

3. Joe Benson, *Uncle Joe's Record Guide: Progressive Rock* (Glendale, Calif.: Joe Benson Unlimited, 1989), 56.

4. Jon Anderson, quoted in Hedges, *Yes*, 51.

5. Robert Wyatt, quoted in King, *Wrong Movements: A Robert Wyatt History* (London: SAF Publishing, 1994), June 10, 1969.

6. Rick Wakeman, quoted in Robert Doerschuk, "Yes: Rick Wakeman and Tony Kaye Face off," *Keyboard* 17 (August 1991), 96.

7. David Gilmour, quoted in Matt Resnicoff, "David Gilmour's Pink Floyd," *Musician Magazine* (August 1992), 60.

8. Peter Hammill, quoted in Bob Anderson, "The Fresh Fruit Interview, Part II," *Pawn Hearts Newsletter* (November 1991), 6.

9. The lyrics to "Jerusalem" were lifted from the opening of Blake's *Milton* and set to music by English composer Hubert Parry in 1918. After posing the question "And was the Holy Lamb of God on England's pleasant pastures seen?", Blake asks "And was Jerusalem builded here amongst these dark Satanic mills?" Thus "Jerusalem" sets forth several social and spiritual concerns engendered by the Industrial Revolution at the beginning of the nineteenth century, including the manner in which the unchecked materialism that resulted from the Industrial Revolution cor-

roded society's spiritual values, and the human and environmental costs of the new industrial society, which seemingly overnight steamrolled over an ancient, stable, agrarian order. Since these concerns were still very pertinent to the hippies of the late 1960s and early 1970s (pointing up how the counterculture can be viewed as an extension of the nineteenth-century bohemian intelligentsia), it is particularly appropriate that ELP chose "Jerusalem" to open their man-versus-machine epic, *Brain Salad Surgery.*

10. The politically charged element of the hippies were most often designated by the term "yippies," who were, as Jerry Rubin once explained, "hippies that had been hit on the head by the police." See Hebdige, *Subculture: The Meaning of Style,* 185.

11. Robert Fripp, quoted in Tamm, *Fripp,* 128.

12. Joan Peyser, "The Music of Sound or, the Beatles and the Beatless," in *The Age of Rock,* ed. Jonathan Eisen (New York: Vintage Press, 1969), 132.

13. Seay and Neeley, *Spiritual Roots of Rock'n'Roll,* 238.

14. Paul Willis, *Profane Culture* (London: Routledge and Kegan Paul, 1978), 128.

15. Ian Anderson, quoted in John Simon, "Ian Anderson: The Codpiece Chronicles," *Downbeat* 43 (March 11, 1976), 16.

16. There is strong precedent in English intellectual life of the twentieth century for the interest evinced by English hippies in Eastern mysticism. Among composers, for instance, one need only mention Gustav Holst and Cyril Scott, who were both strongly drawn to Hinduism in the first two decades of this century.

17. Walser, *Running with the Devil,* 159.

18. Simon Frith and Angela McRobbie, "Rock and Sexuality," in *On Record,* ed. Frith and Goodwin, 371–89.

19. See Straw, "The Case of Heavy Metal," in *On Record,* ed. Frith and Goodwin, 103, 106.

Chapter 5

1. Keith Emerson, quoted in Pethel, "Emerson," 19.

2. Ibid.

3. Ibid., 20.

4. On ELP's live album of 1974, *Welcome back My Friends to the Show That Never Ends, Tarkus* is almost thirty minutes long. The extra length results from the interpolation of part of King Crimson's "Epitaph" into the sixth movement, and from a considerable expansion of the final movement. I must admit I find the live version of "Aquatarkus" especially fascinating because it radically reconceives the studio version. The tempo is much faster, the marchlike quality is lost, and the hypnotic bass guitar/ drum kit ostinato underneath Emerson's "cosmic" Moog solo in the middle of the movement offers a virtually unprecedented example of ELP approaching the "space rock" style of Hawkwind or even Tangerine Dream. Nonetheless, the expanded last

movement does upset the delicate structural balance of the studio version; my discussion here therefore centers on the latter.

5. It is also possible to hear the first part of this couplet as "Where the blades of grass *and* arrows rain." This, of course, would necessitate a revision of the interpretation I have offered here.

6. I am reminded of John Galt, the protagonist of Ayn Rand's *Atlas Shrugged,* whom this description might also be said to fit, although I have never heard Emerson, Lake, or Palmer mention any acquaintance with Rand's novels. Be this as it may, the "Manticore" symbol must have had a deep meaning for the group; when they founded their own record label in 1973, they named it Manticore Records and adopted the Manticore as the label's logo.

7. The English word "Manticore" stems ultimately from the Persian "mandkhora," or "maneater." Ctesias, a much-cited author of antiquity whose works have survived only in quotes by Aristotle, Aelian, and Pliny, describes the Manticore as a creature of the Indian subcontinent.

8. See Pethel, "Emerson," 12–14.

9. Ibid., 16.

10. Ibid.

11. For instance, on a number of occasions I have performed *Tarkus* as a recital piece for solo piano; with a bit of rearrangement of the last two movements it worked quite well. It is of interest to note, though, that one reason that most of the piece was not difficult to arrange for solo piano is that in certain parts of *Tarkus*—and in parts of some other ELP pieces as well—the rhythm section stands on the verge of becoming irrelevant. For instance, while the practice of using drums to rhythmically double melodic lines was not an uncommon characteristic of progressive rock, Carl Palmer doubled Emerson's melodic figurines to a degree that would have been unusual in other progressive rock bands. Likewise, throughout parts of *Tarkus* and other ELP albums there is a tendency for Lake to double Emerson's left-hand keyboard part on bass guitar.

12. I use the terms "modal minor" and "modal major" to denote music that is recognizably minor or major, but which cannot be identified as pertaining either to the diatonic major or minor scales or to a specific mode. For instance, the bass ostinato pattern that dominates the first and third movements of *Tarkus* is essentially locrian, but the motives superimposed over it in the upper register are "chromatic" in respect to the locrian mode.

13. The *Anderson, Bruford, Wakeman and Howe* LP of 1989 reunited four-fifths of this lineup.

14. Thomas Mosbø, *Yes—But What Does It Mean? Exploring the Music of Yes* (Milton, Wis.: Wyndstar, 1994), 129.

15. Ibid.

16. Jon Anderson, quoted in Mosbø, *Yes,* 127.

17. Hedges, *Yes,* 68.

18. The band was acquainted with Blake's poetry, although perhaps not as early as

1972. Drummer Alan White's solo LP *Ramshackled* (1976) contains a setting of one of Blake's *Songs of Innocence* ("Spring") and features Jon Anderson and Steve Howe.

19. I am reminded of Christ's parable of the narrow and wide paths (Matthew 7: 13–14), and of the Old Testament proverb "There is a way which seems right to a man, but the end thereof are the ways of death" (Proverbs 14:12).

20. Roger Dean, quoted in Lehmkuhl et al., *Roger Dean: Views*, 105.

21. Dean modeled his unreal landscape, to a certain degree at least, on lakes and waterfalls seen in the Scottish Highlands, as well as from photographs of Angel Falls in Venezuela. See ibid.

22. Quoted in ibid., 121.

23. See Tamm, *Fripp*, 63; Mosbø, *Yes*, 85.

24. The technique of juxtaposing rhythmic patterns of different lengths against each other to produce ever-shifting accents is known as isorhythm. It can be traced back to vocal music of the late medieval period.

25. However, whether one considers D, A, or F—or all three—to be the piece's tonic, Allan Moore is incorrect to say in *The Primary Text* that the introduction acts as a dominant preparation.

26. See Hedges, *Yes*, 69–70; Bruford, *When in Doubt, Roll*, 8–9.

27. Banks's contribution to Genesis's harmonic style is discussed at length in Dominic Milano's *Keyboard* interview of November 1984 (see especially p. 46). "Firth of Fifth" was largely Bank's composition; he rewrote parts of it after the *Foxtrot* sessions so that Phil Collins could have a more active drum part. See Gallo, *Genesis*, 56.

28. I do, however, hear a real similarity between the harmonic styles of Genesis and of Gabriel Fauré; in the *Keyboard* interview of November 1984, Banks mentioned an interest in the harmonic practice of Fauré's student Maurice Ravel (see p. 46). Genesis and Fauré share a certain "classical" element and fastidiousness as well.

29. Gallo, *Genesis*, 56–57.

30. Barrett's descent into madness is well chronicled in Nicholas Schaffner's *Saucerful of Secrets: The Pink Floyd Odyssey*.

31. Ibid., 199–200.

32. Roger Waters, quoted in ibid., 198.

33. Ibid.

34. Waters claims that this idea was his; Gilmour didn't support the new plan, but according to Waters "Rick did and Nicky did and he was outvoted so we went on." See the musical score *Pink Floyd: Wish You Were Here* (London: Pink Floyd Music Publishers, 1982), 17.

35. Storm Thorgerson, quoted in Schaffner, *Pink Floyd*, 204.

36. *Pink Floyd: Wish You Were Here* (musical score), 11.

37. During their "classic" period (1971–1975), Pink Floyd's harmony could be almost as distinctive as Genesis's, and a major (and neglected) factor in creating ambience. Although I suspect the band would deny any direct influence, I am frequently reminded of late-seventeenth-century English church music (Henry Purcell, John Blow)

when listening to Pink Floyd's music of this period. There are the adagio tempos in common time, the rich Hammond organ backdrops, and the call-and-response between vocal soloist and band's "choral" vocalizations (which may also derive from black gospel). Finally, there are the "affective" harmonies, including not only the numerous cross relations but also prominent augmented triads (*Shine on You* part 3, 5, and 7) the unusual minor triad with a major seventh (D-F-A-C$\sharp$) which recurs throughout "Us and Them," and the movement between B-minor and F-major triads which plays a prominent role in "The Great Gig in the Sky."

38. Parry became almost a fifth member during this period, appearing on *Dark Side of the Moon* and *Wish You Were Here* and touring with the band.

39. The metric shift in question, which is heard again in part six, is an interesting one. There is a shift from $\frac{3}{4}$ to $\frac{2}{4}$, with the bar in $\frac{2}{4}$ taking place over the same duration as had the bar in $\frac{3}{4}$; however, while the beat itself slows, the rhythmic motion increases considerably, because the prevailing quarter note accompaniment in the $\frac{3}{4}$ section is replaced by triplet eighth notes in $\frac{2}{4}$.

40. See especially Schaffner, *Pink Floyd*, 130.

41. David Gilmour, in *Pink Floyd: Wish You Were Here* (musical score), 75.

42. "Welcome to the Machine" offers another characteristic example of Pink Floyd's use of harmony to create mood. The F$\sharp$ of the vocal line repeatedly refuses to resolve into the accompanying E-minor triad; after a while, the E-minor triad with the added F$\sharp$ becomes the predominant sonority, lending the song a darker ambience than a "straight" E-minor triad would have.

43. Roger Waters, quoted in Schaffner, *Pink Floyd*, 200–201.

44. This was a query that the band heard numerous times. Evidentally, Waters had grown tired of it. Syd Barrett named Pink Floyd by conflating the names of his two favorite blues singers, Pink Anderson and Floyd Council (see Schaffner, *Pink Floyd*, 26).

45. Ibid., 202.

46. I hear striking stylistic similarities between part 8 of *Shine on You* and ELP's uncharacteristically "spacey" fusion number "When the Apple Blossoms Bloom in the Windmills of Your Mind I'll Be Your Valentine," from the *Works, Volume 2* LP.

Chapter 6

1. Henry Pleasants, *Serious Music—And All That Jazz*, 197.

2. Dave Stewart, quoted in Milano, "Dave Stewart: Poll-winning British Keyboard-ist," 31.

3. *Marshall Cavendish Encyclopedia of Popular Music*, vol. 14, 1563.

4. Moore, *Rock: The Primary Text*, 78.

5. Ibid., 101.

6. When Genesis hired jazz-rock guitarist Darryl Stuermer to replace Steve Hackett for their live shows in 1977, bassist Mike Rutherford admitted that at first he was disturbed by Stuermer's selection of chord voicings, which he said reminded him of "cocktail music"—not a surprising reaction for someone used to a relatively austere modal syntax when confronted with a richer but more self-indulgent harmonic style. See Gallo, *Genesis*, 92.

7. Dominic Milano, "Eddie Jobson of U.K.," *Contemporary Keyboard* 5 (March 1979), 54.

8. "Gaudete," Steeleye Span's most commercially successful single, is derived from a collection of anonymous school and religious songs called *Piae Cantiones* published by Theodoricus Petri at Greifswald (in modern-day Sweden) in 1582. For a similar arrangement of similar material, The Pentangle's "Lyke-wake Dirge" from their *Baskets of Light* LP is recommended.

9. The rustic clothing the band often wore at concerts also points up this folk connection. Indeed, the group was named after an eighteenth-century British agronomist, Jethro Tull, who invented the machine drill for sowing seed.

10. David Riesman, "Listening to Popular Music," in *On Record*, ed. Frith and Goodwin, 12.

11. John Wetton, quoted in Milly Kusmic and Stephan van de Ven, "John Wetton," *Background Progressive Rock Magazine* no. 35 (June 1993), 6.

12. For instance, when one reads Miles's description of the club scene of the late 1960s British underground (see his *Pink Floyd*), one is struck by the frequent references to female audience participation. This observation appears to be borne out by interviews with musicians active in the club scene at this time (see, e.g., Dominic Milano's "Keith Emerson," *Contemporary Keyboard* 3, 24). There is no doubt, however, that stadium rock—irregardless of the genre involved—was an overwhelmingly male affair. I will leave it to sociologists to explain the difference in female audience participation between the club and stadium levels.

13. Chris Welch, *Black Sabbath* (London: Proteus Books, 1982), 9–13.

14. Ozzy Osbourne, quoted in ibid., 84–85.

15. Even Black Sabbath occasionally fell under the sway of progressive rock during the mid-1970s: hence the use of strings in "She's Gone" and the use of a concert choir and shifting meters in "Supertzar." Indeed, the sophisticated production, the sudden shifts between electric and acoustic passages, and the stream-of-consciousness approach of *Sabatoge* (1975), arguably the band's best album, belies a progressive rock influence. Welch attributes the band's turmoil of the mid- to late 1970s as an outcome of the clash between guitarist Tony Iommi's increasing interest in progressive rock and Ozzy Osbourne's aversion to the style.

16. In particular, a hallmark of the Rolling Stones' rhythmic approach—appropriated directly from African-American R&B—is their tendency to superimpose one bar of 2+3+3 or 3+2+3 in the vocals ("Satisfaction" uses the former) over two bars of

straight four in the rhythm section. It is the resulting polyrhythm that gives much of the Stones' music its "lift" and dancelike character. On the other hand, the accents of the vocals and lead guitar lines in heavy metal tend to fall on strong beats, furthering the effect of rhythmic "heaviness."

17. Eric Salzman, *Twentieth-century Music: An Introduction,* 3d ed. (Englewood Cliffs, N.J.: Prentice-Hall, 1988), 216. Philip Glass, in particular, has gone on to "stardom" in the pop-culture sense of the word.

18. The West Coast minimalists—particularly Riley and LaMonte Young—came out of the same general cultural scene as did the Grateful Dead and other Bay Area psychedelic bands, although the composers were a few years older than the band members.

19. Schaffner, *Pink Floyd,* 25, 27, 50.

Chapter 7

1. Schaffner, *Pink Floyd,* 15.

2. The continued veneration accorded to this club even after the club scene declined in importance is illustrated by the fact that King Crimson performed at the Marquee as late as February 1973, "for pure enjoyment and relaxation" according to drummer Bill Bruford (see Tamm, *Fripp,* 69); furthermore, it was here that Van der Graaf Generator recorded their live farewell album, released in 1978.

3. Jethro Tull and folk singer Roy Harper opened for Pink Floyd at the first free Hyde Park concert on June 29, 1968. At another legendary Hyde Park Concert, King Crimson opened for the Rolling Stones, playing to 650,000 people on July 5, 1969.

4. Hedges, *Yes,* 110.

5. In all honesty, this characterization began to blur during the Thatcher years, as the difference between "blue-collar" and "service industry" jobs (the latter traditionally the realm of the lower middle class) became more nebulous. However, it is certainly true for the 1945–1975 period which concerns us here.

6. David H. Fischer, *Albion's Seed: Four British Folkways in America* (New York: Oxford University Press, 1989), 236–46, especially 243.

7. For more on the role of the art school in English rock culture, see Simon Frith's and Robert Horne's *Art into Pop* (New York: Methuen, 1987).

8. Ian McDonald, quoted in Peter Frame, *Rock Family Trees* (New York: Quick Fox, 1979), 16.

9. Eric Gaer, "Emerson, Lake, and Palmer: A Force to Be Reckoned with," *Downbeat* 41 (May 9, 1974), 14.

10. Dick Heckstall-Smith, *The Safest Place in the World* (London: Quartet Books, 1989), 148, 150.

11. John Wetton, quoted in Tom Mulhern, "John Wetton: Asia's Progressive Rock Bassist," *Guitar Player* 17 (January 1983), 39.

12. Transcribed from "Emerson, Lake & Palmer: Welcome Back—A Musical Bi-ography," Strand Home Video 8121, 1992.

13. Mulhern, "Wetton," 33.

14. Hedges, *Yes*, 15.

15. Janis Schact, *Genesis* (London: Proteus Books, 1984), 92.

16. Hedges, *Yes*, 100.

17. Joachim Berendt, *The Jazz Book: From New Orleans to Rock and Free Jazz*, trans. Dan Morgenstern and Helmut and Barbara Bredigkeit (New York: Lawrence Hill, 1975), 306.

18. Tamm, *Fripp*, 183.

19. Dominic Milano, "Keith Emerson," *Contemporary Keyboard* 6 (September 1980), 20.

20. Andrew Jones, "Fish out of Water," *Montreal Mirror* (March 15–22), 90, re-printed in *Pawn Hearts Newsletter* (April 1990), 5.

21. Curtis, *Rock Eras*, 279.

22. Davin Seay, in his *Stairway to Heaven*, notes how American rock-and-rollers of the 1950s, both black (Little Richard, Sam Cooke) and white (Elvis, Jerry Lee Lewis), were often tortured with a powerful sense of guilt over abandoning their Pentecostal or Evangelical heritages to play R&B, "the devil's music." I suspect it would prove very difficult to find any English musicians who felt a similar sense of guilt over abandoning their Anglican heritage in order to play secular music.

23. Chris Squire, quoted in Hedges, *Yes*, 15.

24. Peter Gabriel, quoted in Gallo, *Genesis*, 14.

25. Anderson, "The Fresh Fruit Interview, Part Two," 6.

26. James Lincoln Collier, *The Making of Jazz: A Comprehensive History* (Boston: Houghton Miflin, 1978), 409–10.

27. Riesman, "Listening to Popular Music," in *On Record*, ed. Frith and Goodwin, 9–10.

28. Willis, *Profane Culture*, 83–85.

29. Robert Wyatt, quoted in King, *Robert Wyatt*, May 5, 1967.

30. See Bangs's "Exposed: The Brutal Energy Atrocities of Emerson, Lake and Pal-mer," *Creem* 6 (March 1974), 74–75, 78.

31. D. W. Meinig, quoted in Jim Curtis, *Rock Eras*, 45. David Fischer's *Albion's Seed* offers a richly developed extension of this idea, demonstrating how four distinct groups of British immigrants have impacted the cultural history of four distinct regions of the United States.

32. Curtis, *Rock Eras*, 45.

33. Deena Weinstein sees elements of northern European mythology in heavy metal themes and artwork. See Weinstein, *Heavy Metal*, 288 and 289, n. 36.

34. Landon Jones, *Great Expectations: America and the Baby Boom Generation* (New York: Coward, McCann, and Geoghegan, 1980), 87.

35. Curtis, *Rock Eras*, 173.

36. Ibid., 264.

37. One issue that comes up again and again in interviews conducted with progressive rock musicians of the 1970s is their dismay with American audiences' inattention and disruptive behavior during quiet passages that would have held English hippies of the late 1960s in rapt attention. See, for instance, Tamm, *Fripp*, 76; Bruford, *When in Doubt, Roll*, 89; Davis, *The Led Zeppelin Saga*, 199; Schaffner, *Pink Floyd*, 179; Barry Harrington, "Progressive Renaissance: Emerson, Lake, and Palmer's Reunion Leads Art Rock Rebirth" (unpublished interview with Keith Emerson), 5. It seems to me that American audiences' rowdier behavior during such passages is indicative of the more blue-collar nature of these audiences; many of these audience members would have never been taught "correct" concert hall protocol in the way the well-heeled English hippies were, and such behavior was at any rate antithetical to their blue-collar backgrounds.

38. Straw, "The Case of Heavy Metal," 107.

39. See, e.g., Eric Salzman's *Twentieth-century Music*, 228, and Robert P. Morgan's *Twentieth-century Music* (New York: W. W. Norton, 1991), 433.

40. Robert Fripp, quoted in Tom Mulhern, "Robert Fripp on the Discipline of Craft and Art," 96.

41. Pleasants, *Serious Music—and All That Jazz*, 79.

42. Jim Curtis sees this tendency being inaugurated by the Beatles' *Sergeant Pepper*, which was never performed live; see *Rock Eras*, 186, 193.

43. Kerry Minnear, quoted in Milano, "Kerry Minnear," 45.

44. David Gilmour, quoted in Resnicoff, "David Gilmour's Pink Floyd," 57.

45. Keith Emerson, quoted in Milano, "Keith Emerson," *Contemporary Keyboard* 3, 52.

46. Eddie Jobson, quoted in Milano, "Eddie Jobson of U.K.," 53.

47. Allan Holdsworth, quoted in Tom Mulhern, "Allan Holdsworth: British Freeform Progressive Rocker," *Guitar Player* 14 (December 1980), 20.

48. I do not intend to address the more general aspects of the rock band as a social unit—an excellent treatment of this topic can be found in Deena Weinstein's *Heavy Metal: A Cultural Sociology*, 69–75, to which I can add very little.

49. Robert Fripp, quoted in Tamm, *Fripp*, 34.

50. Nick Mason, quoted in Miles, *Pink Floyd*, November 1971.

51. Hedges, *Yes*, 68–69.

52. Bill Bruford, *When in Doubt, Roll!*, 39.

53. Peter Gabriel, quoted in Gallo, *Genesis*, 70.

54. Tamm, *Fripp*, 53–54.

55. Keith Emerson, quoted in Pethel, "Emerson," 55–56.

56. Kerry Minnear, quoted in Milano, "Kerry Minnear," 45.

57. Walser, *Running with the Devil*, 104.

58. John Street, *Rebel Rock: The Politics of Popular Music* (New York: Basil Blackwell, 1986), 190–92.

59. The pertinent remark is as follows: "Musicians attempted, with the industry's blessing, to change the meaning of popular music" (ibid., 190). Had the audience no say in this? Were they really merely the passive, mute spectators in this process that Street makes them out to be? If this "attempt" (note again the conspiratorial tone) had no relevance to the values or identities of the counterculture or its post-hippie extension, how did these bands manage to retain their popularity over a six-, seven-, or eight-year period?

60. Ibid., 192.

61. Andrew Chester, "Second Thoughts on a Rock Aesthetic: The Band," in *On Record*, ed. Frith and Goodwin, 315–19.

62. Ibid., 315.

Chapter 8

1. Bangs, "Energy Atrocities," 40.

2. See also Janell R. Duxbury's *Rockin' the Classics and Classicizin' the Rock: A Selectively Annotated Discography* (Westport, Conn.: Greenwood Press, 1985), a reference work that attempts to provide a complete listing of classical quotations in contemporary popular music. Duxbury notes that Procol Harum's "A Whiter Shade of Pale" seems to draw from two sources—the first movement of Bach's Cantata No. 140 (*Wachet auf*) and the "Air for the G-string" from his Suite no. 3 in D major, BWV 1068 (see Duxbury, 50–51).

3. Bangs, "Energy Atrocities," 44.

4. Gentle Giant, *Acquiring the Taste* (Vertigo 1005), liner notes.

5. Jethro Tull, *Thick as a Brick* (Chrysalis MS 2072), liner notes, 7.

6. Curtis, *Rock Eras*, 278.

7. Milano, "Keith Emerson," *Contemporary Keyboard* 6, 23.

8. Dave Marsh, *The Heart of Rock and Soul* (New York: Plume Books, 1989), xv.

9. Bangs, "Energy Atrocities," 44.

10. Robert Christgau, *Christgau's Record Guide: The 80s* (New York: Pantheon Books, 1990), 232.

11. Robert Christgau, *Rock Albums of the 70s: A Critical Guide* (New York: Da Capo Press, 1981), 232.

12. Bruford, *When in Doubt, Roll*, 8.

13. Straw, "The Case of Heavy Metal," 103.

14. Marsh, *Heart of Rock and Soul*, xv.

15. Moore, *Rock: The Primary Text*, 65.

16. Ibid. In fairness to Christopher Small, I cannot find any place in *Music of the Common Tongue* where he uses the phrase "close to nature" to describe black music, and Moore does not cite a page number. To the contrary, on p. 461 Small states that thinking of "black culture" as "closer to nature" is inherently racist, and that liberals

who hold this view as a result of their admiration of black culture "are as deeply in error as the most unredeemed of racists." Nonetheless, Moore is not incorrect to surmise that Small's comparison of the central tenets of European and African music-making (see pp. 42–46) does rather obviously suggest that he considers the latter more immediate and spontaneous than the former.

17. David Ernst, *The Evolution of Electronic Music* (New York: Schirmer Books, 1977), 209.

18. See Peter van der Merwe, *Origins of the Popular Style: Antecedents of Twentieth-century Popular Music* (New York: Oxford University Press, 1992).

19. Bangs, "Energy Atrocities," 43.

20. Christgau, *Rock Albums of the 70s*, 212.

21. See Straw, "The Case of Heavy Metal," 102–3, and Weinstein, *Heavy Metal,* 239–44.

22. Paul Battiste (*Creem* 1972) quoted in Philip Baske, *Heavy Metal Thunder* (Garden City, N.Y.: Dolphin, 1985).

23. Robert Duncan, *The Noise* (New York: Ticknor and Fields, 1984), cited in Weinstein, *Heavy Metal,* 1.

24. Curtis, *Rock Eras,* 287.

25. I realize that critics of this term will argue that I am attempting to trivialize very real struggles over values, justice, and resources. This is not my intent. However, I do believe there is a cadre within academia today that has adopted a "canon" of proposed solutions and tends to engage in self-righteous denunciations of those whose viewpoints may differ. I believe the parallels between certain academicians of the 1990s and certain rock critics of the 1970s are self-evident in this respect and are not coincidental.

26. Anthony DeCurtis, "Music's Mean Season," *Rolling Stone* (December 14–28, 1989), 15–16.

27. Weinstein, *Heavy Metal,* 240.

28. Simon Frith, "Towards an Aesthetic of Popular Music," in *Music in Society,* ed. Richard Leppert and Susan McClary (Cambridge: Cambridge University Press, 1987), 134.

29. On more than one occasion Frith has admitted he is in no way competent to engage in stylistic comparisons on a musicological basis. See Frith, "Towards an Aesthetic," 144, and Frith, *A Sociology of Rock,* 176.

30. Robert Fripp, quoted in Tamm, *Fripp,* 24.

31. Frith, *The Sociology of Rock,* 151.

32. In other words, my own position is that one should not have to choose between a "culturalist" and "anti-culturalist" interpretation; one should be able to draw on both. I accept the anti-culturalist position that the relationships established during musical performances are an important aspect of a music's "meaning"; I think Christopher Small is right to criticize positivist musicology for its refusal to acknowledge this point (see *Music of the Common Tongue,* pp. 49–78). However, it seems rather a leap to take the position that the "text" has no content other than that read into it by

a group or an individual at a particular place or time; I suspect Frith has been forced into this view by his own inability to evaluate the musical "text" as an objective entity. Most uninitiated listeners with no preconceived notions either for or against classical music will probably prefer Beethoven's "Waldstein" Sonata to any of Clementi's. Might this not be because *within the "text" itself* Beethoven does a better job of establishing and thwarting expectations at key moments, avoiding excessive clichés (banality) and excessive surprises (the bane of the post–World War II avant-garde)? In short, while I think Leonard Meyers's views on meaning in music need some revision—especially in terms of integrating the very real impact that the manner in which music is mediated affects its "meaning"—it is too early to reject them entirely. One may wish to consult Anthony Storr's *Music and the Mind* (London: Harper-Collins, 1992) for considerations of the various theories concerning how "meaning" is conveyed through music.

33. Weinstein, *Heavy Metal*, 241.

34. Quoted in Curtis, *Rock Eras*, 125–26.

35. Street, *Rebel Rock*, 166.

36. Roger Waters, quoted in Schaffner, *Pink Floyd*, 251. In his *Rebel Rock*, pp. 163–66, Street makes a similar point when comparing John Lennon's "apolitical" *Imagine* and his "politically conscious" *Sometime in New York City*. Using the criteria outlined above, he finds *Imagine* to be a far more politically effective album than *Sometime;* he notes that the stridency of the latter was a turnoff even for those who were sympathetic with Lennon's socialist views.

37. Walser, *Running with the Devil*, xiv.

38. Jimmy Guteman and Owen O'Donnell, *The 50 Worst Rock'n'Roll Records of All Time* (New York: Citadel Press, 1991).

39. It was not for nothing that a statue of the Greek god Narcissus stood in the foyer of New York's most exclusive discoteque, Studio 54. See Curtis, *Rock Eras*, 300.

Chapter 9

1. Robert Fripp, quoted in Irwin Stambler, *Encyclopedia of Rock, Pop, and Soul*, rev. Ed. (New York: St. Martin's Press, 1989), 374.

2. At the beginning of the *Topographic Oceans* tour, Yes attempted to devote most of each concert to presenting *Tales from Topographic Oceans* in its entirely, much as Genesis were later to present *The Lamb Lies down on Broadway* and Pink Floyd, still later, were to present *The Wall*. However, audience response was so negative that as the tour progressed, the band was forced to drop one-quarter and finally one-half of the piece from its concerts. See Hedges, *Yes*, 94.

3. In classical music circa 1920, these three choices were represented by Schoenberg's atonal and later twelve-tone music (which broke the code of tonal music entirely), by the nationalist music of Vaughan Williams, Holst, Bartók, Villa-Lobos, etc. (which used an expanded tonal palette without abandoning the drama or expressive

qualities of late Romanticism), and the neoclassicism of Stravinsky and the French group Les Six (which emphasized a new simplicity in terms of stripped-down textures, simple, closed forms, less sumptuous instrumentation, etc.).

4. Chris Cutler, quoted in Street, *Rebel Rock*, 148.

5. For instance, Triumvirat and Le Orme show a clear debt to ELP; Epidermis, to Gentle Giant; Eloy and Pulsar, to Pink Floyd; Granada and Ange, to King Crimson. Even the early Italian progressive rock bands such as PFM and Banco, which themselves exerted a strong influence on later European bands, were influenced in their formative stage by Genesis, King Crimson, and *Pawn Hearts*–era Van der Graaf Generator.

6. To be sure, Henry Cow alumni have released numerous solo albums since the late 1970s; however, these albums are stylistically too diffuse to show evidence of a "Henry Cow style." Perhaps the closest thing to a Henry Cow "legacy" is a small American label, Cuneiform, which specializes in releasing avant-garde/jazz/rock music in what might be termed a post–Henry Cow vein.

7. Straw, "The Case of Heavy Metal," 107.

8. Another contemporaneous band from the southeastern United States, the Dixie Dregs, fused bluegrass and boogie with jazz-rock fusion.

9. Emerson gives a detailed account of the role played by Atlantic Records' president Ahmet Ertegun in persuading the band to make their final studio album of the 1970s, *Love Beach*, as "commercial" as possible, in Dominic Milano's "Keith Emerson," *Contemporary Keyboard* 6, (September 1980), 16–17, and "An Open Letter from Keith Emerson to the Readers of *Contemporary Keyboard*," *Contemporary Keyboard* 6 (September 1980), 19.

10. I use the term "rock" here in order to point up the very real difference in the way that the self-consciously "artistic" music of Dylan, the Beatles, and Jefferson Airplane was marketed as compared to the "artless" pre-countercultural pop (or rock-and-roll) of Motown, the Kirschner stable, or the "girl groups" produced by Phil Spector.

11. Virtually all the major British progressive rock bands of the 1970s achieved major contracts early in their careers: the Moody Blues with London's Deram (even Egg, an extremely uncommercial band, recorded two albums on the Deram label in 1970); Procol Harum with A&M; Pink Floyd with EMI's Harvest; ELP, Yes, King Crimson, and Genesis (from 1974) with Atlantic; Gentle Giant with Philips's Vertigo and later Columbia and Capitol; Curved Air with Warner Brothers; Soft Machine with Columbia and later Harvest; and Jade Warrior with Vertigo and later Island. To be sure, the Nice, Genesis (until 1973), and Van der Graaf Generator recorded for Tony Stratton-Smith's Charisma label, while Jethro Tull recorded with Chrysalis. Nonetheless, these two labels were powerful by indie standards, and were in fact extensions of successful management or production companies (later albums by the Nice and Van der Graaf Generator were in fact distributed in the United States on yet another major label, Mercury). Stratton-Smith once said he realized Genesis would likely take three years to turn a profit (see

Gallo, *Genesis*, 24). It is difficult to find a record company executive today who is willing to make that kind of long-term investment.

12. Dave Stewart, "National Health—the Inside Story," liner notes from *National Health Complete* (East Side Digital CD 80402/412). Stewart's frustration over Virgin's refusal to offer National Health a contract stemmed from the fact that Virgin had earlier released albums by a number of prominent Canterbury groups, including Gong, Henry Cow, and Stewart's own Hatfield and the North.

13. Hedges, *Yes*, 104.

14. I must admit that I am not able to offer a satisfactory explanation as to why some of the "classic" progressive rock bands have been more commercially successful among younger listeners during the 1980s and 1990s than others. On the one hand, it is clear that Genesis and the *90125* lineup of Yes were commercial successes during the 1980s because of their willingness to draw elements of the contemporaneous teenage style (i.e., New Wave) into their existing sound. On the other hand, neither Pink Floyd nor the various ELP configurations made many concessions to the new styles of the 1980s and 1990s. Pink Floyd has been enormously successful during this time, attracting a host of new, younger listeners; ELP, on the other hand, has had problems in expanding beyond their preexisting fan base of the 1970s and have not been nearly as successful.

15. Moore, Rock: *The Primary Text*, 184.

16. Ibid., 183.

17. Ibid., 164.

18. Ibid., 165.

19. For instance, some of the owners of the small labels that specialize in neo-progressive music are unwilling to release any new music that is insufficiently "seventiesh." The pervasive conservatism of this stance—and its contrast with the willingness to experiment that characterized the early champions of progressive rock such as Stratton-Smith—is self-evident.

20. Keith Goodwin, correspondence with the author, September 12, 1992.

21. Nick Barrett, correspondence with the author, August 1992.

22. Ibid. Barrett adds that the Marquee was situated just below the Charisma offices and was often frequented by Charisma staff, including Stratton-Smith. Thus one sees even more clearly the persistent interaction between two generations of progressive rock musicians, Stratton-Smith, and the Marquee.

23. Straw, "The Case of Heavy Metal," 105–7.

24. Philip Halper, "Progressive Speculations: The U.K. Scene," *Background Progressive Rock Magazine* no. 23 (June 1991), 17.

25. Hans Rochat, "Twelfth Night: The Sublimity of a Deceased Rock Band," *Background Progressive Rock Magazine* no. 23 (June 1991), 10–11.

26. Michiel van de Ven, "Splitting Image," *Background Progressive Rock Magazine* no. 23 (June 1991), 15.

27. Halper, "Progressive Speculations," 17.

28. Carol Clerk, *Marillion in Words and Pictures* (London: Bobcat Books, 1985), 40.

29. Allan Moore sees this literal repetition in the neo-progressive style as a by-product of the punk revolution. See Moore, Rock: *The Primary Text*, 128.

30. In November of 1994 and 1995, a second and third Progfest were mounted at Los Angeles's Variety Arts Center by David Overstreet and Greg Walker, owners of Art Sublime and Syn-Phonic, two of the better known of the independent labels specializing in progressive rock rereleases and new progressive rock releases. It appears that this will become an annual event; if so, progressive rock has become the first style of rock that is being preserved through historical/nostalgic "festivals" in the manner of jazz, folk, and classical music.

31. Tamm, *Fripp*, xiv.

32. Robert Fripp, quoted in Stambler, *Encyclopedia of Rock, Pop, and Soul*, 374.

33. Robert Fripp, liner notes to *God Save the Queen/Under Heavy Manners* (Polydor PD-1-6266), released in 1980.

34. Ibid.

35. Robert Fripp, quoted in Tamm, *Fripp*, 135.

36. Bruford, *When in Doubt, Roll*, 88.

37. Ibid., 89.

38. Fripp has released several recordings in conjunction with his more advanced Guitar Craft students; these are released under the auspices of "Robert Fripp and the League of Crafty Guitarists."

39. Wayne Bledsoe, "Belew Happy to Play on Smaller Scale," *Riverside [California] Press-Enterprise* (Friday, May 22, 1992), AA-11.

40. Chuck Oken, correspondence with the author, October 19, 1992.

41. Musea is a French label that distributes the recordings of contemporary bands that are stylistically similar to Edhels (i.e., Minimum Vital) and also rereleases "classic" French progressive rock albums of the 1970s (by Pulsar, Atoll, Mona Lisa, etc.) on CD.

42. Marc Ceccotti, correspondence with the author, April 15, 1993.

Postlude

1. It seems to me that Pink Floyd's *Animals* and (especially) *The Wall* rather poignantly symbolize the end of progressive rock's "classic" period precisely because of the emphasis on pessimism, bitterness, and cynicism.

Bibliography

Books

Bacon, Tony, ed. *Rock Hardware*. New York: Harmony Books, 1981.

Banasiewicz, Bill. *Rush: Visions*. New York: Omnibus Press, 1988.

Bangs, Lester. *Psychotic Reactors and Carburetor Dung*. New York: Vintage Books, 1988.

Barthes, Roland. *S/Z*. Trans. Richard Miller. London: Jonathan Cape, 1975.

Baske, Philip. *Heavy Metal Thunder*. Garden City, N.Y.: Dolphin, 1985.

Benson, Joe. *Uncle Joe's Record Guide: Progressive Rock*. Glendale, Calif.: J. Benson Unlimited, 1989.

Berendt, Joachim. *The Jazz Book: From New Orleans to Rock and Free Jazz*. Trans. Dan Morgenstern and Helmut and Barbara Bredigkeit. New York: Lawrence Hill, 1975.

Bowler, Dave, and Bryan Dray. *Genesis: A Biography*. London: Sidgwick and Jackson, 1992.

Bruford, Bill. *When in Doubt, Roll*. Cedar Grove, N.J.: Modern Drummer Publications, 1988.

Carr, Ian. *Music Outside: Contemporary Jazz in Britain*. London: Latimer New Dimensions, 1973.

Chapple, Steve, and Reebee Garofalo. *Rock'n'Roll is Here to Pay: The History and Politics of the Music Industry*. Chicago: Nelson-Hall, 1977.

Christgau, Robert. *Rock Albums of the 70s: A Critical Guide*. New York: Da Capo Press, 1981.

Christgau, Robert. *Christgau's Record Guide: The 80s*. New York: Pantheon Books, 1990.

Clerk, Carol. *Marillion in Words and Pictures*. London: Bobcat Books, 1985.

Collier, James Lincoln. *The Making of Jazz: A Comprehensive History*. Boston: Houghton Miflin, 1978.

Cooke, Deryck. *The Language of Music*. London: Oxford University Press, 1959.

Curtis, Jim. *Rock Eras: Interpretations of Music and Society, 1954-1984*. Bowling Green, Ohio: Bowling Green State University Popular Press, 1987.

Dass, Baba Ram. *Be Here Now*. New Mexico: Lama Foundation, 1971.

Davis, Stephen. *The Hammer of the Gods: The Led Zeppelin Saga*. New York: Ballantine Books, 1985.

DeCurtis, Anthony, ed. *Present Tense: Rock & Roll and Culture.* Durham: Duke University Press, 1992.

Duncan, Robert. *The Noise.* New York: Ticknor and Fields, 1984.

Duxbury, Janell R. *Rockin' the Classics and Classicizin' the Rock: A Selectively Annotated Discography.* Westport, Conn.: Greenwood Press, 1985.

Eisen, Jonathan, ed. *The Age of Rock.* New York: Vintage Press, 1969.

Ernst, David. *The Evolution of Electronic Music.* New York: Schirmer Books, 1977.

Fischer, David Hackett. *Albion's Seed: Four British Folkways in America.* New York: Oxford University Press, 1989.

Frame, Peter. *Rock Family Trees.* New York: Quick Fox, 1979.

Frith, Simon. *The Sociology of Rock.* London: Constable, 1978.

Frith, Simon, and Andrew Goodwin, eds. *On Record: Rock, Pop, and the Written Word.* New York: Pantheon Books, 1990.

Frith, Simon, and Robert Horne. *Art into Pop.* New York: Methuen, 1987.

Gallo, Armando. *Genesis: I Know What I Like.* Los Angeles: D.I.Y. Press, 1980.

Gorman, Clem. *Backstage Rock.* London: Pan Books, 1978.

Guteman, Jimmy, and Owen O'Donnell. *The 50 Worst Rock'n'Roll Records of All Time.* New York: Citadel Press, 1991.

Hall, Stuart, and Jefferson, Tony. *Resistance through Rituals: Youth Subcultures in Postwar Britain.* London: Hutchinson, 1976.

Hamilton, Dominy, with Carla Capalbo and Donald Lehmkuhl. *Roger Dean: Views.* London: Dragon's Dream, 1975.

Harrigan, Brian, and Malcolm Dune. *Encyclopedia Metallica.* London: Bobcat Books, n.d.

Hebdige, Dick. *Subculture: The Meaning of Style.* New York: Methuen, 1979.

Heckstall-Smith, Dick. *The Safest Place in the World.* London: Quartet Books, 1989.

Hedges, Dan. *Yes: The Authorized Biography.* London: Sidgwick and Jackson, 1981.

Hentoff, Nat, and Albert McCarthy. *Jazz.* New York: Holt, Rineheart and Winston, 1959.

Hounsome, Terry. *New Rock Record.* New York: Facts on File Publications, 1981, 1983.

Huxley, Aldous. *The Doors of Perception and Heaven and Hell.* New York: Harper Colophon, 1963.

Jones, Landon. *Great Expectations: America and the Baby Boom Generation.* New York: Coward, McGann, and Geoghegan, 1980.

King, Mike. *Wrong Movements: A Robert Wyatt History.* Wembley, UK: SAF Publishing, 1994.

Leary, Timothy. *The Politics of Ecstasy.* New York: Putnam, 1968.

Levine, Lawrence. *Highbrow/Lowbrow: The Emergence of Cultural Hierarchy in America.* Cambridge, Mass.: Harvard University Press, 1988.

Livgren, Kerry, with Kenneth Boa. *Seeds of Change.* Rev. ed. Nashville: Sparrow Press, 1990.

Macan, Edward. "An Analytical Survey and Comparative Study of the Music of Ralph Vaughan Williams and Gustav Holst, c. 1910–1935." Ph.D. dissertation, Claremont Graduate School, 1991.

Marsh, Dave. *The Heart of Rock and Soul.* New York: Plume Books, 1989.

Marsh, Dave, and John Swenson, eds. *The Rolling Stone Record Guide.* New York: Random House, 1979.

Marshall Cavendish Encyclopedia of Popular Music. New York: Marshall Cavendish, 1990.

McClary, Susan. *Feminine Endings: Music, Gender, and Sexuality.* Minneapolis: University of Minnesota Press, 1991.

Meyer, Leonard. *Emotion and Meaning in Music.* Chicago: University of Chicago Press, 1956.

Middleton, Richard. *Studying Popular Music.* Philadelphia: Open University Press, 1990.

Miles. *Pink Floyd: A Visual Documentary by Miles.* New York: Omnibus Press, 1980.

Moore, Allan. *Rock: The Primary Text; Developing a Musicology of Rock.* Buckingham, U.K.: Open University Press, 1993.

Morgan, Robert. *Twentieth-century Music.* New York: W. W. Norton, 1991.

Morse, Tim. *Yes Stories.* New York: St. Martin's Press, 1996.

Mosbø, Thomas. *Yes—But What Does It Mean? Exploring the Music of Yes.* Milton, Wis.: Wyndstar, 1994.

Palmer, Carl. *Applied Rhythms.* Cedar Grove, N.J.: Modern Drummer Publications, 1987.

Parales, Jon, and Patricia Romanowski, eds. *The Rolling Stone Encyclopedia of Rock and Roll.* New York: Summit Books, 1983.

Pattison, Robert. *The Triumph of Vulgarity: Rock Music in the Mirror of Romanticism.* New York: Oxford University Press, 1987.

Pethel, Blair. "Keith Emerson: The Emergence and Growth of Style." D.M.A. Paper, Johns Hopkins University, 1987.

Pleasants, Henry. *Serious Music—And All That Jazz.* New York: Simon and Schuster, 1969.

Reese, Gustav. *Music in the Renaissance.* Rev. Ed. New York: W. W. Norton, 1959.

Roof, Wade. *A Generation of Seekers: The Spiritual Journeys of the Baby Boom Generation.* San Francisco: Harper-Collins, 1993.

Rosenberg, Neil, ed. *Transforming Tradition: Folk Music Revivals Examined.* Champaign, Ill.: University of Illinois Press, 1993.

Salzman, Eric. *Twentieth-century Music: An Introduction.* 3. ed. Englewood Cliffs, N.J.: Prentice-Hall, 1988.

Schact, Janis. *Genesis.* London: Proteus Books, 1984.

Schaffner, Nicholas. *Saucerful of Secrets: The Pink Floyd Odyssey.* New York: Harmony Books, 1991.

Seay, Davin, with Mary Neely. *Stairway to Heaven: The Spiritual Roots of Rock'n'Roll.* New York: Ballantine Books, 1986.

Shapiro, Harry. *Graham Bond: The Mighty Shadow*. London: Guinness Publishing, 1992.

Shaw-Parker, David. *The Lemming Chronicles*. Sheffield, U.K.: Pandoras Boox, 1995.

Shepherd, John. *Music as Social Text*. Cambridge, U.K.: Polity Press, 1991.

Small, Christopher. *Music of the Common Tongue: Survival and Celebration in Afro-American Music*. New York: Riverun Press, 1988.

Smith, Adam. *The Powers of Mind*. New York: Random House, 1975.

Stambler, Irwin. *The Encyclopedia of Rock, Pop, and Soul*. Rev. ed. New York: St. Martin's Press, 1989.

Storr, Anthony. *Music and the Mind*. London: Harper-Collins, 1992.

Stravinsky, Igor. *An Autobiography*. New York: Norton, 1962.

Street, John. *Rebel Rock: The Politics of Popular Music*. New York: Basil Blackwell, 1986.

Tamm, Eric. *Brian Eno: His Music and the Vertical Color of Sound*. Boston: Faber and Faber, 1989.

———. *Robert Fripp: From King Crimson to Guitar Craft*. Boston: Faber and Faber, 1990.

Thorgerson, Storm, and Roger Dean, eds. *Album Cover Album*. Limpsfield, U.K.: Dragon's World, 1977.

Van der Merwe, Peter. *Origins of the Popular Style: Antecedents of Twentieth-century Popular Music*. New York: Oxford University Press, 1992.

Walser, Robert. *Running with the Devil: Power, Gender, and Madness in Heavy Metal Music*. Hanover, N.H.: Wesleyan University Press, 1993.

Ward, Ed, Geoffrey Stokes, and Ken Tucker. *Rock of Ages: The Rolling Stone History of Rock & Roll*. New York: Summit Books, 1986.

Weber, William. *Music and the Middle Class*. New York: Holmes and Meier, 1975.

Weinstein, Deena. *Heavy Metal: A Cultural Sociology*. New York: Macmillan, 1991.

Welch, Chris. *Black Sabbath*. London: Proteus Books, 1982.

Welch, Chris. *Pink Floyd: Learning to Fly*. Chessington, U.K.: Castle Communications, 1994.

Whitburn, Joel. *The Billboard Book of Top 40 Albums*. New York: Billboard Publications, 1987.

———. *Top Pop Album Tracks, 1955–1992*. New York: Billboard Publications, 1993.

Whitmer, Peter. *Aquarius Revisited: Seven Who Created the Sixties Counterculture That Changed America*. New York: Macmillan, 1987.

Willis, Paul. *Profane Culture*. London: Routledge and Kegan Paul, 1978.

Articles

Aikin, Jim. "Brian Eno." *Keyboard* 7 (July 1981).

———. "Off the Record: An Organ Solo by Eddie Jobson." *Keyboard* 7 (September 1981).

———. "Off the Record: An Organ Solo by Keith Emerson." *Keyboard* 8 (September 1982).

Alexander, Susan. "Phil Collins: 'I'm a Drummer First.'" *Modern Drummer* 7 (November 1983).

Anderson, Bob. "The Fresh Fruit Interview, Part II. *Pawn Hearts Newsletter* (November 1991).

Babbitt, Milton. "Who Cares If You Listen?" *High Fidelity Magazine* 8/2 (1958):38–40.

Bangs, Lester. "Exposed! The Brutal Energy Atrocities of Emerson Lake and Palmer." *Creem* 6 (March 1974).

———. "Jethro Tull in Viet Nam." *Creem* 5 (May 1973).

Barthes, Roland. "The Grain of the Voice." In *On Record*, ed. Frith and Goodwin, 293–300.

Birnbaum, Larry. "Southern Fusion of Power and Polish: The Dixie Dregs." *Downbeat* 45 (October 19, 1978).

Bledsoe, Wayne. "Belew Happy to Play on Smaller Scale." *Riverside [California] Press-Enterprise* (Friday, May 22, 1992), AA-11.

Chester, Andrew. "Second Thoughts on a Rock Aesthetic: The Band." In *On Record*, ed. Frith and Goodwin, 315–19.

Clark, Gary. "Defending Ski-jumpers: A Critique of Theories of Youth Subcultures." In *On Record*, ed. Frith and Goodwin, 81–96.

DeCurtis, Anthony. "Music's Mean Season." *Rolling Stone* (December 14–28, 1989).

Diliberto, John. "Zen and the Art of Fripp's Guitar." *Electronic Musician* (June 1987).

Dillingham, Mick. "Relaxing with Richard Sinclair: Canterbury Tales." *Ptolemaic Terrascope* 2 (autumn 1991).

———. "Van der Graaf Generator: The David Jackson Interview, Parts One and Two." *Ptolemaic Terrascope* 2 (May 1991, and autumn 1991).

Doerschuk, Robert. "Keith Emerson." *Keyboard* 14 (April 1988).

———. "Keith Emerson and ELP Again." *Keyboard* 18 (June 1992).

———. "Keith Emerson: The Phoenix Rises from the Ashes of Progressive Rock." *Keyboard* 12 (July 1986).

———. "Kerry Livgren and Steven Walsh of Kansas." *Contemporary Keyboard* 3 (August 1977).

———. "Rick Wakeman." *Keyboard* 15 (September 1989).

———. "Whatever Happened to Patrick Moraz?" *Keyboard* 17 (May 1991).

———. "Yes: Rick Wakeman and Tony Kaye Face off." *Keyboard* 17 (August 1991).

Emerson, Keith. "Howard Jones." *Keyboard* 15 (August 1989).

———. "An Open Letter from Keith Emerson to the Readers of *Contemporary Keyboard.*" *Contemporary Keyboard* 6 (September 1980).

Ferris, Leonard. "Yes' Bassist Chris Squire." *Guitar Player* 7 (July 1973).

Fish, Scott. "Bill Bruford." *Modern Drummer* 7 (June 1983).

Flans, Robyn. "Nick Mason: Finding His Own Way." *Modern Drummer* 9 (January 1985).

Fripp, Robert. "The Diary of the Return of King Crimson, Parts I, II, and III." *Musician* (December 1981, January 1982, and February 1982).

————. Liner notes to *God Save the Queen/Under Heavy Manners.* Polydor LP PD-1-6266.

Frith, Simon. "Towards an Aesthetic of Popular Music." In *Music in Society,* ed. Richard Leppert and Susan McClary. Cambridge: Cambridge University Press, 1987.

Frith, Simon, and Angela McRobbie. "Rock and Sexuality." *Screen Education* no. 29 (winter 1978/79). See also *On Record,* ed. Frith and Goodwin, 371–89.

Gaer, Eric. "Emerson, Lake, and Palmer: A Force to be Reckoned with." *Downbeat* 41 (May 9, 1974).

Goodwin, Simon. "Jon Hiseman: Interaction." *Modern Drummer* 8 (April 1984).

Halper, Philip. "Progressive Speculations: The U.K. Scene." *Background Progressive Rock Magazine* no. 23 (June 1991).

————. "Sacrifice: Clive Nolan on Pendragon." *Background Progressive Rock Magazine* no. 22 (April 1991).

Halper, Philip. "Progressive Speculations: The U.K. Scene." *Background Progressive Rock Magazine* no. 23 (June 1991).

Hansen, Dwight, ed. (1978–1988) and Mike Spindloe, ed. (1988–present). *Pawn Hearts Newsletter.* Published by the Appreciation Society and Archive of the Works of Peter Hammill and Van der Graaf Generator, 927 6th St. N., Saskatoon, Saskatchewan S7K 2T3, Canada.

Harrington, Barry. "Progressive Renaissance: Emerson, Lake and Palmer's Reunion Leads Art Rock Rebirth." Unpublished interview with Keith Emerson.

Hebdige, Dick. "Style as Homology and Signifying Practice." In *On Record,* ed. Frith and Goodwin, 56–65.

Hedges, Dan. "Steve Howe: Renaissance Man of the Guitar." *Guitar Player* 12 (May 1978).

Iero, Cheech. "Carl Palmer." *Modern Drummer* 4 (June/July 1980).

Jones, Andrew. "Fish out of Water." *Pawn Hearts Newsletter* (April 1990).

Josephson, Nors. "Bach Meets Liszt: Traditional Formal Structures and Performance Practices in Progressive Rock." *Musical Quarterly* 76 (spring 1992).

Kusmic, Milly, and Stephan van de Ven. "John Wetton." *Background Progressive Rock Magazine* no. 35 (June 1993).

Macan, Edward. " 'The Spirit of Albion' in 20th-century English Popular Music: Vaughan Williams, Holst, and the Progressive Rock Movement." *Music Review* 53 (May 1992).

Mattingly, Rick. "Carl Palmer." *Modern Drummer* 7 (December 1983).

McClary, Susan, and Robert Walser. "Start Making Sense! Musicology Wrestles with Rock." In *On Record,* ed. Frith and Goodwin, 277–92.

McRobbie, Angela. "Settling Accounts with Subcultures: A Feminist Critique." In *On Record,* ed. Frith and Goodwin, 66–80.

Mettler, Mike. "Yes: Back from the Edge." *Guitar School* (September 1991).

Milano, Dominic. "Dave Stewart: Poll-winning British Keyboardist." *Contemporary Keyboard* 6 (January 1980).

————. "Eddie Jobson of U.K." *Contemporary Keyboard* 5 (March 1979).

————. "Keith Emerson." *Contemporary Keyboard* 3 (October 1977).

————. "Keith Emerson." *Contemporary Keyboard* 6 (September 1980).

————. "Kerry Minnear: Keyboardist/Composer for Gentle Giant." *Contemporary Keyboard* 2 (May/June 1976).

————. "A New Multi-keyboard Solo by Patrick Moraz." *Keyboard* 11 (July 1985).

————. "Off the Record: Keith Emerson's Concerto Cadenza." *Keyboard* 14 (August 1988).

————. "Patrick Moraz." *Keyboard* 7 (November 1981).

————. "Rick Wakeman." *Contemporary Keyboard* 5 (February 1979).

————. "Tangerine Dream." *Keyboard* 7 (April 1981).

————. "Tony Banks." *Contemporary Keyboard* 4 (July 1978).

————. "Tony Banks and the Evolution of Genesis." *Keyboard* 10 (November 1984).

Mulhern, Tom. "Allan Holdsworth: British Free-form Progressive Rocker." *Guitar Player* 14 (December 1980).

————. "Geddy Lee of Rush, Rock's Leading Bassist." *Guitar Player* 20 (April 1986).

————. "John Wetton: Asia's Progressive Rock Bassist." *Guitar Player* 17 (January 1983).

————. "Robert Fripp on the Discipline of Craft and Art." *Guitar Player* 20 (January 1986).

————. "Steve Hackett." *Guitar Player* 20 (September 1986).

Obrecht, Jas. "Alex Lifeson of Rush." *Guitar Player* 20 (April 1986).

Palmer, Robert. "The Church of the Sonic Guitar." In *Present Tense*, ed. DeCurtis, 13–38.

Pekar, Harvey. "From Rock to ???—A Searching Look at the Pop Explosion." *Downbeat* 35 (May 2, 1968).

Peyser, Joan. "The Music of Sound or, the Beatles and the Beatless." In *The Age of Rock*, ed. Eisen, 126–34.

Primak, Bret. "Patrick Moraz: This Synthesizer Knows No Limits." *Downbeat* 46 (January 11, 1979).

Randall, Mac. "Musician Forum: Robert Wyatt Meets Bill Nelson." *Musician Magazine* (August 1992).

Resnicoff, Matt. "David Gilmour's Pink Floyd." *Musician Magazine* (August 1992).

Rideout, Roger. "The German Model in Music Curricula," *College Music Symposium* 30 (fall 1990).

Riesman, David. "Listening to Popular Music." In *On Record*, ed. Frith and Goodwin, 5–13.

Rochat, Hans. "Twelfth Night: The Sublimity of a Deceased Rock Band." *Background Progressive Rock Magazine* no. 23 (June 1991).

Rosen, Steve. "From England's Genesis, Here's Steve Hackett." *Guitar Player* 10 (October 1976).

————. "Gary Brooker: Rock Piano Mainstay with Procol Harum." *Contemporary Keyboard* 4 (July 1978).

———. "Greg Lake of Emerson, Lake and Palmer." *Guitar Player* 8 (September 1974).

———. "King Crimson's Robert Fripp." *Guitar Player* 8 (May 1974).

Saloman, Nick, with Nick Dillingham. "Curved Air: The Francis Monkman Interview." *Ptolemaic Terrascope* 2 (May 1991).

Santelli, Robert. "Alan White." *Modern Drummer* 9 (January 1985).

Sayrs, Elizabeth. "Deconstructing McClary: Narrative, Feminine Sexuality, and Feminism in Susan McClary's *Feminine Endings.*" College Music Symposium 33/34 (1993/1994).

Schuller, Gunther. "The Influence of Jazz on the History and Development of Concert Music." In *New Perspectives on Jazz,* ed. David Baker. Washington: Smithsonian Institute Press, 1990, 9–23.

Schwartz, Jim. "Steve Howe." *Guitar Player* 20 (September 1986).

Shelton, Kevin. "Music and the Surreal, Part Three." *Surface Noise* 5 (winter 1982).

Shumway, Darrell. "Rock and Roll as a Cultural Practice." In *Present Tense,* ed. DeCurtis, 117.

Simon, John. "Ian Anderson: The Codpiece Chronicles." *Downbeat* 43 (March 11, 1976).

Slabisky, Igor. "Full Frontal Fripp." *Trouser Press Collectors Magazine* 4 (January/February 1982).

Straw, Will. "Characterizing Rock Music Culture: The Case of Heavy Metal." In *On Record,* ed. Frith and Goodwin, 97–110.

Summers, Russ. "Remembering Alan Gowen." *Keyboard* 9 (January 1983).

Teledu, David. "The Talking Drum: An Interview with Jamie Muir." *Ptolemaic Terrascope* 2 (autumn 1991).

Van de Ven, Michiel. "Splitting Image." *Background Progressive Rock Magazine* no. 23 (June 1991).

Willis, Paul. "The Cultural Meaning of Drug Use." In *Resistance and Ritual,* ed. Hall and Jefferson.

Zwerin, Mike. "A Different Rock Group: The Soft Machine." *Downbeat* 35 (July 11, 1968).

Musical Scores

Emerson, Lake and Palmer. New York: Warner Bros., 1977.

Emerson, Lake and Palmer: Anthology. New York: Warner Bros., 1981. (Keith Emerson was directly involved in transcribing the pieces included in these volumes for Warner Brothers, so the ELP volumes tend to be free of the faults that afflict many of the other volumes listed here: faulty transcriptions, entire instrumental sections that are excised without comment, important background motives that are left out, etc. All three volumes are unfortunately out of print.)

Emerson, Lake and Palmer: Tarkus. New York: Warner Bros., 1980.

Genesis: Seconds Out. New York: Music Sales Co., 1978.

Genesis: Anthology. New York: Warner Brothers, n.d.

The Best of Jethro Tull. Port Chester, N.Y.: Cherry Lane Music Co., n.d. (Transcriptions of the pieces on *M.U.: Best of Jethro Tull* and *M.U.: Best of Jethro Tull, Volume Two.*)

Kansas: Two for the Show. New York: Warner Bros., 1979.

The Moody Blues: A Question of Balance/To Our Children's Children's Children. New York: MCA Music, 1970.

Pink Floyd: The Dark Side of the Moon. London: Pink Floyd Music Publishers Ltd., 1973.

Pink Floyd: Wish You Were Here. London: Pink Floyd Music Publishers, 1982. (Contains lengthy interviews with Roger Waters and David Gilmour covering the genesis of the *Wish You Were Here* LP.)

Rush: Hemispheres. New York: Warner Bros., 1979.

Rush: Permanent Waves. New York: Warner Bros., 1980.

Yes Complete: Deluxe Edition. New York: Warner Bros., n.d.

Index

Printed in the United Kingdom by
Lightning Source UK Ltd., Milton Keynes
141091UK00002B/2/A